THE TEN PERCENT

A Scottish Undercover
Police Officer's Story

SIMON MCLEAN

SPELLING DIFFERENCES: UK V US

This book was written in British English, hence US readers may notice some spelling differences from American English: e.g. color = colour, meter = metre and jewelry = jewellery

DEDICATION

Louise
Often, when I know you are near,
My heart skips a beat, just as always,
And sometimes, without warning, you make me smile all over.
Lately, when I think you can hear,
I tell you my thoughts, just like you'd want me to,
And listen, can you hear me?
Such are the mystic ways of time.
Your memory sustains me.
Your image makes me smile.
The echo of our laughter will forever fill my heart.
For my wonderful, beautiful, brave and inspirational daughter
Louise Jane McLean.
I miss you so much.

xxx

CONTENTS

INTRODUCTION

I was on Gordon Street. Across from Glasgow Central Station. Lunchtime. A nice day. I was chatting. Happily smoking with a colleague. Discussing the covert surveillance and personal protection training course we were delivering upstairs. The street was really busy. Taxis, cars and the whole spectrum of life coming and going. Typical city hustle and bustle.

Then, straight out of the blue, a young guy came up to me with his palm open offering me a selection of tablets. I simply told him where to go, and continued with my chat, but from the corner of my eye I saw him offer someone else at the bus stop his wares, where he was met with a similar response. Only then did my old police head flicker to life. I began to see the whole cityscape through an entirely different lens. The street was suddenly transformed to me, as if looking through a night vision scope.

Within two or three seconds, I had spotted the car across Hope Street with the watchful occupants. Dealers. Another pusher punting to a group of young girls outside Central Station, with more apparent success than my guy was having. A crew dividing up their haul of stolen goods under the canopy of the station before splitting. The always watchful and wary opportunist street beggars on their self-allotted squats. A young couple were arguing in the taxi queue, and now there was a real shifty guy watching me from the door of the bookies.

Now, an Asian man, not far away from me, with a totally bewildered expression. He looked as though he had just this minute arrived from the East. He still had his traditional clothes and several huge suitcases around him. I wondered what he was seeing. Initially, I hadn't noticed anything. Then, because of a would-be drug dealer, I began to see all of the nefarious activity going on around me. What was the stranger seeing through his lens, if indeed he had just arrived in the West? Of course, his perceptions and impressions would have been informed entirely by where he had just come from, his experiences and background. Did we all look the same to him?

My point is that this collection of stories, mainly from my career as a police officer with Strathclyde Police, are only and can only be my recollections and memories. Depending on whose memory we rely on, the details will always differ, as we all see the world from our own individual perspective. Ask your partner what happened on your first meeting or date. Ask your boss what was said at your job interview. Ask a sibling or friend to describe an incident from your past. What was said and who did what? You'll quickly discover that everyone remembers different things, different moments and totally different details.

The truth therefore is self-evidently totally subjective, not factual. No one is lying, we just all remember things from our own personal perspective, and can only perceive through our own lens. There are no lies on the following pages. Some facts may even be totally wrong, but they are what I remember, and I apologise up front to anyone who remembers them differently, or not at all.

By way of explanation in case I seem in any way disparaging of the 'other' ninety percent of police officers, who in my estimation don't qualify for my Ten Percent, I need to put on record my admiration, sympathy and pride when I see the job they do day in and day out on our streets, with less than no thanks or recognition. They are the best of us without question, running towards all sorts of situations on our behalf, knowing that they are in a losing position no matter what then occurs.

I really can't speak highly enough of them because I know the pressures and stresses they bear. I know the toll it's taking on them and their loved ones and I know that if we didn't have them the country would soon fall apart under anarchy. My real fear is that as we continue to back them into painted corners, we will make our historic methods of consensual policing extinct, and our streets will then be patrolled by some kind of paramilitary force or, much worse, run by the laws of the jungle.

PROLOGUE

'You'll make it, big man.'

'Keep going.'

'Don't friggin' lose him.'

'Put the foot down.'

These were the words of encouragement I got over the radio from behind me. Miles behind me. I was driving the lead car, about half a mile behind the target vehicle, and he had just made the Baillieston lights heading north from Glasgow. Trouble was there were two civilian cars side by side that hadn't made it through and were now stopped at the red light, like proper citizens, minding their own business.

I had a convoy of about five unmarked vehicles coming up behind me. Fast. I couldn't see any of them as yet, but I knew for sure they were there. I could hear them all shouting at me. We really didn't want to lose this guy and we surely would if I waited for these lights to change. We had no idea where he was going, only that he had said he was intent on shooting a police officer, and we knew he was capable, having just been released from a twenty-three year stint in a high-security prison. That was our official reason not to lose him. The sad reality was that we would all be on an earner if we could get on his tail and establish his route. A whole weekend of overtime and surprises in strange towns and cities. We could end up anywhere and it was all about to be lost if I couldn't get through this one set of lights. We would all just have to go home. God forbid.

John beside me in the passenger seat was totally useless. If he had said to stop, I think I might have. Maybe. But he couldn't speak at all. He was white-faced and white-knuckled. He didn't say to go for it either. Totally useless. I was doing about eighty and the distance was running out fast. Decision time. Of course,

I sunk the foot.

We were easily doing a hundred mph as we squeezed between the two stopped cars. Obviously, we made it, because I'm here to tell the tale, but what a bang. I know I was holding my breath and I can still feel the relief as we shot out the other side. I thought the noise must have been the sonic boom of the sound barrier being broken but soon realised that I had no wing mirrors left. Just hanging wires where they had been on either side. What a scare those two drivers must have got whether or not they saw our big Ford Sapphire coming as it sped through the nearly big enough gap, taking their mirrors with it. I might have noticed their shocked expressions if my eyes had actually been open.

John looked at me with puppy eyes I never again saw from a police officer. He must really have thought he was about to die. He did make some reference to this, but I quickly put him right by stating the obvious.

'We'd be better off dead than costing the team a weekend away on ovies.'

No argument there. Just huge relief. We could breathe again. The target was off on the M73 heading due north to who knows where. The lads were catching up fast to join the follow and good times lay ahead. Just another undercover surveillance operation for the Serious Crime Squad target team. But I'm a wee bit ahead of myself here. Let me take a breath and start at the beginning.

PART ONE:

CAMPBELTOWN

CHAPTER 1: THE BEAUTIFUL GAME – EARLY YEARS

Since I was old enough to walk, football has been an integral part of my existence. Ironically, I can now only play walking football. It has permeated every aspect and almost every day of my waking life, most of my sleeping life and definitely much of my thinking time. This explains a lot of my shortcomings, perhaps.

As a kid, I lived on Allander Street in Glasgow in an old prefab house. Importantly, we had a garden, or football pitch to be accurate, and I was mostly out there kicking a much too big football about. As a result, I was always good at 'keepy-uppy'. I'm sure the only reason I was persuaded to go to school at all was because I could play footie on the way, at the breaks and afterwards. As my mother would often comment:

'He's football daft, that boy.'

So, it was no surprise that for my fourth birthday, my grandfather, also Simon, was taking me to Lumley's on Sauchiehall Street to pick my first proper strip. On the top floor of Lumley's, I had the pick of the shop – almost. The only restriction placed by my mum was that I wasn't allowed a Celtic or a Rangers kit, as they would just attract trouble. Such considerations are perfectly natural in this part of the world. All of the tops were hung along the wall and I narrowed it down to two: Motherwell or Partick Thistle. Of course, at four years of age, it was only the colours that mattered, and the yellow, black and red stripes of the Maryhill Magyars naturally won the day. Destined to be a 'Jags' man for evermore, I can still marvel and delight at my early foresight and wisdom in avoiding that Fir Park mob.

So, I became a Thistle supporter, an affliction I bear to this day. When my son, Simon, was also about four years old, I took him to Firhill and lifted him over the turnstile as I had been by my granddad, mother and anyone else I could coax into taking me to see the 'Harry Wraggs.' It was a cold winter's day and they were playing Raith Rovers or some lower league team. There were few punters huddled under the shed anyway, but by half-time young Simon was bored silly, and took to running about the terraces. There was plenty of space and this was before we were all made to endure the match while sitting for the entire ninety minutes.

I realised that we were going to freeze to death or die of boredom and so I picked him up into my arms and started for the south exit. As we passed an old man on the terrace, I heard him grumbling and realised it was directed at me.

'Bloody disgrace, bringing kids to the fitba.'

Perplexed, I turned to perhaps defend my decision and saw that he was smiling. A toothless grin and wrinkles was all I could see under the Thistle tammy and big scarf wrapped around his neck. He must have been in his seventies or eighties. I smiled hesitantly while frowning at him and he said:

'That's what happened to me when I was a wee laddie, and I'm still fuckin' coming here.'

My son is now thirty-seven, and still the pull of Firhill goes on. He's even taken my wee granddaughter, Fallyn Louise, who was only two at the time. A family curse, I suppose. When my sister, Jane, visited from Brisbane a few years ago with her family, a visit to Firhill was pencilled in early on the itinerary. We had a great time, a lovely family day out, and she must have been lucky because the result was positive. We hammered Dundee 0-0.

Anyway, at four years old I was football daft and when I went to school, I had a confusing time, and not just academically. It seemed to be a big deal what school I went to, for all of my family. For me it was simple, because I only wanted to play football and all of the other stuff just filled the gaps between games. Kicking a ball to school, break times, lunch time and always straight after school. Shoes lasted a matter of weeks, and before Primary One was over, I had even been caught 'dogging' school with my mate,

Kevin Mitchell, to go and play football. So, this all begs the question:

'What school did you go to?'

This is the standard Glasgow enquiry that allows you to categorise someone as either side of the religious divide, a beloved precursor to any job interview, date, or welcome to almost any social gathering.

This is where it gets complicated for me. My dad was a 'Tim' (a Catholic to you perhaps). No question. His parents came to Glasgow from the far west of Ireland (Achill Island) in the thirties just before he was born, one of the youngest in a brood of twelve. He was in Lisbon in 1967, taught me all the Celtic songs and was as steeped in Irishness as only Irishmen who've never lived there can be. So, despite the fact that he had buggered off when I was an infant, I was sent to St Teresa's Primary School in Possil. By this time my mother had also buggered off, most likely on the trail of my dad, but who knows. My big brother, Dermot, was being passed about between our many relatives, and I was settled with my gran and grandpa on Allander Street, Possil. I later had a detective sergeant, Bob Barrowman, who couldn't believe anyone could be brought up on Allander Street and not have a criminal record. He maintained this made me backward or wanting, but more of Bob later.

A memorable night in Possil was 25th May 1967. Most Glaswegians, and certainly those sporting the emerald green hoops of Glasgow Celtic FC, will recognise the date instantly. I had just turned eight. That night Celtic became the first British club to win the European Cup. This was a fantastic achievement with a team of Scottish players, none born far from Celtic Park. I'm sure that most Scots were watching the game and I was no exception, together with my stepfather, my grandfather, my big brother, and with my mum floating about.

Of course, the sporting occasion was immense, even more so in retrospect with over fifty years having passed without a repeated achievement on that scale. My brother, Dermot, was never really a sports buff. He didn't really get it. I remember he and I would play tennis and after hours of slog it could be two sets all and four games apiece in the final set and he would say:

'I'm off home for my dinner now.'

He would leave me screaming and, no doubt, crying in frustration. I would rather lose than leave it as a draw.

Anyway, at half-time in the game that was to create The Lisbon Lions, he asked if I wanted to play football out in the back garden. Daft question, of course I did. I obviously got caught up in the game because at one point I scored a goal and the whole of Possil erupted, roaring their approval. Of course, I quickly learned that the late great Tommy Gemmell had just bulleted home the equalizer against Inter Milan from twenty-three yards. I had the privilege of telling Tommy that story many years later. He loved it.

So, back to my confusing childhood. I got as far as my first communion, but by this time my mother had met my future stepfather, Ian McLean. He was a 'Hun' (commonly known as a Protestant outside west-central Scotland and Northern Ireland) and, of course, my schooling was a big issue, it seemed. It resulted in me being taken from St Teresa's and moved to Keppochill School just over the hill. Simple enough, you might imagine, but just a tad confusing for a wee boy.

Up until then, in the school playground we would look through the elevated fence and shout at the kids going to the 'other' school. I don't remember much about the actual vocabulary but 'Proddy dogs' rings a bell. This was great fun as a six-year old, and it's a pursuit still enjoyed by many grown men in this part of the world. It was much enhanced, in fact it was only fun at all, if the 'dog' below shouted similar abuse back at us. This also applies in the grown-up version today, and it is the absolute vitriol in the resultant exchange between sixty-thousand fans of the Old Firm that creates what is generally accepted here as a 'great atmosphere.' What a place.

You can possibly imagine my confusion when I was sent to

Keppochill School because of my mother's change of religious persuasion, and had to walk over the hill with my new found pals only to be shouted at by my recent pals from above. 'Catholic cat' was the new lyric I had to memorise.

My grandpa worked in Smiths Iron Works in Possil, the type of heavy industry and workplace Glasgow was famous for at the time, and I would visit him there as much as possible when off school, because I got to kick a ball about with the men on their breaks and at lunchtime. He was a massive man, about twenty-five stone, and his appetite matched his stature, certainly for drink and gambling. My job on a Friday from the age of about seven years was to go to his work at finishing time and get his wage packet from him. These were the days when wages were paid in cash on a Friday. This was to prevent him going, via a few pubs, to the dog racing at Shawfield and being skint by Saturday morning. We must have grown up quickly in the sixties, because when I later worked in Possil as an undercover police officer, you wouldn't let a grown adult walk about Possil with as much as an ice cream cone, never mind a week's wages.

He was off to work about six-thirty every day, and my gran wasn't far behind him. I think she cleaned at one of the schools. So, I was home alone for a period every weekday. I was pre-school, no more than four years old. My gran would leave the record player on the floor plugged in. The old gramophone type with the solid lid and built-in mono speaker. She had piled a stack of singles ready to drop. All I had to do was get down off the bed and pull the lever, and off they would go, totally high tech in 1962. The single would drop, the arm moved over and onto the first groove, and off it went.

When they had all dropped and played, I would simply turn them all over, stack them on again, and pull the lever. Gran would be home soon after. Some of the songs I remember well. They must have been engrained in my brain. *It's Now or Never, Return to Sender, Moon River, Wonderful Land, Speedy Gonzales, Runaway.* I'm sure I could go on. Later in life, I became a DJ for my late great friend, Hinton Craig. I played keyboards in a rock band in the early eighties and my children all have music as a focus in their lives, my eldest being an accomplished musician. I'm sure all of this stems in some way from those far-off days when I was left to amuse myself on the record player every morning.

The highlights of my school years, certainly in primary, were all focused around football and, increasingly, sport in general. We had moved to the West End where my stepfather worked in a paper mill. We even took the giant leap of buying a house, which was a huge thing in the sixties. I played football for the school, the 108 Boys Brigade, the 101 Scouts in Hyndland and in every waking hour in between. Around the middle of Primary Seven, I learned that I had 'made it' into Hyndland Senior School, as opposed to being sent down a supposedly inferior route to a junior school – Hamilton Crescent, in this case. All I knew was that most of my mates and the best footballers were going to a different school. I was only interested in football. Even girls, although obviously intriguing, couldn't distract me from my dream of being a footballer. I so wish that focus had lasted much longer. Maybe another fifty years.

I loved playing football and my heroes were all the wingers we enjoyed in that era, and took totally for granted, never suspecting for a second that the position would become a relic not too long after. Arthur Duncan, Johnny Gibson, Dennis McQuade, Bobby Lawrie, George Best, Jimmy 'Jinky' Johnston, Willie Henderson, Willie Johnston, Eddie Gray, Charlie Cook, Peter Lorimer, and on and on. But I think two matches really affected me in a big way.

My first Old Firm game was at Hampden in May 1969, the Scottish Cup Final. I was in the famous North Stand looking down on the spectacle. There were over one hundred and thirty-thousand fans; half in blue, half in green. Totally mind blowing to a ten-year-old. For weeks afterwards, maybe months, I practiced non-stop, and for the first time had some idea of what was required physically to be a football player. Jinky didn't play that day, but the defenders, and in particular the late Billy 'Caesar' McNeil, made a huge impression in the way they dominated the game and the ball in the air.

Again, I was lucky to meet Billy and, as everyone who did so knows, he was an absolute gentleman. He made just as much of a positive impression on me as a man off the pitch as he had on it when I was a wee boy. People say that you should never meet your heroes as they will only disappoint, but that certainly didn't happen when I had the privilege of spending some time with Billy McNeil. This was in his pub off Victoria Road and, unbelievably now, ten of the Lisbon Lions were in the room. I sat with them and, although the camaraderie between them was obvious and the banter flying back and forth nonstop, it was obvious that they knew without question who their leader was. A real icon and role model sadly lost to us now.

The second game was when Celtic played Leeds United at Hampden in the European Cup semi-final a year later, in 1970. This time it was a big crowd of over one hundred and thirty-thousand mostly Celtic fans, and I had the opposite view than the North Stand. We were at ground level. A policeman made me put my legs back over the wall I was sitting on. This view changed my whole outlook. Jinky took some punishment, not only in that game but in general, and yet he bounced up and came back for more, time after time. I was so close to the action I got a real sense of the speed, determination and aggression required to play as a professional. I loved it, and will ever be proud to say that Jimmy was a friend of mine in later life, before we lost him in 2015.

I took it all seriously. I was totally obsessed. Some might say I still am, but as a young boy I lived and breathed football. That's all that mattered. One Saturday morning in Primary seven, we all got on the minibus and travelled to Dumbarton to play St Pats, always a good team. We got changed and were going out to warm up when the referee told us the pitch was waterlogged and the game was off. I was totally devastated. This possibility had not even occurred to me. It honestly broke my heart and I cried most of the way home. I couldn't handle it. My life revolved around the next game.

I think this explains why I rarely get disappointed. I tend to expect things to go wrong. So, if the flight's late or someone cancels a meeting, it's no big deal; if someone changes plans at the last minute or the weather closes in unexpectedly, I'm never too perturbed. A part of me is always expecting the pitch to be flooded. That way I never have to cry all the way home again.

On one winter Saturday morning, again we were on the park ready to go when the stupid referee decided it was too muddy or something. Idiot. We were trudging back in to the Scotstoun changing rooms when I met my mate, Stan, on his way out with the school rugby team he captained. He said they only had fourteen players and more or less co-opted me right there and then. I remember that first ever game of rugby vividly, for all the wrong reasons. They put me at full back and told me just to catch the ball and give it to someone else. That sounded easy enough.

Remember, it was freezing cold and wet, but apart from that I don't have any other excuses. The ball came towards me from space somewhere and I managed to do as I had been told. I got underneath it and caught it. Nae bother. Now what? It was then I looked up and saw a squad of massive guys running towards me full pelt. They looked really angry at me. For fuck sake. I did the only sensible thing available and threw the ball out the park. Now I knew why you give it to someone else, but there was no one around.

Stan was also captain of the school cricket team but I was ready to draw the line at that. Cricket, for goodness sake. Until he told me that you got a half-day off school to go and play. Now you're talking. Always loved that game. I actually really enjoyed it and found it to be every bit as physically demanding as any sport. I should also point out that I played rugby later in life for the police a few times, for RAF Machrihanish and for Kintyre Rugby Club. I just learned how to avoid those angry guys.

From then on, I didn't play at football anymore. It became

a serious endeavour. I was quickly appointed team captain in Primary Seven and this coincided with my slump in academic interest. I captained the school team throughout my four years of secondary, and in second year all my old friends and best players came back to Hyndland, which was now a comprehensive. Perfect.

Despite a few trials and playing for some right good teams over my secondary years, I never got spotted or invited to make the step up that I craved. I obviously wasn't quite good enough and certainly didn't have the posture or build of a player. In retrospect, I played with many lads who have gone on to make a living out of football all over the world, including John Wark and Andy Gray. It seems one of the things I lacked was a mentor or someone with contacts who could put me forward at the right time and place. I can testify without any chance of contradiction that neither my natural father, Eddie, nor my stepfather, Ian, ever saw me kick a ball on a football park, despite knowing that it was my obsession and dream. Perhaps that played a part.

I have a good friend now, Derek Connelly and his son, Ross, plays for Hamilton Accies as a goalkeeper. Derek has travelled all over Europe and beyond, and he or his wife Kate never missed a game during his younger years. Derek tells a story that when Ross was about ten years old, his mother, having watched him play and dive fearlessly at player's feet, insisted he wear some head protection. It wasn't optional and he sported head gear similar to what Petr Čech of Chelsea would later wear. Of course, he was the only youngster wearing such a contraption and a scout from one of the big clubs approached Derek to ask about Ross. His first question was:

'What's with the head gear? Is there something wrong with him?'

To which Derek replied, 'No his head is fine, it's his mother's head that's messed up.'

We now know that Katy was well ahead of her time and, as usual, mums know best. All young players will soon have to wear protective head gear. They both reckon that, apart from the obvious safety benefits of the helmet, it got Ross noticed. It made him stick out from the pack and he now earns his keep as a professional goalie.

I continued to play two or three times a week for a variety of teams and at sixteen years of age was told I was leaving school to get a trade. My mother had lined up an interview in Yarrows Shipbuilders in Glasgow and so that was where I started as an apprentice electrical engineer in 1975. Like most of my peers, I had little if any choice in this development. I would much rather have stayed on at school, but it wasn't an option for me. As Billy Connolly observed, as he had worked in the yards around that time, in those days of full employment the school gates and the gates of the shipyards and car works opened and everyone flooded across the gap.

I played for Yarrows, of course, although this really was a huge step up, not only in quality, but in physicality. This was where I could have done with some advice. I had no right to be playing this level of junior football. Not without a lot more savvy and conditioning than I had. But I just followed the football really and when I got some game time, I played the way I always had for the school, the BB, the Scouts and so on. Foolish. I also played Churches League badminton at that time, so fitness wasn't the issue, just naivety, and when you appear to be a smart ass someone is going to bring you down to size.

I ended up with a serious knee injury and had to have an operation, resulting in a lost knee cartilage. That wouldn't happen nowadays but was common then, and again, without any advice or instruction, I starting playing football as soon as I could walk. No rehabilitation, no physiotherapy programme, no clue really, and of course I just guaranteed deterioration of the knee over a period of time.

I was an apprentice electrician in Yarrows Shipyard, studying an ONC in electrical engineering, which entailed block release studies at Anniesland College alongside my practical apprentice-ship in the yard. When I was injured, playing for Yarrows team, I was off work for some six weeks, came back, slipped on a ladder in a Type-21 Frigate, injuring the same knee, and was laid off for another lengthy spell.

By the time I got back to work properly, not only had I lost my place in the team but I was told that I had missed too much study time and could no longer remain on the ONC course. I wasn't even allowed to drop down to what was termed the Technicians course but was to stop going to college altogether. I would become what we termed a 'wire puller', with no qualifications at the end of my apprenticeship. This was the state of affairs when I passed Strathclyde Police HQ on my bike and popped in out of curiosity. Without the injury, who knows what path my life would have taken, and all of what was to follow would undoubtedly be totally different.

At that time, I was dating a girl from Jordanhill. Her name was Allison. Her dad was a chemist and her mum a staff nurse and, of course, they considered me, with my long hair, Yamaha motorbike and cocky attitude, way below the standard they had in mind for their only daughter. I wasn't allowed anywhere near the house ultimately and, in retrospect, Allison, who went to a private school, was obviously using me to rebel against her privileged upbringing. Bitch. I only just realised that.

Anyway, I played badminton for the same church team as Allison and so I would pick her up on my bike not far from her house, but I almost got caught by her mum one night, and drove off at speed before she could give me any abuse. Her big face was red with rage. She apparently called me some particularly nasty names when Allison got home later that night. You'd think I'd kidnapped her.

I was out of the badminton and everything else for a while then as I got an operation on my knee at Gartnavel Hospital the next day. I had only ever been in hospital to get my tonsils out when I was four-years old and had apparently cried for three straight days, and so went there with real trepidation. In the morning I was to 'go down' with three other guys in my ward who were all much older than me. I was seventeen. We were given pre-meds that knocked them all out, but only made me giggly and full of beans. Stoned, of course. I only vaguely remember how funny it was that all the other guys were asleep, how hilarious it was getting put in a green goony, and how exciting it was getting wheeled down to theatre. It was a real hoot.

I was still quite enjoying this lark when the anaesthetist started talking to me and tapping my wrist. He was telling me that I would be knocked out and everything would be fine, and just before he told me to start counting to ten, I heard a vaguely familiar woman's voice saying cheerily:

'Good luck, Simon.'

When I looked at the end of the table all I remember is seeing the smiling, or smirking, big eyes of Allison's mum looking down on me. Next I knew, on the count of three, I was gone and woke up in agony back on my ward. I have told that story countless times, and with much more melodrama and relief when I got out of Gartnavel.

What I do know is that after the operation I surprisingly woke up in agony back on the ward. I had somehow contrived to get into a sort of foetal position in the bed and I must have been moaning or screaming in agony. When I was lifted and turned, I saw nurses crowded round me and one of them holding a big syringe and needle. She proceeded to pull my gown aside and stuck the needle in my backside, and I can still to this day remember the absolute bliss of those few painless seconds of euphoria before I slipped back into unconsciousness. It really was beautiful and has always been in my mind over the years dealing with all sorts of addicts, pushers and dealers. These substances are dangerous, not just because of the obvious effects and risks of overdosing or getting a bad hit. It's because of their amazing effect they are so addictive. That's why I am so wary of them, and would never even try hard drugs. I could see the dangers clearly.

This also applies to gambling for me. I saw as a boy the hardship and pain that it caused through my grandfather's affliction, although his was a story repeated throughout schemes like Possil. So, although I enjoy an occasional flutter on the National or suchlike, I never partake of that particular pastime, just in case I get caught in its vice-like grip.

I was out of hospital within a few days and played in a football tournament ten days later over on the beautiful island of Islay, congratulating myself on my great powers of recovery. I was limping about, of course, and it really was all downhill from there. What a twat.

With my prospects of becoming an electrical engineer 'up the swanny', as it were, and a gammy knee meaning I would be lucky to kick a ball seriously again, I really was at a crossroads. It was 1978. I was sharing a ramshackle flat with my friend, Stan, in a Woodside tenement. He was at Paisley Tech, as it was then, laying the foundations of a successful future as a civil engineer in the whisky industry. I was actively looking for a change in direction, and that change was to be almost as big a surprise to me as it was to anyone.

CHAPTER 2: THE POLIS!?

I honestly have no idea what possessed me that day. I was nineteen, still an apprentice electrician in Yarrows shipyard on the Clyde and living in a flat with my close friend, Stan. I drove a motorbike, had curly long hair over my shoulders, played in a wee rock band and was well down the road of satisfying my mother's mantra: 'Get a trade, son.'

I was driving through Glasgow City Centre on Pitt Street when, on impulse, I pulled up outside Strathclyde Police HQ. I walked in the main door, asked for recruitment, and was shown down a corridor. I entered a room marked personnel and asked the big sergeant behind his desk:

'How do I join the police?'

What a surprise when I wasn't thrown out the door. The sergeant was smiling as he eyeballed my soaking clothes dripping on his nice floor and my well-worn helmet clutched under my arm. As he put some forms together in an envelope he observed, 'You're tall enough anyway, lad – six-foot one – but you'd need to get that haircut.'

I mumbled some acknowledgement and left for home, for the first time considering actually applying to be a rozzer!

In retrospect, almost forty-five years later, the subtle seeds of this career option had been sown gradually. I had once been awarded a bravery (or stupidity) medal at Glasgow City Chambers for chasing some neds who had smashed the plate glass window of Modatoys, a toy shop at the corner of Clarence Drive and Lauderdale Gardens in Hyndland, right across from my school. I had caught one of them and handed him over to the police. Why I did this will always remain a mystery to me, but I did enjoy the recognition.

Also, in 1978, the police had just been recommended a massive pay rise, much improved conditions and index linked wages by the Edmund Davis report. The incoming Thatcher Government were committed to enacting these recommendations, obviously beefing up the police for the many coming conflicts with the unions. Strathclyde Police were recruiting like mad, even advertising constantly on local radio. This had obviously permeated my subconscious.

In any event, I related this intended lark into the heart of the establishment to my mum, stepdad, brother, sister and mates, who all giggled or laughed and dismissed the whole idea as outlandish. Not one of them took me seriously, not because they thought I was obviously destined for greater things, but because they thought I wasn't smart enough, was too lazy, too undisciplined or too wild. I do know that I filled that form out and handed it in to Pitt Street, personally simply to spite them all, and find out if they were right. In retrospect I think these were the very 'qualities' required to later qualify me for The Ten Percent.

I was subsequently interviewed, sat an exam, and attended a medical. I was then told that a sergeant would visit my home as the final part of the recruitment process. Now, that posed a real problem. There was absolutely no way I could use the address of my shared flat in Woodlands. That would have meant washing dishes and cleaning the place. I had wisely used my mum and stepfather's address in Novar Drive, Hyndland on my application and so an old Highland sergeant appeared at the appointed hour one winter evening in 1978.

My mother proved to be the perfect host, as always. He was directed into the front room (the good room kept for such auspicious occasions) and after some pleasantries she asked him, 'Would you like a wee dram, Inspector?'

The rest was a formality, I suppose, and so, on 27th December 1978, I was sworn into the office of police constable at Oxford Street in Glasgow.

There were about a hundred and twenty recruits at Oxford Street for two weeks, about double a normal intake. The police really were recruiting in droves at the time. One of my lasting memories of this initial introduction to the service was on the Friday of the second week, when we were to be spoken to by the clergy. We were told that the Catholic contingent should all move to another part of the building, where a priest was waiting. The rest were to stay where they were.

There was much grumbling among the ranks; many of them had begun to form what would become lifetime friendships in that intense fortnight, and someone shouted out, 'We'll all stay here together.'

This was quickly followed by what seemed like a unanimous consensus of mumbled approval and no one moved from their seat.

After some huddling and conferring on stage, it was announced that a communal service would follow. And it did. Sometimes the students teach the learned, and what I now know is that the old-school coppers who had been paid a pittance barely above subsistence, and been treated as second-class citizens, would never have dared question any such instruction.

A new era was dawning, a totally new breed of copper. Not interested in bigotry, segregation, colour or class. Joining the Masons would no longer be mandatory. What side of the Old Firm divide you supported would no longer dictate your working environment or prospects, apparently. A new Chief Constable, Patrick Hamill, was seeing to all of that stuff.

An Assistant Chief Constable also spoke to us at the end of that day, and what I remember of his talk was that he said when everyone else was running away from things, as police officers, we would be running towards them. Sobering words, indeed, as we all headed into the unknown together.

CHAPTER 3:
KEYSTONE COPS

By this time we had found out where we would be posted on leaving Tulliallan ten weeks later. The way I discovered this reveals much about just how naive and unworldly we all were. I was given a rough sketch map with all of the geographic divisions and boundaries shown. Highlighted on mine was L Division, which had Dumbarton as the HQ.

I could also see Old Kilpatrick, Helensburgh, Balloch and The Vale of Leven, all just blue train journeys from Glasgow. As a Glasgow West Ender I was naturally chuffed, but, unbeknown to me, Argyll had failed to reach the map. It transpired that there were eight of us allocated to L Division and we were told to report at Dumbarton HQ at ten o'clock the next day, in uniform.

We all met at Buchanan Bus Station and as we got on the bus we were fumbling in our uniform pockets for change to pay the driver. He looked at all of our red faces still quite embarrassed to be in police uniform, and with a quizzical look explained, 'You don't pay on the bus, lads.'

This was our first, but not last, lesson that there is no learner uniform. When you wear the cop uniform you are expected to be one. End of. Total strangers ask you the time – all the time – ask for directions, report things to you, and give smiling good mornings or 'hello officer' on passing. More interestingly, if you initiate the contact by smiling, waving or saying hello, they invariably respond to the uniform in kind. A really useful social tool to a young single man.

We all arrived intact at Dumbarton police office, L Division HQ, in good time and were shown to a massive board room. We were sat around the table expectantly when, a few minutes later, a huge man stepped in, Divisional Commander Watson, with scrambled eggs all across his police hat. There were no niceties or formalities. He didn't sit down or say hello, just simply:

'I need two for Oban, two for Dunoon, two for Campbeltown and two for Rothesay. You have ten minutes to sort it out, lads.'

And off he went.

I quickly said, 'I'll go to Campbeltown.'

I had been there once. I had cycled to Carradale on the Kintyre coast and camped there a few times. I had been to Islay a few times, also camping, and so, at least, had some idea of where it all was. My mate, Graham Kennedy, copied me, and so Campbeltown had its latest recruits.

As we left the building, we were all anxious to discover each other's destinations and my buddy, Rab McCubbin, said he was off to Rothesay. Shocked, I asked him why he chose Rothesay and he just shrugged his shoulders. I said, 'You need to get boats and stuff.'

He laughed. 'Fuck off. It's only a train to Rothesay, big man.'

Fair enough. He must know these things. As it transpired, we were all actually in the same boat. Totally clueless.

As for Graham Kennedy, it transpired he had just copied me, thinking he had a good idea where we were headed. He lived in Alexandria after all. How far could it be?

He actually travelled down to Campbeltown a few days before me as he was going onto a different shift. We both drove motorbikes but were using the bus to get our stuff (albums, stereo, dancing gear, ironed shirts) moved down to our digs. Graham later told me that he had asked the bus driver where to change buses for Campbeltown. In those days you had to complete the latter part of the journey down the Kintyre Peninsula on a West Coast Motors bus. The driver told him to change at Tarbert.

When the bus arrived at Tarbet, just before Arrochar, Graham was off, waiting for his luggage to be retrieved from the hold. The driver said to him:

'I thought you were going to Campbeltown, son.'

'Aye, and you told me to change bus here,' Graham reminded him.

The driver was patient and told him to get back on and he would keep him right. It was, of course, the beautiful Tarbert on Loch Fyne where the buses changed, which felt like the end of the world by the time Graham got there more than two and a half hours later, after a break at Inveraray.

The real shock for Graham was that the West Coast Motors' bus in those days played teuchter Scottish music down the Kintyre road all the way to Campbeltown, culminating on the winding ten mile stretch that was Tangy Bends, a particularly severe series of twists and turns that circumvented the coastal rock formations near to Tangy Farm. This was the location of many an accident, many of them fatal. A traumatic journey for a city boy, who couldn't believe a town actually existed at the end of this adventure.

I wasn't far behind, of course, and actually arrived in 'the Wee Toon' on Monday 16th April 1979, one week after my twentieth birthday. As luck would have it, that Monday was a public holiday and the place was quite deserted. I had to report to the police station, and of course had no idea where that was, but as I retrieved my bags from the hold of the bus, I was approached by a male about my age who asked, 'Are you the new copper?'

He then directed me towards Castlehill, where the old copshop sat, taking great delight in escorting me some of the way. He thought this was all hilarious. Of course, I soon discovered that he was one of the most notorious rogues in Campbeltown. We became well acquainted over the next three years.

In the few months prior to our arrival in Campbeltown, after our initial two-week training at Oxford Street in Glasgow, we were all required to attend probationer training that lasted eight weeks. This was residential, non-negotiable and would much determine if a career in the police was possible or desirable for us as individuals. Before we could travel to our respective postings and begin our probationary period, we had to be tried and tested to the full. We had to be intimidated, belittled, confused, bombarded with facts, laws and information, and our temperaments tested to the fullest degree.

There was only one place where all of this could be accomplished outside Colditz and that was in the prison that the Scottish Police call Tulliallan: the Scottish Police College in Kincardine, Fife.

CHAPTER 4: COLDITZ

My first experience of Tulliallan was traumatic, just exactly as it was intended to be. About a third of the young recruits who travelled there for initial training left within the first week. This was usually achieved by simply running away. Every morning over that first week another few dormitory beds were deserted when we were roused at six-thirty. Gone, vanished. Never to be seen again. And that was the whole point of the first week. Not that I knew that at the time.

From the minute I walked in the front door I had some apparently deranged sergeant screaming at me to hurry up, slow down, get my hair cut, stop talking, tidy myself up, whatever. Usually this was communicated by screaming in my face. My only response was: 'Yes, Sergeant.'

I could see that all of the other recruits were being shouted at just the same and so I was quite happy. I didn't know what was going on really, but as long as everyone was happy, I was too. I could put up with any amount of shouting and bawling. I had been brought up with shouting. I think it all seemed quite normal to me. Everyone was sober, no one was threatening any violence. No big deal, really. I had always been taught to keep an eye on the quiet guy. He was the real danger. I would still prefer shouting to whispering and mumbling, or even silence.

It was a real problem to plenty of others though. Some of these guys were absolute nervous wrecks. They took it all so personally. Some were actually in tears at night. They generally lasted no more than that first week, but the first to leave were the guys who had to shout back, and they were sometimes the guys who had arrived with a swagger you could dry the washing with.

'Who do you think you're shouting at, pal?'

Similar, less polite, responses being a sure-fire way of getting marched straight back out the door.

I think I had my hair cut twice in the first few days. I was made to remake my bed about twenty times one morning and we were all marched onto the parade ground at crazy times of day, or made to double time it to the swimming pool with no notice. It was all so random that I enjoyed it, although I moaned and complained among my peers and new friends, of course. A given. I wonder what goes on at Police College now. I'm quite sure it's no longer acceptable to badger and bully recruits. Maybe they get the same but have signed a disclaimer giving shouting permission beforehand. Oh, and the offer of counselling after a bawling out? Who knows? But back then it was how they 'found you out.'

Throughout all of this we were constantly pressing uniforms, 'bulling up' our boots to a high shine, trying to complete the gruelling physical tests in the pool and on the sports fields and gym and, of course, studying like mad for exams and trying to grasp totally new concepts and legislation. I was told recently by a young cop that there had been an eighteen-year-old recruit on her course who couldn't complete a press up. Yes, one press-up. Honestly.

When you also consider that we were all thrown into this eight-week induction with a hundred or so total strangers, it added up to the most intense, exhilarating, challenging and rewarding experience of our young lives. It really did make or break you, and for those of us who came out the other end and made it to our postings in divisions throughout Scotland, we at least had a level of fitness and a basic knowledge of the law as it applied to our duties. We had acquired and accepted a level of discipline that would enable us to be presentable as cops, and listen to our experienced colleagues and gaffers for the few years it would take to shape us into actual useful police officers, although arguably some never reached even those lowly heights.

We made friends at Tulliallan, some of which would last a few months, some a lifetime, but we were all in it together at that point and so we all helped each other pull through. Of course, the whole spectrum of character types were represented in our ranks. The academics, who excelled in the classroom and in exams, who loved to study or found the learning easy. Or ones like me, who enjoyed the sports and found physical activity rewarding. I was never out of the pool, became the fittest I ever was, played football for the police, and became badminton champion in subsequent years. In those days the police encouraged and facilitated sportsmen and women as much as possible, although I'm led to believe that has changed somewhat now.

There were musicians, artists, representatives of every possible trade, some ex-soldiers or forces personnel, office workers, labourers, teachers, unemployed. In fact, you name it and chances are there was representation, including some barbers who made a few quid at Police College. These recruits were spread across the age spectrum, from eighteen to mid-thirties mostly, and would form the backbone of the Scottish Police Service for the next thirty years.

There was only a token female presence. I would guess that five percent of the students were women as, in those days, policewomen were still much in the minority and definitely treated much differently from their male colleagues. They were still required to wear skirts, had different uniform and equipment, and weren't expected to perform the same tasks as today. I think with hindsight that I was there at the start of changed thinking, especially on the part of the women recruits of the day, who went on to prove that they were every bit a match for their male counterparts in every aspect of the job.

As a young cop in Campbeltown, I was working one of my first night shifts with a PC John Malcolm, a big lad, full of fun. John thought it would be a great laugh to scare a police woman in the early hours one night, and had acquired a realistic full-face rubber mask for this purpose. She was on her own in the old Castlehill Police Office when John started scratching windows and making noises around the building in an effort to spook her.

This culminated in him being at the back door into the car

park when she swung the door fully open and saw him leap towards her making scary monster noises with his grotesque mask on. She, Christine (then) Alexander, proceeded to thump him full pelt over the head with her baton, and I think would have continued to do so if I hadn't intervened.

John was lucky that women PCs were issued with 'sticks' about half the size and weight of the men's baton. He still had a nice lump.

The most dangerous times in that period of initial training at Police College were not at Tulliallan, surrounded by our peers and teachers, but at the weekends when we got home to have our washing done. You see, we all had our police warrant cards, had been sworn in as constables and had a tiny bit of growing knowledge. Life goes on, of course, and I remember several situations where it was only by luck or the swift intervention of a friend that I was prevented from producing my identification in order to 'deal with' some situation in a pub or on the street. A few of my peers came a cropper in such circumstances.

It was only later in my service, and especially working in a rural community, that I realised the dangers involved, where fighting men, or even crowds, can suddenly become allies against a common enemy: a police officer. Many a time, in later years, I made a swift exit or even stepped over fighting men to escape such a scenario. When off duty, of course.

A story from that period of my life underlines how much life has changed in the forty years since. We were told to prepare a ten-minute speech on any subject, to be delivered to our own class. Public speaking like this was a strong feature of all police training, and an attribute I came to be truly thankful for in later life.

I had a few ideas, no doubt revolving around football or sport, but my mate, Stan, was at Paisley Tech at the time, studying civil engineering. He told me a fascinating story about a thing called the silicon chip, and how it was about to transform almost every aspect of our lives. As he explained how typewriters would become obsolete, replaced by word processing, all manner of devices would become miniature and portable, the repercussions began to dawn. Together we made furious notes and came up with what was a ground-breaking, up-to-the-minute talk, giving my peers a privileged insight into the near and distant future.

I'm not sure how well delivered it was, but I know that I was enthusiastic for sure, and that is normally half the battle, but it totally flopped. No one was the slightest interested in this science fiction nonsense, and I was totally deflated by their lack of engagement. I received the cursory round of applause, and cursory average assessment for what was a fantastic peek into the future of mankind! Bastards.

My next effort at speaking in front of the class was to explain where I was going to work, the Mull of Kintyre. This involved me drawing the geographical area on a marker board while I explained where it was, and a huge dick with hairy balls appeared in front of everyone's eyes. This received hysterical ongoing laughter as I filled it in with a straight face and commentary about the area. I received a hearty round of applause, numerous pats on the back and a resounding A+ mark. I make no public judgement about what these responses say about our level of recruitment and tutoring back then.

My assessment at Tulliallan on that initial eight-week training course was decidedly positive. I had passed all of the exams, although with not much above average grades. I had proved myself competitive and was extremely fit with an interest and some proficiency in all sports. I had worked hard to excel in the pool and achieved all of the lifesaving certificates achievable. I had made loads of friends and proved sociable.

I had survived a few minor scrapes with authority, but overall had shown a healthy respect for rank and the discipline of uniform dormitory life. So, Tulliallan had done its initial job. I was a decent, honest individual who was clean and tidy, had a reasonable temperament, was – crucially – teachable and trainable and could get on with people. I was fit to start my two-year probationary period as a constable, and I was raring to go.

CHAPTER 5: DEATH

This came as a complete surprise to me, as it does many. The fact that the police deal with death on a daily basis, and as with most learning curves in uniform, I was deliberately thrown in at the deep end. There I was in my first week on the job, sitting in our Sherpa police van blethering to my big pal, Tam McNab, in the middle of the night, hardly a care in the world, single in those days, on a nice calm night on Main Street, Campbeltown, when – boom. All hell lets loose.

This was my first real emergency, when everything kicks off, when things happen automatically but much more loudly, quickly and intensely, when everyone kicks into an entirely different mode altogether. I learned to do that, to become part of the solution, acting on autopilot, as part of a team; a concerted effort. I took to that emergency mode so well that it became my comfort zone. It still is, I suppose, and I suspect it always will be.

When all of the training kicks in, all the repetition, practice and discussion come to the fore, the instant rush of adrenalin when you drive at high speed, take down a violent ned, switch on that blue light, kick in a door, search for a missing kid, jump in the water, whatever. It really is addictive, and to this day, at sixty-one, I still feel as though I'm constantly on stand-by.

I'm only really fully alive when the shit hits the fan.

An emergency, at a familiar farm address, recognisable names and an unusually frantic response by Tam, who was not easily roused, a blue light dash, ambulances appearing as we pulled up, tears, screaming, more police officers. Mayhem. I really don't remember much of what happened at the scene.

A recently retired police officer, Graham, had gone to bed with a headache and suffered a massive brain haemorrhage in his sleep. I had only known him vaguely from camping trips to Islay before I joined the police, but he had worked there in Port Ellen as a constable and in Campbeltown. He had a young wife and family and was well-known and liked by all of my now colleagues.

The sequence of events and the details have all escaped me now, as I was too new and shocked to process the flood of information, and simply did as I was told. This included removing the remains to the cottage hospital mortuary where Tam and I removed Graham from our 'shell', a fibreglass temporary coffin used to transport the deceased, and placed him on a mortuary slab to await examination.

One thing I did remember, and can still to this day recall with the same internal response, the same shock and feeling like no other I have ever experienced, was that as I took Graham's legs to help lift him, I felt the coldness of death, a coldness that cannot be matched or compared, an instantly recognisable coldness that penetrated my soul, stamping an indelible mark on me forever. A unique coldness, colder than marble, or frost, or ice. The ultimate coldness that penetrated my very being.

Although I would later feel that same cold on many deceased persons throughout my police service and life, including my parents and my twenty-three-year-old daughter, Louise, it is that first time in the mortuary of the old cottage hospital in Campbeltown that still comes to mind when death raises its bastard head.

CHAPTER 6:
THE POST MORTEM

In rural parts, a certain flexibility is required by the local police. This entails utilizing available resources to best effect, including equipment and manpower, forging relationships with local contractors or experts and generally making do and mucking in. It all goes without saying. The job just gets done.

With three or four officers on shift at any one time to cover the array of police responsibilities, I would contest that a rural posting provided a sink or swim environment with the broadest range of duties possible. From school crossing patrols to sheep dipping, from bumps to fatal accidents, petty theft to robbery, and from minor skirmishes to murder, the only certainty being the total unpredictability of any occurrence at any given time on any given day.

On that same week of night shift (my first), I was again with Tam McNab on Main Street, having just finished our first property check. This is sadly a historic function where we would physically check that all of the commercial property in the town was secure, front and back where accessible. 'Pulling padlocks' is how we described it and it was taken seriously indeed.

I was once roused from sleep with no sympathy or apology at nine o'clock after a night shift and asked when I had checked a specific property on my beat as it had been found violated by the proprietor. Our sergeant, Archie Shaw, treated the property check as a primary function, and we took to carrying out two property checks per night where possible. Such was the importance he attached to pulling padlocks he even made us wake him up to help!

Anyway, Tam and I were sent to a nearby address where it was suspected that a male had died. Tam decided to pass the police station, on Castlehill at that time, and pick up the aforementioned shell, which is when our first problem arose. The Sherpa van was at Lochgilphead for monthly service, and due to circumstances they had given us the short wheelbase Land Rover for that one night. Unfortunately, the shell was about eight inches too long to fit in the back of the vehicle.

Resourceful as ever, I was sat in the rear with my back against the wire bulkhead, holding onto the shell by its tiny metal hook handle, which only allowed a three-finger grip. Easy enough on the five-minute outbound journey to the locus. On our arrival, things started to go pear-shaped.

The doctor had just left, having pronounced life extinct. The deceased had apparently choked on his own vomit while sleeping on the couch. Our problem was that the sitting room and couch were on the upper level of the property, meaning we had to negotiate a stairwell with a landing half-way, and a big daft banister. This was tricky with the shell empty, but physically demanding on the way down with the cadaver on board. It was also mentally demanding of Tam, who of course was in charge of the operation. Laurel and Hardy would have made a better job.

We then faced the major task of taking the shell and its contents to the local mortuary in our Land Rover, which was still too wee for the shell. Again, I was perched in the rear, now with my feet braced against the rear stanchions, and off we went with the back door wide open and the shell jutting out the back. It was a five-minute drive to the old cottage hospital, but the Cottage Brae was famously steep and serpentine, and Tam was easily the worst driver I had ever experienced to that point, although he was Lewis Hamilton compared to some police drivers I encountered in the future.

He stalled twice going up the brae, and by the time we reached the summit every muscle in my body was aching and my three fingers holding the totally inadequate shell handle were welded together. I was holding on, though. The thought of the shell and its contents shooting out the rear of the police vehicle is funny in retrospect, but not so funny when a real possibility.

On our return to the office I was asked if I had ever seen a post mortem. Of course, at twenty-one I had only a vague idea of what a post mortem was, and so I was told to go with Tam and transport the deceased to the Vale of Leven hospital in Alexandria where the event would take place later that day.

Before leaving, I was told by an old sergeant, Alec John McLellan, that I should watch the post mortem from start to finish, regardless of how I felt. He insisted that no matter my response, revulsion or physical sickness, this would stand me in good stead, and prepare me for the many gruesome sights I was sure to encounter throughout my career.

I did as instructed and, surprisingly, kept my lunch down. I was fascinated by the whole environment and process, calmed perhaps by the respect displayed by the mortuary attendants, hospital staff and pathologist to the deceased, and by their professionalism and calm demeanour. I watched everything from nearby and stayed throughout, although Tam had gone for a kip, having seen it all before. I would be lying if I claimed to have enjoyed this experience. I'm not one for watching operations on TV or even for reading about the blood and gore in a story, but I enjoyed having had the experience.

I think it was life changing in its way. When you've seen the human body taken apart, the skull sawn off and the ribs parted to expose the major organs, seen those organs put in jars for further examination and heard the pathologist systematically recite his or her observations regarding the condition of the lungs, brain, heart, etc., there's not much more that can confront you. Old Alec John was absolutely right. I was much better prepared for the career to come, with all of its gruesome sights, sounds and smells, after watching a full post-mortem.

More upsetting and thought provoking than the actual dismantling of the human body was when the process was complete and the cadaver was being put away in the fridge. Now shrouded, it was wheeled along to a big bank of fridge doors, one was opened and the trolley was slipped inside. Then another door was opened and a tiny child's body was taken out for examination. As I said, death has a coldness like nothing else and provokes a unique sadness that permeates our soul.

The purpose of the PM is to enable the pathologist to ascertain the cause of death and, if content with his findings, and finding nothing suspicious, issue a death certificate, allowing the deceased to be released to the family for burial or other arrangements. At the end of the procedure the pathologist called us both into his office and stated that he was unwilling to issue a certificate as yet. He had found two small holes in the deceased's forehead and he thought some investigation should be made. This was most perplexing.

As Tam called Campbeltown to relate this development and initiate some CID involvement, I had a eureka moment. The shell. Only Tam and I knew of the shenanigans involved in removing the body from the flat.

I immediately inspected the shell and called the pathologist over. Sure enough there was a tiny screw head sticking out of the shell cover just above where the head would have been. After his own inspection of both the shell cover and the deceased, and our reluctant confession as to our lack of removal abilities, the pathologist was satisfied and duly issued the requisite death certificate.

This was a big lesson for me as a rookie cop. The details and facts are crucial. The truth is an imperative. It was only by luck and because the sergeant wanted me there at the post mortem that Tam and I were there at all. If other cops had attended the PM they would have been totally perplexed as was the pathologist. This would have triggered a whole set of enquiries and investigations before the explanation was found, entailing a lot of leg work and uncertainty, as well as totally unnecessary grief and worry for the deceased's family and friends.

Back in Campbeltown, the local detective sergeant, Arnie Carson, had his first words with me, and explained how he had been aware of every aspect of the case from the first phone call and written incident report to its satisfactory conclusion, and how his department would now interview those involved before the death and at the flat itself in order to confirm that there were no 'suspicious circumstances.' He went over and noted my statement and explanation of the injuries, which had indeed been incurred post mortem.

Although I had only four weeks or so 'on the job,' I think the seeds were sown right there. I wanted to be him. A detective.

CHAPTER 7: BAD NEWS

As a uniform police officer in a rural posting like Campbeltown, dealing with 'sudden deaths' (or 'suddin puddins', as we referred to them) is at least a weekly occurrence and, of course, these deaths take every shape and form: natural causes, road and other accidents, drowning, fires, as well as suicides and murders.

In every instance, bar the latter, the procedure was much the same; the paperwork the same, and the routine the same. Have a doctor confirm life extinct, secure the scene and any property, identify the deceased, inform relatives or next of kin, establish the cause of death and so on. Every rural copper could do this on autopilot through repetition, but despite that, each and every death leaves an indelible mark, or so I now believe.

As a CID officer in Barrhead many years later, I was heading back to the office one lovely Sunday afternoon when I heard a call go out over the radio several times. Realising there was no one available to take the call, and only being five minutes away, I took it. Nice guy. A lady was concerned for her elderly next-door neighbour as he hadn't been seen for a few days and wasn't answering his door or telephone. Straightforward.

I met the lady, opened the gent's letter box and realised immediately what the situation was. There is no smell like death. I told her I would deal with it, smashed a small pane of glass on the door and entered the house. The old man (seventy-eight, I later discovered) was sitting on his lounge chair, half-drunk cup of tea by his side and the TV on in front of him. He had passed away peacefully in his own home. I called for the doctor and started to establish relatives, identity, etc., for the sudden death report. Just total routine.

By this time in my service I had dealt with every shape and form of death, including the most violent imaginable as a Serious

Crime Squad officer, the most horrific road traffic accidents and the most heart-breaking murders and deaths of children. So, an elderly man passing away peacefully in his armchair shouldn't cause too much of a problem. Or so you would think. But the mind is a strange miracle indeed.

The practicalities were purely routine, as stated, but I was still thinking about that old man later that night. I've absolutely no idea why that would be the case, but it was. A few days later he would pop into my head again and this continued for some weeks. I hadn't told anyone about this, sure that it would pass soon enough. But it didn't. It went on for months and sometimes could move me to tears, but always leaving me with a deep melancholy that settled over me for hours.

Eventually I spoke to the police doctor about it, but Dr McClay was old-school. He could only offer the same platitudes that friends and family had to hand. The police were not at all tuned into these things in those days, in line with practically all employers in my experience. I never did get any useful information, far less an answer, but with the passage of time I stopped mourning that old man gradually, and I can safely say that today is the first time I've thought of him for a long, long time. If my story stops here you will understand why.

There were many more deaths where that effect would have been much more understandable, and therefore more acceptable. Cot death, for example, is far too common, and among the most heart-wrenching deaths for any police officer to deal with. I had more than my share as a CID officer in Campbeltown and Rothesay. At one in particular, the baby's mother was only just seventeen, and had what we would now describe as learning difficulties. She was well-known to the local police.

I attended the highly charged scene accompanied by a police woman and when it came time to remove the baby we couldn't use the police shell. It just seemed totally inappropriate somehow. In the event, my colleague sat in the rear of the CID car with the baby wrapped in its blankets, in her arms as if sleeping. I'll always remember the nurse at the hospital morgue taking the baby from us as if handling a live sleeping baby, gently and carefully. I liked that a lot.

In this case the post mortem verdict was cot death, which means nothing to anyone, but the next day the young mum was waiting to see me at the office when I arrived. She told me a really sad tale of friends visiting, drinks being on offer, fun being had and the baby crying in the room for attention, a feed or a change no doubt. She said she had only tried to hush the baby, and did so, and only later discovered her mistake when baby could not be roused.

I arranged a further post-mortem, but the results were totally inconclusive. Medical professionals don't rush to contradict colleagues, ever. So, no charges were brought. In Scotland, a confession is never enough to convict anyone without supporting or corroborative evidence. Thank goodness. To the best of my knowledge that young mother later went on to raise a family.

On another occasion, an elderly man had gone out walking around the hills and never returned. Missing persons are a daily occurrence for the police, but the vast majority are tracked down or returned within hours. It's the tiny minority that are troublesome. There was no trace of this chap, and eventually the physical search has to come to an end. This is a devastating time for the family, but inevitable just the same.

If there is no evidence of foul play, or obvious leads as to the whereabouts of the missing person, the physical search ends, and the private attitude of the police is that the person will turn up sooner or later, hopefully, but rarely, alive (of course, this is totally different where children or young persons are involved).

This particular old man had been 'a bit down' since the death of his wife and had wandered off onto the hills, it seemed. We were aware that a close relative worked at the local hospital, and this was useful knowledge if identification was needed at a later stage.

Sure enough, a few weeks later, a body was recovered at sea.

I can't remember if it was washed up or brought in by a fishing boat, but from the age and description there seemed little doubt that it was our missing old man. We collected the remains and conveyed them to the mortuary. This is not a popular job as remains brought from the water are never pleasant to deal with.

We managed to place the cadaver on the mortuary slab and prepare it as best we could for identification. His relative, who was working in the hospital at the time, was called to do the needful. With the usual inevitable upset, tears and preparation, I eventually folded the sheet down covering the face of the deceased to allow the relative to see the victim. She immediately let out a wail and a scream (I'm not sure of the difference) and ran from the mortuary shouting, 'It isn't him.'

Shit. Wrong old man, obviously. The danger of assumption, eh?

There's no happy ending here, of course, but there are usually endings. Her relative did eventually turn up dead on the hills and was laid to rest. It transpired that the body recovered from the sea had made its way over from Ayrshire, and he too was reconciled with his family, but only after a post-mortem.

Again, the post-mortems were carried out in Alexandria, and of course the deceased had to be transported there by the police. John Malcolm and I were given that job, but the problem with remains brought from the sea, especially after several weeks decomposing, is the smell. We devised a plan, which was sanctioned by the hierarchy.

We took the Sherpa van, and the driver wore a gas mask type thing. Even so, the smell was so overpowering that we changed over every twenty minutes or so with the other cop following in a police car. In this fashion we conveyed the remains to Alexandria and back, a round trip of over two-hundred miles. Not my best shift, for sure, and every stitch we had worn that day was destroyed.

The Sherpa van was off the road for over a week. It was washed, scrubbed and treated with every detergent and disinfectant known to man. It was hosed out three or four times a day. It was left with all of its doors and windows open twenty-four hours a day. Our wee handy man Harry Hutch made it his mission to get that van back on the road. Yet every copper who ever sat in it could smell the unmistakable odour of death as he or she entered. It never did go away. It never really does.

Again, with Tam McNab, I attended a call to a quite remote cottage on the outskirts of Campbeltown one back shift. A post man or delivery driver had raised the alarm due to a lack of any activity at the premises, where an elderly man lived alone. When we arrived, the doctor was just leaving. I doubt he had even gone into the bedroom, far less carried out any examination of the deceased. He had died in his sleep and in his bed, and was still there with the covers around him.

Tam and I took up our positions in this by now well practiced job, and simultaneously placed our gloved hands under the remains in order to lift him from the bed and into the shell, and both of us quickly drew our hands back as if bitten. The body was still warm. This was totally counterintuitive as the one thing everybody has in common in death is that definitive coldness. Our brains couldn't process this for a few seconds, the first thought being that he's still alive.

Of course, he wasn't, and as we regained our composure, I realised that the electric blanket was still on, and obviously had been for a few days, hence the smell. I don't need to go into further detail here, but suffice to say the undertaker agreed that we could place the body straight into his shell and miss out the police shell part. Of course, I helped him do his stuff and when I was stripping another uniform for the cleaners that night I found a five-pound note in my top tunic pocket. I never did find out for sure, but I think the undertaker, who I would unfortunately become well acquainted with in years to come, stuck that fiver there as a gratuity for the help I gave him with that particularly bad job. I'm quite sure it was the one and only monetary tip I ever received as a cop. Then again, maybe it was a wee fiver I had forgotten about …

Another part of the process that most people forget falls squarely on the shoulders of police officers is the delivery of the dreaded 'death message', a thankless and hated task undertaken by every officer on a regular basis. The loved ones, usually a wife or husband or other close relative, have to be informed quickly, and often need to assist with the required identification. I can remember my first death message delivery in Campbeltown as if it was yesterday. As a rookie, I was an observer, but it demonstrated at an early stage just how unpredictable life can be.

An old man had passed away peacefully in the local cottage hospital. He had been there a while and there had been no drama or commotion. Tam McNab and I were passed the details and instructed to attend his home address and inform his now-bereaved wife. It doesn't get any simpler, and Tam talked me through it. He said we would go to the downstairs neighbour and inform her, and ask her to accompany us when we delivered the death message to the elderly lady, just to help keep her calm. Simple enough plan that, for Tam, seemed well thought out.

We chapped the neighbour's door and when she opened it and saw the two uniforms and glum faces she screamed and went into hysterics. (Someone told me once it's never good news when that uniform appears at the door and that kind of sums up the job.) We had to go in and try to calm her down. She was supposed to be helping us go upstairs for the hard part. We were there maybe ten minutes consoling this neighbour and eventually convinced her that we needed to be calm for the next bit, and so she came with us up another flight, and we waited to go through the whole rigmarole again.

The new widow opened the door and saw the three of us and said, 'That's him away then. I knew it wouldn't be long. Come in and have a cuppa, lads.'

We left her a while later comforting her neighbour, who was still visibly upset. Folk never cease to surprise.

In the same vein, Sergeant Barnett and I went to visit a lollipop man who was giving it up. We had to gather his stick and coat and bits and bobs as well as complete some paper work. He was a really nice old guy, Archie. His wife had passed away a week or so ago and he was a deflated character. They had been married for almost sixty years. Sad.

We went in and were seated in the living room and pleasantries were exchanged. Archie remembered his manners and offered us a wee cup of tea, and we accepted, thinking it churlish to leave him on his own too soon. He had been a school crossing patroller for over twenty years, after all. He disappeared into the kitchen and left us sitting listening to the old clock ticking away in the eerie silence of loneliness.

After a wee while we couldn't hear any movement in the kitchen and Alastair signalled for me to go and check it out. On entering the kitchen, I found old Archie standing in the middle of the room with tears rolling down his face. He had no idea where to find the cups or the coffee and just broke down. Having had tea made for him and guests for fifty-eight years, he had no clue where to start and no real desire or motivation to learn.

I made light of it and quickly sorted out the refreshments, but Archie was only going through the motions. As often happens, Archie also passed within a few months of his wife and I related this tale at his funeral, adding that I was sure he was back to being catered for as he was accustomed.

As previously stated, dealing with deaths of all varieties, ages and circumstances was and is a daily and routine function of the police service. These are just a few of the countless I've encountered, with more to follow in later tales, but it would be totally remiss of me not to mention Mike Greville of Govan Community Police a few years down the line. Mike was affectionately known as PC Gadget. He could regularly be found browsing crime magazines and it took him half an hour to get kitted out with the police aids that he had strapped, hooked or buckled to his person.

One Friday night he appeared in the community police office (portacabin) that my plain clothes unit shared, and threw open his tunic to reveal his latest life- saving contraption: a stab proof vest. He looked like the Michelin Man that night, heading off on foot patrol in the Wine Alley. Imagine my surprise when I was told the next morning that Mike was injured on-duty and had been in hospital overnight for observations. He had been hit over the head with a plank of wood. What a man.

One early evening Mike came into our room looking particularly thoughtful and certainly not as chipper as usual. When I asked him how he was, he told me this horrific tale. He had been sent to deliver a death message. An elderly man had taken a massive heart attack on a bus and was pronounced dead on arrival at hospital. Mike was tasked with attending his home in Penilee and informing his wife of this tragic turn of events in her life, and had attended straight away. So far, so good.

When she answered the door and was confronted with the police uniform, she immediately started and asked, 'Is everything okay?'

The police don't often, if ever, bring good news, after all.

In this case the police lost it completely, and said words to the effect of:

'Everything's fine. No need for alarm. Your husband took a wee turn on the bus, but he'll be okay.'

How do you explain that? Mike had about ten years of police service. Like everyone else he had delivered dozens if not hundreds of death messages. I immediately grabbed the keys and we went back to Penilee as fast as I could get us there. I left Mike in the car while I grabbed a neighbour and broke the sad news to the new widow. Not a good job, always tinged with sadness and always requiring respect and understanding. But much better than the kind lie. I have delivered hundreds of similar messages and the only rule about them is to get right to the point. Ensure you have the right person and tell them the news. Often the person you have to inform has an inkling of what's coming. Put them out of their misery quickly.

I was once shouting at my football team, Lomond Vale AFC, on Glasgow Green as they fannied about as usual in some cup fixture. My phone went and it was the doctor from the hospital where my daughter was a patient. Her best friend, and fellow cystic fibrosis sufferer, had died overnight on his way home with his parents. Louise was gravely ill and they wanted me to tell her. I did so and as her frail body racked, trembled and sobbed in my arms, I thought maybe all of those other death messages were just practice for this one.

'I'm very sorry to have to tell you that …'

I think Mike just got a bit blasé. Maybe he forgot to prepare mentally because you have to get into the right frame of mind a few minutes before doing the job. But you must realise that it's a kindness to deliver the message and be totally unambiguous about it. That's the mind-set. Be totally frank and to the point while showing empathy in words and tone. I think Mike just went up to that door and had other stuff on his mind. It's the only explanation I have for Mike's mishap but I know that I was worried more about it at the time than I am now. Because I didn't even take the piss or slag him off in front of our colleagues about it. That's even more unbelievable.

In Campbeltown, death messages were always much more personal. The chances were high that you knew the people involved or knew some of the extended family and it was likely that you would meet these people again, be served by them in a local shop, or even pass them in the Co-op. But it was always a uniform job where possible, the uniform providing doubtless identification and, perhaps, some reassurance.

In just those first few weeks of my police service I had watched and learned as the many routine functions of the rural police were attended to night and day, but I was soon to have my eyes open to the other end of the job's scale. A murder investigation.

CHAPTER 8: MURDER

This inkling of a future in the Criminal Investigation Department was certainly reinforced on another night shift a few months later. A body, later identified as the remains of Anna Kenny who had vanished from Glasgow city centre over two years before, had been found buried in a shallow grave near to Skipness, a tiny village on the east coast of Kintyre. I now know the area well, having walked the Kintyre Way, cycled the road many times and in the summer used the Skipness-Arran ferry as an alternative route back and forward to Glasgow with my daughter, Louise. But on that night shift I could have been on the moon – the dark side, at that.

I was a city boy, remember. I was still scared of cows. All I knew was that Tam McNab and I were tasked with an important role in any murder enquiry: guarding the locus. This entailed sitting in that big daft police caravan thing you see at the scene of murder loci. It has all of the facilities. A table and two chairs, a light via a generator, a phone and a kettle. That's it.

Apart from 'guarding the locus', the purpose of these portable offices is in order to facilitate the door-to-door team, encourage any potential witnesses to come inside and impart information, and generally create a police presence right in the middle of the community, at the scene. There was more chance of Tam staying awake than anyone passing by. Two or maybe three cars passed in a shift, and this was our major excitement.

All of the Scenes of Crime and Forensics teams had long fled back to the city, and when I suggested to Tam that we go and inspect the actual gravesite, he commented, 'Have you never seen a hole in the ground before?'

Fair dos.

For most of that murder enquiry, I was night shift. Constant night shift. No days off, seven to seven. We would joke that we only went home for a fresh shirt. I swear that within a few weeks we were going a bit mad. Especially as the good weather made its usual, brief visit to Scotland. It became increasingly hard to go to bed with the sun shining and we broke out occasionally, staying up to play golf or share a few cans. One night, I was working with John Malcolm, who was always up to some lark or other. We were in the old Black Maria van with the sliding front doors on an especially gorgeous dawn. We were out Machrihanish way when John pulled into the side of the road adjacent to a big field. He said 'watch this', and took the mike for the PA system from the dash. He then began to 'Moo' into the mike, his voice being projected far and wide from the mounted megaphone on the roof.

At first, I wondered what this was supposed to achieve, then, after another rendition from John, I saw far-off movement. A cow's head lifting, ears twitching. Then one stood up, quickly followed by some of her pals. Within a few minutes, and a few more calls from my talented colleague, we had a steady procession of cows heading our way. It was amazing. They just all followed each other mesmerised by the deployment of the blue light as an added feature by me that I insisted hurried them along. I know that John was sceptical of my contribution, but before long we had seventy-four cows lined up at the fence in front of us. That's a lot of pissing and shitting going on right there.

Deciding that this gathering deserved some reward I took the mike from John and slid the door fully open. Addressing my attentive audience, I said:

'Good morning, girls. Thank you for attending. You are probably wondering why we have gathered you together at this time ...'

I never did get to finish that thought. A loud thump-thump-thump on the rear of the van pre-empted the appearance of the smiling local farmer who waved aside our embarrassed attempts to apologise, assuring us that we had saved him the job of rounding up the herd. That was how I knew there were seventy-four of them.

This trick was repeated many a time, usually whenever I had

the kids out for a run in the country. It never failed, even with the high-pitched moo of three and four-year-old girls. Naturally, they were expertly trained and, although I never told John this, it seems the blue light was not a contributory factor. John Malcolm taught me much about being a police officer, granted, mostly about how to cause a barney, but of all his gifts, the cow whispering was by far the most valuable. It provided great amusement and hilarity and if there's a better, more heart-warming sound than that of your young children laughing, I've yet to hear it.

After our seven nights of twelve-hour shifts, seven till seven, 'guarding the locus', we had a few days off and then commenced back shift back in Campbeltown. This is when I discovered that the Strathclyde Serious Crime Squad were in town in some force, or as they were quickly renamed, the Serious Drinking Squad. A well-earned nickname, at that.

I got to sit in on a few debriefings, share a few beers after my shift with some of them, and generally listen to the stories they generated through mostly drunken escapades in the Wee Toon. These included fights in pubs between themselves and locals and drunken brawls where no locals were involved at all, the locking up of local worthies in order to generate court citations in future, a hush-hush encounter between a Crime Squad officer and the local dignitary's wife, and the ongoing tally of the bill they were running up at their hotel of choice.

The locals were well used to regular influxes of male specimens. At that time, RAF Machrihanish, four miles away from Campbeltown, was a thriving military base, and home to an American Squadron and Navy Seals. There were also weekly visits from numerous Royal Navy vessels, and so the local women were always busy trying to maximise on these opportunities, and the local males were always busy trying to prevent these inevitable liaisons taking place. A powder keg, indeed. So, the Crime Squad lads – some of whom took to this gene pool diversification project enthusiastically – were well entertained throughout their stay in Campbeltown.

Just to add to the crazy and volatile mix of interests, most weekends would see a Chinook helicopter land on the town green and dispatch its load of twenty or so soldiers fresh from Belfast, only twenty-six miles away by air. These were troubled times in Northern Ireland and the guys were simply being given some respite and the chance to relax and enjoy a few beers in relative safety. Sometimes they were glad to leave again.

On one such occasion around that time, Tam McNab and I were tasked with helping the Chinook land on the green. This entailed standing near the landing spot and shooing away the town's kids who naturally wanted to run underneath it and wave at the soldiers. This was traumatic as I was at least four stone lighter in those days, and while Tam hung onto his police hat, I hung on to Tam.

The helicopter landed and the waiting soldiers jumped aboard in practiced fashion. Now, the big double side door of the Chinook always had a guy hanging out of it. He was presumably the spotter making sure that there were no hazards underneath when landing or taking off. He was naturally strapped in to either side of the open doors and this time he was waving to us to come over. He then indicated that we could have a spin round the town for five minutes. Speaking wasn't an option near to that beast of a machine.

Tam looked at me and I shrugged my shoulders and so we both clambered aboard. Tam was pushed into a spare seat across from the door, but that was the only one there was. I could only see rows of smiling drunken squaddies staring back at me, but the spotter guy signalled me to hang on to him. He became my best friend right then, as the massive bulk started to shake like mad. I remember seeing the dashboard shaking and couldn't believe that this thing could actually get off the ground. The noise as it lifted away was magnificent, that bass whoop-whoop penetrating my very core. And off we went.

When we were airborne and moving, the sound settled down to merely thunderous, but by then I was amazed to see the town below us, and as we banked anti clockwise I was excited to spot streets, farms, Campbeltown Loch, and, finally, Davaar Island, as we circled the town at a thousand feet or so. Throughout this time the spotter was unruffled by my two-arm vice grip on him and all too soon we were landing back on the green and waved our new friends away back to Belfast. Great fun.

The soldiers were never a problem. I think they must have really appreciated their few hours of freedom. Perhaps they never really got time to acclimatise, as they were only a few miles from active and vigilant duty, with dangers all around them. The navy lads were a different proposition altogether. They always sent a shore patrol into the town with the sailors, and although these guys, with their three-foot night sticks in hand, were of great benefit in the many brawls we broke up, they were of most use when it came time to return the crew to the waiting frigate or suchlike.

They could identify their own and so helped greatly when we had to chase these drunken sailors down the streets or drag them from parties in order to get them back aboard. They rarely came quietly. Our efforts were regularly rewarded by the delivery of copious amounts of Navy Cut tea or other provisions to the police station.

So, this gives some idea of the environment the Crime Squad lads found in the Wee Toon in 1979, and they, of course, did their best to fit right in.

The flipside was that there actually was a murder enquiry taking place, but as an absolute rookie, still much on my probation, I was almost totally on the far periphery of that. I wasn't a police driver or even a civilian driver of cars at that point.

I did get involved in a door-to-door enquiry one day in Tarbert, some eight miles away and the nearest town to Skipness. We were given clipboards with newspaper clippings, notes of TV programmes, films that were showing at the time and anything else that might jog someone's memory. We were asking people to remember their movements over a week or so period more than two years before, when Miss Kenny first went missing, with a view to uncovering a stranger or a strange vehicle, or anything really.

We were dispatched in pairs around six in the evening and told to chap all of the doors in our designated street and come back for debriefing around eight. Simple enough. But one of our local lads was sent on his own up the hill out of Tarbert, north on the A83 towards the town boundary. His name was George Kaja, a legend. George had been a soldier and, as I was to relearn many times, some soldiers take instructions literally. They just act under instruction.

We all found our way back to the Tarbert office around 8pm, as arranged, but before our debriefing it was noticed that George was missing. Someone was dispatched to find him as he was obviously out of radio range. It transpired that George had got to the top of the brae leading out of Tarbert, where the houses stop, and had seen a farmhouse further up the hill. So, off he went. He then came out and saw another farmhouse in the distance and off he went again. And so on and so forth. He was eventually traced halfway to Lochgilphead still looking for the end of the street.

This was unbelievable to the Crime Squad but not to us who worked with George daily. He had once taken his dog for a walk and it became so exhausted he had to carry it home over the hills. I had spent my first ever morning on the beat with him in Campbeltown when he raced between different schemes to make it look as though they were more cops on the beat than just us. He had even attended a road accident in a Panda car and walked back to the office without it. He was legend. But he could fight like fuck, and was built like a brick shithouse. Useful attributes that can override most failings.

Needless to say, the murder enquiry petered out in our neck of the woods, as the focus of the enquiry moved back to Glasgow, along with the Serious Crime Squad detectives. Enquiries became focused on Anna's disappearance and I believe the case is still open to this day, unfortunately.

A word here on that enquiry – although from my perspective, as a young officer with no more than a few months service – the

'Serious Drinking Squad' were a hurricane-force mystery blowing through Campbeltown, leaving so much debris and confusion in their wake. I would hate anyone to think that the murder enquiry they were engaged in was compromised in any way. Just the opposite is true. I came to see this from the inside, as an SCS detective later in my service.

These were the cream of the crop, taken from their respective divisions because they lived and breathed 'The Job.' There was literally nothing these men wouldn't do to catch any murderer, and in particular an evil that could take a twenty-year old woman and dump her a hundred miles from home. These men all understood the tragedy of that, how it made all of their wives and daughters vulnerable, how that evil undermines all of our lives, and especially how that victim's families would never recover from such a loss.

All of this knowledge, born of sad experience, is the reason they drank so much, gave the impression of a teak exterior and usually flaunted authority at every turn. They were tasked with identifying, tracing and incarcerating the worst among us, the most dangerous and callous of us all, who would take life unflinchingly, and most likely keep doing so until stopped. This was quite a responsibility that was shouldered in different ways by us all in order to keep functioning in that abyss.

They left quite a footprint in Campbeltown, for sure, and apart from the pubs' and hostelries' coffers they had inflated, the locals they had either terrified or infatuated depending on their gender, and the many stories they had sown into police folklore in Argyll, they had again left a lasting impression on a young constable who liked their style. Their no-nonsense approach to the job, their dedication to the task in hand, and their obvious respect for the victim and her family really impressed me to no end.

When I was spoken to by Detective Superintendent, Joe Jackson, some years later, on my first day as a Serious Crime Squad detective, he impressed on me:

'In this place, son, we work hard and we play hard.'

I already knew that, boss, and I now know why. I had

unknowingly met some of the Ten Percent.

CHAPTER 9: FISHY BUSINESS

There's always a price to pay. Sometimes there and then, like an entry fee or surcharge, sometimes with the return of a favour when called upon, and I suppose these prices can be summed up with the all-encompassing catchphrase, 'there's no such thing as a free lunch.'

No one is more aware of that than a police officer. Every free coffee, offer of shelter from the elements or snippet of information invokes an unwritten and unspoken but well understood contract, mostly never enforced or called upon, and almost certainly never mentioned directly. It's a subtle but equally powerful force in the dynamics of interaction, especially where authority is involved in the relationship or transaction. It's that relationship aspect that's all-important, but there's no need for us to explore those of parent and child, or siblings, or, God forbid, husband and wife. There are many other books on those troublesome subjects. Thankfully, we're only interested here in the complicated dynamics of copper and civilian.

The traffic warden in Campbeltown lived roughly twelve miles south, down towards the Mull of Kintyre. She had no transport and, so, relied on the local bus service. But this meant that she was always tight for time, with little, if any, room for delay or mishap, and she only arrived at the old Castlehill police office with a few minutes to spare before taking to the streets to pursue her job. Living in a small village, she had little trouble in locating someone who drove the required journey every weekday, and with a contribution towards petrol costs she was in the town bright and early every day. So much so that she was able to take on a wee cleaning job in the Sheriff Court, situated, handily enough, across the road from the police office. Perfect.

Now, Ann was quite fastidious. I suppose you have to be

wanting in some regard to be a traffic warden in the first place, but she tried to enforce the parking restrictions as best she could. A difficult task when you know almost everyone you encounter. When does a warning suffice? Are tourists and visitors, who are less familiar with the restrictions, more likely to get a ticket than the local, who knows fine well that a chance is being taken? I suppose the best I could do would be to devise some criteria including a warning system, and stick to it the best I could. I'm not sure if Ann did this or what her system was, but whatever her strategy, it let her down really badly one day.

She came across the car she was the passenger in every day parked illegally. I don't mean dumped in the middle of the road or blocking a vital artery of the town's traffic system. There was no complaint received initiating a police response. Perhaps just left for a few minutes too long outside a shop. It couldn't be ignored, apparently, and a warning would certainly not suffice. Out came the black book and a ticket was slapped on the windshield. Another tenner (or whatever the fixed penalty was in those days) earned for Argyll and Bute Council, but at what cost?

I often wondered in the months that followed, when I saw Ann rushing about to get on the street for nine, if she ever regretted issuing that ticket. Did she not realise that her morning lift was at serious risk? Did she think that she was morally obliged to issue the ticket because of her relationship with the driver? Just like how a father refereeing his son's team is liable to favour the other team. I know for a fact she wasn't stupid, but perhaps there was some personal motive everyone else was unaware of. In any event, it serves to highlight nicely the moral dilemmas often faced by persons in position of authority or power. It's at times like these that the oath to carry out your duties 'without fear or favour' can be less than straightforward.

When I was in uniform in Campbeltown, I got friendly with the local mobile chip van owner, Robert. His sister-in-law, Tina, was married to my friend, Hinton, who warrants his own chapter later in my story, but you can see how people are connected in rural communities. His lifetime companion in the van, and later in Roberts Chip Shop in Fishers Row, was John McIlroy and his brother, Billy, was married to Tina in those days. Tina later married Hinton. You always have to be careful who you're speaking about in places such as Campbeltown.

Anyway, Robert was aware that I was looking to buy my first car and he told me that he knew someone who would give me one for free. Even as a twenty-one-year old I was sceptical, but it transpired this was true. I phoned the man and he explained how he would be delighted to get rid of it off his driveway. It was a manual Peugeot with only minimal mileage, but I would be doing him a favour if I took it. He and his wife both drove automatics now for personal reasons. I went to see the car and it was in good nick and certainly above my budget without debt being involved but he was vaguely familiar to me and that rang some warning bells in my head. Perhaps this wasn't the happy coincidence and good fortune that it appeared to be.

Making a few cursory enquiries revealed that this chap was a local criminal lawyer, and although he was heading towards retirement he was still acting for clients. I declined the offer for obvious reasons and, to this day, never knew if the offer was innocent and generous or whether there were more sinister underlying motives. I did have a few minor run-ins with him in court over the next few years, but nothing controversial or particularly dramatic, so it's hard to imagine when he could have reverted to the favour or tried to call me in. I do know that he was charged with careless driving in future years, (not by me, I should add), but the truth is that these gratuities are often an insurance against future circumstances, and of course, no one can foresee what might lie in store for us. I certainly made the right call.

So, what about the free coffees or breakfast rolls at the cafés, public buildings and hotels on our beats? These are undoubted perks of the job but they don't, for me, cross the thin line into the realms of dodgy-ness, though perhaps, like most things, they are forever in that shady, murky, grey area of human transacting.

My view, reinforced many times, was that the owner, proprietor or manager of most legitimate commercial enterprises valued a visible police presence. They wanted the local 'bobby' to pop in and spend time. It did business no harm and perhaps discouraged behaviours best kept at bay.

The Argyll Hotel in Campbeltown was a great favourite of mine. I had my first wedding reception there, I played in the band upstairs every Sunday night for a few years, my children enjoyed playing in the big hall and learning duets with me on the upright piano beside the stage. I DJ'd at so many functions of every description and compèred the New Year Hogmanay party on numerous occasions and in those early days there was always a bacon roll and a coffee with my name on it. Every day. That was because when Tam McNab and I were on night shift we always kept an eye out for old Kate.

Kate had worked in the Argyll Hotel for a lifetime, and she was in her late seventies back then in 1979. She had long since passed her days of productivity but still went into the hotel at five-twenty every morning to open up. Of course, a hotel never really closes but Kate went through the ritual of putting the water on in the kitchen and pottering about for a few hours in her mind making vital preparations for the coming day. The lift we gave her, after we manhandled her up into the Sherpa van, saved her twenty minutes of laborious walking and, often, a right good soaking into the bargain. The truth was that the good deed made us feel useful, too, and I like to think it helped us sleep better when we went home to bed at seven, but was it worth a free roll and a coffee? We never refused. That would be rude.

Then we move on a step to local shopkeepers and businesses. There were many examples, but perhaps the best for my purposes here is the fishmongers on Longrow South in Campbeltown. Donnie Gilchrist was old-school, the Gillchrist fishermen going back umpteen generations. There was never a chance that he would get into a situation where he required good favour from the local constabulary, and I feel sure he would have been totally mortified to be in that position. As a total rookie I went into the shop with Tam and we went straight through the back where Donnie and his staff were constantly preparing fish. He and Tam exchanged pleasantries, I was introduced as Campbeltown's latest acquisition from the city and, a few minutes later, each of us was handed a white, paper-wrapped parcel, and off we went. I was mortified. I had no idea what had just occurred.

This was called a fry and, as far as I'm aware, every officer in the town, about thirty of us, collected a regular parcel. That's a lot of fish even at prices when there were still decent stocks in the sea. So why did Donnie do this? He certainly wasn't the only shop keeper doing so. My suspicion initially was like yours. He or his family must be up to no good somewhere. Running a dodgy business side-line or driving home drunk every night and buying off the police with his fish. Nothing could be further from the truth. Donnie was an elder in the Lowland Church and beyond reproach. Tam was totally bemused by my questioning of the fry parcel. Never one for philosophical analysis, he just shrugged it off. Tam had about twenty years' service in Campbeltown and it had always been thus. That's the way things were and no one apparently ever questioned it or discussed it.

What I discovered as time went on was that all of the older cops had these contacts but they were always proper people. Businesspeople or clergy, office bearers or professionals, who were establishment people. Folk who supported the police and conducted their business and personal lives with decency and civic duty. The last type of people who would ever do anything illegal, and whose only dealings with the police were through everyday life and death, or the Masonic lodge. This was a prerequisite to being able to give the officers freebies. If you were a rascal, or even might be a rascal, you didn't get into that club. Not until you had attained a certain level of regard, and wealth was no measure of the person.

All of this was totally unspoken. I never ever heard any officer refer to this system and so it is entirely my perception. Perhaps that was because of how it had come to be in the first place. You see, until 1977, police officers really were paid a pittance. They were tied to their houses, negating any possibility of buying property, there was no such thing as paid overtime and their wages were derisory. The police wages nationally lagged about thirty percent behind the national average of thirty pounds per week in 1970, the gap growing year-on-year. This was all recognised in local areas, where the police officer was highly valued and regarded as a vital part of the community, often providing the line between the haves and the have-nots, but himself being firmly positioned with the latter in any material sense.

This was where the gratuities came in. It was a way for a businessman to express his gratitude or thanks for the vital job the constable carried out, while ensuring that he could continue to do so and provide for his family. Officers really were on the poverty line, and this was recognised. This shines an entirely different light on the fry of fish, parcel of meat cuttings, bag of chips or even a wee back door dram. It was this black-market economy that supported the welfare of the officers and ensured that the job of protecting those business interests was continued effectively. If this was corrupt then it was caused entirely by necessity on everyone's part, a direct result of the total neglect of the constabulary nationwide by successive governments.

A DCI once told me that you would have anything from thirty to forty detectives at a murder locus, standing about all night doing little but wait for instruction. This was because there was no such thing as overtime. It didn't cost a penny to call officers out from their beds and have them on-duty, just in case you needed them. When I was a murder squad detective, overtime was only ever grudgingly used when all other avenues were closed, and a call out really was a thing of the past.

I didn't go into Donnie's fish shop often. I would go in more off-duty for a blether if he was quiet and I confess that I did occasionally accept the fry he pressed on me, but mainly because it gave him pleasure and spoke volumes of the unspoken bond we shared. He was a real character. I did put a cystic fibrosis collection can on his counter top which I thought appropriate and certainly assuaged my conscience somewhat. We younger modern police officers had an entirely different mentality. Our wages and conditions were much more in line with the standards of the day. We enjoyed housing and other allowances, our salaries were index linked, and we could and did buy property, including the police houses that had imprisoned our forebears. We didn't need or want charity, as it appeared, or, much worse, someone currying favour against some future decision we would have to make.

I read somewhere quite recently a comment by some superstar regarding his poverty thinking. He said that if you were brought up with little or no money then you would forever be cursed or gifted, depending on your outlook, with 'poverty thinking.' You would always be frugal to a degree, abhor waste of any kind, and forever watch the pennies. From stories I heard back in the day, Paul McCartney was renowned on his farm for keeping a close watch on expenditure, despite his enormous wealth. I found this to be true with the older senior cops who had spent most of their service close to the breadline. Those habits and customs of mutual community support only died when they did, because I know for a fact that the fry or meat parcel went on long after they retired from any position of influence, killing the suspicion of corruption stone dead.

I have written this chapter because the most common question I am asked about my days as a police officer is:

'Was there police corruption?'

The truth is that we all have our own views about what are acceptable behaviours and what are not, often determined by the particular circumstances and motives involved. I was once marching an armed robber from a dwelling in Castlemilk. Cuffs on, in a hold, after an armed raid, and he was still resisting. The house had no carpets, little furniture, a tiny portable TV, and clothes everywhere. The kitchen was rancid and the whole place stank of dampness, urine and sweat. There were two children with bare bottoms and his woman who could hardly keep her eyes open or raise her head such was her state of heroin-induced relaxation. My colleague had just recovered the sawn-off shotgun in a roof space and made some comment to him about the futility of his crime. The robber railed against my grip and looked me in the eye.

'You'd fucking try something if you lived like this, big man. Believe me.'

I did believe him.

I know of a traffic cop who was asked by his next-door neighbour to look into a fixed penalty with which he had been issued. I'm not sure if it was speeding or some other traffic offence. Within a few days or weeks, the ticket was withdrawn and the neighbour left a bottle of whisky in for his friend. Unfortunately, there were undercover officers watching when the pay-off took place and a good officer was lost to the force. To my knowledge there was no evidence that he solicited the payment or put any price on the favour, but the acceptance of it was sufficient.

I knew a traffic officer who would send HGVs to the nearest weighbridge, suspecting that they may be carrying a load exceeding the vehicle's legal limit. This incurred a cost to the carrier, whether it was in excess or not, and rumour had it that the officer received a commission on every weigh-in. Another traffic cop was allegedly conducting wide load escorts at a rate reduced from that of Strathclyde Police. It should be noted that these were all white hat traffic offences, as CID officers were always well beyond reproach.

Was there police corruption?

It's like the questions lawyers employ when interrogating witnesses in court, and demand a yes or no answer. A colleague of mine, Mike McKenna, was once pressed like this in the High Court, and he stood his ground, insisting certain questions could not be answered in this simplistic way. Eventually the solicitor became infuriated and Mike offered an example. Mike said:

'Now, sir. You answer only yes or no to my question. Are you *still* beating your wife?'

It's definitely not a Yes or No answer.

CHAPTER 10:
THE BLAME GAME

Thinking about this always makes me smile, and sometimes laugh out loud, even today, forty years after the event. I suppose part of the reason for that is that it occurred in Campbeltown Sheriff Court on the most beautiful summer's day. I have always loved The Adventures of Tom Sawyer since I was about ten or eleven-years-old, and the feelings it conjured up in my pre-teenage mind are still vivid and treasured. I have no doubt that it was Mark Twain's masterpiece that awakened the love of reading that some of us are so fortunate to nurture and enjoy. I still resort to it every few years, and still get goose bumps when Injun Joe's entrapment in McDougal's cave is revealed.

Another valid reason that I remember this incident so well is that it was just funny. Anyway, the court room had that hazy, relaxed, clammy feel to it that I associate with Tom, trapped in his classroom when the Mississippi summer is coming into bloom outside the massive school windows. That's how it felt to me, and still does. The Sheriff was in his throne and his clerk busying with papers in front of him. There were a few lawyers around their table, an accused in the dock, and around a dozen people with a variety of interests in court business filling most of the front two benches.

There were no seats in the public part of the courtroom at that time, just a theatre-style series of ten or so benches in two sections facing the Sheriff. I had noted subconsciously that there was a woman sitting at the rear of the benches on her own, or else I just got really lucky. I was in the middle of the court, at the edge of the second-row bench with almost everyone in front of me. I was the court officer that day, which simply means that I was to record the outcome of the matters brought before the Sheriff, and assist the running of the court in any way required.

It really was hot. Sleepy hot. I was struggling to keep my eyes open. I had drifted off a few times, waking with that start and gasp of horror before realising that I was unobserved and I was somehow still in an upright position. The long and the short of it is that I was wakened abruptly on one occasion by the loudest fart I ever remember hearing. Now that's saying something. It woke me with a start, accentuated by the smack off the wooden bench. I was compos mentis immediately, realising that my bottom had let me down badly, erupting in the silent courtroom like thunder, as if I was in bed at home.

My eyes sprung open and to my absolute horror every head in the room was turning towards me. The Sheriff looking over his specs, the clerk looking up from his important papers, all of the lawyers with scrunched up faces turning towards me, and all of the members of the public, including the local Campbeltown Courier reporter, turning round to identify and vilify the culprit. I mean to say, who could be so common, and lacking in any kind of decorum, as to let one go in the Sheriff Court, while in session and in the presence of His Lordship?

What was I to do? Within a second they would all be staring at me. I would be the talk of the town, forever more the farting policeman. How would I even be able to function as an officer of the law when no one would take me seriously? Why would they? My life and fledgling career were about to go down the river. I am so sorry to report that I did the only thing available to me in that tightest of corners. It was totally cowardly, a despicable act for sure, and a source of deep shame to this day, its only small and slight redemption being that it was and is so amusing.

I turned my head at the same time every other person was turning theirs towards me, and looked over my shoulder at the poor girl sitting all alone at the back of the court. She of course began gesticulating, waving her arms and shaking her head at everyone, silently mouthing the useless phrase:

'It wisnae me.'

We were all shaking our heads by then. What can you do? No wonder she was on her own, smelly wench.

Farting, of course, is for some reason a constant source of humour in male circles. Or at least the chaps I've hung out with. I'm not sure what the equivalent would be in female circles. Men, perhaps.

I was in the High Court waiting room one day, playing cards in order to pass the time. Inevitably, the Procurator Fiscal came in just before lunch time on the third day of the trial and told us that a deal had been struck, a plea had been entered, the trial had folded, and our services would no longer be required. As he explained the ins and outs of the matter the most disgusting smell enveloped all of us. It was revolting. Normally something to be proud of if you were responsible, perhaps on public transport, in a car full of male colleagues, or at the bar, but not to be shared in esteemed company. No one cracked a light until the Fiscal had made a speedy exit, no doubt wondering what a CID diet consisted of exactly that could explain the smell emanating in that room. At that point someone piped up:

'For fuck sake. Who farted in front of the Fiscal?'

I'm not sure who was responsible, but Donnie Hardy, who ran our football team, piped up immediately:

'I'm sorry. I didn't know it was his turn.'

Priceless moments.

I perhaps need to give some explanation here, as I move from a flippant tale of public farting to a tragic subject of great concern to the police and society as a whole. This tendency to jump from humour to gravitas is a vital part of the emergency services psyche. Doctors, nurses, ambulance crew, firemen, forces personnel and veterans: we all shared a dark humour that would seem totally inappropriate and totally out of place to an observer. Childish humour sometimes, the cheapest of jokes and even senseless banal comments that could elicit roars of laughter or otherwise, embarrassing giggles. Like a fart.

There is absolutely no doubt in my mind that this was a coping mechanism we all shared, without ever discussing it or wondering at its validity or value. It was like a valve and we could help each other by releasing just a little of the tension, emotion and sometimes terror we were feeling. Sometimes the situations we found ourselves in, from Lockerbie to a simple cot death, were unimaginable. Only the most macabre mind would contemplate these horrors and yet someone has to deal with them. Make decisions, be reassuring and sympathetic to family and loved ones, sometimes face the media and give accurate factual and sensitive information to the world.

We often faced serious injury or death as a routine occupational hazard. Taking down armed criminals, addicts with needles and countless knife-wielding madmen or drunks who would kill us in a flash. These are the pressures we ask our emergency services to face day after day, and humour is one of the tactics they employ to retain their perspective and sanity when it's all over.

It becomes a habit. Part of the unwinding ritual. I'm sure there are dozens if not hundreds of psychology books on the subject, and there are certainly plenty who have suffered the effects of Post Traumatic Stress Disorder over the years. It's perhaps why I do it here. To give us a break. Realise that life goes on regardless and whatever horrors we all have to confront at different times there will be an afterwards for most of us, and it will all seem a bit better tomorrow.

There really is little we can do about the accidents, mishaps, violence and problems nature will throw at us. They will occur. But we can all come out the other side, more or less intact, if we help each other. A hug or pat on the back, often a raised glass between us, and even a joke or some laughter, go a long way to helping us move on as we must.

CHAPTER 11: SUICIDE

Nowadays, being a regular player of 'walking football', it's hard to believe that I was once among the fittest of probationers at Tulliallan Police College, or that I could outrun the Campbeltown Fire Engine along the town esplanade. I don't even remember seeing the fire engine, but I do remember the crew screaming and shouting encouragement. You see, I was chasing someone as I overtook the tender on the Esplanade.

I was good at chasing people. Not just because I could sprint fast, but because I learned early on in my service to pace myself. When neds bolted, they tended to go flat out for the first forty or fifty yards and then look back to take stock of their pursuer. If I was that copper, I was running maybe half sprint, building up to a steady three-quarter pace, and so they had put some distance between us.

I would shout at this point, just to wind them up even more, and put on a spurt, encouraging them to increase their sprint and keep going flat out. No one can run flat out for long, and when you max out it is really difficult to get your wind. The next time they look back they see me, steady as she goes and hardly out of breath, obviously in for the long haul, and catching up.

I actually learned this trick when my mates and I were being chased by a man through the streets of Hyndland in Glasgow's West End. We had thrown a few bangers onto his doormat, watching with childish glee through the glass front door as his wife threw the house telephone up in the air when the bangers exploded a few feet from her. We ran away the customary twenty or thirty yards and slowed down, still laughing at our smartness and huge success. But then it got better.

Out of the house a big guy came running up onto the pavement, shouting some insult, and he started chasing us. Off we went, all five of us running over the bridge from the Broomhill side at Hyndland station and down through the foot tunnel that leads onto Queensburgh Gardens. Surely far and fast enough to shake off the old codger. But no, on he came, now with a slight smirk on his face as he saw the look of shock and surprise on our young coupons. And off we went again …

As we spilled out of the station entrance there was no need for debate. Instinctively, we split up. I only know that I went up Novar Drive, and that when I glanced round to see who the old git had followed, I discovered it was me. He was starting to wilt now, though, and I was much on home turf. I ran for the school in those days, thought nothing of cycling a hundred miles a day and of course I had the much better incentive of escape. I ran full pelt to the top of Novar Drive and leapt the fence into the play park. From a pedestal at the top of the kids' chute I could see all around me and well down Novar. He had given up or hopefully collapsed in a heap somewhere behind me, but I had learned a lesson about pacing myself that would stand me in good stead over many a foot chase, when I was the pursuer.

We all met up at Stan's house and recounted our various forms of escape, but someone remembered the nameplate on the door of the house we had attacked with our bangers. We looked the number up in the phone book and sure enough there it was. The address and phone number for the old guy who had terrified us. When he answered his phone, he was met with a chorus of:

'Run faster next time, ye old git.'

So brave, so proud, so smart.

An added bonus to this method of hunting down a ned is that when you catch up with him, he is absolutely knackered. He's almost glad you've caught up with him, and of course has no fight left in him. That was most certainly not the situation when I overtook the fire engine, but then this was no criminal.

This was actually a sad situation. A gravely-troubled young man had called the police station in the early hours a month or so before, when we had also been on night shift. He said that he had taken an overdose and gave his address. When we got there, we had to put the door in, and sure enough found him semi-conscious in the bedroom. We got him to hospital and he was sorted medically. I always remember that we charged him with a breach of the peace, which was our only recourse in those days, in the hope that the court system could source some support for him, as this was an obvious cry for help.

So, when he called again in the early hours saying that he was going to jump into Campbeltown Loch, we took him seriously. As we drove towards his home, I spotted him running towards the sea front, and as the passenger, I was out the door and off after him. I remember running round the corner of the old job centre and being hit by the wind. It was freezing. I could see that the tide was in and registered immediately that if this guy hit the water, I was obliged to go in behind him. That is real motivation.

I must have run like the wind. The fire brigade were apparently going to a call out and saw the chase along the esplanade. They swore that I overtook them. My 'slowly, slowly, catchy monkey' theory was long discarded, and I managed to get within striking distance when he was about ten yards from the end of the pier. I executed a most determined rugby tackle that Gavin Hastings would have risen and applauded for, and hung on to him tightly until the van caught us up. I was delighted to still be on dry land. We could easily both have drowned in the freezing Campbeltown Loch that night.

Yet again this poor lad was sent back to court charged with a breach of the peace and, yet again, whatever help he was seeking and obviously needed, just wasn't there, it seemed. I was away at Tulliallan Police College a few months later when I heard that he had taken his own life with a car and a hosepipe. So sad.

The pier held some strange fascination for those suffering depression or wishing to harm themselves in a public way. Another night, Tam McNab and I were called to attend the old pier as a woman was threatening to jump off the end into the loch. Sure enough, as we parked the van and started heading towards her, off she went. Plop, right in the water.

Now she had gathered quite a crowd of onlookers prior to our arrival, and was now screaming and shouting in the water, in great distress. The good thing, from our point of view, was that she was only chest-high in the water, as the low tide was well out. Still, one of us had to go in and 'rescue' her. In the best traditions of the force our training kicked in and we decided on a course of action based on sound common sense. We tossed a coin. And he lost! Ya beauty.

I was elated. I must have almost peed my police trousers that night. It was just so funny. As Tam climbed down the metal ladder on the end of the pier, her screaming and splashing got worse, and the crowd were egging her on continuously. Tam waded out to get her and I'm sure ambulance control thought I had lost it, as I tried to speak to them, all the while trying to curtail my hilarity. I do remember throwing a big lifebelt at Tam, which only added to his grumpiness somehow.

My recollection of those times in the early eighties is that we, as police officers, had little or no contact with social services. They were always seen as problematic to us and seemed to be working to a totally different and alien agenda. I'm sure they felt exactly the same about the police. The attitude of the police to social workers is summed up by a joke that was one of numerous constantly circulating through our ranks.

A man is lying in a doorway. He has obviously been beat up, seems unconscious and is badly in need of medical attention. The passing public are ignoring him, giving him a wide berth. No one wants involved, crossing the road to avoid him and his situation. Until, thankfully, a social worker happens on the scene and immediately runs over to the injured man. The social worker takes one look and says, 'This is terrible. I must find the person who did this and help him.' And then runs off into the crowd.

No doubt about it, that made absolutely perfect sense to me. So when it came to finding help for people crying out for some support we had no tools at our disposal. Only a court system geared up to punish offenders and make money for solicitors. I certainly don't remember any mention of mental health matters at any time on the streets, during our training or in the courts.

I pray that it's different now.

Suicides always created mixed emotions for police officers, and maybe for everyone. On one hand, the loss of life is always so sad. A reminder of our mortality; the inevitability and finality of death. There's also the sadness and emptiness left behind which can never really be mitigated or consoled other than on the surface, but, on the other hand, it seems such a selfish act. It leaves so many questions behind for loved ones, questions that can never be properly answered.

Things were more black and white then, whereas today we are much more aware and willing to talk about mental health issues, and it seems that there are many more safety nets and support networks in place. I sure hope so because there also seems to be much more to be depressed about.

CHAPTER 12: DRIVING

A police officer in Campbeltown, or any other rural posting for that matter, who couldn't drive police vehicles was a liability, really. So much of the job depended on mobility, and so it was always desirable to have young cops trained up as soon as possible. To this end, I was much encouraged, if not ordered, to pass my civilian driving test post-haste. I had a full motorcycle licence, but had hardly ever driven a car, and when I moved to Argyll, I had no great desire to do so. That attitude soon changed when I made the bitter winter journey up the A83 a few times on my motorbike.

Through my friend and mentor, Ian Andrew, I bought my first car, realising that it would be much easier to have folk take me out driving if I had my own vehicle. Investing two-hundred pounds, I became the proud owner of my very own and white Hillman Imp. A wee cracker. With my test booked for December, I headed off to Tulliallan Scottish Police College in Fife for my two months probationary training, with the possibility that I could return to duty as a driver.

My test date was allocated in Campbeltown for a Friday in the middle of my stint at Tulliallan, and so I had to travel from Fife on the Thursday to be at the test centre at nine. The journey between Campbeltown and Kincardine by public transport was a trying experience, and exceptionally time-consuming. But I had a car. Somehow, I contrived to drive up and down between Campbeltown and the Police College with no licence at least half a dozen times. I say somehow because it now seems totally bizarre that I would risk everything like that for the sake of a few hours on the bus.

As I said, my driving test was in Campbeltown on a Friday, and so I drove back from college on the Thursday night, and got a licensed friend, Alastair, to sit with me driving to the test centre, which was the old job centre in the town. My test was booked for nine o'clock, and so at the allotted time I presented to the examiner, who visited the town especially every few months to conduct driving tests. He had just returned with an examinee and looked up his list to tick me off. I'll never forget his smirking wee face as he looked up at me and said I wasn't on his list. He shouted out another name and off he went, with a bounce in his step. Just a horrible wee man.

I got on the telephone to DVLA, who realised their mistake immediately and told me to get wee smirky face to call them as soon as he came back from the test he was on. I did so and after he made the call, he grudgingly told me that he would do one more test and then take me. That would be at eleven o'clock. It is almost unbelievable to write the next sentence, so rare was such an occurrence on the Argyll coast with its Gulf Stream winters. It started to *snow*. A few inches dropped in the space of the forty-five minutes the examiner was out, and when he arrived back with his learner, he took great delight in walking straight over to me and stating with a smirk, 'All tests are cancelled today.'

He then crept away and drove off in his Rover. A real little shit.

There was nothing to be done. Ever confident and presumptuous, I had arranged to drive back to Glasgow, giving a young policewoman, Isabel, a lift to Alexandria, and so we drove off at about two o'clock. What neither of us knew was that if there was some snow in Campeltown, then mid-Argyll, some fifty miles further north, and the Rest and be Thankful, would have some serious winter conditions.

The following winter I had been walking the beat in Campeltown when I was told I was being picked up by the Land Rover to travel up the coast. Alastair McKinlay duly picked me up and told me to put on the wellies under my seat. He said we were going to try to rescue people caught in a snowdrift. This was fair enough, but it wasn't snowing. It was raining in Campbeltown. At best, it could be described as a bit sleety.

This changed gradually as we headed north up the west coast of Kintyre, until we reached Clachan and turned easterly and upwards. Within a few hundred yards, we were in blizzard conditions. I'm not sure where we were but when we stopped, Alastair told me to tie the rope on the floor around my waist and to the vehicle door. He put on the blue flashing light and told me to follow him when he got to my side. I thought this was all just a bit dramatic. Okay, it was snowing heavily, and the snow was up to my knees, but how bad could it be?

I found out immediately.

Within a few feet of the Land Rover I could see nothing at all. Well, just whiteness. I swear that, although we had only moved a short distance, I was totally disorientated. It is amazing how this happens when there is nothing from which to take a bearing. The rope around my waist became the only thing that made any sense of this new white world. I just followed Alastair closely and we happened upon the district nurse in her Mini. She had become stranded on this side road trying to get to a patient.

She reluctantly came with us back to the Land Rover on the main road but she wasn't happy to be on the move back to Campbeltown, and certainly not in the slightest grateful to be rescued. She wanted us to take her to her other calls in the area.

Isabel and I were blissfully unaware of all of these perils brought about by heavy snow and snow drifts when we set off for Glasgow that Friday afternoon. We learned the hard way, persevering in my Hillman Imp in the face of a blizzard. The fact that neither of us had a driving licence helped as I simply crawled along, concentrating on staying on the road.

This was a feat that many motorists failed at that night and we passed dozens of cars abandoned in ditches or drifts at the side of the road. Between Lochgilphead and Inveraray I noticed a wee man looking lost and forlorn next to his silver Volvo. I quickly dismissed any idea of lending assistance when I realised he was my smarmy examiner from earlier that day, who had messed up my test and took great delight in calling off all activities that day. He must have stayed for his free lunch and was now stranded in the middle of nowhere.

As we crept past him, I noticed his car half-way down a ditch. Would it be churlish to reveal my delight at his misfortune? Would it reveal too much of my real character to refer to my self-congratulations at my negotiating the atrocious driving conditions, while my would-be examiner stood by the road side like a newly made snowman? Would it be just a bit too much if I laughed out loud, slapped the steering wheel and smiled every time I've thought about it over the past forty-odd years?

I got home to my mum's eventually that night, was back at Police College the following Monday, and was contacted by an apologetic licensing authority who offered me a new test date this coming Friday in Glasgow. I made it perfectly clear that Anniesland test centre in Glasgow was a big ask as opposed to Campbeltown, but rather than wait two months I would make that sacrifice. I had grown up in the West End and knew the Anniesland and Knightswood area inside out.

I passed the driver's test that day, thankfully, and now only had to wait the required six months to sit my police driver's test and become an advanced driver. Only then would I be allowed to drive police vehicles when I had successfully passed a week's driver training and examination. During that time, my colleague, Ian Andrew, made sure I got lots of practice, and I learned so much from him, not only about driving, but every aspect of policing. Where Tam was disinterested and would cut corners at every chance, Ian was keen, enthusiastic and thorough. I have a lot to thank him for.

CHAPTER 13:
ADVANCED DRIVING

Most of my driving lessons on the shift were off-road. Not because we were worried about the legalities or anything like that. It was mostly the Land Rover, so that my shift colleagues could shoot rabbits and suchlike out the windows when I caught them in the headlights. You had to have hobbies to help pass long winter night shifts. I would get 'wee shots' sometimes when things were quiet, but I couldn't wait to be summoned to my police advanced driver's course, and in the spring of 1980, the day finally arrived. The even better news was that I wasn't required to travel to Glasgow and stay for a week, as the road traffic officers of Argyll would be conducting the course.

Our teacher and tormentor for the week was to be PC Bob Stewart, a big traffic cop. He really was big. I remember once I was holding a local worthy on the ground, face first against the Sherpa van, unable to get cuffs on him or move him. He was the local scrappy, and strong as an ox. Bob arrived on the scene in his Capri traffic car, sauntered over, and lifted us both off the ground. He proceeded to despatch both of us into the rear of the van and haul me back out, feet-first. His police shirt cuffs had to be cut and re-stitched to accommodate his massive wrists. He was my pal.

There were two other lads on the week long course with me, Bruce from Dunoon, and Bannie from Oban, who had failed the course a few months previous. They would both be living in quarters at Lochgilphead and we would travel up to mid-Argyll every morning to pick them up. So, every day I drove those first fifty-two miles to Lochgilphead with Bob instructing me, and after each day's driving, I drove the return journey back south.

Our test drives were to be on the Friday with other traffic officers. The only other variation to this was that on the Wednesday we would travel to Glasgow and conduct our city drives, staying overnight at Oxford Street Police College near Glasgow Sheriff Court.

It was a great week. We really had some laughs, learned so much about driving and formed lasting friendships. There were a few highlights that can be revealed now and some that can never be discussed at all. If they even happened, that is.

On our city drive we had finished the day's instruction and gone out for a pint on Byres Road. The Curlers bar to be precise, home territory for me as they had great jam sessions on Sundays. Bob and I went to the gents at one point, and as we used the urinal, a wee guy was looking up at Bob quizzically. Bob still had on his police trousers and shirt, an anorak counting as plain clothes in his mind.

Eventually Bob looked down and said, 'What is it, pal? What's up?'

The wee guy asked, 'Are you DS, big man?'

As if the Drugs Squad would have reason to enter the Curlers at all.

Quick as a flash Bob retorted while zipping up his trousers, 'No, we're the ADS.'

As we left the toilet, we could see the total confusion this had caused and so, as a parting shot, Bob cleared things up for him: 'Argyll Driving School.'

Brilliant.

Before relating this next story, I should say that drinking and driving wasn't as illegal in those days as it is now. I'm not sure when it became illegal – the nineties I think – but certainly in the seventies and early eighties, it was a little bit illegal. I mean, the legislation was pretty much the same. The penalties were largely the same and the threshold to pass a breathalyser was a bit more lenient. The only thing that has changed significantly really is the public attitude to drink driving, and so it is taken much more seriously these days, thankfully.

This is a theme I will certainly return to later in this tale, as police stories and histories are often punctuated by or pre-empted by drinking copious amounts of alcohol. It is only with hindsight that these drinking sessions stand out at all, as at the time, and in many other walks of life, drinking was as much part of the routine as eating or having a shower. I would point out that any officer who didn't enjoy a wee drink was at risk of not being fully trusted by his peers. It really was a totally different culture which I am finding it impossible to defend or justify in any way now. It's just the way things were. Just like smoking in all sorts of confined and public spaces such as restaurants, cinemas, public transport, and so on, taking a drink was much the norm, and if you had to drive, you just took care. It was often the least pissed who was elected as the driver.

In my defence, I had never booked a drunk driver throughout my probationary period of two years. This was a bone of contention for my gaffers who liked to show that our probationers in the sticks got a broad experience of every aspect of police work, and so my 'probationers card', which recorded cases as I ticked them off as done, had a glaring gap where drunk driver should be. At least I wasn't a total hypocrite.

On this morning, the four of us were driving towards Glasgow through Inveraray. Bob had a trick to keep us all attentive and would ask any one of us what a road sign had said that we'd just passed. On this particular morning I was much under the weather, snuggled in the back seat, when Bob asked me about the last sign. I had no idea, made a decent guess, but failed miserably. Sure enough, he made Bruce stop the police car, told me to clamber out, and dispatched me on foot to go back and read the sign. This caused much mirth among my so-called colleagues, and off I went. En-route, I passed a shop and nipped in for a bottle of Irn-Bru (a well-known hangover cure to this day). Being in uniform, some conversation was struck with the young shop assistant and I belatedly scurried back to the waiting car, got in and saw the expectant faces around me.

'Well, what was the sign'?

Shit. I forgot to look. Would you believe he made me go all the way back again to read it? I still can't remember what it was to this day, but I can remember that nice shop assistant. Funny that.

CHAPTER 14: ISLAY COVER

Being a police driver was a big change. No longer was I just along for the ride, making up the numbers. I became an equal part of the shift, could participate in escort duty to Barlinnie, or wherever, and generally carry my weight at last. A job that had been unavailable to me until then, and was despised by any of the mostly married cops, was cover duty in Islay when the local lads took their leave. This was no hardship for me, a single man living with the domestic imbecile that was Kenny Rhodes. It was a jaunt.

On my first such visit to relieve Dougie in Islay, I arrived the day before he left on holiday with his family. I was to stay in the single man's quarters, a wee self-contained flat that formed part of the Port Ellen Police Station. Dougie's police house dwelling was part of the same building. I travelled in uniform, which was always good for a free coffee on the CalMac ferry from Kennacraig, and so I was easily recognisable to Sergeant Jimmy Dorwood, who met me at Port Ellen.

He introduced me to Dougie, showed me around the upstairs flat and gave me a brief tour of the Island. Of course, I was familiar with the geography, having visited with my camping buddies several times as a teenager. The sergeant was based in Bowmore, about ten miles from Port Ellen, and I had the use of the wee Ford Panda car. My shifts were basically nine till five, and I would join up with the sergeant at the weekend on a back shift, all straightforward and civilized. If only.

When Jimmy had left me and returned to Bowmore, I went for a drive. It was a nice day and the funny thing about an island is that you eventually tend to end up back where you started. In any event, I found myself back in Bowmore and as I turned past the round church at the top of the hill, I saw a girl at the side of the road waving at me. Being the ever-vigilant policeman, I did a U-turn and made my way back up the hill. She could have been in distress for all I knew. You can't be too vigilant in my book.

I pulled up and she leaned in the passenger window proceeding to bombard me with questions, the strange face in town. Now, call me old-fashioned, but young blonde girls, on a warm summer's day, leaning in your car window, all smiles and friendly. Come on, what chance did I have? We had a few laughs and I told her I was finishing at five and could meet her for a drink later. We agreed that I would pick her up at seven. She was adamant that she would come to Port Ellen and we would have a wee drink at my digs. I swear that by that stage I would have agreed to swim back to Bowmore.

Changed into civvies, but obviously still driving the Panda, because I had no other transport with me, I was in Bowmore at the appointed time and place, and there she was, now dressed, made up, and beaming that I had arrived. I still remember the dress she was wearing and that her hair was loose now down her back, but the thing I remember most was her perfume. It was absolutely gorgeous and is still recognisable to me now in airports, lounges, restaurants or wherever I happen to be. Needless to say, I was in a bit of a state.

She didn't want to go for a drink or a bite to eat. Who was I to argue? So, we went straight to the single man's quarters I had spent about five minutes in earlier. I hadn't even unpacked my bags. I was dispatched across the road to get some drinks and when I came back the place had been cozied. There was music playing, the curtains were drawn and the glasses made ready. Only with hindsight did it occur to me that this woman seemed to know her way about that flat quite well. Such is the 'rush of blood' that we males have to contend with.

I'm not a hundred percent sure of the timescale, but maybe an hour or so later (I do know that there was now no doubt that the evening was heading quickly towards a natural conclusion), the telephone rang. I didn't even know there was one. I left it for a while but no one was answering and it wasn't going away.

'Hello.' Hoping it's a wrong number.

'It's Jimmy Dorwood here. Sorry, one of the local worthies is kicking off. We need to go and sort it out. It's in Lagavulin. I'll pick you up in thirty minutes.'

Laga what?

I was dumbstruck. How could this be? Talk of bad luck! We really were pissed off. Plus, I had the slight problem of a half-dressed girl in my police flat, in another officer's home, a few hours after arriving in Islay. Was that allowed? I had no idea, but knew that anything before marriage in Argyll was pretty much frowned on.

I had no way of getting her home to Bowmore. I would have passed Jimmy on the road as he sped towards me. I told her the call shouldn't take too long and after it I would take her back. The night wasn't over, hopefully.

I was waiting outside in uniform when Jimmy drew up and filled me in with the details. It was a well-known drunk, called Islay, who had kicked off and was threatening to batter someone and generally keep everyone awake all night. He needed locked up for a night to sober up, a regular occurrence apparently, and routine. We travelled the twenty minutes or so to Lagavulin and sure enough, an arrest was made. Now, throughout this tale, arrests are made almost without comment or note. That's what the police do, after all. But I feel it appropriate to point out the significance and importance of an arrest, especially in these enlightened times when every Tom, Dick and Harry likes to expound about their inherent rights.

My first arrest was a few days into the job, on Campbeltown Main Street, with my first mentor, Ian Andrew. It was busy with shoppers, and a drunk man was causing a real nuisance, being abusive, loud and generally threatening to passers-by. Not only did he completely refuse to desist when we approached, but he became even more remonstrative and loud, now directing his anger at us. As my neighbour Ian made his move and grabbed his right arm, I did likewise and secured his left, and we immediately forced him facing against the wall with his arms behind his back. Ian had cuffs on him within a jiffy and called for transport to get him off the street.

My point here is that in that few seconds of getting a grip and control of the guy, I felt the real anger and strength of this drunk. No one wants cuffs put on them, and no one wants their liberty taken away. In that brief moment, I was made forever aware of the dangers involved in making an arrest of any kind. The act is a really decisive and forceful move. It can't be wishy-washy or half-measured, or everyone's in danger. More especially, it is a real act of force. Physical violence towards a person of the most intrusive kind that is legal, as long as no excessive force is used to affect the arrest, and totally necessary in order to protect those 'rights' we hear so much about.

Then, the real lesson was learned. After we stripped this man of anything he could harm himself with and placed him in a police cell, it was left to me to close over the heavy cell door and turn the massive key in its lock. This struck me as a profound act, locking up a fellow citizen, depriving him entirely of his freedom, and deciding that he could do nothing, see no one, and be entirely dependent on the police for the foreseeable future. His life was on hold until we, the police, or a court, decided he could go back to it. I accepted this responsibility with some personal gravity and soul searching, as the realization of our power hit me hard.

Ian's decisive, positive action and practiced method of detaining, immobilising and controlling the big drunk was a really important lesson for me. I never, throughout my career as a police officer, made a casual arrest. It was always carried out with a degree of respect, consideration and self-justification, but above all decisively and positively, and on that night in Islay, it was tinged with a real resentment that my interesting night of diligent carnal community policing had hit the buffers.

Our drunken nuisance was brought back to Port Ellen and placed in a cell, in the downstairs operational part of the building, and then the real bombshell was dropped, almost casually by the sergeant. I was to check on this idiot every half hour until three o'clock, and then every hour until someone would come and take him to court at about nine-thirty in the morning. I would be up all night and had to prepare the report for the Procurator Fiscal to go with him to court. Suddenly this rural policing lark, and the jaunt that I had supposed it to be, were taking a totally unexpected turn for the worse.

I still had the slight problem of a – hopefully fully dressed – woman upstairs in the quarters, and with hindsight, I suspect Jimmy suspected or knew something about that. He knew everyone and everything that went on in Bowmore, but at the time I thought I was flying by the seat of my pants. I even asked Jimmy if he wanted a coffee before heading back to Bowmore, a simple courtesy, but boy was I relieved when he said he would speak to me in the morning, and waved goodbye. Phew.

A good few hours later (I had to make sure the sergeant was away to bed) I returned my date to her street in Bowmore and only felt safe when I was back in the office in Port Ellen, but as I sneaked in the back door, I was greeted by a wall of sound. Or so it seemed. My drunk had moved into the noisy phase of drunken merriment and was singing his heart out at full volume. At least he was still alive after my jaunt, which was some relief. I told him to shut up and went upstairs to get the paperwork done, but within a few minutes he was off again. The same song I think, no doubt a Gaelic classic, but at three or four in the morning, just a pain in the backside. I was a new face to him and I would imagine he was enjoying my confusion and obvious lack of imagination in how to deal with him.

Eventually, Dougie appeared, obviously irate, out of his bed and still in his night clothes. He only said, 'Follow me.'

And I did.

Downstairs we went and into the cell corridor.

'Shut up, Islay, last warning.'

Ah, a recognised and familiar voice, and off the singing went again, with even fresh vigour. Dougie grabbed the nozzle of the fire hose fixed to the cell corridor wall and told me to turn the tap on when he said. He then opened the door and gave me the nod. As the door opened the jet spray begun and what a force. It might just be my memory playing tricks now but I feel sure that old Islay was pinned to the rear wall for a minute or so by the force of the single hose jet. Dougie then told me to switch it off, wound it back on its wheel type cradle and headed upstairs again. All he said to me was, 'He'll be quiet now.'

And he was.

I stayed up the remainder of the night, checking on the prisoner as instructed. I had no idea if this actually happened under normal circumstances, but I knew that in Campbeltown we had a twenty-four-hour bar officer, and that a large part of his responsibilities was checking on prisoners every hour (when they were sober) and so I was taking no chances. To be fair, staying up all night was no big deal at twenty-one or two years of age. Not like now, when staying awake all day is a challenge. It had been a long and eventful day, with my journey, first shift on the island, an arrest and report, not to mention my delayed but acceptable and satisfying (at least for me) first effort at community policing. I love Islay.

CHAPTER 15: THOSE YANKS

Campbeltown was a different place in the early eighties from what it is today as far as employment is concerned. Whether it is better now is a matter of opinion, and perhaps depends on what stage of life you have arrived at. It was certainly much wilder back then, mainly because of the employment opportunities available in those days and the resultant disposable incomes available. In the Highlands there is much less available to divert funds from the important things in life, such as alcohol. Some truths are global, and certainly no reader will disagree with the fact that where there is copious alcohol consumption, there is trouble for sure.

The world-renowned Campbeltown Shipyard, the Jaeger clothing factory, the Campbeltown fishing fleet and the Machrihanish Air Force base were all in full flow. The MOD base at the mouth of the loch had regular ships docking and the Royal Navy had frigates and suchlike berthing at the town's quay most weekends. In short, the town was booming, and when you threw the American forces into the mix, including a squadron of their elite SEALs, it was some melting pot. As they say, light blue touch paper and retire.

You quickly learned how to survive when the inevitable clashes occurred. One night, when I was new, the doors of the Victoria Halls burst open at finishing time, and out spilled one big massive barney (or fight to the uninitiated). About twenty-five to thirty males, battering lumps out of each other. Great stuff. I couldn't wait to get in amongst it, but as I opened the van door to run across and arrest everyone, the sergeant, Alastair Barnett, grabbed my right arm and told me just to sit tight for a minute or two. He summoned some assistance from the other two officers available to us and, even when they arrived a few minutes later, we waited.

Eventually he put on the blue lights, sounded the twin tones a few times and slowly drove across into the middle of the fighting. Of course, it had dispelled to some degree by now, and only the most determined remained. He then told me to get out, stay close to him and to collect as many jackets and items of clothing as I could and throw them into the van. We did that for a few minutes and began grabbing the tiring boxers and putting them into the rear of the van. There was some token resistance but I think most were happy to be pulled from the fray. Then the gaffer caught my arm and pointed to an enormous guy who was standing on one spot despatching kicks and punches that were really hurting the recipients. He was in a different league and could likely have killed someone if he wanted to.

We approached him from behind in classic sneaky police fashion, and simultaneously grabbed an arm each, intending to pull him into the yawning rear of our Sherpa van. Somehow, he was rooted to the spot. We couldn't budge him. Not an inch. He then realised we were there and, thankfully, who we were, and simply shrugged us off. I feel sure he could have rag dolled both of us right there. I've rarely felt such raw power from an individual. I then distracted him while we edged him backwards to the van where about ten arms shot out and grabbed him inside. He did manage to get his hands onto the sides of the van in an effort to stay outside but I kicked the door and even giants hate getting their fingers jammed, it seems.

The Americans were a constant source of bemusement and amusement, but always great fun, just because they were so respectful of the police, full of mischief and behaved with us as though they were still stateside. I pulled over a big American car (a lot of them brought vehicles over) one summer's night on Kilkerran Road and approached the vehicle from behind. The window came down and I asked the guy to get out of the vehicle. He did so, and put both hands on the roof with his legs spread. I realised immediately this was what he would be required to do at home and when I asked to see his ID he moved his hand towards his inside jacket pocket and asked if could fetch the ID from inside. He didn't seem to know I couldn't shoot him, even if I wanted to.

He brought out his military SEAL ID and said to me, 'I'm sorry, officer, I don't have my driver's licence, but I don't need it tonight.'

'And why would that be, soldier?'

'I ain't driving, sir, he is.'

He pointed to his colleague in the driver's seat of the left-hand drive piece of shit. Enough said.

When we did lock up any of the Americans, they invariably gave us a hard time verbally. Drunk, of course. Them, not us. They would demand their rights under such and such an amendment and threaten all kinds of legal action against us. What was great was the next morning when their military police came to collect them. They would sign out any property, be escorted to the cell and the door flung open for them. They would march into the cell and scream stuff in American at the sleeping guy, who was on his feet and at attention before the smile hit my face. They were then marched out of the office into a waiting vehicle and off they went, never to be seen again. They were on the next transport across the Atlantic. No court. No messing about.

The real issue with the Yanks, as it always has been, is that they are red-blooded males and, for some reason, love Scottish women. They did seem to have a thing about the Scots lassies. I was in a bar one night, off duty, and a young girl known to me turned round to her six-foot-six American date and said:

'See you, ya bam, a'll batter fuck oot a ye, ya wanker.'

This smiling Adonis turns to me, happy as Larry, and says;

'Ain't she so cute?'

For goodness sake. She obviously hadn't completed finishing school in my book.

They were a real source of escape for Campbeltown girls, just like in towns near forces bases across the world, and many girls have found happiness and a new life stateside over the years.

Although only tolerated at the time, the American servicemen are an undoubted loss to towns like Dunoon and Campbeltown, for, apart from the diversity and fun they brought to the community, they contributed significantly to the local economy.

How sad it makes me to see the current riots and unrest, suspicions, claims and counter-claims going on in the States. It really is a powder keg and it must be a nightmare to police the streets just now. Treading on eggshells is never easy when you are tasked with enforcing the laws of the land, and I think some perspective has been lost in that regard. What does society want, expect or demand of its law enforcement?

If we discard the extremists on either side who would either do away with the police or clamp down with an iron fist on any dissent, we surely have the majority who have reasonable expectations that their lives and property will be protected and that their streets will be kept safe. That the laws laid down by the democratically elected government of the day will be enforced with some common sense and good judgement.

Now we come to the enforcement when people break those laws, become a danger to others, refuse to desist and want to resist arrest when confronted. Sometimes with weapons, often with firearms. Unfortunately, only force can combat force, no matter what some keyboard warriors might think. And even more unfortunately, when force is used, things can and do go wrong. Firearms are discharged, restraints are overused, some officers overstep the mark, and obviously all sorts of demons such as racism, homophobia or anti-Semitism can raise their ugly heads under stressful and dangerous situations that develop.

I can make no defence for officers who misuse their powers or authority. Truth is, I have no time for them and feel the courts should be harder on those who misuse the trust we all put in them to be controlled and fair to all. What I can understand is that when anyone carries a weapon or behaves in a manner which threatens lives or serious injury, they have instigated the response and circumstances that follow, and ultimately are to blame for the sadness we all feel in the aftermath of these events.

CHAPTER 16:
DEAD OR ALIVE

As a young probationer I reported for duty one nice summer's night and at the briefing I was told to accompany the old sergeant, Alec John McLellan, a real character, as most of these teuchters were. He was going on holiday the next day and didn't want to get involved in anything that might interfere with his getting away sharp in the morning. Fair enough.

He was serious about this and, instead of him and I walking down the Main Street from Castlehill Police Office, he took me down the back streets, away from any possible trouble. We strolled down the hill past the community centre and down towards the esplanade and the town's two piers, deserted at that time of night.

Sergeant Alec John was nearing retirement in 1979, and for his thirty-odd years of police service had been part of the Argyll Police Constabulary, a force of maybe a hundred or so officers and staff who all knew each other and each other's families, business and family's business, and so on. In 1976, reorganisation had seen the birth of new police force areas, and Argyll was swallowed up by the biggest of the Scottish regions, Strathclyde. As a recruit of Strathclyde Police, I was one of maybe ten or so incomers to Campbeltown over the last few years who knew little or nothing of rural life and nothing about policing, and so the daily frictions between the old and new are obvious.

In retrospect, these older cops and sergeants were patient. Police officers hate change and complain about it constantly, but despite all of their protestations and moans, the job goes on irrespective. New friendships are formed and the natural bonding of those wearing uniforms and having common purpose prevails. It was interesting that these old-school Argyll men or 'coonty cops', as they were known, would regularly slip into Gaelic when chatting to each other.

'If you don't use it, you lose it, laddie,' is how it was excused to us toonies.

One sergeant, Angus MacLeod, was almost indecipherable at times. On one occasion he had shouted an instruction to me in the middle of a melee on Main Street, while I had some drunken yob pinned to the bonnet of a car, and as I looked over at Angus quizzically, the ned managed to put the head on me. I had two loose front teeth for some time.

Over the radio it was pure guesswork with Angus. I remember him giving some instruction to my mate Kenny Rhodes over the airwaves. Kenny heard:

'Go and get your piece, lad.'

Quite soon, Angus came across Kenny sitting in the kitchen eating some chips and went ballistic, as only he could. He had told Kenny to go and direct traffic on the main street, it seems. Easily lost in translation.

Anyway, back to my evening stroll down the back streets of Campbeltown with Alec John on that lovely Saturday night. We were just about to pass the now old library site, where a beautiful statue of Linda McCartney now stands in remembrance, with the dark esplanade in our sites, when we heard the unmistakable sound of a car skidding around the main roundabout and accelerating along the shore front. It would have passed in front of us in a few seconds, but we heard it break sharply and skid around the junction straight in front of us, almost lose control and accelerate straight towards our position on John Street.

From first hearing the car to it actually speeding past us took a few seconds, the blink of an eye really, and I would be lying if I said I can remember what actually happened as it passed. The problem is that the statement I eventually wrote was drummed into me for months, as the driver was scheduled to appear at the High Court on trial for attempting to murder me. I can only relate what my statement said, as it is actually now ingrained in my mind.

Seeing the car turn onto John Street, having heard him speed along the esplanade, I stood onto the road shining my torch up and down (in the prescribed manner, of course) indicating that the driver should stop. The driver then drove onto my side of the road and attempted to run me over, accelerating straight up John Street and over the spot I was standing on. He would have hit me without doubt if Alec John hadn't had the presence of mind to pull me out of the speeding car's path. All hell then broke loose.

Alec John radioed for other vehicles to pursue the speeding car and for transport to be brought to us in order that we could join the chase; a chase that went on for about an hour. Someone drove the police Sherpa van to our location and Alec John took the wheel. By this time, the out of control car, an XR3, had been spotted several times throughout the town, and members of the public were phoning 999 to complain.

There was at least one police car in pursuit, and so we were aware that he had driven out of town and was now heading back towards Campbeltown on the west road, the main Glasgow road. Alec John took us onto the Longrow, which eventually becomes the west road. We were heading straight towards the lunatic.

Now, locally we all had personal radios that were controlled from Campbeltown office, and their range was limited to a few miles around the town, and so everything said over them was local. But the police vehicles had a fitted VHF radio with which we could communicate directly with Pitt Street in Glasgow and force wide for that matter. I have no problem remembering exactly what occurred over the next few minutes.

We were driving west along the Longrow and sure enough the totally out of control XR3 comes towards us travelling at high speed, closely pursued by a police car with its blue light flashing. Alec John decided to use the Sherpa van the way I had apparently used my torch earlier, and began weaving across the road in the path of the XR3, blue light birling, headlights flashing. As he did so, the XR3 driver decided to ram us, or at the least force a game of chicken. We were never going to win that game of nerves, not with Alec going on holiday in the morning, and he took evasive action, swerving into the county garage and back out the other side at some speed. Alec was raging now, all composure gone, and as he stopped to turn the Sherpa and continue the chase he grabbed the VHF radio from the dashboard and shouted into it:

'Get the bastard, dead or alive.'

Goodness only knows what they made of that outburst in Glasgow HQ or Dumbarton control room. Hopefully, the strong Gaelic accent confused them.

The rogue vehicle then spun around town a few times and headed off up the east road onto a much trickier B-road towards Carradale. But we had backup in Carradale, the local constable Willie Robertson, a real county cop. Alec gave instructions for Willie to be telephoned, called out as he was off-duty, and told to block the road to all traffic at the Carradale bridge. Simple enough.

As it transpired, our maniac driver had turned off onto some forestry road before reaching Carradale, but when our traffic car got to the bridge, they found the Carradale Panda car parked across the width of the bridge. It lights were on and its blue light was lighting up the surrounding woods but Willie was nowhere to be seen. He had simply parked the Panda as instructed and buggered off back to the police house a few hundred yards up the road. What a character he was.

There was no big dramatic ending. The XR3 was found abandoned at a closed gate on a forestry road and the driver apprehended not too far away trying to walk some six miles back to the town. I did learn a valuable lesson that night, though. The big traffic cop, Bob Stewart, filled out the crime report which formed the basis of the police custody report that was to be submitted to the Fiscal on Monday morning and the charges read as follows.

Charge 1. Attempted murder of police officer, Simon McLean, in John Street.

Charge 2. Attempted murder of three police officers by trying to ram them at high speed on Longrow.

Charge 3. Driving whilst under the influence of drink or drugs.

Charge 4. Reckless driving at various loci in and around Campbeltown

Charge 5. Speeding at various loci in and around Campbeltown.

Charge 6. Driving without insurance.

Charge 7. A bald tyre on the front offside wheel of the XR3.

Charge 8. A faulty windscreen wiper.

Being a curious rookie, I queried this leap of seriousness from attempted murder to a worn tyre and a broken wiper. Bob then told me a truth that would stand me in good stead.

'Throw enough shite, son, and some of it will stick.'

I suppose I should finish this tale with a posthumous thank you to Sergeant Alec John McLellan who, through his quick thinking and selfless act, plucked me from almost certain death in the path of that lunatic driver. Thanks, Alec. I think.

CHAPTER 17: ROAD TRAFFIC

Road accidents were a constant source of fatalities, especially since the Tangy Bends were then still a feature of the A83 between Bellachuntuy and Campbeltown, a perfect trap for a tired driver almost at the end of his or her long journey (apparently the majority of accidents occur in the last ten percent of journeys). Or of a morning when the rising sun doesn't quite penetrate the still shaded west side of the road, leaving the night frost intact, awaiting unsuspecting travellers.

Lorries leaving Campbeltown were guilty of filling their diesel tanks up to the brim and, a few minutes later, as they headed north and negotiated Tangy Bends, they left deadly pools of fuel behind. All in all, a recipe for carnage.

One fine summer's day, my colleague, Ian Andrew, and I were dispatched to attend the site of a lorry having left the road and landed on the beach. There was no further information other than the location. Tangy Bends.

When we got to the locus, sure enough, there was an HGV wedged between the rocks and the sand, and its rear end was up in the air. It had shed its complete load, many tons of cattle feed chips, each about two inches long. The lorry's windscreen was gone and the chips had landed in a giant mound right in front of the driver's cab. There was no one about at all.

We immediately started digging with our hands into the massive pile of chips, our assumption being that the driver had been thrown through the windscreen on impact, and then covered by the pile of chips. It was really smelly stuff, and it was warm. We quickly discarded our tunics as we franticly dug into the mountain, all the while listening for any sign of life below. This went on for at least ten minutes when a man appeared above us, asking:

'How are you doing, lads?'

He was the driver, and he explained that he had gone to find a phone to call his boss. We weren't in the slightest relieved that he was alive and well. I thought Ian might strangle him and bury him in the chips.

One evening close to Christmas, I was heading south towards Campbeltown on my own in the CID Cortina (what a car it was). It was while the Tangy road works were in full swing. It took about two years to build the current stretch of road to replace 'The Bends.' As I got to about fifteen minutes from home I came up to a red light at the single file road works, near to Clachan. There was one car waiting in front of me.

When the light turned to green, I prepared to go but the car in front didn't move, and by the time I thought to go around him the lights were back at red. Fair enough, he must have stalled or have some mechanical problem. I decided to wait for the next green light and see if he moved. He didn't. Not an inch. I now realised that his engine was still running and so there must be a problem.

I got out and approached the driver's door, and quickly realised the male driver was totally unconscious. Thankfully there had been no heart attack or stroke, just a lot of well-meant drams from his customers as he did his insurance round before Christmas. He had been sociable and was still asleep when the uniforms arrived on the scene to arrest him. I had two and a half years' service and this was my first drunk-driving case.

I had no enthusiasm for road traffic law. I could never understand colleagues who were the exact opposite. They would talk about cars all day and night and aspired to join the traffic department – or white wooden tops, as I called them. One of them in Campbeltown in those early days of my career was Dougie Bones. He was a nice guy, and car daft.

As a single cop I had asked a girl who worked in the bank out for a drink. Like you do. She had said yes, but asked if she could bring her friend and I could bring another copper. I got Dougie to come along. To the best of my knowledge he had never been seen with a woman. Sorted.

We had a nice wee night in a few local hostelries, I never saw her again (she actually married a friend of mine) and, apart from not getting any shirts ironed for me, the night was pleasant but uneventful. Other than for one detail.

We had been in the pub for an hour or so when I went to the toilet. As I was attending to business, Dougie appeared behind me and I asked him how he was getting on with his blind date.

'Great,' was the response. 'Thanks a lot for bringing me along tonight.'

'Do you think you might see her again?'

'Oh yeah, it's sorted. We're going to the car show together.'

Shocked, I automatically acknowledged that this was great news, a real success that they got on so well. We went back to join the girls and then slowly it dawned on me. This was in February.

'Dougie, when is the car show, this weekend?'

'No, it's in October in Glasgow,' he innocently replied.

As someone who thought a long-term relationship lasted all night, I simply couldn't compute any of this. I still can't to be honest, but I can see the whole thing through a new lens now. A perspective only offered by hindsight. They went on to become Mr and Mrs Bone and had a lovely family. Dougie spent the majority of his career in fast cars with his white-topped hat on.

CHAPTER 18: NIGHT SHIFT

I had two years of night shift in Campbeltown, throughout my probationary period, and being a bit of a night hawk in those days I enjoyed it. Not everyone did. The early part of the shift, starting at eleven, was always taken up with the pubs and clubs closing, and of course, this could go on until much later at weekends. We learned that the rain was the best policeman there was because it would get them off the streets and home much more effectively than we ever could. When the streets were quiet, we would carry out our first round of padlock pulling, checking that all of the business properties were secure, front and back.

I have had some real scares doing that, once walking into the old fish factory yard where noises had been reported. Pitch black, shining my torch, and there, under an old trailer, revealed in my spotlight, two sets of feet, stock still. My scream soon put paid to that and we were off on a chase. Another time again, a report of possible intruders at the coal yard in Rothesay, me on my own with my torch, walking through the tight pedestrian tunnel into the yard. As I came out into the yard, I shone my torch to the left. What a sight. Three big faces lined up no more than two feet away. For fuck sake, another suit ruined. One of those big faces grew up to be my son's father-in-law and he remembers the incident more for the scare I gave them.

But back to Campbeltown. At some point during the night we would check the shipyard, explosives store and other outlying property. The shipyard, now long closed, lay across Campbeltown Loch, looking back towards Davaar Island and the MOD naval base. The naval base was manned round the clock by the MOD police, who worked the same shift patterns, got paid the same wages and basically had all of the same conditions and benefits of the real police, but stood guard and let vehicles through a barrier.

I would tell a joke about the three policemen going to heaven, and St. Peter asks the first one where he worked.

'In London, with the Met.'

'Och, away you go in. Next.'

'I worked in Govan in Glasgow, Sir, with Strathclyde Police.'

'That'll do me, big man, in you go. Next.'

'Oh, I worked with the MOD police all over.'

St. Peter is delighted.

'Thank goodness. Watch this gate while I go for a piss.'

It was always the same lad who was on night shift, and every other shift alongside our pattern, Dick McFadyen. When we were at the shipyard, we would flash our blue light for a few seconds and our reward was that Dick would flash his lights. The whole hillside above the loch lit up for a few seconds. What a sight. This was a serious storage facility in a strategic position with regards to the Atlantic. The whole hillside was illuminated, marking the enormous underground storage facility that it was.

When Dick responded, this was the complex coded message that meant it was clear for us to proceed over and get a cup of coffee in his gatehouse. A nightly ritual when all was quiet. He would come out when we drew up, unlock the big padlock, and remove the chain holding the gates and drape it back over while we were inside having a well-earned break.

Dick was forever reminding us of his vast responsibilities and the fact that he was an authorised firearm officer and had access to a gun, kept in his gatehouse safe. He had shown it to us several times. So, we hatched a plan, and one quiet night three of us went in the van, with me in the rear out of sight. When we got to the base, Dick came out and greeted Tam and Ian as usual, while I waited until they were all in the gatehouse. I then jumped out of the van and into the base through the gates that were left with the chain dangling.

After a recce, I climbed up on the roof, started thumping my feet and jumped off onto the big grass embankment alongside. Of course, Dick was out to investigate, closely followed by my two colleagues winding him up. When they were back inside, I threw a handful of pebbles at the window, which apparently sounded like shrapnel from inside. By now the boys had Dick in a right tizz, goading him to get his sidearm out of the safe as we were obviously under attack. I got back on the roof again and after a few hefty thumps I was off, but this time when Dick came out, his car doors were lying open. That was the final straw, apparently, but rather than go for his gun he was in the process of calling his boss in Faslane to report goodness knows what. The boys had to tell him the truth and I was brought in for my hard-earned coffee.

The night shift was often a time for larking about and practical jokes, mainly because it was quiet, we had the streets to ourselves and crucially there were no bigwig gaffers about to hinder us. In Glasgow it was sport to have the new start out cleaning the traffic lights with a mop and pail and we would often carry the spare Sherpa van keys with us on foot, and steal it if we found it lying outside an obvious skive or doss. Always good fun.

The night is usually when all sorts of nefarious activity takes place and the police were no different. A police woman in the squad once told me that she had slept with everyone on her shift, about thirty men. Like you, I was struck speechless until she explained that, come four o'clock, she just couldn't keep her eyes open as a passenger in the police car, no matter what, and that every single cop on her shift could vouch for it.

It was also a time for ambush. Maybe we had an old score to settle or someone we had been trying to get a word with but they had been evading us. Closing time was always good. One night, Ian and I came across a rammy on the Main Street in Campbeltown. Just some locals having a square go and it quickly dispersed as we walked towards them. We recognised one of them as a guy who was always there or thereabouts, an opportunist thief and a real horrible sneaky character, who had been putting the boot into someone on the ground. Just his style. Of course, he had slinked off into the shadows, but we obviously knew where he lived.

We were waiting in his back court in the old Park Square flats.

It was pitch black and the obvious route for him to sneak home, and as he came into the square we were hiding near his back close in wait. He was singing or mumbling away as he came near and then we heard a window being pushed up in a hurry and the unmistakable tones of his wife echoing all across the square and beyond.

'You, ya fuckin idiot, yur a useless arse.'

I don't need to repeat the tirade of abuse she gave him, at full volume and fully descriptive of his faults, as only irate Campbeltown women can aspire to. I would know – I was married to one.

Just as I was getting ready to grab him, I saw Ian shaking his head and signalling not to grab him. We just let him go to his fate, and Ian convinced me quite easily that what awaited him was much worse than we had planned or could even dream of. We would get him another time.

We used this principle quite often with drunks. A night in the cells on a charge of drunk and incapable would result in a free breakfast and bed for the night, and a measly five-pound fine. Much better to take them home and watch them be dragged those last few steps by the hair, inside to pay forever more for the embarrassment of being brought home by the police. What would the neighbours say?

Night shift was often playtime, but it is also when most people die, when domestics regularly kick off, and when serious crime is committed. It was seldom boring, that's for sure, and I always enjoyed going home to my bed at seven when everyone else was going to their work.

CHAPTER 19: ARCHIE SHAW

Sergeant Archie Shaw got promoted from Oban to Campbeltown with about twenty-eight years' police service. He had served in Dunoon and Inveraray, as well as Oban, and so certainly qualified as a 'coonty man.' I think it was fair to say that his promotion was as much of a surprise to him as it was to the rest of Argyll. And so, with only a few years' service remaining, he and his wife were forced to up sticks and move to Campbeltown, widely regarded as the arsehole of the county.

From the off, Archie hated the Wee Toon, but it was worth a few years' sacrifice, I suppose, for the increased pension rights the sergeant rank offered, and, in any event, Archie was nothing if not loyal, and would have moved anywhere if asked to do so, without question.

He became our shift sergeant, as our gaffer, Alastair Barnett, had been moved to the Campbeltown CID as detective sergeant. There were four or five cops on each of the four shifts, and on our shift, Group 4, there were Tam McNab, Ian Andrew, Ian McCallister, me and Isabel McArthur in order of service. Each shift had a policewoman. With a three-shift pattern, early turn, back shift and night shift, there was always a group off-duty, and so twenty-four-hour cover was provided.

Like Tam, Archie was old-school, and he used to regale us with stories about his county days. They sounded dreadful. In Tam's case, the old copper stories were interspersed with tales of the merchant navy. They were also dreadful. Apparently county police officers were never paid overtime; in fact, I don't think any forces were. This apparently explained why you would see twenty or thirty detectives called out to a murder scene in those days. It didn't cost any money. Instead, Archie explained, they were given time in lieu. In other words, for any hours spent working over and above your forty hours, you received time off in the book. This was a ledger still kept in my day that allowed you to save time for emergencies or to supplement normal time off.

Archie's tale was that when he was working at Inveraray, and being called out to road accidents night and day all through summer, all of this time was going in the book. He then received a visit from the Chief Constable of Argyll, who would exclaim at the hundreds of hours in the book and order Archie to take two weeks off in order to use this time up. Of course, this would be in the middle of winter when the schools were still in and with no notice. By the time Archie went back to work he would discover that those hours had simply transferred to a colleague who had been forced to cover for him for two weeks, and that he was about to cover for him. And so it would go on.

Archie was a nice man. Once when he had crashed a police car he apparently presented himself at the boss's desk the following morning and handed over his warrant card, prepared to resign there and then. Of course, he was sent packing, but it was good to work with someone who had that genuine loyalty, integrity in himself as a man, and absolute faith and belief in the system. I didn't meet many like Archie Shaw over the years. No one did.

His one insurmountable problem was some form of sleeping sickness. I'm not sure if it was ever diagnosed as narcolepsy or anything else, because Archie would never discuss it at all. He must have thought that if he never mentioned it, no one would ever notice and so there would never be a problem. But it was profound. He could fall asleep anywhere at all. Sometimes you were speaking to him and he was trying to converse but his eyes were fighting to close. It could be standing up, driving, walking the dog, you name it.

On the shift we all learned to accommodate this. It was never mentioned in his presence and we always drove the police vehicles. We always knocked on his office door before entering to give him time to come to. He invariably had a big mark on his cheek where he had been resting it on his hand. There were dozens of stories about Archie falling asleep over the years. Apparently, he had been found by his sergeant in Dunoon sound asleep in a doorway on his beat, standing up. Our understanding and loyalty to our sergeant meant we would protect and defend him to the hilt, but we still had a lot of fun.

My favourite trick was driving the police Sherpa during the night and waiting for Archie to start nodding. On a quiet night in the early hours, it never took long. When he was sound asleep, head lolling about, I would stamp on the breaks and jump out the van as if chasing someone. A few seconds later out would come Archie, only half awake, wondering what all the fuss was about. It was always a false alarm, but good fun at the time.

On one occasion we almost took it too far. The whole shift were to report a few hours early for a back shift and attend what served as our games room (a pool table and a dart board) upstairs. The pool table had been removed and seating put in, and we were all to be briefed about the new Civic Government (Scotland) Act 1980. A major piece of legislation that, among lots of other things, changed the way we could detain and deal with suspects, and the paperwork involved in doing so. It basically introduced what became known simply as Section 2, when a suspect could be held for up to six hours without charge.

We all had to be trained up to use this new procedure and every shift was briefed separately so as not to interfere with normal policing. We all attended together with Archie, our leader, but when we were setting the chairs out, we realised that there was one radiator in the small room and it was belting out. We informed everyone else that his was to be Archie's seat.

Poor Archie, he never stood a chance, and yet he tried so, so hard to stay awake. In those days you could smoke anywhere. Hard to believe now, but confined spaces never seemed to be an issue. Archie smoked like a lum, and it was one of his favourite tactics deployed to help him stay awake. The conscious effort of puffing away on his fag, coupled with the inherent dangers involved, could normally be relied on to keep him at least semi-conscious.

Not in this room.

The radiator did its job. I would say he lasted ten or fifteen minutes. He had undone his tunic in order to ventilate (this was a big deal for Archie, informal) and was on his second smoke already when the chin started to drop. The real problem here was that he had a lit fag in his hand, and as his head drooped so did the hand holding the lit cig. He would drop it to his shirt, feel the heat of the burning fag through his shirt, and jolt awake with a start.

How we all managed to suppress the laughter is beyond me. You see the real problem was the secrecy. None of us had ever discussed this with Archie. We couldn't. He was our sergeant and obviously felt he had to lead by example in every aspect of his work. He would have been totally mortified by any mention of it, as would we. In the normal course of things, we could compensate for him whenever required, and work round his obvious disability. No problem.

But here we were in circumstances where he was a danger to himself and to everyone else. He certainly burned his shirt a few times down his chest and belly area, and of course had ash spilled everywhere. I think Ian pretended there was a call for him downstairs in order to extricate Archie from that room. This allowed everyone to save face but, man, it was so funny.

I learned a lot from working with Archie Shaw. Not about investigative work or procedure. Not about interviewing suspects or witnesses, or even report writing and paperwork. What I did learn was that a certain simple integrity can go a long, long way in life. It can earn a man respect and peace of mind, and can underpin many of his actions and decisions on a daily basis. In most cases it can allow a man to rest and sleep peacefully in his bed at night or, in Archie Shaw's case, almost anywhere.

CHAPTER 20:
OPPORTUNITY KNOCKS

On 28th December 1980, the day my two-year probation period ended, I started work in Campbeltown as a CID officer. This was a strict six-month secondment designed to broaden a copper's horizons, give him or her some insight and experience of the investigative side of the job, and gauge the likelihood that you had the makings of a detective or, indeed, had any desire to take that career path.

Alastair Barnett, who had been my first uniform shift sergeant, was DS and the DC, Neil Kennedy, had just been promoted when I took his seat in the CID office. Alastair badly damaged a nerve in his back simply lifting a sack of potatoes a few months into my stint, and so for about four months I worked alone. Due to these circumstances, my six months was extended to ten months, a period when I really found my feet, or even my wings. I was still single, had an active social life based around sport, played for the local amateur football club and shared a flat with a colleague, Kenny Rhodes. Happy days, indeed.

I shared a flat with Kenny Rhodes for about six months – long enough, for sure. He really was totally and utterly useless on the domestic front. I know many people would laugh at me slating anyone's housekeeping prowess, and I wouldn't claim to be Felix Unger, but this was ridiculous. The problem being that Kenny had been brought up the youngest of five kids, and he was the only boy. He had never done anything at all, and this was patently obvious.

There is a definite warning primarily to mothers here. I have met so many males who have never acquired the most basic of knowledge, far less skills, about how to look after themselves, many of them young police officers who had obviously had everything done for them all of the time. There are mums who think they're doing the best for their boys, but who then send them into the world in a moronic state of total dependence on carry-outs and unable to even understand how to wash and iron their clothes, make their beds or wash a dish.

I lived with Kenny, and so I witnessed all of these shortcomings. He believed that just because you buy a tin of soup, for example, and eat it all yourself, this must apply to everything. A packet of biscuits, a loaf, a half-dozen eggs. He once had scrambled egg everywhere across the cooker because he used the whole pack. His room became so messy and dirty that he slept on the settee in the lounge for months on end. He simply didn't have the tools to deal with the mess.

One night, a Royal Navy ship was berthed at the quay, guaranteeing a night of entertainment. Many a time we had to try and round up the sailors who were due back on board, but had found something much more interesting ashore. Girls. We would sometimes chase them along the street and have to take them back to their ship in handcuffs. In fairness, the Navy always provided a shore patrol of their own, who didn't mess about. They carried massive night sticks and weren't slow to use them, and so we managed to keep a fleet at sea, just about. The shore patrol officers were always grateful for our help and cooperation, and invariably left some beautiful navy cut loose tea at the office for us.

On this particular night, things had calmed down around three or four, and the sergeant told Kenny to make a brew for everyone before we resumed our patrols. He threw him a quarter-pound packet of the navy-cut tea. No one thought any more of it. Ten minutes later, Kenny appeared with a big tray. He had put mugs on it, sugar, spoons and maybe even milk. I remember thinking that he wasn't such an imbecile after all, or was totally taking the piss out of me at home. By the look on his face you would think he was Jamie Oliver's advisor.

We all gathered round expectantly for a well-earned cuppa, and someone decided to pour. Alas, nothing came out of the teapot. Then a few dribbles of black liquid escaped. Then someone lifted the lid. It was almost a solid mass of tea-leaves. Kenny had tipped the whole lot into the teapot, then some boiling water. No one on the shift that night could quite believe it. I could. He told me later he had searched for instructions but found none on the packet.

I could relate many tales about Kenny's domestic exploits but my favourite was when he tried to make mince. I came off shift after eleven one night and saw his plate lying on the carpet. It was obvious he had eaten off this plate but I couldn't for the life of me make out what was on it, hardly touched but unrecognisable. I casually asked Kenny, as he lay on the couch as usual:

'What's that you had for dinner, mate?'

I had to be careful or he would go in a huff, as he didn't know anything about the world where ordinary people can shop, clean and cook food. It was all a mystery, or even a miracle, to Kenny.

'I made some mince, but it was shite, nothin' like ma maw's.'

'How did you cook it?' I couldn't tell if it had actually been cooked.

'I put it in the oven on a tray thing, but it was really dry and hard. I just got Chinese.'

'You know you're best to use a pot for mince, buddy?'

He was upset now.

'Don't start all that cookery class shite, mate. Just leave it.'

And the subject moved on or we drifted off to bed.

On back shift the next day, I was approached by one of the cleaners, who told me that Kenny had related the 'shite mince' tale to her, looking for some tips. She was astonished that a young man couldn't perform such a simple task, and I think she was wondering if I was the same. In any event, she had told him to use a pot and advised that an onion through the mince would give added flavour, etc. I thought no more about it.

A week or so later I found him eating his mince with a puzzled look on his face. He had used a pot and browned the mince to a point where it would have at least been edible. But the onion was sitting on top of it, still whole and in its skin. He had simply plopped a whole onion on top of the mince as he had heated it.

'How's the mince tonight, mate?'

'Aye, much better, but still no like ma maw's.'

You really couldn't make it up, but there's no doubt my life was enhanced, and much more fun, with Kenny in it.

My instinct here is to say that I was a lucky detective, but I can see those years now with the clarity only time can provide. Certainly, being in the right place at the right time can be classed as fortunate to a degree, but even then opportunities have to be taken, and I was determined to seize mine. The secondment was for six months but I was retained in situ beyond that time due to my undoubted success in the role. I had some notable arrests in that ten-month period that certainly did me no harm.

The local soft drink distributor in those days was a company called Daniel's. They also supplied sweets, crisps, confectionery and suchlike to most if not all of the local businesses, and they had a warehouse on the north side of town. Their manager was well-known to the police (he liked a dram, in other words) and he called me one day, asking me to visit, as he had a strange problem.

He explained that Daniel's had a number of storage places throughout the town and that stock was going missing from one of them with no explanation. He was noticing that a few boxes of this or that would be short every few days, but he had no idea how this could be possible, as the only keys for the store were accounted for. I asked to see the store and to my surprise it was on the Main Street, across from Woolies, next to the old book shop.

Just a locked door with a single-room store inside, a door that I had passed hundreds if not thousands of times and had no idea what lay behind it. I subsequently learned that no other cops knew what was behind that door either. The room was perhaps ten by ten by ten feet and, although a kid would consider it an Aladdin's Cave, it had a modest amount of stock stored head high. Sweets of just about every description, loads of crisps and some crates of 'ginger.' There only was the one door and there were no signs of any forced entry. Jimmy assured me that stock was steadily disappearing.

The key for the store was a massive iron mortice, much like the cell keys that we had in those days, and I physically checked that the two existing keys were in the possession of Jimmy, himself, and his main driver. They assured me that the keys, along with many others for the business, never left their possession. It was patently obvious that there was another key somewhere, or the driver was 'at it', but someone was going to have to be caught in the act. Jimmy refused to accept that it was anyone connected with Daniel's. In fact, he didn't really agree with me that another key existed. I'm sure he thought there was something supernatural going on. There was little point in explaining to him that these mysteries generally turn out to be the result of good old-fashioned theft by mere mortals, always in my experience to date.

I started with an inventory, noting batch numbers, delivery dates and details etc. I knew every Smartie and every Wotsit in that place and, sure enough, every now and then, a box of this or that would disappear. I put a mat down inside the door that would activate if stood on. It did, maybe two or three times a week and this would send a silent signal to the radios of whoever was on shift at that time. The place was always locked when they got there, then sweeties were missing the next day.

The problem with alarms is that they activate by mistake on occasion, eliciting the same response from the cops on-duty, and where at first the response is like a scene from the Sweeney, the novelty soon wears off with false alarms, and the 'cried-wolf' syndrome kicks in. Eventually, it's just a pain in the backside. The problem was that the thefts were so random, sometimes weeks apart, sometimes days, and so it was infuriating that we couldn't pin down the culprit. Weeks went by, which ran into months and, gradually, other things took over completely, and although still an ongoing enquiry, it was no longer at the front of anyone's mind or the top of their inbox. Maybe the supernatural explanation had more substance than we thought?

A few months later, in the summer of 1981, one of the local lock-up garages, quite near the police station as it transpired, was broken into overnight. Inside was an ice cream van fully stocked and unlocked. It certainly wasn't fully stocked by the time I got there. It had been ransacked. The till had been emptied and nearly all of the cigarettes stolen, as well as a wide selection of confectionery.

I liked these types of crimes. I had such a good network of informants, friends, local businesspeople and fly-by-nights that I could generally pick up an idea of who had the goods pretty quickly. I played in both the pool league and the darts league in the town, and so was mixing constantly on a social level with a wide demographic. I was personable, played football, refereed, and played golf.

Most importantly, I considered myself part of the local community and was always what I considered to be fair. I would rather take a drunk home than put him in a cell. I had a large dose of common sense when it came to booking people for road traffic offences or minor misdemeanours. I tended to give people the benefit of the doubt, and although I had little time for thieves, I was more sympathetic to the fighters, certainly where only fists were involved and no weapons used or liberties taken.

All of the above meant that I was able to approach people who maybe wouldn't generally talk to a police officer, because I had played football with or against them, gave them a word of warning or marked their card in some way over the months. I never acted on stuff I was told through drink, certainly not without a further sober conversation having occurred. There had to be a trust that they wouldn't end up in court as a witness and I always protected that relationship as much as possible.

A good example of how that long game can pay off was when a wee girl of three or four was almost abducted one sunny, uneventful Sunday afternoon. She went missing from her garden.

The panic button was pressed. Roads were blocked, searches commenced and cops called in from their time off, but thankfully she was found within forty minutes by her big brother, playing in a swing park at the old paddling pool on Kilkerran Road in Campbeltown. She was fine.

A description of a man with a beard was gleaned from her and other kids in the park. He had taken her to the park and had taken off shortly before we arrived. We had no idea who this guy was, but he had certainly taken this wee girl about half a mile from her home.

Later that night I saw a notorious Campbeltown worthy standing at the town's main junction, nodding to people as they passed. Everyone knew him. He was a real rascal, could fight like mad and was behind just about every violent public incident in town. The last time I had spoken to him was in the rear of a police van when he was missing an ear. Someone had bitten it off but he hardly noticed. He and I had a long history of rolling about the streets together. We also played football in the same team for a while (until he went back to prison). He was actually the guy who had directed me to the police station on my arrival in Campbeltown.

Anyway, I parked up the car and joined him at his post. We stood side by side, both looking ahead down the Longrow. Everyone who passed gave us a strange look or a double take, the local detective and the local crime lord passing the time of day. I don't think we looked at each other. I had just crossed a line, approaching him in public, and we both knew it. He couldn't move away, that would show a weakness or fear. He couldn't turn towards me or engage in conversation openly, that would indicate an exchange of information, a common thread, a relationship between us. And so, we both faced down the Longrow. The conversation went as follows.

Me: 'Wee girl, ponytails, taken from her garden. Four years of age. I'll pay for a name. I'll leave my personal number at the office. Help me out.'

Him: 'Try the Argyll Hotel, chef or kitchen staff. I don't want paid. You sort it, big man, or I will.'

That was it. I walked away, straight across the road to the Argyll Hotel and summoned the owner, a friend of mine. Twenty minutes later the new chef was arrested. His car was packed with his belongings as he intended to bugger off later that night. He was identified and convicted and, more importantly, flagged up as a suspect for similar and much worse crimes in other parts of the UK.

Time and time again, I benefited from my philosophy that the long game was what mattered. I know for a fact that no other policeman in Campbeltown would have approached that individual asking for help. I also know that he wouldn't have given them the help. We'll never know what we prevented that day, and never can. All we can do is try to shorten the odds in our favour bit by bit and, in my case, make the lines between the 'good guys' and 'bad guys' a little less defined so that we can all benefit.

It's interesting that in all the dealings I had with that rascal, his partners and his much-extended family over the following years, and there were many, that incident was never ever referred to by either of us. In fact, it's fascinating. I've met hundreds of police officers who wouldn't give away the information he did without a promise of reward or recognition.

Once, when the sergeants' mess club at Machrihanish had been broken into, the chief inspector asked me to go out on the Friday with Kenny in plain clothes, as if off-duty, and find out what had happened to the large amount of spirits stolen. He felt sure the booze would be in circulation locally.

He was absolutely right, and we found the booze. We had crawled diligently round the local pubs, secured invites to any parties being organized for after hours, and showing great dedication and persistence attended all of them. In the process we had become exceptionally intoxicated, managed to get into a few scraps along the way, lost the CID car (later found totally unharmed behind a pub) and made a lot of new friends. A huge success, we thought.

On the Sunday, I rounded up a few troops and, armed with a search warrant, revisited an American serviceman's flat in the town where we recovered the vast majority of the stolen booze, or the bottles at any rate. Only the dregs were left for the most part, but the bottles were easily identified as stock from the violated mess bar. The fact that Kenny and I had helped empty the bottles never raised its head. Some things are best left unsaid, I suppose, as long as the job gets done. I digress again, but informants were increasingly the lifeblood of my career as a divisional detective and I considered the nurturing of them as a key skill and attribute. I also enjoyed it.

So, back to my burgled garage and looted ice cream van. Where cigarettes are involved, the starting point is obvious. In fairness, it's the same starting point when hoping to catch a whiff of any stolen goods being sold. The good old pub. In those days I was a bit of an expert in pubs. I could go into establishments that didn't normally get frequented by cops or their associates (other police officers) because they tended to get verbally harassed by the clientele. Looking back, the police officers of that era were starting to see themselves as middle class, and only frequented a select list – maybe two or three of the twenty-odd pubs in the town.

I, on the other hand, could go anywhere because I played football, pool, darts and so on, and because I would never think of myself as anything other than working class. My mum would kill me otherwise. I once was offered the chance to sell 'stuff', sale or return, at the Barras in Glasgow, when it was at its peak. A prime stall, all mine for the weekend, no outlay or risk. My mother went through the roof.

Her words are ingrained. 'We don't do that son. We don't sell stuff. That's not what we do.'

This wasn't said with any regret or sympathy. There was no sign of apology to accompany this announcement. It was a fact. It would be a disgrace, a 'showing up' of some kind, and as we all know, these are the worst possible kind of crimes. I took it that the 'we' encompassed the whole working class the world over, and so my glimpse of an entrepreneurial future was terminated right there, with no room for debate on the subject.

It was thanks to my mum and her sociable lifestyle that I could go anywhere and talk to anyone, on just about any subject. Some would call it the gift of the gab. It was and is a serious gift to bestow on anyone.

Consequently, it didn't even take me a whole pint to find out who was selling cigarettes off cheaply. I had the name so quickly that I could still drive, and I knew just where to find him on a nice summer's night. I picked up a uniform cop, arranged for someone to get a warrant signed, and headed north up the Carradale Road.

I parked on the bridge, on the main road, and leaning over, surveyed about a dozen fishermen lining the banks of the river which was in good spate. Many a summer's night I had spent among them. Sure enough, there was my suspect, innocently casting without a care in the world, until I called his name.

'I need you up here. Now.'

'I paid a fiver for this, Mr McLean. I'll come in to see you later.'

'Do I need to come down and get you?'

I think both him and I, together with all of the other fishermen there, knew that if I had to go all the way down to the riverbank in my suit and shoes, he was going in the river in a bid for escape, before being rescued by me and detained for questioning via the hospital. That was generally how these things unfolded, ensuring a much better chance of future cooperation with me or my colleagues (it's sometimes a big shock to civilians that policing is carried out by force, or at least it was in my day).

He was duly packed into my CID car with all of his fishing gear and given every possible opportunity to confess his sins and tell me where the loot from the ice cream van was. He chose to decline this offer and so we ended up at his flat, where he stayed with his mum and dad, with a search warrant and a few uniform cops in tow.

I can understand why he chose to take his chances. On balance, he judged firstly that I was bluffing and wouldn't actually go to the trouble of getting a warrant and carrying out a search of his parents' house and, secondly, that even if I did all of that, there was a good chance I wouldn't find the stolen goods as they were so well hidden. He was wrong on both counts.

His parents were angry. His protestations of innocence were compelling. On more than one occasion, the uniforms looked dispirited and were certainly not searching with the conviction I would expect. As always, this only made me more determined. I sent one of them off to get a Phillips screwdriver. While never claiming to have the powers of Sherlock Holmes, I always had a good instinct about when people were lying. I've learned to trust that instinct more and more as the years have passed, and I certainly did that night.

We found nothing in any of the cupboards, spaces under beds, cabinets and so on. After twenty minutes or so, everyone was against me, my colleagues included. This wasn't helped when I started lifting the edges of carpets looking for under floor spaces. When I told our prey that the screwdriver was to start removing things, I knew immediately that he had some secret and, when it arrived, I set to work on the covers over the central heating vents.

It is hard to explain the feeling when a search such as this pays off, especially when you are the only one who is in the slightest bit enthusiastic about it in the first place. Suffice to say it's really, really good. I put my hand into the vent, quite a way in actually, round the corner, and felt something papery in my hand. Out it came into the light. A few rolled up cheques made out to the owner of the ice cream van. Bingo. I love the look on a ned's face as it goes from total innocence and outrage at the police for wasting his and everyone else's time, for picking on him and harassing him and his family for no reason, to abject misery as he realises he's caught.

This is when the excuses start. I was given them, I forgot about them and so on, but I quickly put a stop to that. Handcuffs applied, searched, cautioned, all formal now. Parents cautioned about considerations of reset or even aiding and abetting a crime and harbouring a criminal, you name it. The boot was on my size ten now and the tables had turned.

The search concluded with a few hundred pounds cash, the cheques I mentioned and about two dozen boxes of cigars, all taken from air vents in our man's bedroom. Not a good haul considering what had been stolen from the ice cream van. I realised I would be busy interviewing our suspect for the next few hours in an effort to cajole him into telling me where the rest of his loot was stashed. Always a joust I loved.

We were all traipsing out of the flat, our prisoner now in cuffs and being closely followed by me. I'm not sure why, maybe he looked upwards sub consciously, but I certainly did. The ceiling was really high. Maybe twelve feet, and there in a wee corner of the hall ceiling, almost imperceptible, was the outline of a loft hatch.

'What's that up there?'

I asked him. His shrug of the shoulders and attempt to keep walking made me even more curious. His father piped up at that point:

'I think it's a loft officer but no one's ever used that. It's too high and small.'

Maybe he was being truthful. Who knows?

'How about we get the ladder from the police garage, put it in the van and bring it down here?' I asked my colleagues.

I had to be careful at this stage of my career as I was invariably younger both in years and in service to most of them. I was dependant on them every day for assistance, corroboration and information, and so had to remain on their good side as much as possible while knowing that most of them totally resented me being the CID out of turn.

It took some time to organise but, sure enough, the shift sergeant appeared with the van and the ladder, curious to see what I was up to no doubt. They were always waiting and hoping I would fuck-up, showing that the boss was wrong to put me in this role too soon.

Of course, it was me who climbed the ladder and, slim as I was in those days, it was a tight fit to get into the loft. I couldn't find a ladder strong enough now. A torch was passed up and revealed to me was an Aladdin's Cave of booty, much more than I could have hoped for, and obviously not only the proceeds from the recent ice cream van break-in. Ya beauty.

A chain of coppers was established and it took us a good fifteen minutes or more to pass all of the stolen property down and out to the van. Cigarette cartons, more cigars, loads of sweeties, crisps, more cash, some bottles of booze, tools. There may even have been a cuddly toy. It was a substantial haul of stolen property that ultimately would prove to have come from four or five break-ins over the previous few months.

Satisfied that I had cleared the loft space, I began my descent. This was no easy matter. I dropped both of my legs through the hatch, taking my weight on both hands, placed either side of the hatch. My plan was to bend my elbows, dropping my feet down to be guided onto the top rung of our ladder. From that position I could then squeeze my torso down through the hatch and climb down the ladder.

My feet were just about on the top rung, with cops below me shouting directions, when my right-hand fingers touched something metal, just at the side of the hatch ridge on the floor of the loft. I immediately reversed and pushed my arms straight again, taking me back up into the loft. This generated much shouting and cursing below as my buddies thought I had bottled it.

I sat on the hatch edge and found this metal object. A large iron key. I honestly think that my subconscious knew immediately what it was and what it was for, but my conscious brain took some time to catch up. I got onto the top rung again and this time came out of the hatch. I looked at our prisoner and held up the key with a huge grin on my face. Only he and I knew what was going on in that instant. His face was a real picture. He hated me so much.

I said to the sergeant I had to make a quick detour on the way to the office, and he came with me. He nearly killed me with the huge slap on the back he gave me on the Main Street when our new-found key opened the door of Daniel's Store. Mystery solved and not a ghost in sight.

It was October that year when I was summoned to Pitt Street and made a fully- fledged detective. I had made the best of my opportunity.

CHAPTER 21: NO SUSPICIOUS CIRCUMSTANCES

As the detective constable in Campbeltown, I only ever saw my detective chief inspector twice in the Wee Toon. The first of those occasions was a suspicious death, when I was an aide with the CID, with no detective constable and a detective sergeant on long-term sick leave. In other words, on my own. I should say that this death was apparently suspicious only to me. No one else found it to be of any interest and life went on for everyone else, other than the deceased obviously, as if nothing had happened. See what you make of it.

The early shift had received a call that a Chinese male was dead in a top floor flat on Long Row, Campbeltown. These flats were and are above the main Chinese restaurant in the town, Mr Wong's Golden Ocean, and Mr Wong also owned these flats which he used to accommodate staff for the restaurant.

The uniform cops had attended and sure enough found a young male of about twenty to twenty-five years old, dead. He was in a room at the top of the building, which he shared with two other Chinese men. The room looked as though it had been totally ransacked. The cops had wisely backed off, sealed the room, and called their sergeant, as well as the doctor, etc. It was quickly passed to me and, after one look in the room, and a look of blank expressions from the Chinese staff and management, I called my detective inspector in Lochgilphead, Roddy MacDonald.

While waiting for Roddy to appear, I sealed off the whole block of apartments, had all of the Chinese staff at the police station awaiting an interpreter, and had made arrangements to have the young deceased man moved to the mortuary. I hoped that the pressure of the restaurant lying idle on a Saturday afternoon would focus the minds of the potential witnesses, who, so far, were acting as if nothing had happened.

The Sherpa van arrived, driven by a uniform colleague, John Malcolm, an enormous man. He reversed the van across Long Row, parking the open rear doors at the pavement, a few yards from the entrance to the property. He and I then removed the grey police shell and carried it upstairs. All of this activity, coupled with the police tape draped across the pavement, had inevitably attracted a small crowd of onlookers, which, in turn, attracted more people, and so on.

It was a bright and warm June day, and John and I had a real struggle bringing the now-occupied shell down the four flights of stairs from the top flat, mainly caused by the restricted three-finger grip we each had of the shell's two wire handles. By the time we reached the bottom landing, we were knackered. The plan had been to bring the shell out and hoist it straight into the back of the waiting Sherpa with minimal fuss and only a few seconds exposure to the public.

The problem was that as we came out into the sunlight, we both realised that we didn't have the strength left for that final lift into the van, and at the least would have to change hands on the handles. Not realising that the crowd had swollen tenfold in our absence, we stumbled out onto the pavement and put the shell down. Both of us immediately sat on the shell for some respite and shared moaning and John came out with his usual totally inappropriate one liner:

'This is the biggest Chinese carryout I've had for ages.'

We both burst out laughing, only then realising that about fifty other people were laughing as well. At us. Not our finest moment.

In due course, Roddy arrived from Lochgilphead and, to my surprise, he had Detective Chief Inspector Adam Hay with him. This needs some perspective, because relating this now, thirty-five years later, I still find it inexplicable. I had roughly two years and six months service. I was the aide to the CID, and so was hopeful of being made detective someday, but if that was to happen it would normally be with about eight to twelve years' uniform experience. If it were to happen at all it would be totally dependent on the favourable recommendation of these two senior officers. At that time, I was *never* going to contradict or question anything that they said.

They had a call to make, and it had to be made there and then. Murder, or no suspicious circumstances, and they made the latter. At the time I was totally nonplussed. To my mind, there had been a fight in that room and the result had been a death. I was geared up for my first local murder enquiry as part of the CID, but within twenty-four hours, the gaffers had written a report, washed the police's hands of the whole thing, and life went on as if nothing had occurred.

With the benefit of hindsight and many such decisions later, I can accept that I wasn't party to any of the discussions that took place between high ranking officers that might have involved the pathologist or the medics, or for that matter, the restaurant staff and owner. Perhaps the budget just wasn't there for a major enquiry. No one ever explained to me why there was no murder enquiry, no proper interrogation of the Chinese staff that I knew of, no forensic scenes of crime carried out at the locus. I was only the boy.

What I do know through bitter experience is that those decisions aren't made with only the cold facts in mind. The biggest question isn't what happened, but who it happened to. This was a Chinese lad, with no relatives in the UK. The Chinese staff and restaurant proprietors weren't interested in any police involvement. The Chinese community were and remain insular indeed. If it had been a young Campbeltown lad in that room, the murder balloon would have gone up before I had put the telephone down.

I feel sure that Adam Hay made what for him was a mammoth trip to Kintyre specifically to ensure that the outcome was 'no suspicious circumstances.' There had to be some good reason. I should also say that the only other time DCI Hay travelled to

Campbeltown was when I had raided an American servicemen's flat in town for drugs and in the process seized some serious porn. Apparently, it takes senior detectives to assess this type of material and it must be done thoroughly in a darkened room.

Many years later I was involved in a similar scenario in Govan. A woman had been found dead at the foot of her stairwell. She lived on the top landing. She was found naked. The consensus was that she had fallen over the banister in her state of intoxication. To this day I believe that the fact that she was an active prostitute was the crucial fact in deciding 'no suspicious circumstances.'

In this instance I made my feelings known to the boss, Detective Superintendent Joe Jackson. He gave me the case. He let me run with it. Told me to do whatever I could until I was satisfied, and if I could come up with a witness or a suspect, or anything worthwhile, he would reconsider.

I worked night and day on my own. I had no leverage anywhere. No media exposure, no uniform presence round the doors of Paisley Road West, no useful forensic evidence. I had re-interviewed the boyfriend at some length but he knew what cards I held (none at all). After a week or so, the woman's family, who had come together to lay her to rest, summoned me to a pub in Ibrox. They all thanked me for my efforts and gently let me know that I should let it go now. It was over. It still rankles to this day, though, and maybe explains why my favourite fictional detective is Harry Hieronymus Bosch of the LAPD. His mantra is that either all murder victims matter, or none matter at all. I believe that.

I recall that one of the strangest cases I was ever involved in became the Campsie Murder case, another story for later, and I know for a fact that for the first few hours after the first naked body was found in a mountain stream, the case was classed as a suicide by the then-boss of the CID for the north of Glasgow. There was real pressure from above to avoid costly murder enquiries.

CHAPTER 22:
THE MCCARTNEYS

Every summer in Campbeltown, the June Show is held, invariably in August. I know, don't ask me. This is when farmers all bring their tractors and livestock into a big field on the outskirts of town, stalls are set up, competitions take place, throwing cabers and suchlike, and there's a massive white beer tent. There's also a roped-off section where horses congregate and a variety of horsey things take place. I was reliably informed that Paul and Linda McCartney always attended the event with their horses and children. As my DS, Alastair Barnett, was off on long term sick with a serious back injury, I was the only CID presence in the sub-division.

Listen, I was twenty-three years old. McCartney was a god-like figure to me and he spent his summers with his family a five minutes' drive from Campbeltown. I was an aspiring musician. I was never going to pass up an opportunity to actually meet the man.

Also, John Lennon had been tragically assassinated not that long before the summer of 1981, and I thought it was perfectly legitimate that I take some interest in Paul's safety arrangements. That was my excuse, anyway.

The day before the July Show, a Friday in early August, I decided to pay him a visit and familiarise myself with his planned movements at the show, for safety reasons of course. This was easier said than done. The former Beatles' farm was only accessible along a narrow and bumpy dirt track. I was fortunate not to remove the sump of the CID car, an old Ford Cortina Mark 3, on my way to meet Paul.

After satisfying the armed guards carrying shotguns that I was, in fact, a police officer, I came to the house of his farm manager, a local called Bobby Cairns. I had a blether with him, and all of Paul's staff were reluctant to let anyone through to the actual farm house. Cairns couldn't understand why anyone would want to speak to McCartney. My story that I was there on important police business eventually got me through this cordon.

I drew up outside the actual farm house where the McCartney family lived while in Kintyre and, as I got out of the car, I was immediately confronted by the final and most serious line of defence. A stern-faced and intimidating woman with her arms folded and a face like thunder. I immediately showed her my police warrant card, but surprisingly this didn't have the usual effect. She was supposed to ask me, 'How can I help you officer?', or suchlike, but she didn't know the script. Instead, she moved closer to me, totally blocking any progress I might make towards the farm house.

'And why are you here?' asked Linda McCartney. 'This is private property.'

I was totally out of my depth. I'm quite sure I stuttered and mumbled my excuse that had seemed so credible in my head a few minutes before, but now seemed totally pathetic and weak. They had their own security arrangements and employed only the best to protect their family. As I was making to get back in the car, red-faced, all of my bravado gone in the face of this formidable woman, my obvious discomfort must have had an effect on Linda, because she visibly relaxed. I wasn't much older than her oldest step-children, after all. I was on my own, so no threat, and was obviously totally star-struck just to be in her company. In any event, she completely surprised me and said:

'Would you like to meet Paul and have a cup of tea? Come on in.'

And off she walked towards the farm house door.

Before relating any of what followed in the hour or so that I was with the McCartneys, I have to get one thing down on paper. Linda was an absolute gem. She was charming, really funny and fun. She totally relaxed me and made me feel entirely welcome in her home. Even that word cannot be used lightly here because what I discovered in that short time was that this was an actual home, with a real family inside. She was the exact opposite of her public image as portrayed by the media, and totally devoted to Paul and her family. I so wish I could have known her better. In the brief time that I spent in her company I knew for certain that she was an amazing person. She had a twinkle in her eyes that was so knowledgeable, so welcoming, so fun and so real. I was as amazed as Paul was.

I just smiled broadly and followed her into the lovely cosy kitchen of the farmhouse and, as directed, took a seat at the enormous wooden table. Soon, children of varying ages started to appear, as did Paul. The place was really alive, but I was the centre of attention. My impression was that so rare were visitors, especially strangers, that this was a real novelty for the kids. I became the celebrity. They were firing questions at me left, right and centre, about being a policeman in particular. Paul told a story about always being stopped by the police on Merseyside when he was a teenager because he drove about in an E-Type Jag.

He had to reassure me that young Jamie, who was three or thereabouts, wasn't insulting me when he kept repeating the word 'pig'. This was just the word of the moment apparently. I gave him the benefit of the doubt. It was a farm, after all. He also told me that the whole family had been watching *Top of The Pops* recently and when Paul's current chart hit was playing Jamie kept looking at the screen and then looking up at his dad. After a few minutes he asked:

'Dad, are you Paul McCartney?'

We blethered with the kids for a while and then Paul asked if I would like a tour of his studio and stuff. He and I then wandered round the farmhouse. He explained some of the workings of the studio, how it was kept at a certain temperature to keep the instruments in tune, and, en route, we passed amazing furnishings, like the piano from *Magical Mystery Tour*. There was kids' art everywhere for mum and dad's birthdays and all the usual family portraits, hundreds of photographs and mostly homemade but priceless gifts. It really was surreal.

I was once told that as a general rule you will be quite ambivalent about four of any ten people you meet at random. You will not hit it off with, and will maybe dislike, three, and the other three you could be friends with. I know that Paul and I were in the latter three, for sure. We just chatted and joked naturally. So much so that I told him my band were playing in a local Campbeltown pub that weekend and he was welcome to come down for a pint. I actually believed he might appear, perhaps with his bass, but alas, he didn't.

We spent a while longer in the kitchen and it was me who said I'd better leave. To be honest, my bottle had crashed by then and I certainly didn't want to overstay my welcome. It just seemed to dawn on me where I was, and who I was with. Paul walked with me to the CID car. When we got to the driver's door, he asked me if I could do him a favour. He produced a packet of John Player Special cigarettes from his pocket and explained that he had found these on the farm earlier that day when horse riding. He thought he had spotted the flash of binoculars on the surrounding hillside over the last week or so and was worried that some stalker-type person was hanging about. Could I have them fingerprinted or checked out?

I immediately put them gingerly into a plastic bag and said I would have Interpol (I watch telly, too) check it out. I drove back down that treacherous road, nipping myself, desperate to tell someone where I had been.

The next day, I visited the June Show, parked up the CID car, and walked into the Anderston Park field, which was really busy as always. The sun was out and the festivities, competitions and drinking were in full swing. Suited and booted, I walked round the perimeter and eventually came to the horse jumping and riding section in the far corner. This was a roped off area and there was Paul's Land Rover sitting facing the crowd, with him in the driver's seat reading his *Glasgow Herald*. There was a crowd of about eighty people standing facing him, on the public side of the rope, just staring at him.

I was walking behind the crowd, baffled by their fascination and rudeness. I had no intention of going anywhere near Paul and was just about past the crowd when I heard a shout.

'Hi, Simon. How are you?'

It was Linda McCartney, smiling and waving while she held a horse with a small child in the saddle. As she did this the whole crowd turned and looked at me to see who this obviously close friend of the McCartney's was. I was totally embarrassed and completely chuffed at the same time. I simply smiled and waved back. So many times over the years I've dreamt of the clever things I could have said, or wished I had gone over for a chat, now knowing, with hindsight, of course, that I would never have the chance to meet her again. What a gift is hindsight.

On my way out of the field, I saw a local and distinctive car driven by the daughter of a well-known farming family. The Blacks of Tangy Farm. It was parked with the windows down and the two teenage girls chilling out, feet on the dash. I then noticed that the girl in the passenger seat was Heather McCartney, who I had met the previous day in her parents' kitchen. As I approached, they both recognised me and Heather said:

'You're the policeman that was at our house yesterday.'

I smiled, knelt down beside the passenger door, said hello to Lorna, and asked, 'Does your dad know that you smoke, Heather?'

She nearly died on the spot.

'Please don't tell them, please. They'll kill me.'

'Is it John Player Special that you smoke?'

She was totally confused now.

'You throw them away when you go home, don't you?'

A nod of cautious but baffled agreement.

I then told her of her dad's concerns and the packet he had found near the farmhouse. She promised to never throw the packet away carelessly again, reassured that I wouldn't tell her parents if she was more careful.

I never did tell my mate Paul of my solving the case. I thought it best that he remain vigilant, and he's still with us after all, so it worked.

I met Paul once more, a year later when I revisited the farm on some equally trumped-up story. I was warned this time by Bobby Cairns that he was, 'into his music' and that I was wasting my time. He was absolutely right. I parked outside the farm and saw Paul at the kitchen window washing dishes. He came out and met me in the yard, still with his towel in hand, but he wasn't really there. He was civil but not chatty. The family were all away somewhere and he was totally preoccupied. I later discovered that he was starting a world tour in Scandinavia later that week.

He couldn't wait to get back indoors and I doubt if he would even know I had been there at all. He was obviously in some creative or preparatory mode at the time, and as I drove back to the main road, Cairns simply smiled and mouthed, 'Told you.' It was my friend, the wonderful Linda, I wanted to see anyway …

CHAPTER 23: THE WHISKY TRAIL – CROFT TO CROFT

As a young detective I was sent back to Islay. I was relieved to hear that I was still allowed after my first disgraceful stint on holiday cover. This actually occurred while I was on stage in Carradale Village Hall, playing in the band Horizon. We were a cover band, but we were good, loud, and had a good following throughout Argyll, including Oban and Dunoon, and played all over Scotland at times. In any case, we were in the middle of an Ike and Tina number, specifically *Nutbush City Limits*, when the local bobby, Willie Robertson, came onto the stage next to me. He screamed into my ear that I was to get the first ferry to Islay the next morning. In about five hours' time, actually.

I was picked up by the night shift about five-thirty, having had about two hours sleep and dispatched on the two-and-a-half-hour ferry journey across the sound to Port Ellen, where the local PC, Dougie, who I had covered for when he went on holiday, took me to a remote hill in the far north of the island and pointed me towards the peak. He would wait in the Panda for me at base camp reading his paper as this was obviously detective work now. My expedition took me to the summit, where a shed was situated.

By this time, I had been told the story, such as it was. Inside this shed, no bigger than a telephone box, there were banks of racked computer equipment which had been vandalised. The cost of the damage was in excess of thirty-thousand pounds apparently, which, believe me, was a lot of money when I was a young detective. This was a naval appliance, to do with shipping in the North Atlantic, and apparently justified some cursory investigation and the expense of sending a detective, albeit of the trainee variety, over to investigate.

Dressed totally inappropriately in my Ralph Slater suit and brogues, I was busy taking photographs of the area when I was joined by an equally frozen Royal Navy Investigator. After quickly establishing that we were both totally clueless and baffled to be stranded out in Bear Grylls country, we took exactly the same photographs as each other. We then slid and slipped back to sea level, discovering that we had been booked into the same hotel.

Work over, we retreated to our sanctuary where we proceeded to enjoy the local hospitality to the full, and on Scottish Islands this is a serious business. Such was the merriment and community bonding that night that we both missed the only return ferry the next morning. Towards what should have been closing time and the end of our night, I remember the aforementioned Dougie telling me to slow down when he caught me about to finish off my pint.

Last orders had been called and almost every other customer was leaving or had left. The barman pulled down the shutters, and the tourists and uninitiated wandered off into the bitter gales and rain to retire. Only when the last of them had closed the outer door did the barman raise the bar shutter again, and another round was quickly acquired. It was my first, but certainly not my last, lesson that all is not always as it appears in the western isles of Scotland.

Another time long before, as a lad camping on the island, we had found ourselves at a party in Port Ellen, having retired there when the pub shut. During the course of the joviality we were directed out of the back door, through a garden, over a wee fence, and into the kitchen of another house. Most of the men from the party were congregated here, and there were no snacks on the table. Only copious amounts of whisky. There was little joviality or merrymaking here. This was serious drinking business.

When most people had crashed out or staggered off there were only three of us left awake. My mate, George McFarlane, our host, Sid Bowman, and me.

'We need more booze, lads. Let's go,' Sid announced, as if it was five in the afternoon and not five in the morning.

Off we went and, sure enough, the storm doors of the Royal Hotel were half open, enough for us to slip in behind Sid. At this point, Sid slowed down and put his fingers to his lips to keep us quiet, and we could soon hear unmistakable sounds from inside. When we peeped round the corner of the bar, there was the barman cleaning his pipes and the nooks and crannies of the young barmaid, astride the pool table. He was going about this with some gusto and whatever questions he was firing at her were being answered much in the affirmative. I was only sixteen.

Sid whispered to George to go and bang the front doors and, copying Sid, we pretended to make a noisy and boisterous entrance and thankfully they had cleared the table by the time we stumbled into the bar. Our business was quickly concluded with no negotiation. I'm not sure that any money changed hands, and we were on our merry way. The next few hours were spent dangling our legs over the end of the Port Ellen pier, enjoying the dawn of a new glorious summer's day while we discussed the pressing issues of the day and laughed at our timely visit to the hotel.

Back to my big investigation. My chief inspector, John McKeegan, must have lost young officers before to the island environment, because he told me in no uncertain terms the next morning (not for repetition here) that if I missed the following day's ferry, I needn't return at all. My lame excuse that I was 'following a lead' and was 'working closely' with the RNIU (Royal Naval Investigation Unit) carried no weight. He'd heard it all before, no doubt. Such was his wrath that I may have stayed up all night to ensure being on that boat, but I found myself up and about well before dawn, with several hours to kill before I had to be at the ferry terminal.

The island was deserted, so I took the Panda car and headed back to the locus for a bracing (freezing) walk. The hill and the hut were still there and, with no more photographs to be taken, I spent a few minutes admiring the wild countryside and bleak grey sunrise before heading back down the hill, hoping to find a source of coffee and warmth before heading to the ferry terminal in Port Ellen.

Not far into my descent, braced against the wind, I passed an old man heading up the hill with his crook, and as I passed him, I gave the customary 'morning' greeting, hardly lifting my head. I was just past him when he uttered:

'You'll be the detective from the mainland, then?'

How he blew my cover of shirt, tie, suit and muddy brogues in that location I'll never know. I affirmed his assertion, as denial seemed futile, and he went on to state, 'Terrible, the damage these young holidaymakers do.'

I know that I had walked a few more steps before my powers of deduction latched onto the clue he had just imparted, but I was never at my sharpest at six in the morning, with a hangover, preoccupied by the rollicking I was to receive on my return to the office. I stopped and asked, 'Aye, the holidaymakers, terrible, do you know which ones that would be?'

'Those youngsters in the cottages, always causing trouble, every year,' he said, pointing down the side of the hill towards the sea.

I headed off in that direction and, within a minute or so, saw a line of seaside cottages no more than half a mile away.

I wasted no time in chapping those doors and, at my second or third door, I hit the jackpot. A stressed woman in her dressing gown answered the door, and I had no sooner identified myself before the two young criminals behind her were shouting denials, crying and blaming each other.

My trip home was gleefully spent preparing a summary case for submission, and I managed to keep a straight face as I placed it on the Chief Inspector's desk nonchalantly. My DS was also present, no doubt to witness my dressing down, which naturally was delayed due to my success. Their open mouths were a vision.

Never again was I so blasé. Door-to-door enquiries became my mantra. Speaking to residents, passers-by, businesspeople, delivery drivers, anyone I could find near to a locus. I can assure you that this was and is the totally unglamorous function of police work but easily the most basic and rudimentary source of information and clues. Especially if you can canvass on the same day and time as the event occurred or even better just after it's happened. It perhaps partly explains why Harry Bosch, the fictional Los Angeles detective, is my hero. He has a sign above his work station.

'Get off your ass and go knock on some doors.'

If it's good enough for Harry Bosch … He calls it the grind, the leg work, repetitive, boring, routine and mostly fruitless. He also maintains that you have to earn your results with the grind. I believe him. No, I know it's true.

For completeness I should say that I shared my good fortune with the Royal Navy Investigator, who later told me that I most likely saved his fragile position. He later retired from a senior ranking job with the MOD, and was instrumental in my future involvement with our security establishment. But that is for much later. I still had a lot to learn …

CHAPTER 24: THE MANTRAP

What a name for a pub. I had never heard of it until I was sent to Oban to work undercover for a week. I was twenty-four, a newly appointed detective, and excited to get away at the job's expense. I'm not sure who came up with the idea but it was unusual in Argyll. I certainly wasn't complaining.

I was to go to Soroba House in Oban on the Monday and meet a guy, Tam, who was a DC from Dumbarton, about the same age as me. We were to spend the week drinking in the Mantrap Pub in the town centre and monitor any activity involving drugs. We would update the gaffers daily and things would proceed from there. Nae bother.

We were purporting to be electricians that were working on a job somewhere up in Oban. I certainly don't remember the details now, but we were dressed appropriately, and would go into the Mantrap about tea time. We were there about five-thirty that first day, suitably thirsty after a hard day's 'electricianing.'

Tam and I got on fine and socialising wasn't any problem for us at all. The Mantrap had a pool table and it certainly served its purpose that week. I've always had a problem with pool tables. Under normal circumstances, you buy a pint and decide to have a game of pool. Usually, before you finish your pint, someone has put money up on the table, indicating that they want to play the winner. Sometimes there can be five or six people in that queue.

When you either get beat or win, the chances of you having finished the pint are slim, and so you or your mate continues playing. Remember that one of you has put your money back up in the queue, and a refill is soon required. This process can easily lead to last orders, missed dinners, late nights and serious domestic disputes. I know that from hard experience.

Tam and I didn't have any such concerns or constraints, as

our remit was to be in the pub as much as possible. So, we played pool and blethered with the locals happily. Our one concern was pacing ourselves to still be in the pub come closing time, and so we were deliberately drinking slowly in order that we would still be compos mentis come closing time. This was where we made a rookie mistake that fateful Monday night.

We had assumed that the pub would close at eleven on a midweek night, a reasonable assumption with hindsight, but, as we all know, assumptions often make you an ass. At about ten to eleven, we went up to the bar and bought a few drinks, intending that they would keep us inside until everyone had left or was leaving, but as eleven o'clock came and went, there were no last orders shouted, and the place got busier. We quickly established that closing time was one in the morning. We weren't prepared for that, and our pacing was way out. We were well pissed.

The result of this was that we fell out over a game of pool. In our defence, neither of us had eaten, and we had taken on board a good few gallons of beer. We ended up arguing heatedly, resorting to fisticuffs at one point, although no blows were actually landed as far as we could establish. We were too drunk to fight effectively, but we were loud. We did have to be split up and held back and this caused quite a commotion apparently. I don't remember much about it.

I do remember realising what had happened the next day and thinking we might have blown the whole operation by getting ourselves barred from the Mantrap. We presented ourselves at the pub that Tuesday, prepared to grovel our way in, and luckily the manager accepted our apologies and let us stay. We were worth a lot of money ...

We could not have ingratiated ourselves to the clientele any better had we planned the whole thing. Everyone knew us and wanted to take the piss about our carry on. We were accepted as characters and good guys and regarded as a fixture around the pool table.

We had some food that Tuesday and had our wits about us all

night and, over the course of the week, scored every kind of illicit substance known to man. We also knew that on Friday night there would be substantial amounts available for sale through all of the usual outlets.

Tam and I were worried about the bust. The gaffers wanted us in there when it went down, in order to ensure that all of the main culprits were hoovered up, and we were prepared for the looks of disappointment and let-down when these guys realised we were actually coppers. We needn't have worried. The overriding vibe and comments that were made about Tam and I were shock and horror that the police would actually employ reprobates like us.

To me, this showed that I was a real undercover cop. I had managed to be a totally convincing ned, a drunk and druggie in the biggest den in Oban, maybe Argyll, or, for all I knew, the world at the time. Some might say I was a natural ...

CHAPTER 25:
COCO THE CLOWN

Please keep that thought. The one you just had when you read the title of this story. Exactly. Few would be able to rhyme off the story of Coco. See, I bet you didn't even know there was a story about him. Well that's exactly the state of ignorance I was in when I was told he was the suspect for a significant fraud in Campbeltown. Give me a break. Someone had to be having a laugh. I went to the Royal Hotel across from the old pier expecting to meet Jeremy Beadle and company with their cameras rolling. In the event, it was a serious hotel owner who was waiting for me.

It seems that a man had appeared at the hotel the previous weekend. He was well presented, spun a fantastic tale about being a professional clown, and proceeded to stage a show in the hotel that night. There were only a half-dozen or so kids there, but he put on three more shows during his week-long stay, all more successful than the last. He had all of the gear, a full clown outfit, all of the makeup, the wig, all of the clownish props and, of course, a big red nose. He was a roaring success and took no money. All of his performances were for free. What a guy, until he upped sticks this day without as much as a farewell, and missed out the part where you pay the bill.

He'd run up an invoice of over two-thousand pounds and the hoteliers were anxious to track him down. Not the most gruelling day's work for me, you would expect, especially with the fantastic description provided. Added to that, I had what we call in the profession a wonderful thing called, 'a lead.' He had told all and sundry that he was playing in Glasgow, and, sure enough, the hotel staff had an advert for Coco the Clown appearing that night at the Kelvin Hall.

For whatever reason, I wasn't allowed to go and get him, but had to pass it on to my Glasgow compatriots who would get all the fun, and get to see the circus for free into the bargain. I had a chat with the late-shift CID at Cranstonhill in Glasgow, and they promised to go and arrest this character for me at the Kelvin Hall. The plan was that they would detain him and call me, send me a fax of his photograph (out of clown uniform obviously) and I could get him identified at my end. They could then charge him and we would send someone to get him the next day to appear in court in Campbeltown on the fraud charge. Simples.

It was an irate detective that called me back later that night. They had gone to the Kelvin Hall where the circus was on. They had managed to get through really strict security and secured an audience with Coco the Clown in his dressing room, thirty minutes before he was due on stage, or whatever clowns go on. When they met him, they discovered he was German. He actually was Coco the Clown, one of the handful of clowns permitted to wear the red nose, apparently. How was I to know? He was actually an Auguste, and took exception to being called a clown, and it was patently obvious that he hadn't been in Kintyre doing kids parties for the last week. Oh dear.

I never did catch my Coco, although he was arrested down south a few months later, doing exactly the same thing. He appeared at a court in England and my case was one of over a hundred and forty to be considered. Of course, it made all the papers at the time because of the headline fun it could generate, and he did make plenty for charity apparently. I wonder how his act went down in prison.

CHAPTER 26: THE BEAUTIFUL GAME – AS A YOUNG COPPER

When I passed my sergeant's police exam, it was a really big deal. It was my first attempt, I was only twenty-four years old and it opened many doors in my police career. I would estimate that only about ten or fifteen percent of cops had their 'tickets' in those days and so I was confirmed as a real flyer. On the day, the results were announced I was called into the Chief Inspector's room first thing and told the great news. There was much back slapping, congratulations and plans for celebratory drinks later. I went back to the CID room at the rear of the station with a real spring in my step and smile on my coupon.

An hour or so later, I was at my desk dreaming of the changes I would make as Chief Constable, when a call was put through to me.

'Is that DC McLean?'

'Yes it is. How can I help you?'

'Is it Simon McLean?'

'Who is this? Who's calling please?'

'It's a Stewart McLean in Dumbarton. I think there's been a mix up of some kind with the exam results.'

I was interested now. The park is always flooded, remember.

'What kind of mix up. What's the problem?'

'I think I've got your results and you've got mine. I don't know how this happened. I'm sorry. How did I get on, do you know?'

'I'm sure you've passed, Stewart. How did I get on?'

'I'm sorry. You've failed the exam.'

Hook, line, sinker.

Archie McCallum had learned of my news quickly and decided to wind me up and put my gas at a peep. He only let the disappointment last a few moments before bursting into his familiar laughter and congratulating me. He never ever let me forget that day either.

On my arrival in the town, I had signed for the Campbeltown Pupils, the local Scottish amateur premier league team. I also played five asides for the local police and we won the league the following season which was a great feat in a weekly competition where everyone wanted to beat the local polis. Through the football in Campbeltown, I also was befriended by Archie, a local Justice of the Peace, who took a shine to me. Archie was behind most of the boys and amateur football in Kintyre, and was a real character, sadly missed even now.

We became good friends over the years, mainly through our love of football, and he has been sadly missed in the town for many years now, but never forgotten. Old bastard.

A great example of how football was just fundamental to so many of our lives is a comment made during the Pupils' training on Kilkerran Green. It was a dirty, horrible winter's night. We were exposed to the howling wind and bitter rain being blown across the loch, and only those fortunate enough to have visited the West Coast of Scotland on such nights can really understand just how utterly freezing and miserable it can be. We were lying on the wet grass, on our backs at this point, doing some sit ups together. This was training night and we were at the edge of the grass near to the road in order to utilise the street lighting. We suddenly became aware of an elderly man standing on the path about ten feet away. He had his dog on a lead and, although he was well wrapped up, he was 'drookit' for sure. In between grunts and groans, one of our number commented on his presence:

'Look at that madman, walking the dug on a night like this.'

It took a few seconds before we all burst out laughing at how stupid we must look to him, lying on the wet grass in sports gear, doing exercises. You can be assured we didn't stop though.

Although I trained with the Campbeltown Pupils for a short time, my shifts didn't really allow for time off and travel every other week that took up most of a Saturday. This was my excuse, anyway. The other part of it was that my knee was starting to swell after games and training, and I was never really fit enough to play football at that level.

I still played though. I formed and ran the Kilbrannan Amateur Football Club. The Kilbrannan is and was a pub in Campbeltown and, although we played our first season in the local pub league and won it, we moved up into the Kintyre Amateur League, which was run and administered by the abovementioned Archie McCallum. We had a great team. Well, a great bunch of lads at any rate.

At our height, in the close season after our title triumph, I organised our participation in the annual Islay Tournament. Islay is a place I have alluded to a few times here without going into any detail. There are quite a few reasons for this, the first being to protect the reputations of some of the characters involved and, secondly, because memories are always a bit hazy when it comes to visits to these parts. Suffice to say that it's always eventful.

On one of the many occasions I was there, and I have been visiting the island since I went camping there when I was sixteen years of age back in 1975, I was speaking to the Port Ellen milkman, who told me he was in the bad books both at home and at work, and had to go up the road early from the pub. About midnight. He explained that he had been doing his rounds that morning when he parked outside one of the Port Ellen hostelries to leave their milk and discovered that the front storm doors were open slightly. This was a serious breach of security and protocol, as the unwritten rule was that anyone leaving after official hours would leave via the back door, as a sign of respect to the local constabulary. In any event, the milkman, George, decided that further investigation was required, and entered the still-lit bar area. It was there that he discovered about six patrons in various sleeping poses dotted around the bar area, and the barman flat out on the floor behind the bar itself.

George, having 'a serious drooth' himself from the previous

night's indulgence, decided that a wee 'hair of the dog' would give his system a boost, and proceeded to pour himself a 'wee hauf' from the optic, careful not to disturb the well-earned sleep of the barman. In doing so, he did manage to rouse one of the customers from slumber, no doubt attuned to the sound of a filling whisky glass, who was also in need of some resuscitation and so another whisky was served up. As in most things, one thing led to another and, soon, a new day's drinking had begun, breakfasts ordered, and all was well with the world. Except that the milk float was sitting outside on the street still with its undelivered load aboard. It was the afternoon before many of his customers received their awaited milk and why George was expecting, at best, a rollicking from his boss, and was reluctant to go home that night.

I initially visited Islay as a biker, aged seventeen, in 1976 when we camped just outside Port Ellen in Port Righ. We returned many times, had many adventures, and made some great friends. I also visited when working as a police officer, initially covering for uniform holidays, etc., and later as a CID officer investigating particular crimes. (see the Whisky Trail.) I have also visited socially over the years with wives, and a few times with my late daughter, and played discos and with my band at a few gigs, but for the purposes of this particular chapter I will stick to the visits related to playing football for a variety of teams, and latterly of refereeing.

My first visit as a footballer was with that Kilbrannan team. What a lark. We caught the CalMac Ferry to Islay at lunchtime on the Friday, and by the time we arrived in Port Askaig, we were already the worse for wear, despite the fact that we had a game later that night in Bowmore. There were fourteen of us and as we disembarked from the ferry, we were welcomed by a fleet of private taxis awaiting our arrival, in order to convey us the ten miles or so to our digs in Bowmore; the Bowmore Hotel, no less.

As stated, we all had a few beers and so were directed towards the taxis that would convey us, and I was led into the last taxi in line, together with two or three others of our team. I later learned that I had quickly been identified as the police officer from the mainland who was coming over to play football and, as such, I was singled out to be brought slowly to the hotel in order that the driver could quiz me and ascertain if I was likely to cause any problems for the islanders in their settled way of life.

I was questioned all the way to Bowmore by the driver, whose name was Blue. I know, but that was his name. Honestly. I was up front and anxious to get to the hotel to meet up with the rest of the squad and get organized for the game later. I was led into the busy bar of the Bowmore Hotel and my driver, Blue, got to the bar and turned to me.

'Will ye huv a wee whisky?'

I said, 'not at all, I'll get this one,' and proceeded to order doubles, indicating him and my teammates from our car. I swear that he turned to the guy next to him at the bar and said in a stage whisper:

'It's all right, he takes a fucking dram.'

I had passed muster, it seems, because everything got a bit louder and more relaxed from then on, and I would imagine that word spread through the island pretty fast that I was not a great threat, just another piss artist, as expected, no doubt.

We had a great weekend. I know that we played our three games, and won at least one of them, possibly two, but it really was about participating and entering into the spirit of the weekend and, such was the success of this visit that we were invited back repeatedly over the next few years, but never managed to get there as the Kilbrannan team. Never likely to refuse an invitation to Islay, I did continue to go as a referee for the tournament and, on one such occasion, took the Serious Drinking Squad with me as participants. Over that weekend, I played all three of our matches and refereed two other games, including the final. I might have been limping, but I was limping a lot.

The refereeing was beginning to become more attractive than the playing now, as my knee was a serious problem, and when I moved from Campbeltown to the Isle of Bute, I had no real aspirations to play for the local amateur island team, The Brandanes. I really couldn't handle the training regime anymore. Instead, I played for a local pub team, which meant not having to travel off the island for fixtures, being able to play without serious training, and stepping down a level where serious injury was much less of a concern. I could also take up more refereeing duties which were manageable, and enjoyable for some reason.

CHAPTER 27: HINTON CRAIG

I've named this chapter after my old friend, Hinton, (James Hinton Craig), who sadly passed away on 2nd June 2007. I miss him a lot, as do many. Everyone who knew him, basically. When I first arrived in Campbeltown as a complete rookie copper, I was befriended by Hinton and his 'crowd', and they are all still fond friends to this day. The ones that are still with us, that is. Unfortunately, those casualties include my ex-wife and mother of my three children, Margaret. At that time, Hinton owned and operated the main disco unit in Kintyre, the Hinton Craig Road Show. He was also an accomplished musician, owned and ran the local record shop on Longrow, The Sound Centre, and was soon to invent a local video rental business as well. His only real competition was Woolies in those far-off times.

If football has been the common thread running through my life, then it is closely followed by music. Right from those early formative years when our old gramophone player was my babysitter, to the peak years of playing with Hinton and the lads in our local Campbeltown band called Horizon. We travelled all over Scotland playing mostly rock covers and had some fantastic laughs along the way.

My first 'gig' was with my mother, aged about ten. I'm guessing I was the only victim she could drag along to the Odeon picture house in Renfield Street, Glasgow, to see Engelbert Humperdinck live on stage. From vague memory, I was the only male in the place and it was my first, but not last, experience of actual female hysteria.

My first proper gig had been David Bowie playing Green's Playhouse in Glasgow. It was May 1973 and I had just turned fourteen. We had bought the tickets months beforehand, and that in itself was an adventure. I stayed over at my mate Stan's house in Clarence Drive, Hyndland. His mum's flat was one story up, and there are ridges across the tenement stonework which made perfect hand and foot holds. We were 'tucked in' at a respectable hour by Stan's wonderful mum, Kit, who informed us that she had put on brand-new linen for us, and left us reading peacefully, like proper children. She even reminded us not to read too long and put the light out soon as we had school the next day.

A short time later, being obedient lads, we put the light off, and lay blethering for ages, then when Stan judged that Kit would be sound asleep, we got dressed, stripped the beds of their sheets and tied them together and then to a piece of solid furniture. Off we went out the window. I know that Stan stood on the fence on the way down, because apparently, I let go of my end at that point, thinking he had landed, and he jumped from there. I followed him down and off we went walking into the city centre to get Bowie tickets when they went on sale at nine o'clock. It all seems so melodramatic now. Why didn't we just go out the door quietly?

I'm sure we got to the Third Eye Centre in Sauchiehall Street at about three or four in the morning and joined the queue. Yes, there was a couple already there. By the time the office opened, the queue was away up into Garnethill, but we got our precious tickets. We knew absolutely nothing about Green's Playhouse or any other concert venue, and just bought our one-pound tickets that we thought were the best ones, the front row. This was Row C for some reason. In actual fact, these turned out to be the worst tickets possible, as Green's had one of the tallest stages in Europe at the time, and so although we spent the whole gig standing on the back of the seats, we still had a restricted view.

Bowie had no support act and our next gig was to see Nazareth, a superb Scottish band. We only knew their one massive hit at that time, *Broken Down Angel*, and when they finished without having played it, we were a bit miffed. We got up to leave and realised that no one else was, so we hung about for a while. Only then did we learn that we had just watched a support act (in this case Silverhead, who were superb) and that Nazareth was still to come. They were brilliant and played *Broken Down Angel* in their second or third encore.

I could write another book about the bands we saw over the following years at Green's, and as it became, the Apollo. We saw Queen, backing Mott the Hoople. Jethro Tull, Uriah Heap, Sabbath, Wishbone Ash, Genesis, AC/DC, E.L.P, Rory Gallagher, Alex Harvey, and on and on. When I started work in Yarrow's as an apprentice electrician and prospective electrical engineer, I made a lifetime friend, Kenny Little, who was and still is a wonderful musician. He and I went to see the Stones I would guess around 1975 or '76 and we agreed on the way home that Jagger and Co. were past it and just going through the motions.

It was Kenny who decided that I was to be his keyboard player. He had heard or read a story about Ian Anderson of Jethro Tull defending his then bass player being of limited ability, by stating simply that he was his friend. This obviously appealed to Kenny – and to Paul McCartney, of course –who utilised Linda on similar grounds on keyboards. Kenny persuaded me to buy a Casio electric piano and all of a sudden, I was in a band. The No Entry Band, no less. We played quite a few gigs, but nothing really memorable other than Kenny punching the manager of the old Wellington bar for making a pass at him. All I did was play the chords Kenny had taught me, and I did incorporate an old stylophone thing to play the start of *Band on The Run*.

Kenny wrote most of our music, so no one knew if you got it right or not, and it was a real hoot playing live. I took great stock of the many great keyboard players of the day like Rod Argent, Jon Lord, Keith Emerson and so on.

As related earlier, I left Yarrow's when I messed my left knee up playing football and didn't do any rehab or physio, joining the police and moving to Campbeltown, but I will be forever grateful to Kenny for allowing me to be in his band. He taught me the basics of keyboard play but, more importantly, I got to play in public, and that experience was to stand me in good stead.

Almost as soon as I arrived in Campbeltown, I became friends with Hinton, his main DJ, Billy McIlroy, and the whole crowd of relatives and friends that are so close in rural communities. Hinton also played in a local rock band and I was a good friend and golf partner of the keyboard player, Kevin McMillan. If I tell you that Kevin's father, George, was a local JP who sat in the Campbeltown District Court and that his sister, Ann, was a best friend of my future ex-wife, Margaret, you'll start to have some idea of how everyone's somehow connected in these parts of the world.

When my shifts would allow, I was either DJ'ing for Hinton at some function or other in any number of pubs in Campbeltown, and beyond, or I was driving Hinton's van to a gig where Billy would be doing his stuff on the decks. Billy was a great guy and quite a gifted DJ, which I always found strange because he had the most horrific stammer. It was pretty bad and only got worse whenever he had a drink, which was quite a frequent occurrence. The only thing I ever saw defeat his handicap was a microphone. While he was behind the decks, I asked him if he wanted a pint. He raised his hand for me to wait a second.

'Good evening, this is the Hinton Craig Road Show here in The Royal Hotel Ardrishaig, getting things started with everyone's favourite.'

He would turn the music up, and as it got louder, he would turn back to me and say, 'Wisit, wisit wisit, can I get, wisit, a pint of wisit, wisit, of lager, please?'

We had some great fun all over Kintyre in pubs, hotels and clubs, and covering weddings, anniversaries, beach parties, sponsored twenty-four-hour dance events. And on a good many nights we provided the warm-up music for Horizon before they went on, and the disco after the live music. I was also at every Horizon gig when I was off-duty, as all of my mates were in the band and got a wee shot of keyboards from Kevin during practice and sound check sessions. Sometimes, if Kevin couldn't make a practice for whatever reason, I would sit in on keyboards just to help work out the tune. Usually a current chart hit.

And so, when Kevin announced that he was accepting an offer from Freddie Star to travel the world playing on cruise ships, it left Horizon with a calendar full of bookings and no keyboard player – until Hinton had the bright idea of me stepping into the fold. Hinton was the drummer, owned the PA and a good proportion of the equipment, and it was his van we used to travel the country. So, I went along to Tuesday practice in the school and auditioned. I recall we played *Another Brick in The Wall*, *Delilah* (The Alex Harvey version) and *All Over Now*, and I formally accepted the lads' invitation to join the band that night.

This was a proper gigging band. We had a five-thousand-watt PA and a serious amount of gear. Hinton helped me get a brand-new Fender Rhodes piano, which was integral to their sound, and I bought a Korg synthesiser and a Yamaha hundred-watt combo amplifier. I had just started my stint as Acting Detective Constable, so that was 1981 and my only regret is that it only lasted two years. I eventually had to leave the band as I was moved to Rothesay on the Isle of Bute to take up the post of Detective Constable, and for the first six months on the island I was almost suicidal, such is the grip and lure of live performance.

However, with a wife from Campbeltown and a host of friends and in-laws there, we were regular visitors to the Wee Toon and I played with Horizon at a few events, and did my DJ for Hinton when possible for many years.

Over the following years, when my youngest of my three children, Louise, was born and diagnosed with cystic fibrosis, Hinton was forever helping me out with charity work, lending me a PA system, speakers, or a deck for some charity event, providing transport. You name it, really. He was like that with everyone. Seldom did he refuse anyone assistance. So, when he asked me to help out and DJ at a gig in the Victoria Halls months later, I had no hesitation in saying yes.

It was months away but, as happens if you're lucky, time goes by and all of a sudden you have to be in Campbeltown next Friday night. I hadn't given it a minute's thought until then, but on the Friday headed down to the Wee Toon with my second wife, Karen. All I knew was that there was a band playing the Victoria Halls, the main venue in Campbeltown, holding about five-hundred people, and that I was to provide music before and after the gig. Or so I assumed.

Hinton told me that all of the gear was set up and that the doors would open at seven-thirty. When Karen and I went in just before that I did notice that there were only the decks on the stage, off to the side, and I wondered that the band hadn't set up their gear or sound checked as yet. There was no drum kit or amps anywhere to be seen, other than the DJ set up for me. I got organized, put on some music for back ground and we went for a drink at the bar.

The hall filled up quickly and we were shortly behind the decks, cranking up the volume and preparing the discs, etc., for the night ahead. I had asked someone who the band was, but the name meant nothing and I just did as required. Then this big guy came up behind me and handed me a mini-disc. He introduced himself and said, 'Just stop and start it as we go through the set.'

'Nae bother.'

I actually considered that they were going to mime to music. I don't know what I was thinking, but a few minutes later he came back.

'Are you ready to go?'

And then he walked onto the stage without waiting for an answer. The curtains opened and the place erupted. I stopped the music dead, ready with his disc. Only then did I notice that the pitch of the audience was off. On looking out, I could see that it was exclusively women, and as the guy introduced the 'band' I hit play for the disc.

Out they came and five other guys walked past me, each one bigger than the last. All dressed in Highland regalia, kilts and all. At least, they were dressed on the way onto the stage. On the way back, they were virtually naked. The 'band' was the Clansmen, the popular Scottish male stripper and dance band. I now realised why Hinton wasn't here.

The place was in an uproar. I've never seen anything like it. I've been at Old Firm games, Cup Finals, Scotland v England games, even the Ayrshire Junior derby, and never seen anything like this. Grown women, grown women, crowding the stage, screaming, in tears for goodness sake. These guys knew how to work a crowd, all right, but this was ridiculous. For ninety minutes or so, they teased and cajoled the frantic crowd, who were feeding off each other. I now knew why there were security guys at the front of the stage. It was as close to out-of-control as you can get, without actually tipping them over until the final encore when the Full Monty made his appearance. Even I was quite excited by then, and it wasn't an anti-climax. Absolute bedlam.

Hinton was so laid back, everything under control but always on a tight schedule, picking up gear here, dropping kit off at a venue, always in a rush going somewhere, but always with a plan and in total control. One day, someone fell out with our sound engineer Russell Carol. I can't remember the details but he was being an arse, apparently, so it all blew up and he left. Internal politics and not much to do with me. In any event, as luck would have it, we were playing at McTavish's Kitchen in Oban that night, a really good gig that we all enjoyed.

We arrived as usual about eight and humped all of the gear up the long flight of stairs, my Fender Rhodes being the major obstacle. It took us a good hour to set all the gear up and then ten or fifteen minutes to sound check. Then we could relax for an hour or so before going on. We had an H&H thirty-channel mixing desk with everything hooked up on stage. The desk had taken a painstaking few hours to set for every single instrument. I had spent at least an initial three hours on it with Russell and, since then, countless tweaks depending on the dynamics of the hall or pub we were playing in. The mixing desk and the settings thereon were absolutely critical to the sound of the band.

I suddenly became aware of a commotion, some raised voices, swearing and some glum faces, as the desk was taken out ready to be cabled up. I made my way over and Jim the guitarist, Russell the bass player, and Chris, our brilliant vocalist, were obviously distraught. Russell, our sacked sound engineer, had left a parting fuck-off message for us all. He had zeroed every dial on the desk. This was a major catastrophe, an hour or so before our biggest regular gig. We were pretty much speechless, just standing there in shock. We were not yet ready to figure out how to address the problem when Hinton appeared carrying some of his drums. He stopped.

'What's wrong with you lot?'

We promptly all pointed to the mixing desk and someone told him. He didn't flinch. He just put his gear down, fished for his wallet and from it produced a piece of paper. He unfolded it and handed it to me, a complete list of every setting for every dial on the desk. Hinton just carried on without a word or even a smile of triumph. He would have had a wee piece of paper for every piece of gear he owned, no doubt. The day was saved. That's why he was Uncle Hinton. He looked after everyone.

The truth is that those few years, and the time spent as a DJ and driver for Hinton prior to that, encompassed countless adventures. We travelled all over Scotland, including pubs in Glasgow, forces' bases as far north as Elgin, most of the west coast islands, including Islay, and the stories gathered along the way would be substantial.

Alas, I had been identified as the candidate for a solo gig. With a son just a few months old, we were on the move, still within Argyll, but to an unsupervised posting as the only detective on the Isle of Bute.

PART TWO: ROTHESAY

CHAPTER 28:
DRUGS, DRUGS EVERYWHERE

When I arrived in Rothesay on the Isle of Bute as a young detective, the environment could not have been any better for a lad wanting to make a name for himself and lock up lots of rogues. There hadn't been a drugs case submitted by the local police in three years. This wasn't because illicit drugs hadn't found their way 'doon the watter', but because the local police weren't in the slightest interested. This included the detective I was replacing, who had been born and bred on the island. They had pretty much legalised most drug misuse in that beautiful part of Argyll, an hour from Glasgow. Way ahead of their time.

On my first day in Rothesay, I had gone out for a pint at night and almost choked on the cannabis smoke in the local disco. *Relax* by Frankie Goes to Hollywood was Number One at the time. I had no particular axe to grind with regards to drugs, but resented their use being flaunted publicly in this way. When I mentioned it to the uniform cops who policed the island, they just shrugged as if it wasn't their problem. Over those first few days, I decided to at least force this underground, where it surely should have been.

I was no expert in the narcotics field, but, having worked in Campbeltown, with its large American base nearby, I had enough knowledge and experience to get by. In comparison with the local island cops and users, I was a world expert and, to be honest, drugs were everywhere I looked. I must confess I did nurture a cannabis plant in a wee pot on the windowsill of the CID office in Campbeltown, but it really was for 'recreational purposes only,' not smoking. I had rescued it from some drugs search and just innocently enjoyed the cleaners and the DS admiring it regularly, and nurturing it like a baby, oblivious as to what it was. The simple things …

On my first back shift in Rothesay, I brought a local guy in for questioning about a theft of some sort from his workplace, the local coal yard. I really can't remember the details, but it was quite routine. The parent company, based in Dunoon, had reported losses of industrial amounts of diesel from their Rothesay yard. It was yet another ongoing matter that had been left lying about. When we searched him before placing him in the police vehicle (my old Cortina), I found a nice lump of hash in his jeans pocket. He was quite surprised when I told him he would be detained in custody for this, as I felt there was enough to establish that he was supplying hash, a much more serious offence than possession, an offence that could easily carry a prison sentence. The uniform sergeant and every other officer at the local station were equally surprised by this revelation.

When it eventually dawned on this guy that he was going to stay in a cell overnight, he became cooperative, which was my intention. Not only did he tell me who had been stealing the diesel fuel at his workplace (over a long period of time), but he offered to tell me who had supplied him with the hash, in exchange for his freedom. I called the local Procurator Fiscal, who was way overexcited by this turn of events, and she enthusiastically agreed with my trade.

She actually asked me, 'Do you think there's a drug dealer on the island, Simon?'

This became a busy first shift for me. I should explain why the police had this discretion (whether to keep an accused in custody to appear at court on the first lawful date available or to release him or her for report).

Of course, this only came into play under certain parameters. The seriousness of the crime was the major yardstick. No one gets charged with murder and gets released for report. Released for report means that he or she is released and a written report is sent to the Procurator Fiscal, who will then instigate proceedings by issuing a complaint on the accused, citing him or her to appear at court on a designated date. In the eighties, we moved on and the station duty officer could release a person on bail, requiring him to appear at court within a week or so, on a designated date and fixed time. This was an undertaking taken by the accused.

So, in order to 'release someone for report', they must have a fixed address that has been confirmed by the police, in order that they can be duly cited to appear. If the alleged crime was some type of theft or fraud it might be that there is outstanding property that might yet be recovered, or other enquiries that the police want to pursue, like interviewing witnesses or chasing an accomplice. All of these factors would help determine whether a person could be 'released for report' or 'detained to appear.' When the latter applied, a full report had to be submitted to the Procurator Fiscal and the accused would be taken to the court in handcuffs on the next lawful day, meaning a day that the court was sitting. The day begins and ends at midnight for these purposes, a fact that made Friday arrests interesting, and resulted in many an accused being charged just after midnight, giving us a chance to get the paperwork completed and gather further evidence. In my case, as a new guy on the block, it made perfect sense to gain the Fiscal's approval, as that superseded anyone else's opinion on the matter.

With the Fiscal's enthusiastic approval, I took this guy out in the CID car and he duly pointed out the house where he had bought his hash the night before and, through the Fiscal, I applied for a warrant. I also acquired a warrant for the house of the coal yard worker, a manager of some sort, who I suspected had been stealing diesel fuel over a period of time, a busy first day that was about to go into overdrive.

I seconded some of the uniform shift, something local shift sergeants weren't used to at all, and we visited the alleged 'drug dealer' first. It transpired this was a young guy who lived here with both of his parents and some siblings. The subsequent search was more or less confined to the bedroom of this young guy, and he was cooperative. He had never been in trouble with the police before and this was a nice family. His problem was that along with the lump of hash in his bedside drawer was a list of names with monetary amounts accredited to them. Some of them scored out, some not. The name of the guy who had shopped him was there as well. This was obviously a 'tick list', or drug dealer's customer ledger.

A nice wee capture that gave weight to my charging him with possession with intent to supply, a much more serious offence than simple possession, and which proved to have serious consequences for him. The great thing about drugs cases is there's always someone else up the chain to get shopped. I nearly always had the discretion of release at my disposal with which to trade, and it nearly always paid off in some way. Naturally, when I then had the information regarding the supply chain, I could choose to use it immediately, or save it until a time when it suited me or when I had some firm intelligence to back it up. It was never-ending. In this case, it had come from a Greenock supplier who was well-known to my colleagues across the water.

When the young lad eventually went to court, he pleaded guilty on the advice of his learned lawyer, who told him that he wouldn't get a custodial sentence as a first offender and had been in possession of a modest amount of cannabis, a then class C drug. Sheriff Irvine Smith suspended sentence in the morning and told him to reappear at two o'clock that same day. He obviously had some homework to do.

I was off-duty, but got a call to appear at the Fiscal's office at one-thirty. No reason was given, or required. At her office she asked me about this case. As the lad had pled guilty, there were no details or circumstances known other than in my original report. She specifically asked me if this lad was a drug dealer. I explained to her the significance of the tick list, and the fact that I had only visited his address due to the recovery of drugs he had sold.

That afternoon, Sheriff Irvine Smith sentenced the young man to one year in prison. This drew gasps from the court, shock and bewilderment from the lad's family, lawyer and friends. The common opinion, after much canvassing of current sentencing trends and facts, was that he would get a suspended sentence or a hefty fine, as a first offender. Not from Irvine Smith. He had decided to put a marker down to every other dealer or would-be dealer on the island. In this, he definitely succeeded. It was the talk of the town, not only among the drug users and dealers, but in the police station, where no one had even considered a drug case for years, if ever.

This was a fantastic result for me. I now had real clout when I caught anyone with any quantity of drugs. I had really made a mark on the drugs scene, ignored for so long, and I intended to make full use of this new perspective, together with my new best pals, the Procurator Fiscal and the sheriff, no less.

In the shorter term, that same night, I had to get a few night-shift cops to come on-duty early to help visit the house of the suspected diesel thief. It was to become a trend that these cops from all four shifts would at first reluctantly come on these 'turns' with me. This was a typical example. In this particular case, the suspected diesel thief was a well-to-do manager of a local business, living in a beautiful detached home with his school teacher wife. He was most likely known personally to all of the cops and they were totally uncomfortable standing behind me when I explained the contents of my warrant and my intention to search his home.

I was used to this from Campbeltown. Quite often it had been my own DS standing beside me with the red face, because he had lived there too long and knew everyone. All of these coppers, or certainly the older ones, had been in these communities too long. They couldn't or wouldn't do their jobs effectively anymore. It was actually the best thing about regionalisation and the invention of Strathclyde Police that these areas were infiltrated by fresh blood. I should point out that this scepticism and reluctance to back me up soon turned to grudging respect and acceptance, especially as it earned everyone overtime and actually had an effect on a community used to a totally passive, if not inept, police force.

The result of that first reluctant search by the uniforms was spectacular. I'm not sure of the details now, but it was a big house and we recovered jerry cans full of fuel from every place of concealment. The basement alone had over thirty containers, and it took us nearly two hours to remove all of the diesel. This family were literally living on a bomb. No one could believe the amount we recovered, and we were all shocked at how irresponsible this guy was to store highly inflammable liquid in the home of his young family. He didn't go to prison, but he did ultimately lose his job. Quite a first late shift for me, and it didn't let up much afterwards.

When I had been in Rothesay for about a year, the place was almost closed for drugs. It was much on a par with other rural communities in that we were totally conversant with all of the main players, were informed quite quickly when strangers came to town, and had our eye on all of the up-and-coming potential dealers. We had a good handle on it, and I say we because the younger of the uniform cops were quite enthusiastic about drug enforcement now, and were a great source of information themselves.

That year prepared me greatly for the drugs units I was to create and head up in operations throughout Scotland, and beyond in years to come, but at the time it was just really good fun and a steep learning curve.

CHAPTER 29:
CELTIC CONNECTION – THE FIRE

As the only detective on the Isle of Bute, I was basically on permanent call. I practically always had an AID to the CID, a uniform officer seconded to CID for a six-month learning curve, as I had done in Campbeltown, but when he or she was off, or we were both rostered the next day, I would get the call. This always happened at the most inconvenient times possible, and it really couldn't have been any more inconvenient this time.

My late wife, Maggie, had gone home to Campbeltown for a week or so break with my son. Her family all lived there and my kids loved visiting with their gran, great grandfather, etc. My oldest, now thirty-five, still does so virtually every week! I couldn't join them every time and, on this occasion, I was working and playing quite hard. I played darts for the Hillside Hotel, at the top of the Serpentine Road in Rothesay, and I was really friendly with the proprietors, Bob and Margaret. (A few years later I brought the SCS over to play football and we all stayed at the Hillside Hotel.)

I played keyboards in a three-piece that were resident there, so I could always be assured of a warm welcome and they were just genuine and nice people who worked hard and liked me. They were also great fun and had a regular clientele due to their location at the top of the notorious hill. It wasn't somewhere that had a passing footfall trade.

I'm not sure if there had been a darts match on that night, but, in any event, I was there late, drunk and in the company of a few fellow team members. It's all a bit vague, but what I do remember is that a young guy came in late on and I didn't like him much, maybe his tone to Bob or Margaret, maybe I caught him giving me a look. Whatever, he was a strange face and I realised that I would fall out with him quickly if I stayed and so I got a taxi summoned and went off home. I definitely had to be in court in Paisley the following morning and this, no doubt, was in the recess of my drunken mind.

I have no recollection of going home or getting into bed, but what I do remember starkly is the phone ringing incessantly when I had only been asleep for ten seconds or so. That's how it felt. No sooner had my head hit the pillow when the phone started ringing, and wouldn't stop. When I answered it, all I heard was the fact that I had to get up to attend a fire and take photographs. If ever someone was on autopilot, it was me that night. I got picked up by some night shift cop and we went straight to the locus of the fire.

The fire was out by now and the place was a real mess, as doused fires tend to be. I had to put up with the obvious banter from the firemen there, who could tell that I was still pissed, half-asleep and not best pleased to be there in the middle of the night. I took as many photographs as I could (they all look the same in a house fire, to be honest) but a pile of ash at the front door caught my attention. I got a hold of the fire chief and he briefed me properly. What I took in or registered at the time, I have no idea. Not much, I fear. But the story was compelling and certainly sobering in the telling now.

The flat was situated top left. Unusually, if not uniquely, in Rothesay, this block of sandstone tenements was four flights high. That is, a ground floor with three landings above. This is one higher than anywhere else on Bute. It was significant in this instance because the local engine could only get a ladder to the third flight. The people in the flat could not have been rescued by the fire service, not by ladder anyway. When I asked the chief about the pile of ash outside the door, he told me what he believed had occurred, and when firemen tell you a theory, it is invariably fact. Otherwise, they don't tell you anything.

The father of the household and his twelve-year-old son had

been at Parkhead that night, watching Celtic play. They had caught the last ferry home and got soaked in the rain on the way home and when going into the house they had both dropped their wet Celtic scarves on a pile of other old clothes lying there waiting to be binned or taken to the charity shop. They had gone in and joined the mother and nine-year-old daughter, who were already in their beds. They went to sleep.

At twenty-three minutes after two, the husband was awakened by a bang in the close outside his front door, and luckily went to investigate. He was met by a wall of fire, the whole door being on fire. He instinctively closed the door and started screaming and shouting to rouse his family. They also dialled 999, of course. He then huddled his wife and kids together and, using wet towels and blankets, managed to get them all out of the flat and down the stairs safely.

What had happened was that someone had set fire to the pile of clothing lying on the landing outside his front door. This, in turn, had burned the doormat and the door had caught fire, generating enough heat to burst the conduit pipe running up the wall beside the door. This was the explosive bang that the man had been awakened by; otherwise, the house may well have caught fire quickly, an incredible close shave.

I do remember taking a statement from the man. He insisted I have a coffee, perhaps detecting a certain fragility about me. Everyone's a detective, eh?

I recall telling this story on paper in the police report, and then having to explain it to the chief inspector, then my detective inspector and then the Fiscal. Eventually, I had to tell it to a jury at the trial, who were the only ones that really mattered, but in the telling, there were still some obvious leaps of intuition that could not be rationally explained. Perhaps if I had been more candid and divulged that I was undoubtedly pissed, everyone would have understood my ability for creative deduction.

The man of the house told me that he had forty-three badges pinned to the front of his Celtic scarf. These had been collected over many years and each was significant in its own way, especially to him. He was most anxious to have them retrieved from the pile of ash.

I had someone contact the firemen and requested they be saved. I continued taking the statement. The obvious question was who had started this fire, and why? Given the fire chief's theory and the statements from the dad and son, it was looking increasingly suspicious. An attempted murder of the whole family, perhaps?

The father worked in one of the Port Bannantyne yards and had done so for years. We went over his movements, associates and routines in great detail, but the only thing of any note that had occurred was that he had argued with some young guy in a pub and punched him. So he said. He maintained that this had happened two or so months ago and he hadn't thought anything about it since. He couldn't name this guy, but gave me a description.

I then met the fire chief and told him I wanted to search the ashes from the door in order to retrieve the Celtic badges and we rummaged through it together. There was no metal there. Not a trace. The chief assured me that they would have survived to some degree.

Starting to sober up, I made my way back to the Hillside Hotel, not for more drink, but for information. It took me ages to wake up Bob, who was most displeased. Everyone wanted me to leave it until the next day but I have always understood the importance of momentum. In any case, I had to catch the ferry in a few hours, so sleep wouldn't be an option now. When Bob eventually came to the door, he had to go back to rouse Margaret to ask her my questions. She was a local lass and, as a popular publican, knew everyone and their granny.

He came back and gave me the name of the lad I had taken an instant dislike to earlier in the bar. He also told me that he had left just after two o'clock. He was so pissed at me that he didn't even ask why I wanted this information, and why it couldn't wait a few hours. Within minutes I had established this guy's address. He had to pass the scene of the fire in order to get home, and when I went back to the locus, a few telephone calls soon established that this was the clown that the complainer had punched in a Port Bannantyne pub before Christmas.

Within a further twenty minutes, and with a pissed off Justice of the Peace added to the list of disgruntled Brandanes that night, I had a warrant for his house to search for two Celtic scarves, Celtic badges or memorabilia and anything associated with the now attempted murder of earlier that night. (When you have an accused the crime is always as heinous as possible; when there's no accused or little likelihood of catching one, it maybe wasn't so bad after all. Maybe a freak accident?)

I, the shift sergeant and two of the night shift cops executed the warrant straight away. It was his mother's house and she was really upset. It's always a shame for family, especially mothers who are cursed to love their sons, no matter what kind of idiot or scumbag they've turned out to be. When she showed us into his room, he was sleeping like a baby. The two Celtic scarves sitting folded nicely on his bed stand, all of the unique badges still pinned on.

He wasn't pleased to see me either.

In those days I had to send spools of film to Dumbarton to be developed, the pictures returning a week or so later, and these photographs would become evidential in the subsequent sheriff and jury trial. I got a call from the laboratory a few days later. There were no photographs on the spool, none at all. This tends to happen when you forget to remove the lens cover. The scenes of crime guy at HQ was sympathetic. Easy mistake, we've all done it, lesson learned and all that shit. It sure was. Try to be sober when attending scenes of crime examinations.

CHAPTER 30: DAVID ROBERTSON

There was an unsolved mystery that was bugging me, but it was only of concern to me, as I was responsible for the Bute crime figures. No one else gave a jot about them, but I took great pride in having the highest detection rate in Strathclyde, hovering around eighty percent. In the cities, anything from ten to fifteen percent was the norm and, in Campbeltown, we had always kept it above fifty. To put this into some perspective, a lot of minor crimes such as thefts from cars and vandalisms were undetectable with limited resources, and obviously what resources we had were deployed towards more serious and solvable crimes, such as housebreaking, thefts and frauds, serious assaults and so on. This was only vandalism, but it had gone on for many months and accounted for maybe fifteen or twenty unsolved crime reports over that period. It was pissing me off.

The problem was that it made no sense. It was spray painting, going up mostly at weekends and always giant in size. Each letter about two feet tall, always done overnight and always the same message.

'COME THE DAY, FALKIRK RAGE SYDT'

The same bloody message, in bold, white capital letters and not a clue to be had. It wasn't a spray painter, per se, who enjoys appending his 'menchie' all over the place. Like Stayo, or YPT (Young Partick Team). I had some knowledge in these matters. The letters weren't crafted and there was no flourish of artistry, just letters. Not even joined up, for goodness sake. Here was someone who couldn't even do joined-up writing and I couldn't catch them.

I had photographs of every graffiti job, and from the ones I had attended I had secured paint samples, so I knew it was spray paint, and I knew that I could prove the case if I found any physical evidence. So, I turned my attention to solving this ongoing problem, and catching the serial vandal, for no other reason than improving the crime figures and stopping him or her taking the piss.

I started where every proper investigation should start. At the various loci, looking for any physical evidence left behind, and chapping doors around the vicinity. Door-to-door enquiries, in other words. Most, if not all, of these vandalisms had been reported and attended by my uniform shift colleagues, who had then submitted the crime report for each one, so, a whole variety of cops on any one of the four different shifts. The only thing they had in common was that each cop in turn had treated it as of nuisance value only and submitted the 'green' with no enquiry made. Every green I ever laid eyes on throughout my career said that door-to-door enquiries had been made with negative result. Invariably, it was absolute nonsense. Seldom did anyone ever bother, but it was such a passion of mine that I was later to become the go-to guy for door-to-door organization on major crime enquiries. You always generate knowledge, often leads and, hey, as an added bonus, it even gave the residents the impression that the police gave a shit.

I had a policewoman with me to lend a hand. She was just young enough to be chuffed at helping the CID, but just old enough to be disenchanted within a few hours of chapping doors. Fortunately, door-to-door enquiries are simple. You knock the door or ring the bell, and make a note of the number, time and day if no one answers in order that you can come back at a different time of day or week. If someone answers, you ask the questions you have had written down by a thoughtful detective, and note the answers. Boring, perhaps, but the beauty of it is that anyone can be effective on the doors if they follow the simple rules. Speak to everyone, and do it as soon after the incident as possible, and ask about the neighbours.

For these reasons, we started at the most recent locus and worked our way back in time. The various incidents had occurred all over Rothesay, so we were busy, and I think at the second or third locus we had some progress. I hope that the policewoman having had some success encouraged her to carry out door-to-door enquiries throughout the rest of her career, but I seriously doubt it. It was a dying art even then, but she got the first crucial clue. An almost empty tin of spray paint had been thrown into a hedge not far from a sprayed gable end, found by the homeowner and was still lying in their big garden bin waiting to go to the dump. Lovely.

I did all of the scenes of crime examinations on the island and I did manage to get a few decent fingerprint lifts from the can, but what I could tell was that it was small fingers we were after. A school kid was my guess, and he or she had to be getting the paint from somewhere. My next stop was the Rothesay High School and it happened to be an in-service day, when the place was eerily quiet without screaming weans everywhere, but with only the teachers in, supposedly working. I do remember the head teacher saying to me when I commented on the delightful lack of children:

'Simon, it's the only time we get any work done around here.'

I laughed out loud, but he didn't. I think he was absolutely serious.

Any good beat man should know all of the businesses on his patch. In rural offices like Rothesay or Campbeltown, no one would have a specific beat, but the geographical area was still divided into beats for crime recording purposes. In the city, it was a different matter. Before the invention and proliferation of 'community policing', uniform shift cops would have a designated beat or area that was their responsibility to patrol. What a source of information he or she was for everyone, and especially detectives. This was usually a first port of call on any enquiry, as the beat man knew the lie of the land, the local routines, who was locked up, wanted or on the make. The point here is that this should always start with the school, if there is one on your beat.

Even primary schools were of great value. I always tried to encourage parents to be positive to their children about police officers. I hated it when I'd walk into a shop and the parent would say, 'Now behave or that big policeman will take you away and lock you up.'

What an idiot. What a pathetic excuse for a parent. What a wally. Of course, I couldn't say any of that directly, but I could certainly imply it. I would generally get down on my hunkers to eye level with the kid and explain that if he or she ever needed help or was lost, a policeman or woman was the best person to go to for help, because they would always, always be safe and get home to mum. This was much easier if the 'beat-man' had built bridges at the local school, or even nursery, and popped in occasionally for a cup of tea or just a blether.

Once, in Campbeltown, I was in the school across the road from the then police office in Castlehill. I might have been on proper police business or just 'popping in', as described, but at any rate, I was at one point cajoled into producing my handcuffs, and don't ask me how, but a wee girl of about ten ended up with them on one of her wrists. This would have been okay if I had the key for them with me. Thankfully, it was so close to the police station, but I tried to sneak her across to get her unlocked and got clocked by the handyman, Harry Hutch. If you wanted to spread a rumour or story, Harry was the place to start it, so it was a long time before I was allowed to forget the day I brought a ten-year-old into the office in cuffs. So, back to Rothesay …

Head masters were always good guys, pragmatic, protective of their school, staff and pupils, and inquisitive. They always wanted to know everything that was going on and invariably had loads of great stories to tell about school life. It was never a hardship sharing a coffee with the heady, and they always seemed to enjoy the reciprocal stories from the outside world that we brought to the table. In this instance, with the mystery of the serial vandal to solve, the head was intrigued and on the case immediately. I'm not sure if it was his idea or mine, but we agreed that a note would go home with each child at Rothesay High School pointing out the damage being done and the costs involved and asking for any information that might help stop it. I think this was included in a note to parents covering other routine calendar stuff for the school.

I then turned my attention to the spray paint. Where was a kid sourcing this? Who would sell spray paint to a teenager? They would surely remember doing so, although admitting that to me would be a stretch. In these circumstances it's always best to be assertive. If I went in, produced the used can, and asked:

'Have any teenagers been buying this type of spray paint over the last few months?'

The only possible answer, really, is 'no.' It's hard to move on from there, and always tricky to get anyone to change a 'no' to a 'yes'. Anyone who's been married knows this.

There are much better approaches. For example, ask for a tin of spray paint the same as the one you have, without showing it, and see what the response is. Now you know whether they stock it or not, and whether they have any in stock. If he produces a can or says we're out of stock (because the serial teenage vandal has bought it all) we can then identify ourselves and get down to business. I would maybe ask, 'Can I see your record of sales of this going back maybe six months?'

This is a favoured one of mine because it can put the proprietor of any business on the back foot. There are some things that do require proper records, such as pawn shops, chemists and firearms dealers, but the question implies that there should be a record. Similarly, I could ask, 'Can you tell me how many of these you've sold over the last six months?'

I get a similar result because every shop keeper or business owner would love to be right on top of their sales. They know this is how proper business is done and want to appear to be proper businesspeople, with strict systems in place, and so, I get a positive answer, or some lame excuse, all of which keeps me on the front foot. Only when I've established that they stock or sell the same brand as our vandal has been using will I move on to the purpose of my visit. By that time, if I've done my job at all, there should be some rapport going on. This all may sound simple and basic, and it is to some of us, but only when you've tried to teach these ways of manipulating outcomes to others (similar to teaching sales) do you realise that not everyone finds this a natural behaviour. In fact, some, especially those with warrant cards or uniforms, will never use anything but brute force, bullying and intimidation.

In a similar way, I learned early on about closed and open questions, the simple rule being that if you asked a question that could be answered simply with a 'yes' or 'no', then that was a closed question and not much use to anyone where you hoped to learn something. For example:

'Were you at home last night between ten and midnight?' Closed question.

'Where were you between ten and midnight last night?' Open question.

I have marvelled at how difficult some people find it to incorporate these basic principles to their job, and especially the last part of asking an effective question that every salesman understands fully. Shut up after you've asked it and wait for the answer, which is always revealing.

To cut a long story short, there were only two stores on Bute that stocked spray paint and, despite my sophisticated questioning and interviewing technique, neither stocked the brand I was interested in. I also had a word with the vehicle repair business on the island, but again to no apparent avail. That was okay. This is the grind, the leg work, and the more negatives I got, the more I was stacking the law of averages in my favour. What I did learn was that the particular brand I was tracking was mostly used in marine work.

What we all perceive as luck always plays a part in any successful endeavour but equally, I believe, we make our own luck to a large degree. For example, if we hadn't gone door-to-door we wouldn't have found the white, branded spray can, and if I hadn't gone to the local outlets I wouldn't have been pointed towards the shipyard in Port Bannantyne, and without that visit I certainly wouldn't have been tracking an off-sick apprentice in Greenock on the day I popped into an ironmongers-come-chandlers in Gourock on my way back home. A shop that did stock the exact brand and colour of paint Rothesay walls had been decorated with. The trail was heating up, my favourite part of an enquiry. A guy called Neil. Good description, stayed in Rothesay, drove an old blue pick-up, regular customer, mostly white paint, did up boats.

I think it took me about ten minutes to find this Neil when I visited the harbourmaster the next day. His name was Neil Robertson and he was a real character, becoming one of my best ever friends over time, together with his lovely wife, Anne. By the time I went to visit Neil, I pretty much knew I was on the right track. I had phoned the school first thing and the headmaster confirmed that there was a David Robertson in first year. He also had a younger sister and his dad was listed as Neil and they had moved from Falkirk over the previous summer. I also had the address and a request for a warrant pending with the Fiscal.

Neil knew right away that I was on the right track, and the missing paint that he had noticed made sense immediately. It's fair to say that he was equally mortified and mystified as to why his thirteen-year-old son saw fit to put graffiti up and he couldn't figure out what the bizarre message being painted actually meant. He asked me if I could let him approach his son at home before I came to the house and, for some reason, I knew this was a decent guy and there would be no issues with that. Sure enough, when I got the call from Neil and went round to his house later that day the whole family were present and there had been tears shed.

As agreed, we formally arrested David and conveyed him to the police station. Neil had agreed that we make it as official and intimidating as possible in order to hopefully cut short David's criminal spree and prevent, or at least make him question, any future acts of stupidity. As far as I'm aware, that's exactly what we achieved and David has gone on to become an upstanding member of society. His dad would be proud of him.

If only more parents adopted Neil's attitude and used the police in this way. Most kids probably come to police attention at some point growing up, and if it's handled properly, with cooperation between parents or carers and the cops involved, the outcome can be positive. All that matters is that the culprit can admit their mistake, understand that there are consequences for your actions and they have many choices ahead of them, but sadly even then parents were beginning to talk of their kid's rights, and look for a lawyer's involvement straight away. I suppose it's much worse now. What a shame.

Neil and I would always speak if we bumped into each other, sometimes in the Golfers Bar or the Esplanade Hotel, and our association was to last way beyond my time as the detective in Rothesay.

CHAPTER 31:
THE ROTHESAY FLASHER

Rothesay was still part of 'L' Division, as it was then known, with the HQ in Dumbarton. My DI, the late Roddy MacDonald, was based in Lochgilphead and would still be my boss. The major difference was that I would be unsupervised on a daily basis as the DC was the only CID presence on Bute, which was isolated by the Caledonian MacBrayne ferry service to Wemyss Bay (and the much smaller Western Ferry to Rhubodach on the Cowal peninsula).

It was also a personal upheaval, moving with a young baby, and as my wife, Maggie, was Campbeltown born and bred, this was a major event. Having to quit Horizon was a huge disappointment but, on the plus side, we were much closer to Glasgow, my family there, and our mutual friends in the city.

On my first week in Rothesay police office, Roddy came over and showed me round the office and explained what was expected of me. I had recently passed my police sergeant's exam (my first ticket) and his wise advice was that I should use the next year or so to ensure that I passed my second ticket, the inspector's exam, and that this would pretty much guarantee my promotion out of Rothesay not too far down the line. Another posthumous thank you is due to Roddy for that wise guidance. I only wish that I had listened at the time.

I was introduced to the local Procurator Fiscal, Caroline McNaughton. To describe her as a character would be to vastly understate her huge personality, flamboyance in and out of court, her sharp intellect and insatiable appetite for the theatrical. She was also a recluse, only being seen in her office building within Rothesay Sheriff Court and in the courtroom itself, always wearing the most outlandish wigs and hats, and her stated mission was to ensure that she travelled off the Isle of Bute as little as was humanly possible.

The problem for her was that her job in Rothesay barely justified a full time Fiscal posting, and she was constantly seeking more work from the police in order to prevent her being asked to cover at Greenock Sheriff Court, which she hated with a vengeance.

She loved me. I remember sitting in her office chatting one day and she spotted someone through her window, taking something out of a workmen's skip across the street.

She leapt to her feet and shouted at me, 'Get him quickly, Simon. He's just stolen something from the skip. Quickly.'

I, too, had leapt to my feet in reflex, but when I heard her, I started laughing, thinking she was having a laugh. Cases were no laughing matter to Caroline and I had to sheepishly pursue this guy and take the old broken chair from him. I called for a cop to come and corroborate me and had to caution and charge the culprit with theft from a skip, and later submit a report to the Fiscal (who was also a witness). Not my greatest moment, but Caroline was content that her figures had been boosted, and if she was happy, well, I was happy. I find that philosophy usually works with women.

I should also mention that the sitting sheriff in Rothesay was the legendary Irvine Smith. More of Irvine later, but suffice to say that he was feared by accused persons throughout the land, and with good cause, as he was unforgiving, blatantly pro-police, and severe in sentencing. He was also prone to ridiculing not only accused persons, but their family or other supporters in court, but this fear was not reserved for the accused, the guilty and their unfortunate friends or family.

Defending solicitors could also expect to be grilled and slapped down at every opportunity afforded and, me being a police officer, he demanded the highest standards in court at all times. The stories of his antics in court are now drifting into folklore, but I have many untold tales for later.

He and Caroline were an amazing double act in court, often relating cases and scenarios to the plots of their favourite operas of which they were both passionately fond.

But back to my first day as the 'Jim Bergerac' of Bute. I had my own large office at the rear of the building and even a scenes of crime room complete with a darkroom for developing my own photographs. I had more office space than the sub divisional officer, Chief Inspector Ian Gillies, a real gent. As Roddy introduced me to civilian staff and the on-duty shift working throughout the office, I spotted an egg box lying in a corner under a table in my room, and asked what it contained. Reluctantly, Roddy hefted it out and put it on my desk.

'This is the Rothesay flasher,' he explained. 'About eighteen months ago he stopped and thankfully hasn't been heard of since.' Noting my furrowed brow he went on. 'There were over a hundred women and girls attacked or flashed at over a three-year period, at a variety of locations, but mainly in the Port Bannantyne woods. These are the reports and all of the statements gathered over that period.'

'Did you catch him?'

'No, he was never charged. People are scared of him and no one would identify him. He's a real bastard and would never admit to anything but he was interviewed numerous times.'

'Who is he? Is he still here?'

'Oh aye, he's still here all right, and you'll get to know him soon enough. His name's Charles Contini.'

Roddy was right. I had many run-ins to come with Mr Charles Contini, a full cousin of the late Scottish singing sensation from Rothesay. The egg box of misery and intrigue was resettled under my corner desk and forgotten about for the time being.

I have no doubt Roddy and I enjoyed a few whiskies that night, as we did every time he travelled to Rothesay, every few months throughout my tenure on Bute. He had an incredible constitution when it came to whisky and it took me days to recover from his 'supervisory visits.'

About a year after my initial posting to Rothesay, I was called at home late one night and told that there had been an incident where two young girls had been indecently assaulted. I asked a few questions of the sergeant, old Willie Young, as he was a clever old bird and wouldn't be calling me without good reason. There was a policewoman on-duty and enough experienced manpower to deal with initial enquiries. I could sense that he wasn't happy and made my way to the office.

Willie had been on the island for many years, and it was with a sadness that he took me to his room and broke the news to me.

'Contini's up to his old tricks again.'

Willie had dealt with many of the historic cases and been involved in the many failed attempts to capture Contini over a period of years, and he could envisage it all starting again. It had been a real frustration and embarrassment to the local police, and none of those involved wanted a repeat. The egg box was about to be dusted down.

I discovered that two young girls, aged about twelve or thirteen, had been walking home around eight that night, through an uphill path to their housing scheme that cut through some woodland. It wasn't quite dark. A man had come up behind them and grabbed the bigger of the two, pinning her to him with one hand and pushing his left hand up her skirt. He had started to touch her privates inside her knickers but she struggled violently. Her friend ran off immediately but, to her credit, was screaming at the top of her voice hysterically.

Due to the struggle and loud screaming the actual attack only lasted for a minute or so maximum and the culprit, a male in his thirties and with a good build, had let the girl go and disappeared into the thick undergrowth. I arranged to interview the girls myself the following day with their parents.

I can remember the next few days well. Roddy came over, as did Jim Clarke, a DS from Dunoon. Everyone I spoke to, cops, civilians, even my next-door neighbours, looked at me strangely as if to say:

'Contini, eh? Tough luck. You'll not catch him either.'

A small incident room was set up and it quickly became totally obvious that the perpetrator was the same guy from the egg-box cases. No question. I can't convey strongly enough how everyone on the island knew it was Charles Contini, and it was our job to nail him. This assumption was ingrained in every single person's mind: the cops, the gaffers, the cleaners, the shopkeepers, everyone knew.

It was only with real difficulty that I eventually persuaded the DI to let me interview the girl who had been assaulted. Roddy wasn't one to change his mind easily and he had been scheduled to speak with her and her parents. My rationale was that I would have to live with this case long after everyone else had buggered off home and I was untainted by the numerous failed attempts to capture this guy over the years.

He and I went with a policewoman and I took a detailed statement. The story about the attack was just as I summarised it earlier, with much more detail regarding the girls' movements earlier in the evening and much fuller descriptions, etc. We now also had the doctor's report, and sure enough the culprit had scratched her internally with his 'jaggy' nails. When we left nearly two hours later, I think Roddy felt I had just been trying to impress him by being so thorough. After all, everyone knew who had attacked the girl. This statement paled into a brief chat when compared with statements later demanded of me in the SCS.

In the pub that night for debriefing, I got brave with a few pints in me and voiced my doubts about the case to all and sundry. Remember, I was twenty-five, easily the youngest detective in Argyll – the youngest there had ever been in the division up to that time – and, in effect, I was questioning some experienced detective officers and their work. I later realised how delicate a situation I was in, but at the time I thought I was helping. Basically, a few things were troubling me.

There was now no doubt that the attacker had used his left hand to touch the girl's privates.

We also knew for sure that he had 'jaggy' or ragged nails.

The girl knew who Charles Contini was.

Charles Contini was right-handed, for sure, and quite an accomplished artist. He drew cartoon images on cigarette boxes in Barlinnie for payment.

He was extremely vain and always well turned out, bling and all. I didn't see him having 'jaggy' nails. He was a cool customer and certainly wasn't a nail biter.

If the wee girl knew him and said it wasn't him, surely it wasn't him?

I needn't have worried. I was ignored completely. A few smart-ass comments were made as more drinks were ordered and the evening continued without anyone giving the slightest cognisance to the youngster's ramblings.

The next day, Contini was brought in for questioning. The DI and a DS conducted this cursory exercise, as many before had done. Charles Contini was a would-be gangster with the perfect technique in any police interview. He always refused to engage at all. He would confirm his name and details and then refuse to answer any questions. He wouldn't deny his involvement, would never provide an alibi or give any account of his movements, nothing. He would just smirk and often ask for a lawyer. He was totally infuriating, especially as he wore a cocky, arrogant expression on his coupon throughout.

I now believe that Charles Contini enjoyed being thought of as the perpetrator of these crimes. It all added to the legend that he was in his own mind. Even at the cost of being thought a pervert, he enjoyed being known as uncatchable, as the tormentor of the police. The whole thing fed his enormous ego.

As he left the office jauntily after his fruitless interview, I just happened to be outside. Honest. I surprised him totally by approaching him directly and shaking his hand firmly. He and I had enjoyed many run-ins over the previous year, and never had a handshake been involved or considered by either party. He had almost killed a good friend of mine and the lines were clearly drawn between us. I kept hold of his hand and pulled him towards me watching the casual smirk turn to something much more defensive and threatening.

Looking in his eyes I asked him from a range of a few inches, 'Can I ask you something, Charles, man to man, just me to you?'

He liked this. I could feel the tension in him, and sense the badness in his heart.

'Go on, big man, you and me.' No cockiness now. Just violent tension.

'You didn't attack any wee girls, Charles, did you?'

Sometimes, silence can be the deadly weapon of the questioner. And I was silent then, watching every nuance of Contini's reaction from close range. He smiled, broke my grip, and jogged off to some lair without further comment, but for a split second I had seen the subconscious flash across his eyes. I knew I was right. He was a dangerous guy. He was a drug dealer, a thief, a bank robber, a real bully, wife beater and a violent man. But he didn't have jaggy nails. And he wasn't the Rothesay flasher.

Cops love to get away on an enquiry, especially detectives, but after a few days of freebies in the hotel, late night drinking sessions and catching up with old friends and meeting new colleagues, they love to get home again. The work has been done, stories have been created for future telling and they just want to get back to their own patch, dry out and make their excuses. Life goes back to normal, and after a few days in Rothesay they all started to drift off to all corners of Argyll.

The last to leave was Roddy and I reminded him of his last words to me that day many times over the years to come, even after we had both retired.

'You can't win them all. He'll make a mistake and we'll get him.'

I had a few days off and when I came back to work, I knew I couldn't put the egg box back in its place. Not yet. I spoke to the Fiscal, but even Caroline gave me no encouragement. She adored Roddy (he was a real charmer) and, like everyone else, she knew it was Contini. My uniform colleagues, some of them good friends, took the piss out of me – even my wife told me to forget about it 'for goodness sake.'

The only encouragement I received was from the most unlikely source: my good friend, Neil Robertson. He had been seriously assaulted by Charles Contini six months earlier. I had come back from a weekend away with my fledgling family to find that he was in hospital with a fractured skull. I was told by the cops who attended that he had fallen in the toilets of a local pub and bashed his head on the urinal. He was in a serious condition in hospital having had a stroke and other complications. He never fully recovered but only recently passed away.

I went to the hospital to visit but he was still unconscious at the time. After paying my respects to his lovely wife, Ann, I was leaving and did so via the doctor's office, simply to hear what the prognosis might be for Neil. I then discovered that Neil had two fractures to his skull, one on each side of his head. Even I knew how difficult it would be to fall twice in a gents' toilet, no matter how drunk you might be.

When I visited the pub (let's just say it wasn't an establishment that police officers would frequent off-duty), I had three uniform cops with me. I had two of them stand at the door as me and my mate, Andy Bannister (who was six-foot-seven) announced that the pub was now a crime scene and everyone could go home. This caused some real consternation. I put tape over the gents' toilet door and let the barman call the proprietor, who was present within minutes.

Within a short space of time I had attained the enthusiastic cooperation of the landlord and his staff (as they wanted to reopen the pub), compiled a list of who had been in the bar on the night Neil was taken away in an ambulance and, in a private conversation, I learned what had happened that night.

Neil had been drunk and playing pool. He had failed to show the requisite respect to Charles Contini, who had then followed him into the gents with a pool cue in his hand. Contini walked out a few minutes later and Neil left on a stretcher. This was exactly the kind of cowardly and vicious behaviour for which Contini was renowned and feared. The problem was that I could not obtain an official statement from anyone. No one would speak up against Contini. They and their families would still live in the town long after I was gone. I had no evidence. Forensics were of no use as every patron uses the gents at some point and fingerprints on a shared pool cue would be useless in court. It was also almost four days after the event.

This was my first interview with Charles Contini and he blanked me completely. No denial, no alibi, nothing. I was happy to bide my time, though. I knew the value of patience.

I was eventually called to a criminal compensation hearing in Glasgow, a claim made by Neil who was still recuperating months later. I had given evidence at many of these hearings, invariably blowing some ned's spurious claim entirely out of the water. On this occasion, I was in the room for two minutes. I told the panel the truth. This was a vicious assault committed by a violent and dangerous man who was well-known to the police, but unfortunately due to the fear he created in our community, I didn't have enough evidence to charge him.

Neil won his claim and was awarded a substantial payout. It was a life-changing event for him. Not because of the many thousands of pounds he received, but because of the lasting effects of his injuries on him and his family. He was due every penny.

And so it was Neil who I was with on a visit to his home, to which he was almost confined to at the time. During the course of our chat, in a private moment, he asked me if I was going to catch Contini for the indecent assaults, which were big news in Rothesay. I told him I didn't think Contini had done them. Neil, who had more reason than anyone I knew of to see Contini in prison, didn't flinch or bat an eyelid. As a local man, he, too, had been drawn into the folklore about the 'Rothesay flasher' being Contini, but he looked me square in the eye and told me:

'That's a pity, mate, a real pity. I know you'll get whoever it is, though.'

First thing the next morning, I went to see the chief inspector, as usual, for our daily chat. He was a solid man in every way, a pillar of the church. A good guy who gave me much leeway over the two years I spent as his detective and, for whatever reason, he heard me out and told me to follow my instincts, promising that I was acting under his direct instructions.

His only word of caution was to tell me, 'There's no overtime available.'

So, I went to work. With hindsight, these enquiries seem so simple. When you know the answer it's so obvious, isn't it? No one knows the leg work, the false leads and information, the dead-end avenues that prove fruitless. At least ninety-nine percent of the hundreds of phone calls, interviews, visits to the local registry office, searches of historic voter rolls, visits to schools, and on and on, are totally spurious and useless at the end of the day. I was utilising my spare office wall and it was plastered with photographs, newspaper cuttings, birth certificates and snippets of information as I created a fantastically detailed Contini wall chart.

I should say that although the majority of the Contini family were respected business people in Rothesay, they were of no help to me. Charles was a source of great embarrassment to the extensive family and they had no desire to have more bad press. This was understandable, especially since they had been thrown into an unwanted spotlight globally through the Scottish superstar that was a full cousin of Charles's.

Over a period of weeks, while still attending to my daily duties, I ploughed through the information I was gathering from all points of the compass. The egg box was now empty and I knew every detail of those unsolved crimes. I also knew instinctively that, through elimination, I was narrowing the field and then it happens, almost imperceptive at first, a shadow deep under the surface, just enough to cause a ripple of thought. A few phone calls, read a few more statements, a night's sleep, and it comes nearer the surface, still teasing, but just out of reach. A third cousin left the island as a young boy. What age would he be now? What did he look like all those years ago? Where is he now?

Eventually, as the boxes are ticked and people are interviewed, the more closely it emerges, rising from the depths into full view, a wondrous thing, the most beautiful thing, the most profound of all things to a detective – the truth.

I've just had a fax from the British Army base in Colchester (quite a feat of persuasion on its own) with a picture of a squaddie, Paul Baxter, who I know was originally Paul Contini, who has taken his stepfather's name. Much more important than his details is the faint black-and-white photograph of the soldier attached with the fax. I'm looking at Charles Contini. I swear he could be a double.

If I could convey in written words the feeling an investigator gets when this happens, everyone would become a detective. It still wells me up just recalling that moment of realization. I was going to catch this bastard. I spent hours on the phone persuading the army hierarchy that I was simply hoping to eliminate this guy from my enquiries, and eventually secured a verbal report of his leave periods going back five years. Totally off the record, of course, and only when I had alluded to the press having a great interest in this matter.

The records were perfect. He had been off sick for lengthy periods (from depression, it later transpired, for which he was prescribed Valium), and he was a left-handed nail biter. He had recently been posted overseas for two years while the egg box gathered dust, but all of the dates fitted perfectly with the outbursts of indecent behaviour in Rothesay. Much later, I collaborated with detectives in the areas he had been posted with the army and they, too, had egg boxes, or at least files in cupboards, that had remained unsolved. Until now.

I went to the Procurator Fiscal's home with the CI. I wasn't Harry Bosch just yet, and I needed some proper guidance how best to proceed without jeopardising any future case. I was out on a limb with the army for sure, but it was agreed that I would concentrate on the most recent and historic victims with a view to securing a formal identification. The Fiscal and the DI would deal with the undoubted politics involved and go about securing the desired evidence through proper channels.

I needed help, of course. When Roddy saw my wall and the filing system I had created, his reaction was a rueful shake of his head.

'You're some kid, McLean. Some kid.'

I'm still not sure if that was complimentary.

Under the Fiscal's instructions, the most recent victim identified Paul Baxter (Contini) from a selection of photographs. It was a positive identification. No doubt. And it was enough to give us all the leverage we needed to crave a warrant for him. I didn't get to arrest him initially. His employers had him transported to Scotland and he arrived at Rothesay Office in shackles, where he was handed over into our custody.

In the meantime, I had been given a wee team and we got back to work, now with a specific target and purpose. We managed to trace and contact seventy-eight of the girls and women who had been complainers and witnesses, just over sixty percent. Of them only forty-two were prepared to speak with us at all. Many of them were now married or settled elsewhere and didn't want to dig up the past. Of the forty-two, twenty-seven agreed to attend Rothesay Police Office to view a formal identification parade. This was quite an undertaking with ferry crossings and the like. Fourteen appeared on the day, and twelve of them, including the most recent victim and her friend, picked out Paul as the person responsible.

Copious amounts of alcohol were consumed that night and, the next day, I took great delight in removing the egg box from my office forever. The floor in my old CID room will still have the box shape ingrained on its surface for frustrated cleaners to fret and worry over.

CHAPTER 32: THE SHERIFF CLERK

The Rothesay Flasher was an important case for me. It was regarded as unsolvable and, in solving it, I laid down my credentials as a serious young detective. You see, when I got the case, everyone knew who was responsible but could never prove it and so it just sat in its big egg box in my office, and the world seemed content at that. After this case, whenever I spouted forth, people listened with a new gravitas. My CI looked at me strangely, as if he wasn't sure how to deal with me. My DI, Roddy, called me lad now, and didn't harass me for not being behind my desk at eight every day. Even the Fiscal, always encouraging and positive, was now my new best pal, and would have me over to her office for chat and coffee. Life was certainly changing, but whether for the better remained to be seen.

Throughout my tenure as the detective in Rothesay, the notorious Irvine Smith was the sitting sheriff. He lived on the island, so it made perfect sense to have him sit in Rothesay Sheriff Court once per week. He travelled to Greenock Sheriff Court on the other weekdays. You would think that having the most pro-police, hard-hitting sheriff in Scotland would be a real plus for the good guys, but this was much a double-edged sword for the local police.

While Irvine was unforgiving with the criminals, and ruthless in his dealings with them and their solicitors, he was also equally demanding of the police, or indeed anyone giving evidence in his court. On one occasion, I was meeting with the Procurator Fiscal in her office within the court building, when Irvine stormed in and upstairs to his chambers. From the brief glance we had of him, he was obviously raging at something, and I discreetly sneaked off to let Miss McNaughton deal with it.

I later discovered that he had been sitting at a court case involving the Faslane peace camp, when some of their number had been arrested and appeared on charges connected with their efforts to keep nuclear submarines out of Scottish waters. The police had messed up their evidence in the witness box. This had resulted in Irvine being unable to convict, hence why he was so angry. He would and did back up the police and give us great leeway in the witness box, but demanded that officers be professional and present the evidence succinctly, clearly, and without contradiction or flaw.

As a young officer, I had been told that when giving evidence in court it was the sheriff I was giving the answers to (other than a jury trial, where I addressed them), as it was he or she who was making notes and making a decision whether there was sufficient evidence to convict based on those notes. I used this to great effect in court. When the Fiscal led me through my evidence in chief, I would look at him or her and give my answers in a loud, affirmative and positive voice. Then came the cross examination from the defence lawyer.

At this point I would shift my body position and turn to face the sheriff. I would listen to the question and give my answer to the sheriff, never looking at the defence lawyer at all. I knew this infuriated them, but apart from that obvious gratification, it made the attorney's life so much more difficult as my body language wasn't affected at all by my eye contact with him or her. It also gave me a direct link with the sheriff, and, many a time, paid off handsomely. I strongly suspected that the sheriff enjoyed it, too, although obviously that was never discussed.

I would give my evidence and the defence lawyer, doing his job, would take me back through it and pick holes, ask obtuse questions, and basically try to cause some confusion and create a wee grey area that could sow some seed of doubt. On many of these occasions, especially in front of juries, Irvine would step in, summarise my evidence in a few sentences, get my affirmation that this was the statement, and tell the lawyer to move on. Priceless.

I was the only CID officer on Bute and so having Caroline McNaughton as the Fiscal and Irvine Smith as the sheriff was a great stroke of fortune to me personally. While demanding, as both were clever and dedicated, I was forced to perform to an exceptional standard.

Every aspect of my work benefited, from investigation to police procedure in the field, decision making, dealing with prisoners, interviewing, handling evidence, scenes of crime examination and photography, record keeping, identification processes, report writing, giving evidence in court and everything in between these daily functions I had to perform, in the certain knowledge that my actions and my work would be expected to withstand the most arduous forensic scrutiny in due course. This grounding as a young detective was to stand me in great stead later in my career, and beyond.

In one Rothesay case, a businessman from Port Glasgow travelled to see me by appointment. His name was John Friel and he was the boss of Robertson's, a TV hire and retail company with branches throughout Scotland. There was a branch in Rothesay town centre.

He explained that this branch had been run by a woman on her own for some years and that most of their business was TV hire on weekly rental terms. Their problem was that this woman had been off sick for a few weeks recently and they had sent a replacement over to mind the shop in her absence. This woman had subsequently reported that people were coming in to pay their weekly rental instalment but no record of them as a customer could be found anywhere in the shop's system. These customers didn't exist, apparently.

After much researching of records, accounts and books, together with interviewing of the customers, we could find it was established that Robertson's had lost in excess of seventy-thousand pounds in business over an almost three-year period. I was incredulous that so much money was being generated through this one branch, but I had all of the paperwork and records to prove just that.

Eventually, after the trial, I spoke to John Friel about it and he explained how this had happened. Robertson's were a modest business mainly based in the Greenock and Inverclyde area, when they got into a deal with three other similar operations. Together they created and financed a TV advertising campaign. Glenns, Hutchison, Robertson and Stepek. It was a huge success and all of their business took off through the roof – great result.

The problem for Robertson's was that their administration operation consisted of his wife and a few girls in a portacabin in Port Glasgow. This was totally inadequate when the business exploded, but who was bothered? They were too busy banking the money to worry about the details. Hence, seventy-thousand pounds being siphoned off gradually over a period of years was never going to be flagged up until their admin caught up. A lesson for any business and a scenario I was to see repeated many times and in much greater scale.

In my first six months in Rothesay, I had really gone to town. I still played in the local pool league, played football for the Black Bull Pub and the Brandanes, and nurtured as much local goodwill as was possible. The flow of intelligence was constant and reliable. Having the Procurator Fiscal firmly on my team, and a sheriff who was totally predisposed towards the police, the world was my oyster.

I quickly knew all of the top drug dealers, all of the 'hard men' and the persistent thieves. Once or twice a week, I was executing sheriff warrants and, every time, I learned more and more. A well-run drugs enforcement operation is really an administration task, collecting information, cross referencing and making the connections. The old adage that a 'junkie' would shop his granny is accurate, except we would add onto that 'for having no lights on her bike.' An addict would do literally anything for that next hit and so every one of them is a potential source of information. It was with this backdrop that I encountered a problem.

I was turning up to execute a drugs warrant, either at or after midnight, or just early in the morning, depending on what my intelligence sources dictated, to be met by a smile and a welcome.

I should say that I knew all of these people – for the most part, anyway. They were either on bail, had been convicted because of me, or had been in a house when I had raided it. It was and is a small community, after all, and any strangers in town stuck out a mile. Equally, I was well-known to all of them, if not from meeting, then purely by reputation.

I walked into the Black Bull in Rothesay, a police pub if ever there was one, along with my late dad, who was over visiting for a few days. The place was quite busy, as usual, but as soon as I crossed the threshold, the whole place went silent for a few seconds. Just long enough for everyone to be made aware that the CID had entered the premises. Just in case someone wasn't tuned in. My father was mortified, but quickly caught on when I simply hailed the owner, Len, and ordered our two pints of beer – skipping any queue, of course. Len always obliged with a smile on his face. A good publican like Len liked cops using his bar. It sent out a good signal, kept out the worst of the riff-raff, and made him a right few quid as well.

As in Campbeltown, I frequented all of the bars in Rothesay, not as a drinker, but as a welcome or unwelcome observer. I could sit with my paper and have a coffee, making everyone uncomfortable without any problem, and always I would learn. In my first few weeks on the island I had walked into a bar supposedly run by the 'hard men' and rogues of the town and, would you believe it, a drunk was sleeping in the corner. He wasn't doing any harm and he wasn't committing any offence. But the owner was, and so was the manager who was in charge. When I told him this, he was a bit cocky. Big mistake. Huge.

I called for back-up and, when the uniforms appeared, I told them we were closing the bar. When they realised I was actually serious, we proceeded to throw everyone out. The owner appeared pretty promptly, but the bar was clear by then. He was in good time to be charged, along with his manager, with allowing drunkenness on his premises. I know that he made a complaint and that the charges were dropped. I also know that I had made my point.

It's all about respect in my book, but that respect has to be earned, and the police in Rothesay had let that slip over a period of time through over-familiarity. I brought it back pretty quickly.

Back to my drugs raids. I wasn't finding any drugs, which is fair enough. You can't always hit the jackpot. But there was something about the attitude of the dealers and users when I visited their homes. It wasn't right. Somehow, it was as if they knew I was coming. How was this possible? My immediate suspicions fell on my colleagues, especially the younger cops who were in the pubs and clubs, no doubt being offered substances and maybe partaking. They were certainly 'hanging about' with the right crowds, and especially the girls. I spoke to my DI, the late Roddy McDonald, based in Lochgilphead.

As a result, I started keeping the warrants under lock and key, and left a few false documents on my desk where I normally kept live warrants. Nothing we tried over a period of time had the slightest effect. I still knew that things weren't right. So, I went to the Fiscal, Caroline McNaughton. She then explained to me the process for obtaining a sheriff's warrant, with all of its sweeping powers of forced entry and search, valid for twenty-eight days from the date of signing. This was where the problem lay.

I filled out a warrant and sent it over to the Fiscal. She made sure it was a valid request and that I could back it up, then arranged for the sheriff to swear me on oath, ask any questions, and as long as he was happy, append his signature, making it valid from that moment on. I should have known Caroline would make the most of the procedure for her own purposes in order to look busy.

In actual fact, what she did was ensure that the warrant was recorded in the big court book, increasing the work load of the court and lending weight to her arguments against having to cover Greenock Sheriff Court, which she despised. There was only one person who wrote in the official big court ledger, and that was the sheriff clerk. He travelled over once a week on a Thursday from Greenock to clerk at Rothesay Sheriff Court, and nobody knew much about him at all. I soon did.

I applied for a warrant at the home of a well-known drug user and dealer, a local lass. She was a real rascal, although I had always got on alright with her. The main thing was that I knew she would talk if I got her in the right circumstances. I needed to know what was going on, and this was my plan. I was sure it was the sheriff clerk, but needed to know the setup, why he was doing it, and who his contact was. What was he being paid, or was it a relative? A friend? Was it that someone was being fed information by him? If so, who? I targeted her because I felt sure she would either know or have suspicions and because I was confident I could get her to tell me. Boy, did I hit the jackpot.

I had to wake up everyone that night. Roddy said he'd be with me first thing in the morning. My local CI, Ian Gillies, was shocked, amused and, I'm sure, quite content that it was a CID matter and he didn't have to get involved. And the Procurator Fiscal was absolutely ecstatic at the scandal that was about to unfold.

I had executed the warrant, and I can still see the woman's smiling face as she opened the door to me.

'Hello, DC McLean. I hope you don't think there are any drugs here?'

I could also see the smug faces behind her in the sitting room. They were all quite drunk, and were obviously in on the joke.

I told her I wasn't here to execute a drugs warrant, we were here about stolen property. I had information about a stolen video player, a stolen TV and other electrical items stolen over the last two weeks from various places about the town. She wasn't ready for that. The cops I was with were well-briefed and within two minutes they had the stereo, TV and VHS recorder downstairs, and I had her handcuffed to a policewoman and detained.

Safely back at the office, I started to question her about the stolen goods. I had no idea at all whether any of the stuff we had seized was stolen and, to be honest, couldn't care less. People tend to be not quite so cocky in the confines of an interview room at a police station, and it wasn't long before I got to the crux of the matter. To be honest, and with the benefit of hindsight, she couldn't wait to tell me. This is the story that unfolded that night.

She had formed a friendship with the sheriff clerk. She had met him in a pub in Greenock and had arranged to go out with him the next time he was over in Rothesay. He had stopped over one Thursday after court and they got on well. One thing led to another, and he started meeting her at the actual courthouse at lunchtimes. She said that he took great delight in leading her upstairs to the sheriff's chambers, where he would service her over the sheriff's desk, while both wearing court regalia, including Sheriff Irvine Smith's cloak and wig.

She didn't seem emotionally invested in this 'relationship' at all. It was as if it was a real lark, a bit of fun with this guy, the bonus being that he would tell her every warrant that passed over his desk. It reminds me now of the casual attitude to sex that I've encountered many times. For example, when taking a statement from a worthy after a stabbing and attempted murder in a pub in Govan, the comment was something like:

'A wis jist leavin, big man. A spoke to wee Bettie an says "ur you wantin tae cum up the road fur a shag? Av goat a drink in," and she says, "No the night, mate, av goat the weans gettin drapped aff. A'll catch ye later."'

No big deal, straightforward. That was her attitude. The fact that there was sex involved was neither here nor there and I think it was perhaps her couldn't-care-less outlook that led to me having the most worrying three days of my life later in court.

We all ended up in the High Court in Paisley for a jury trial. What a circus that turned out to be. It was my first time giving evidence in the High Court, which is a daunting experience at the best of times, but this was a high-profile case. Our Fiscal, Caroline, was a witness, as she had processed the warrant applications I submitted, and she milked it to the fullest degree. She had made me travel through to the crown office with her several times pre-trial and this was her stage where she could play to the gallery full-on. She really was a character, with her enormous wigs and hats to match. She loved every single minute of it. I wish I could say the same.

Ian Hamilton QC (of Stone of Destiny fame) was leading the defence team and, from the first minute, it was obvious that I was his target. I was stranded in the witness room awaiting my time in the box, but the feedback I was getting at every break was that he was gunning for me, and my name was coming up all of the time. Everyone was telling me I was in for a really hard time. It's strange when people think you're up for the chop. Hamilton must have been mentioning DC McLean constantly, and it was obvious that whatever defence he had lined up for the clerk centred on me and my credibility and evidence. Cops started distancing themselves from me.

Even Roddy must have had his doubts. He must have asked me a thousand times to go over my notes and procedures and what was going on. After lunch on the second day, I got into the witness box. The strange thing here was that I was playing with a totally straight bat. I had simply gathered the statements and some forensic evidence, together with paperwork that I had compiled during the course of the enquiry, requests for warrants and suchlike. I hadn't even interviewed the accused. This had been done by senior officers in Greenock or elsewhere.

Nonetheless, such was the vibe I was getting from all of the court officers, the Fiscal, and my own bosses, it was obvious I was the big target here. If I had known what the allegation was then, I would have been relaxed about refuting or explaining it. I could have led Hamilton down the garden path, had some fun, totally embarrassed him. It was not having any idea what was coming that was so disconcerting, together with being totally alone if things went badly. That much was plain to see.

I went through my evidence in chief that afternoon with the advocate. Plain sailing as I've described. I couldn't think where the trap was that the defence were preparing to spring. We went on the cross examination and Hamilton had the knowing smirk of a prankster. Every question was loaded with amusement and every answer of mine treated with a nodding sarcastic agreement. It was all so painfully slow and drawn out, the purpose being to make me reappear as the first witness the next morning. It was obvious to all that he could have finished the cross examination easily that afternoon, but wanted me back in the box. He made a big show of that when asking his Lordship to adjourn for the day, emphasising that he much had more business with me and my evidence. Bastard.

The next day saw the court room full and the front benches were taken up almost entirely by members of the press. I'm not sure if there were TV cameras lurking outside but it really wouldn't have surprised anyone. This caused great excitement. Everyone raised their game. Looking back, they were all showing off. His Lordship sat straighter, the jury all looked much more serious, the lawyers and their clerks all ran about with more bundles of paper. To cap it all, Caroline McNaughton was holding court herself wherever possible, being too loud in every possible way. There was a real buzz, the only problem being that I was back in the witness box and this whole show of melodrama was in expectation of my exposure, disgrace and demise as the case collapsed around me. I really was alone now.

I learned a fantastic lesson that day, a lesson that stood me in great stead through the Serious Crime Squad, in the CID at Govan and especially in the specialist work that was to follow my police career. When the chips are down, where the rubber meets the road, there's only one person in the world you can depend on. No matter the bravado, camaraderie, declarations of support and mantras of teamwork, and having one another's back. When it comes right down to it and crucial – sometimes critical – actions and decisions are required, you're on your own. The look over your shoulder for support is an error and, in the wrong circumstances, can be a fatal error.

There's no one there.

I was let down badly that day, and I was left alone to deal with all of the pressure and the spotlight, with no support. The Crown should have seen what was coming, but were too busy trying to mitigate the fact that one of their own, a sheriff clerk, no less, was up on a High Court trial. My own Fiscal and senior officers were too busy preening and protecting their own pathetic careers and the police, in general, are always quick to sacrifice their soldiers in order to protect their image. And so, a young detective with no more than four years' police service was left in the loneliest spot imaginable, the witness box in a High Court trial, at the mercy of a legendary and ruthless defence advocate.

Thankfully, he was also a twat. Or, at least, he was that day. He had done his homework, made all the connections in his head, and then came to totally the wrong conclusion. He had obviously been intent on discrediting the only Crown witness of any real import, who had struck up a relationship with the clerk in order to help her circumvent the new anti-drugs regime I had brought to the island. This wasn't really a difficult task as she had a real history, a pretty drastic present, and went on to have a spectacular future.

He learned that she, herself, had been up on a murder charge a few years before this case. She had been the co-accused initially charged in relation to the death of her baby, together with her then boyfriend. She had turned Queen's evidence and testified against him and he had been convicted and sentenced accordingly. He was still in prison. The officer who had dealt with this case was another McLean, who had taken my place in Campbeltown, but had been acting detective constable on Bute at the time of this case. Mr Hamilton had seen the 'detective' and 'McLean' parts and assumed it was me throughout. Idiot.

On the strength of that, he had planned to build me up into the lynch pin of this whole case against the sheriff clerk and then produce his trump card: that I had struck up a relationship with this woman during the child death enquiry, had an affair with her, and had concocted this whole case from there. A fantastic allegation that may not have had legs in the long run, but would certainly have given the press their splash headline and sordid story, cast total doubt with the jury over my character and evidence, and seen his client walk away unscathed.

Of course, it was the biggest damp squib possible. Everyone was on the edge of their seats waiting for his revelation. I was ready to have a heart attack or faint in the witness box. He had built it up perfectly with a real flair for drama and expectation. Then he asked me:

'Is it the case, DC McLean, that you have had dealings with witness X [I can't give her name here, for obvious reasons] in recent years?'

'Yes, it is, sir. That's correct.'

I had charged her a few times with possession of illegal drugs, and raided her house on several occasions, including the seizure of her stereo.

'And is it also the case, Officer, that you negotiated, with Miss X, a deal to have her exonerated from a case involving the death of her child?'

'No, it's not, sir.' I was always taught to keep my answers as short as possible in the witness box.

Hamilton smirked at me and all around him.

'Come, come, Detective, isn't it the case that you investigated the death, if not murder, of this woman's baby in Rothesay, and struck up a relationship with her during the course of that enquiry?'

'No, that's not the case at all, sir. I was only posted to Rothesay in October 1983. I believe the case you're referring to occurred a few years previous.'

If only I had shut up at that, job done, it wisnae me, I wasn't there, ya fanny. I was still in Campeltown, hardly aware of the Isle of Bute. Get it right up you, Mr Hamilton. What else have you got? Oh, nothing at all. Fancy that.

But, no. I was so relieved to be off the hook, so happy that he had nothing with which to slaughter me and my case, and the truth of his error was just dawning on me when I blurted out:

'It was a different DC McLean in Rothesay at that time.'

Shit.

I threw the whole case out the window with that simple sentence. It now looked as though Ian Hamilton had been right, but had got the wrong man.

Shit.

Of course, I didn't immediately realise the damage I had done. I was honestly just delighted to be going home intact. I remember Roddy coming to meet me as I was dismissed from the box, my evidence complete. It seemed there was a mad rush to escape the court by all the vultures that had been waiting for a dramatic revelation. I'm sure I was in some kind of shock. I remember being led down a corridor with the DI actually holding my wrist. I suddenly knew why when I came face to face with Ian Hamilton and all of his gowned cronies coming in the opposite direction.

'Ah, DC McLean. First time in the High Court, eh? Well, you've been well blooded.'

And off they all trooped up the corridor, giggling and patting each other's backs as they do. Jolly fucking good.

I then realised why the DI was holding my wrist. It was now sore and uncomfortable and as I tried to pull away, he looked straight at me and said, 'Are you okay now, Simon? It's done and dusted. Let's get home, eh?'

He then released me and my wrist was marked. As I rubbed the circulation back into it, it dawned on me that Roddy had known Hamilton would have his final dig at me, and he was worried that I might hook him right there in the corridor. He was just ensuring that I didn't give the little shit his headlines after all. Once again, Roddy – thank you.

I had been the last witness for the Crown and the case quickly wrapped up after that. I believe the jury returned a not proven verdict, but I was frankly past caring by that time. They had obviously been influenced by the implications made by Hamilton and the doubt about police propriety over their dealings with this woman.

At least it meant that I could go back to craving warrants that would remain private until I chose to execute them, which was all I really wanted in the first place.

CHAPTER 33: MR SCROGGIE

A few months after I had charged young David Robertson with twenty-three counts of malicious mischief (did I mention that when someone's charged, even a juvenile, the crimes are invariably more serious?), his dad, Neil, called me at the office. He asked if I would phone him when I got home, or come and see him, about a personal matter. He was serious when I got to his home and he then explained to me that he was only looking for advice for a friend, and that he trusted me to do nothing without his friend's say so. I agreed.

He then related a troubling story about a guy who lived nearby on his own, and who wasn't apparently quite the full shilling. He had been taking young kids into his house and had done so with Neil's friend's wee girl, who was about eight years old from memory. The wee girl had said enough to her mum and dad to have them worried sick that he had interfered with her in some way, but not quite worried enough to phone the police. In fairness, I should point out that in small rural or island communities, everybody knows everybody else and all of their business, and any stigma can last a lifetime and greatly influence a person's quality of life and future choices. Such are the considerations of caring parents and so we shouldn't be too critical.

This father wanted to go and confront the guy head-on, as most dads would, but luckily his wife had confided in Neil and Anne, and they had convinced him to wait and take some advice. Thank goodness because such confrontations don't generally end well for anyone.

I came to an agreement with Neil that he would relate to his neighbour or friend. I would arrange to interview the wee girl properly, with a policewoman, and with her mum present. We would ascertain if anything untoward seemed to have occurred, and take it from there, only proceeding when the parents were fully informed and prepared to do so. I did take some advice from the Fiscal here, but I was on solid ground. Until an official complaint was made, I could call the shots. We spoke to the wee girl for no more than fifteen or twenty minutes and realised that this needed specialist involvement and so we adjourned. We were more than satisfied that this guy had tampered with this kid and, with the parents now on board, arrangements were made for the specialist team to come over the next day and take a more detailed account of events, carry out a medical examination, and secure any samples or other physical evidence that could be found. The truth is that the women allocated and trained to conduct child interviews and medical examinations were also the officers utilised to interview allegations of rape, and were generally the investigating officers into such crimes. This was all arranged as such for political reasons, in a supposed effort to protect the victims of such crimes and ensure they were dealt with sympathetically. None of these officers were detectives. None had prosecuted or prepared the evidence for a major High Court case until their secondment into the female and child unit, and none had real experience or expertise in interviewing suspects. But, hey, it looked better. I just wanted the guy in a cell and to find out how many other kids he had abused.

As it transpired, there were a few other children who had stories to tell, but the initial wee girl was the most serious victim that we found out about. I think we actually nipped this thing in the bud for a change. My problem was that when I detained the accused straight from his bed at five-thirty the next morning, I was quite restricted in any interviewing I could conduct, as this guy was obviously suffering from learning difficulties. Nothing he told me was ever going to be of any use (this was long before tape recorded interviews were introduced) as any decent lawyer would have it thrown out of court, on the sustainable and reasonable grounds that I could get him to agree with just about anything, and that his chances of understanding the caution or his rights were, at best, in serious doubt.

I had to be content with a search and examination of his house, where carpet samples and suchlike were obtained, and the seizing of all of the clothing he might have been wearing. The three hair types – plucked, cut and combed –were taken from both ends by the doctor and all of the samples required were bottled up and despatched to the lab. By mid-morning, the Fiscal and I were happy that we had a decent case and so I cautioned and charged him with attempted rape, gross indecency and a few other sexual offences (throw enough shite …) and he was locked up awaiting his court appearance on the Monday.

I took a precaution here and, prior to the caution and charge, I called the duty solicitor. I expected just to brief him on the circumstances and then I could say that I had done so, but the lawyer said he would attend the station. Even better. I always, at every stage of a case, considered how it would look in court, under forensic examination by a judge or jury, and so was more than happy that the lawyer was coming to witness the caution and charge personally, a highly unusual occurrence. I had never heard of the lawyer, him being new to the island. His name was Mr Scroggie.

When he arrived, he stuck out right away. He was ungainly, quite scruffy really, and was actually respectful and pleasant to me and the uniform sergeant. What he always had was the oblig-atory bunch of papers carried about by every brief, but, in his case, crumpled in a pile under his arm. I never saw Mr Scroggie without this accessory, whether in court or out, and wonder now if it was perhaps a special criminal lawyer's suit that you can buy, with the papers already attached to the side of the jacket.

We gave him a few minutes with his client and then brought them to the charge bar, where I cautioned and charged the accused as later libelled and stated above and, as expected, there were no replies to any of the charges. A lawyer will almost always advise his client to say nothing at all in the early stages of a police enquiry, advice that, despite being given constantly by briefs, is often circumvented by the good guys, simply by persuasion. For the avoidance of any doubt, the good guys were us, the police.

He was placed back in his cell and Mr Scroggie asked if he could have a further chat with him. No problem. I promptly retreated to my office suite in order to catch up with developments elsewhere and, no doubt, begin the reporting process that would facilitate our guy appearing in front of the sheriff on Monday morning. To say I was surprised about ten minutes later would be a real understatement. Mr Scroggie wanted to speak to me as his client wanted to give a voluntary statement. Totally unbelievable. Let me explain.

A voluntary statement made in front of a solicitor was tantamount to pleading guilty before you even knew if the police had a decent case. I have taken many voluntary statements, but never with the accused's brief present, and they were always so disputed in court that they were almost worthless or worse. It gave the defence a chance to accuse me of fabrication and lies, and to, at least, cast some doubt on the veracity of such a statement. You see, as soon as an accused is cautioned and charged, he or she cannot be asked any more questions about the crime or offence. He's just been cautioned that he doesn't have to say anything, told what he's accused of, asked if he understands it, and any reply or comment noted. After that, it's all over. He needn't say another word until he appears in court and is entitled to a lawyer to represent him and speak for him. He doesn't even have to give evidence. The exception to that is a voluntary statement.

In this instance, Mr Scroggie was to be present when it was taken and, therefore, if done properly, it would be indisputable at a later date. You can bet your bottom dollar it was done right. There were strict rules and guidelines about voluntary statements. This was to cause much consternation in a murder case some years later (see Campsie Murders). There was no questioning allowed, other than to confirm his details, the date, time and place. He must be cautioned again, and the caution written out in full. It had to be hand-written and had to be contemporaneous, noted on blank lined paper and signed by the accused and those present, with no space for additions. There were to be no omissions or changes at all and it had to be done in one sitting. Most of all, it had to be a record of the exact words used by the accused, and only those words.

Suffice to say that his statement was short and sweet and as much of an admission as it was an apology for any harm done. It pre-empted any future trial, saved a lot of paper work and preparation and, most of all, it saved the wee girl and her friends and their families a lot of heartache and pain. I believe the sheriff would have considered all of that when sentencing, although I seem to remember this guy needed some help and support more than the jail. Without trying to remember his voluntary statement, one phrase from it has always stuck with me, and kind of sums up the case, when he refers to 'Kissin her Virginia.'

The troubling part of that was that Mr Scroggie didn't bat an eye when it was said. I just wrote it down as prescribed.

A guy I had worked with briefly in Lochgilphead had moved to the city and become a detective officer in Stewart Street Police Office. His name was Graham and, during the course of a murder enquiry in the city, he had taken a voluntary statement from the accused. The key thing was to note exactly what was said. This one read along the lines of 'On Tuesday the 3rd of April, I was to convey my wife to a local hostelry for a refreshment…'

I am obviously exaggerating here, but the fact was that the defence could prove that the guy making the statement was virtually illiterate, and could certainly never construct a sentence of that nature. The case was thrown out, a schoolboy error.

Mr Scroggie was totally different from any other lawyer I ever met. He actually cared that the truth be exposed in court. There was one occasion when he stood up in the middle of a trial and told the sheriff that he was invoking some section or whatever, and the sheriff immediately adjourned the trial, sending everyone home for the rest of the day. I later found out that this was a phrase or code to be used when lawyers no longer believed that their clients were innocent, felt unable to continue representing him or her, and wished to be withdrawn from the case. It was the only time I ever heard of that happening and I've known a lot of cops and lawyers over the years.

I was called to a housebreaking (a break-in) one morning. It was an office and the front door on the first-floor landing had been kicked in and the place ransacked. I was waiting for the proprietors (accountants, I think) to take an inventory and tell me if anything had been stolen. I was actually dusting the front office door for prints when Mr Scroggie appeared up the stairs. It transpired that his office was directly across the landing from the one violated and I explained to him what had taken place, asking him to check his office and make sure everything was okay.

I followed him into the interior (well, I wasn't going first. The bad guys might still have been there) and as he opened his office door I gasped in shock. They had really gone to town in here. There were files lying on the floor, the desk was awash with paper, and there was hardly a place to walk across the floor such was the array of papers. Mr Scroggie turned to me and said:

'Everything looks to be in order here, Simon.'

CHAPTER 34: BLIND PANIC

I know myself well enough to say, without any fear of contradiction, that I don't tend to get in a panic. I'm not sure why that is, or if it's just that we're all made different, but, invariably, when the button is pressed, I step up. I become calmer and more focused and, truth be told, absolutely thrive on the adrenalin. Perhaps it's a throwback to my upbringing, where chaos and totally random drunken behaviour was the norm, where you quickly learn to keep your head down, but it's certainly not a conscious thing. I don't think 'Right, don't panic' any more than a flapper says 'Right, let's start screaming and running about silly and that should help a lot.'

It's just part of who I am. I like a deadline to focus my mind, but on one day in particular, I was as close to panic as possible, without completely tipping over the edge. It was a normal day. Quite a nice day as I recall, late summer, and the call came in about two o'clock. A woman reporting that someone had stolen her seven-month-old baby girl and her pram from outside the post office. Unfortunately, I didn't hear the call. Rarely would a control room give a call to CID. It would always go to a mobile uniform car in the first instance, and might be overheard by CID or not. As it transpired, a few precious minutes were wasted because no one grasped the severity of the situation immediately.

The uniform car went to the locus, met with the mother and started taking a statement from her. A description, details of the baby and the pram, all of that stuff, and it was the radio messages in relation to the description that I heard. I intervened and suggested to the sergeant in the office that an immediate search be commenced, starting from the locus. The reply I got was:

'She's definitely not at the locus. She's made off with the baby.'

The one thing that could push me to the panic stage is the

total incompetence and stupidity of my colleagues. I told them to keep everyone in the post office and search the immediate area, residential common closes and other businesses, primarily for the pram. I also called for more officers to be called on-duty ASAP, but it seemed I was the only one who immediately grasped the gravity of the situation, perhaps because my son, Simon, was about one year old at the time. Who knows, but somehow I got it right away and no one else seemed to.

I must have got to the locus within five minutes and before I got there the pram had been found out in the back court behind the post office. The policewoman who found it was so chuffed you'd have thought she'd found the baby. I immediately arranged for a car with one cop to head to the Rhubodach to Colintraive Ferry Terminal, a twenty-minute drive away, and for someone to phone the ferryman and make sure it didn't sail before he got there. His instructions were to physically search any vehicle trying to leave the island on the ferry.

I spoke en-masse to the five or so customers and two staff members of the post office and we eventually gleaned that it had most likely been a woman who was seen hanging about outside around the right time. She was blonde, about sixty to sixty-five, and well dressed. Knowing the times of the main Calmac Ferries off the island, we now had an hour or so to take stock. I'm not sure why, as there was a senior and competent uniform sergeant on-duty, but I seemed to have control of this thing. I just seemed to know what to do and no one interfered or questioned me.

We had it on Radio Clyde within thirty minutes, we had the island shut down quicker than that and, at a quarter to four, I had everyone converging on the pier to search every vehicle and check every foot passenger going on the ferry. Crucially, I had also had CalMac link me through to the captain of the ferry and he was fully aware of what we were doing. I asked him to make all of his crew aware. The baby had now been gone almost an hour and I had whatever cops were available walking away from the locus and speaking to everyone they met, and every publican or shop keeper they passed. Everyone. My thinking was that we couldn't get the story out far and fast enough. We needed to find someone who had seen something.

I knew there was a real urgency and, by now, the others were starting to catch on. This could end badly for everyone, especially the baby. I was also looking for expert help and had called the DCI at Dumbarton HQ to see if he could source some specialist knowledge or advice. He did. A woman from a unit at the Met in London called me about an hour in, and among all the things she told me was the sobering fact that this woman wasn't well. The chances were that she would not have any food or a change of clothes for the baby. She had acted on a growing impulse and this was a well-known phenomenon. The sad fact was that when the baby needed a feed or a change of nappy, she would start crying, and the woman would panic, get agitated and, at best, abandon the child. I didn't even want to consider the other options.

We discovered that she had walked north from the locus, towards the police station. We had a better description of her now. Sharp features, pale complexion, short-ish blond hair, slim build, wearing a dress of some kind, possibly blue. Carrying the baby wrapped in a blanket. (A pink blanket from the pram?) I immediately passed this on for distribution as far as possible, and we all headed to the pier to search cars. This was the big advantage of policing an island. Everyone had to travel on one of two ferries to get to and from Rothesay, and the CalMac ferry was by far the main route, coming over from Wemyss Bay near Greenock.

When the ship came in, the captain stepped off before it had even been tied up and came straight over to me. He knew me from a variety of enquiries on the ferries.

'I might have something for you, Simon. Someone you need to speak to.'

He took me on board and a girl in CalMac uniform was waiting in the lounge. Meanwhile, the troops were searching every car waiting to get on board. I'm not sure of the legality of those searches now, but as I would do many times throughout my career, I made a judgement call. If everyone voluntarily allowed us to search their car, there was no problem. If they didn't, they weren't moving off that pier, and would immediately become a suspect. This is clear Ten Percent thinking in my book.

The girl was in her early twenties and a bit shy, but with encouragement from me and the captain, we eventually gleaned that she had seen a woman fitting the description we were looking for on the lunchtime boat to Rothesay. At first, the girl thought the woman was carrying a baby in her arms. She had been in the lounge with a baby held close to her chest. She had been looking at the baby and fussing when the girl passed, but when she looked more closely, intending to comment on the child, she realised that it was only a doll the woman was holding. She had backed off immediately.

The best piece of information to come from this was that the woman was a regular on the ferry. The CalMac girl thought she must be a resident on the island, and so did I. Then I got lucky, as you do when you do the leg work. We had planned to speak to the taxi drivers who were always on and around the pier, especially when a ferry was arriving, but hadn't had time yet. I got one of the lads to stop all vehicles getting off the pier right away and raced down the gang plank to speak to them.

At first, they weren't too pleased at my interfering in their trade (as if I cared) but they soon came round when they realised why. None of them had picked up this woman with the child doll, but Alex, who I had given a lift home to from the roadside when he crashed his bicycle, remembered seeing her walking off the pier as he drove off with a hire. We were closing in. I'm surprised Alex remembered me getting him home as he was so drunk that night. We now had a direction of travel, at least, up the hill past Rothesay Castle towards the police station.

We met back at the office to gather information and plan our next moves. I remember fielding calls from gaffers wanting to set up an incident room and send manpower over the next day. This horrified me. I had no intention of resting until we had the baby safe. There was a policewoman in tears due to the stress of the whole situation, but I remember being totally calm, and when I spoke with the parents of the baby afterwards, they both said that my determination and confidence kept them sane for those three or four hours.

I'm not sure exactly when, but I eventually had a brain wave. I was sitting with the CI, bringing him up to date, because by this time it had been on national news bulletins and he was getting grief from HQ in Pitt Street. It suddenly dawned on me. I sat down for five minutes and noted all of the corner shops and newsagents in Rothesay and, starting with the ones closest to the police office, had all of them visited right away. Bingo.

Within five or ten minutes, we had a convenience store owner who had served this woman not so long ago. He was sure it was her from the description, and knew her from past visits, although she wasn't a regular. He was sure she lived in the block where his store was situated, because she was sometimes in her slippers or casual, and off we went. Although I was buzzing now, I was also shit scared. It had been over three hours. Anything could have happened. We started banging on doors of the big tenement blocks looking for her and, within fifteen or twenty minutes, we got the break we needed. I had pressed the intercom for a close entry system, ground floor buzzer 0/1, and when the guy answered, I told him it was the CID, could he open the door.

'Is it that woman with the baby thing?' he asked.

'Yes, it is, can you open the door so that we can check the close, please?'

'Nae bother, I think she might be in 2/2.'

When we chapped the door, I was with a young cop, Scott, and, sure enough, the woman we now felt we knew so well answered the door. I didn't caution her, I just told her we were looking for a baby and walked in past her. To be fair, she didn't protest in the slightest and was calm. She wasn't right at all, or perhaps she'd had enough of this baby lark. The baby was on the settee, still wrapped in the pink blanket, and thankfully breathing, sleeping fitfully. I know he would deny it, but Scott had tears on his face, as I have writing this. What a relief. Scott took the baby away downstairs and I waited with the woman until a policewoman arrived. She seemed totally oblivious to everything.

I could see the doll lying on her bed, discarded when she acquired the real thing. After a few minutes, she got her coat on and, with the policewoman, we headed to the office, where she was charged and the doctor called. I know that she appeared in court the next day and was sent to hospital somewhere. There was never any trial or anything. For days afterwards, I was busy taking and collating statements, searching her house and another property she had in Paisley and generally tidying things up for the Fiscal.

When I got home that night, we had recovered the baby, I was emotionally drained, but I recall phoning the office to make sure someone had stood down the cop, Danny, who had been at the Rhubodach ferry all day. It had been all over the news, of course, and when I related the bones of the story, and the happy ending to my wife, Margaret, she in turn told me a story that sent a shiver up my spine.

She had been out around lunchtime with my almost one-year-old son, Simon Jnr, in his pram. She had gone into the Bank of Scotland, leaving the pram and our son outside, as the revolving doors of the bank were a pain. She had only been inside a few minutes and when she came out a woman was holding Simon in her arms staring at him. When she grabbed Simon and asked her what she thought she was doing, the woman had said, 'What a lovely wee girl. You must be so happy.'

Simon was apparently dressed from head-to-toe in blue and should never have been mistaken for a wee girl. He sure wouldn't be now. It was without doubt the same woman, maybe thirty minutes or so before she snatched the wee girl from outside the post office. My wife only proved how ineffective my publicity efforts had been at spreading the word. She was totally unaware of any drama until I walked in the door, and equally unimpressed by my moaning. What a day she had had.

The next day I spoke to the Fiscal prior to taking my report over to her, and she confirmed that the charge should be *plagium*, the Scottish crime of theft of a child under the age of puberty. She had never had such a case and didn't recall hearing of one, so she was quite excited. I was less so, just being totally relieved that the baby had survived her ordeal. I wonder where that wee girl is now.

CHAPTER 35: ISLAND VISITORS

Although I was a city boy at heart, over the course of five years, three in Campbeltown and two in Rothesay, I had pretty much become used to the rural life. I certainly wasn't up to speed on major crime in the city. So when I got a call from the detective superintendent of the SCS, I was all ears. I didn't ask any questions and just did exactly as I was told. An address, a Daimler vehicle and registration number, and get back to him with an update. No explanation. Yes, Boss.

It was a flat on the seafront in Rothesay and, sure enough, the Daimler was parked nearby. The flat looked occupied to me. I was subsequently told that a team of detectives would be arriving on the island that afternoon. They were looking to affect a warrant and arrest a certain Mr Paul Ferris. To be absolutely honest, the name meant little, if anything, to me; likewise, the names of the detectives from the SCS, who were to become my colleagues in the not too distant future.

When they arrived, I checked them all in to the Hillside Hotel with my friends, Bob and Margaret. I always knew that if the accommodation and facilities were a bit limited, this would always be more than compensated for by the hospitality received.

From memory, we hung about for ages and there was a lot of whispering and side meetings going on between the four Glasgow officers, two sergeants (DSs) and two constables (DCs). I wasn't sure what the delay was about and I certainly wasn't party to any of the discussion, my main role being to 'keep an eye' on the flat and the car. I assumed correctly that if the guy they were after was going to be arrested, they were making sure that it would occur after midnight. This would give them a whole day to speak with him or carry out enquiries before he would have to appear in court. I had recently passed my shooting course and was now an

AFO (Authorised Firearms Officer) but my own boss, the Local Chief Inspector, had decreed that I wouldn't be carrying a firearm, despite the fact that all four of our visitors were armed. I was just to 'Listen and watch and do as you're told. No more.'

He also insisted that I call out the lad who was my assistant at the time, Jack Russell (I know.) At the time, I thought this indulgent, but now realise he wanted me to have a witness. When I briefed my own DI in Lochgilphead, he was equally cautious on my behalf and was dismissive of my question as to whether he was going to head over. He thought that was funny, even. What my bosses knew that I didn't fully appreciate at the time was that no one who wasn't a ten-percenter wanted anything to do with a SCS operation. If you wanted a quiet life, as little grief and hassle as possible, and the nice police pension at the end of the road, you stayed as far away as possible from anything they were involved in. I was the exact opposite. It was where I wanted to be.

I learned during the course of this from one of the Squad DSs that I was later to be neighboured within the Squad; that they had been told to include me as much as possible, but not to compromise me in any way. It seems my name was known in the corridors of power at Pitt Street, but I couldn't have even taken you to the corridors. I knew that the four of them suffered my presence, but I didn't know why. I assumed it was for my local knowledge, or to use me in any search or dirty work.

We executed the warrant not long before midnight. It was my first taste of proper police work in my mind. When the door was opened by Paul Ferris himself, he was on the ground within a second and had three or four hand guns pointing in his face as he was cuffed. He had been wearing a dressing gown, and was totally unfazed. I was peeking round the stairwell as I had no gun, but my lasting recollection is of Ferris lying on his back, pinned to the floor with shaking guns in his face. He was chilled. He just looked up and said:

'Is that a snub-nosed S&W 38?'

I didn't get past the house threshold. Jack and I were given the

Daimler keys and told to take it to the police station, which we did. Not long after midnight, Ferris was marched in and charged with possession of a large quantity of cocaine, I think. I was told to carry out a thorough search of the Daimler. Well, I have never searched anything as well as that car. We had it in pieces before we were told to stop, and would still be there if we hadn't been dragged away. You see, I was sure that I was going to get a using. I thought that whatever they had found or wanted to find would be left for me and Jack to discover. In that way, we would have gone to the High Court as innocents telling the truth and would, perhaps, have been believed by a jury. Much to my surprise and consternation, we found no drugs at all, and when we were told to stop searching, I apparently said, 'But we haven't found anything yet.'

The result was a High Court trial and a not proven verdict for Ferris. His brief had spent the duration of the trial discrediting the squad officers, calling one of them 'The Magician of Strathclyde Police', and he successfully sowed a seed of doubt in the minds of the jury. He couldn't have done that to me and Jack, two naïve and innocent lads from the sticks.

We retired to the Hillside Hotel late but, as always, a nightcap was in order. In Pitt Street, or any police office for that matter, there was a rule that firearms were always unloaded and laid out in full view away from any drinking or card playing, or anything that could cause an argument or fight. (Just about anything could do so, truth be told.) Ten percenters are typically quick tempered, highly strung, volatile and opinionated. You only want them to have a gun for the shortest spell possible. In the Hillside Hotel, these guys still had their Smith and Weston's in their shoulder holsters. Suffice to say the nightcap went on for some time, and the evening culminated in a walk along a beach and some target practice. I should draw a veil over the rest of the night.

I never had any real desire to carry a firearm. I am a strict believer that arming the police would just escalate the odds, and many more crooks would tool up as a result. The fact that we can generally police in this country without side-arms should be a matter of pride. In my case, I had always been dependent on my sergeant, Alastair Barnett, as he was carrying the gun. I didn't like that either and, although it had only happened on a handful of occasions, I had always felt that I would rather be in control of my own destiny.

I never did need to be armed in Rothesay, but I was to get more than my fill of firearms in my next posting at the Strathclyde SCS and surveillance unit.

CHAPTER 36:
THE BEAUTIFUL GAME - ROTHESAY

By the time I had left Campbeltown my stint at serious amateur football was over. My left knee was gubbed and the prognosis was not rosy. I had a young family, my son, Simon Jnr, having been born in August 1983, only a few months old, and by the time we left Rothesay two years later, I would have a daughter, Tracy-Ann, as well. So, for once, football was being pushed down the list of priorities, but I still managed to play for The Black Bull pub team in the local league and I took on many more refereeing duties.

I had only been on the island a few months when I was approached by a lad, Gordon Pollock, who had a local covers group. In actual fact, there was only him and a drummer left and he was anxious to have me on keyboards. I really wasn't interested. I had only just begun to get over the withdrawals from playing with Horizon and was reluctant to rekindle that flame all over again. But he kept on at me and all of a sudden his persistence paid off. I'm not sure what was responsible for that, but he told me they had a gig in the Glenburn Hotel where there would be four-hundred punters and I would be paid a hundred and fifty pounds - Yes, I know, One Hundred and Fifty *Pounds*.

Let's just put this in perspective. I was earning about two hundred pounds per week as a police officer with nearly four years' service. A typical gig with Horizon meant leaving Campbeltown around seven and getting back into the town about two or sometimes three in the morning. If we made a tenner each, after paying fuel, etc., and got a free pint, we were happy. This was a three-man-gig locally, finishing before midnight, and I was getting almost a week's wages cash in hand. I actually didn't fully believe it, but agreed to play. Who wouldn't? I just wondered what the catch would be.

As it transpired, it was all true, but there was a catch: the captive audience. We were playing to about four-hundred, but they were all on coach tours – McGill's, Dalziel's and suchlike, and they had been travelling on the bus all day. They had their dinner and then we went on stage. The sound of snoring was louder than any applause we got, but one wee group of ladies were determined to do the slosh, which was quite new at the time, I think; new in this country, anyway, and certainly new to me. I'd never heard of it, and when Gordon told me how the *Birdy Song* went, I couldn't believe my ears. I had to learn it on the spot and I swear I got good at it as we played it and *Beautiful Sunday* about a dozen times. No Google in those days.

From then on, I played regularly with them, maybe once a month but the money was the only motivation, really. The gigs were always local and so there was no travelling involved, but there was a healthy live music scene in Rothesay. I think this was a remnant of Lena Zavaroni's talent and fame. A lot of her extended family played locally and, although good musicians in their own right, the name helped fill any bar or hotel.

I recall a gig in the Masonic Lodge. I'm sure it was a golden anniversary. Not a young crowd, anyway. Again, the money was silly, but the problem with these types of nights is that they can drag on and on, and this particular one did. Then you have the singers. This was my first experience of this phenomenon. You see, the lads I played with in Horizon had all served their apprenticeships playing ceilidhs, weddings and parties for drunk people. I had missed all of that but was now getting found out. As everyone, including the band becomes more inebriated, you start to get requests. This can be almost anything, but any band can call on a back list of hundreds to pull them through when put on the spot. I had to learn these standards on the hoof.

The other problem as the night progressed was that there's always the 'chanter.' The family want to hear Uncle Bill sing his version of whatever. No, it's not a request. It's happening, whatever anyone says, including Uncle Bill. He's virtually pushed or dragged up onto the stage. Him pretending to be reluctant is all part of this ritual and then he announces the song he's sung at every family gathering for the last hundred and fifty years, and the only person surprised or expectant is me. New York, New York was a favourite and of course any keyboard player worth his salt will know large chunks of it. The real problem with these celebrity singers is that they can change key at any second and, of course, whatever key Uncle Bill is in is the right key. He then looks back at me as if saying, come on, you should know this one. What a carry on. The things we do for money. I'm sure the drink helped me cope.

The football was good on Rothesay but the only serious game we played was when we went over to Dunoon to play them. We also had them back over and both teams were full of ringers, but we won both games. I remember I was voted man of the match in Rothesay. I scored the winner, a screamer with my shin from about one foot out. But the only thing I really remember about the away leg was the return journey, or at least part of it. We had a minibus with a sliding side door and for some reason everyone peed out of it, while we were moving. It was fortunate we didn't lose anyone into a ditch. Or maybe we did. Just to reiterate, this was a minibus type vehicle full of mostly serving police officers. Thank goodness we didn't have mobile camera phones in those days.

One of the lads on that minibus was Ian Currie. What a boy. He always took things just that bit too far. He just never knew when to stop. For example, he would go along the bar at clearing up time just finishing off the drinks that had been collected or left there for washing. A madman, for sure, but he was reliable, totally fearless, and a good lad. We always got on well, until it was time for him to leave the island. He moved on from Rothesay to take up a position with the Strathclyde Police Support Unit, in particular the underwater unit. That was his dream.

I came in one wet dreich winters morning, and hadn't even had the cursory cup of coffee, when I was told there was something suspicious washed up on the beach at Port Banantyne. Shit. I grabbed a policewoman and off we went. Sure enough, when we stopped at the designated spot, we could see a bundle of something near the water's edge, about eighty yards away; a decent wedge of it, anyway. So off we trundled and, as we neared, it seemed more and more like the report had suggested. This was a body washed up. The policewoman held back and I approached, checking all around for any signs or tracks, and just as I got down and went to move the cloth from its face, it jumped up shouting some ludicrous insane obscenity at me. For fuck's sake. After screaming and shitting myself simultaneously, I registered Currie's big hysterical face filled with obvious glee. Wanker.

He had been on night shift and when he'd finished, he'd gone bloody windsurfing in his wet suit in the wind and rain. Ideal conditions, it seems. He's obviously concocted this plan, although I refuse to believe he could have conceived it on his own meagre mental resources, and set the trap. I told you he was a wanker. That beach front at 'The Port' was the scene of a few embarrassing incidents for me over the couple of years I spent as Jim Bergerac.

One time I attended a call of scrap theft going on at an old derelict hotel just up the hill. The premises were just a shell really and had been disused for years, certainly throughout my time there. The report said there was a vehicle and people inside stripping metal away, so off we went. I jumped into the marked Sherpa van along with a couple of colleagues. Please don't ask me why. When we got there, they dropped me off and carried on to the other side of the building, clever. Within a few seconds, I saw a guy making a run for it through the hotel, and I pursued. I had a big grin on my face. I loved these chases.

Before I could quite lay hands on him, my lazy uniform colleagues stepped out of their hiding place and nabbed him. As they did so, we heard a vehicle start up and drive off at speed. Buggers. We would soon catch up with them, though, once we got a word with the guy we had in the back of the van. And so we made our way back to Rothesay, with the three of us in the front of the Sherpa. But something was wrong. I thought I had maybe stepped on a nail or a piece of glass. My big toe was sore and, within a few minutes, it was agony. I took my shoe and sock off and it was badly swollen, pure red and absolute agony. What's more, it was getting worse. A guy, Danny Quinn, was driving and I told him to stop. Just as well, as he could easily have crashed the van with the laughing he was doing.

I jumped out, clambered over the sea wall and hobbled down the stony beach. Thankfully, the tide was quite high and the relief was amazing when I got my foot in the water. Not quite on a par with the morphine injection I had got in my bottom in hospital, but at least this was totally legal. When my colleagues calmed down, they went away and dropped the prisoner off at the office, and came back with a bucket. I filled this with water and off we went to the hospital. Apparently, it was acid. When chasing the thief through the hotel I vaguely remembered splashing through some water. It transpired that it wasn't water at all. It was acid from old batteries that were leaking. The doctor said I was lucky that I had got it into water right away, especially sea water, as this had stopped the burning process, undoubtedly saving my toe, and maybe even my foot.

To this day, I have terrible trouble with my big left toe nail, which renews itself every year or so, but never grows properly. No wonder I'm shit at football now.

I digress. My second child, Tracy-Ann, was born while I was based in Rothesay, just before we left the island. It was a strange move to be made in those days, but I had got to know the Divisional commander of L Division quite well through the various high-profile cases I dealt with. His name was Willie Anderson, and he was a real CID man. Old-school, clever, and so well respected and, hence, connected. I had made no secret of the fact that I wanted to be a SCS detective someday and, sure enough, not long after I attained my firearms certificate, I got the news. I was to go to Glasgow and start looking at police houses. I had made it to the Serious Crime Squad. Quite a step up for a twenty-six-year-old with less than seven years' police service.

CHAPTER 37: THE BEAUTIFUL GAME – SERIOUS CRIME SQUAD

The boss of the squad, DSI Joe Jackson, welcomed me to the department with some scepticism. I was young to be there and, coming from the sticks, I didn't have any of the street learning of my colleagues, and none of the friends and contacts that they had all made over their years working the CID offices around Glasgow. I was a bit sceptical, too, but we needn't have worried. I think it's fair to say I took to it like a duck to water and if there's one thing that will always ingratiate you to a new environment of men, it's being able to kick a ball. Joe had told me that in the squad we worked hard and played hard and he wasn't exaggerating.

Over the years in the squad, I played for the squad team and my mate Stan's work team, Clyde Bonding, but these were only bounce games, and I now played at centre half, so could pace myself accordingly. But in this period I took the squad team on a variety of trips to play, the first one being back to Islay for their spring tournament. I thought it fitting that the Serious Drinking Squad should visit the home of serious drinking.

That weekend I played in all three games and refereed two games on top of that, over a three-day period. Crazy. There were many stories that came from those Islay football trips, some of which may be fit to be told in another forty years, but my lasting memory is that we needed to score in order to draw our last game in the group, and then progress to the final. It was 2-2 with a few minutes left when after a corner the ball landed at my left foot, the supposed good one, no more than six yards out. I hit it first time for the top corner and saw it in slow motion sail agonisingly over as it clipped the cross bar on the way. I couldn't believe I'd missed. It was perhaps just as well because I'm not sure we had the strength for another match.

Suffice to say that on the ferry coming home on the Sunday we managed to coerce the captain to open the bar for us. I'm not sure if it was the carrot or the stick on this occasion, but we all congregated in the bar, joined by some surprised, but grateful, regular travellers, when one of our number appeared distraught. When his low mood was queried, he dropped his shirt collar to reveal some prize love bites on both sides of his neck. He was in the horrors at the prospect of going home to his wife/girlfriend/partner (or all three) in that condition, but he needn't have worried.

We were nothing if not resourceful and a plan was hatched to save his relationship, albeit only temporarily. Cameras were produced, long before sophisticated mobile phones of course, and we proceeded to attack the lad, quickly restraining him and stripping him down to his underwear. While he was pinned to the floor and helpless, still fighting but useless against at least a dozen of us, a few of us made a show of attacking his neck, as if biting him. Of course, the flash bulbs were popping. The idea was that he would show the bites, and explain that they were a result of our twisted sense of humour. The resultant photographs would back this up. I never did learn how that story ended. I suspect sadly, like so many others.

On another adventure, I took the team to Rothesay to play against a local select side, this time just one game so as not to interfere with the social side of the trip. We all stayed at the Hillside Hotel with Bob and Margaret, my old friends. (See Rothesay Fire.) I do remember that we won the game 2-1, Les Darling scoring a last-minute clincher when he headed in a perfectly delivered free kick from yours truly. I did miss that sitter in Port Ellen, though. But the most memorable and hilarious part of that summer's trip for me was the journey across the Clyde Estuary from Wemyss Bay and back.

I had put the trip together, just like the Islay jaunt. It was my old pals we were playing, and since I had worked on Bute and knew the lay of the land, I had booked the hotel, etc. Everything was left in my hands. I simply told the squad to be at Wemyss Bay Railway Bar at whatever time. Around lunchtime, I would imagine, for the one o'clock crossing to Rothesay courtesy of good old CalMac ferries. There were about sixteen of us, and the lads were all in the bar by opening time, downing a few pints before heading on our overseas adventure. Only there was a problem I hadn't told them about.

I had taken a chance. All week leading up to our trip, the CalMac staff had been threatening strike action. From memory, they were part of the railway union, and weren't happy about something. It had been fifty-fifty on the Thursday as to whether they would strike and I had to make a decision whether to cancel all of the arrangements, or say nothing and hope for the best. I opted for the latter, but took the precaution of having a boat on standby to get us over the Firth of Clyde to Rothesay. It was the middle of summer, thankfully. I had made a few phone calls and eventually had a boat and driver lined up which I summoned that morning, and was assured that Lachie and his son would be at Wemyss Bay to pick us up. I didn't tell any of the squad. I suspected that if they knew the truth, some of them would call off, which could lead to a mutiny and would at least upset all of the other arrangements, and our chance of winning the challenge game against the islanders.

At noon in the Railway Bar, no one seemed in the least concerned. They must never have watched the news, or couldn't relate the industrial action on CalMac to our Rothesay trip. We had one team member on crutches from a midweek game, and he had brought a 'bird' dressed up for their weekend away. I'm not sure where she thought she was going. I was just starting to get anxious when a young lad of about twelve pulled at my T-shirt and asked if I was Mr McLean.

When I looked down, he said, 'That's my dad waiting now.'

'We'll be there shortly, son.'

I announced to all that the ship was in, and we should board now, and we all began moving to the exit. I did hear a few comments alluding to the fact that there was a bar on the ferry. I honestly don't think they had any idea.

For those who have never had the pleasure of travelling from Wemyss Bay as a foot passenger (I don't think I had until that day) the well-worn travellers' path is straightforward. On exiting the bar, there follows a walk of a few minutes or so undercover, through a big hangar that runs the length of the pier, eventually bringing you out into the broad sunlight and the substantial old wooden pier. Right about where the gangplank would be for boarding. Can you imagine the perplexed expressions as we came out rubbing our eyes and there was no boat there, nothing, just an expanse of sea where our car-ferry should've been sitting in all its splendour?

I just kept walking, following the young lad, right to the end of the pier. And looking down, there it was: our transport. About twenty-feet long, bobbing happily, awaiting us to climb down the ladder and get on-board. There was much mumbling and grumbling, but again I just asked someone to hold my bag and climbed down behind the laddie. I shouted for my bag to be thrown down and my neighbour, big Donnie McQuade, followed me down.

There was now a line forming and I'm sure that having had a few pints in the bar in the preceding hour helped decide a few minds. When 'Hoodsie', with his right leg in plaster, handed his girlfriend the crutches and stepped onto the ladder all bets were off, and the clincher was when his 'bird' managed to make the descent in her short skirt and heels. It became a real laugh and an adventure then, and later, when we had all returned home unscathed as champions of Bute, the consensus was that the trips across the Clyde on those beautiful summer days, with our hands dragging in the water, were one of the highlights of a rather eventful weekend.

The one other squad trip I want to mention briefly (because much of it is lost in the haze of my memory, thankfully) is a trip to Newcastle to play a regional semi-final. We had travelled with a pool of seventeen, but on the day were down to a bare twelve fit players, the usual, really, where an overnighter was involved. I do remember a team visit to Gray's Nightclub, but not much else.

Suffice to say, it was a late night, not really conducive to winning any sports competition.

In the event, we were drawing 1-1 into injury time and got a corner, which would transpire to be our last chance of victory that day.

Tam, my partner in the centre of our defence, was easily six-foot six-inches tall, and built like the side of a big house. He was as hard as nails. When we got the corner I said to Tam, 'On you go up, big man. Glory beckons for Scotland.'

In my mind, to this day, it was Scotland v England, naturally. I couldn't believe it when, holding his cheek like a big pansy, he said, 'I'm finished, mate. I've got a sore tooth.'

A bloody sore tooth!

The last minute against the Auld Enemy. A chance to enter folklore, to put the English to the sword, and get some revenge for those clearances and every other injustice, real or imagined, over the centuries. What a wuss. I trekked up for the corner, and would give anything to say I got on the end of that corner and banged it in the top corner of the net. I wish. I got nowhere near it and we had to play them again back in Glasgow a few weeks later. We eventually lost in the final but I missed both games through injury. You don't get many chances at such glory.

My friend, Donnie Hardie, managed the crime squad football team. He was also a detective sergeant in his spare time. Although he was one of the grumpiest old farts I ever knew, and there was some serious competition for that pedestal, he was also really funny, and as devoted as any football manager could be. He merely arranged the fixtures; booked the parks; organized the transport and sorted accommodation, if it was required; made sure we had enough players; acquired, washed and looked after the strips; and ensured there was a referee on the day. Oh, and he picked the team, as well.

I got picked for one more big game, although I'm not sure why. It was a Strathclyde team against an English team in some regional trophy or other. This was during my stint with the squad and my mucka, Gerry Gallagher, had also been persuaded to play in goals. I had never been able to coax him to play before this, and with hindsight, maybe they asked me to play so that Gerry would come along with me. He had been voted player of the year during a season as a professional in Sweden and was generally regarded as top notch. I knew this but had never seen him play. If he was half as good as he said he was, he could play for any team he wanted.

The game was played at Ashfield Juniors ground in Possilpark, Glasgow, and when I got there Gerry hadn't yet appeared. I knew most of the lads, but only one or two of them had played with Gerry and were wary of him. I knew him really well and, sure enough, he turned up at the last minute. But he looked different. He was in the zone, his eyes slightly bulging and he immediately stripped naked. We were all just about ready to go for a warm up and he goes straight in for a shower. A cold shower. We could hear him shouting and bawling. Out he comes, bollock naked, scrubbing himself with a big towel. He was almost red raw. I threw him his top and shorts and made some smart-ass comment about the cold not doing him any favours, but he ignored me, no cutting reply, or come back at all. He just stared right through me. That wasn't right.

Strathclyde won that game 2-0, no thanks to me as I was substituted at half time, but that was a good thing. It meant I got to watch Gerry in action in goal. He really was something else. He totally dominated his six-yard box. He was an animal. There was no way anyone was going near him in there. His handling, throwing and kicking were exceptional and I'm so glad I got to see him in action.

After the game, I told him he was lucky our defence were so good and that he was nothing special. I doubt I ever told him the truth, because Gerry didn't drink, and any praise or affection we had for each other was only ever expressed through drink. If that's true, I'm sorry, Gerry. You were not too bad at all.

We played all over the country, but mostly in Glasgow, and

it was just random friendlies against whoever was available and looking for a game. We played most of the divisional teams, a ladies' team from down south (the stink of perfume could have blinded you, and that was before we got on the park) and against a host of civilian teams that the lads were affiliated to or knew. A prison officers' team which was almost a riot, and on and on. I'm not sure how many games we played over a season. We just played all the time and only being tied up on a major enquiry would keep me from playing, and even then I could generally nip away for a few hours.

In one special game against the drugs squad, Donnie had arranged drinks afterwards at Victoria's Nightclub in the city centre. It transpired that he had contrived to have medals bought for us all and presented us with our Bounce League Champions medals over drinks. We proceeded to get blind drunk and I actually gave my medal away, presenting it in turn to Terry Hurlock, an English player who played at the heart of Glasgow Rangers midfield at the time. I like to think of it among his other medals and ribbons, and how he explains its origin to any one showing curiosity.

We had some great laughs and times playing football and socialising throughout my four years in the SCS, but if the standard of football had dropped significantly from my earlier years, the opposite was true of my police work. I was now where I had wanted to be, dealing with murders, organized crime, terrorism, major drug dealers and firearms offences on a day-to-day basis. Despite the 'playing hard' part of it that I had been assured of from the start, I also learned how intense an enquiry can get and how manic an operation can be when your life is on the line. This really was the sharp end.

PART THREE:
THE SERIOUS CRIME SQUAD

CHAPTER 38: DOOR-TO-DOOR

We came on-duty one summer's morning only to be told to make our way to Dumbarton HQ, as there had been a murder. Off we all went, four of us in our team, led by our intrepid detective sergeant, Bob Barrowman. We got there quickly and the incident room was in a big gymnasium I had never seen before. This was my old stomping ground, being the HQ of 'L' Division, which covered Campbeltown, Rothesay, etc. The man in charge of the enquiry was DSI Adam Hay, my old boss, but he wasn't there when we arrived. He had left instructions for us to start the door-to-door enquiries.

The murder investigation was two, or maybe three, days old by this time, which in itself was unusual as you would normally get the invite to assist on day one. The second thing was that door-to-door would always be the first thing on the agenda of a major crime. It can take many weeks to complete, and can throw up vital witnesses and information quickly. It gets officers on the patch near the locus and that's where the information and snippets of gossip are to be found. It obviously shows a uniform presence straight away, usually with a marked caravan on site, therefore reassuring the public that we're on the case.

But no one had bothered. More upsetting was that the major incident box holding all of the door-to-door forms and schedules had apparently been tipped onto a table and left lying. Either no one knew what to do with them, or couldn't be arsed.

At this moment, Bobby chose to come out with one of his profound orders. In a loud and authoritative voice he looked at me and said, 'McLean, you're on door-to-door. Just put all of the appropriate forms into the appropriate folders, in the appropriate order, and then we'll get started. We're off for coffee.'

He proceeded to turn on his heel and march off to the canteen. What a man.

My mate, Mike McKenna, hung back to see if he could help me, and when we stopped laughing at Bob's typical instruction, we trekked after them to the canteen. If no one had started the door-to-door three days into an enquiry, it could wait another ten minutes.

I got the door-to-door up and running that morning, with everything in the appropriate places, and the routine plod of a major enquiry began. The only slight problem here was that within a few hours, and certainly by the next day, I had a good idea of who the culprit was, as I'm sure nearly everyone on the case did. He had battered a woman to death, wrapped her in her own blankets in bed, and then set fire to the house before running off. Because I knew the senior officer in charge of the enquiry, Adam Hay, I was pointed towards his office to ask him if we could go and bring this suspect in.

He was candid with me, explaining that he was waiting for the lab reports and fingerprint results to come back. These would, hopefully, make the case a slam dunk. He knew me, though, and I would never wait for these things. I would just go get him, interview him and speed up the laboratory by having him on the clock in custody. So, he made me a deal without spelling it out for me. If I waited for his instruction, he would let me and my team go and bring him in, which was fair enough. He could just have told me to fuck off back to Pitt Street with my new pals, after all. It transpired that Adam was going for an interview that day for a job as an Assistant Divisional Commander in another force. Our reading of the situation was that he wanted to be able to say that he was Officer in Charge of a major murder enquiry at his interview, hoping to impress.

The next day we got the green light and had a full confession in the bag before we knew it. We then had the payoff in the Milton Hotel with the mixture of my new colleagues in the squad and my old friends from Argyll. We had a nice time.

CHAPTER 39: THE BABY KILLER

The harsh fluorescents of the squad room highlighted the strain on every detective's face at muster, the signs of sleep still apparent as their eyes adjusted to the unforgiving light. Most mumbled greetings went unanswered as they congregated, waiting for the briefing and issue of side arms, another routine turn in the SCS, when the hunt for some unfortunate ned would hopefully come to a fitting climax.

An enterprising sort had poisoned baby food on the shelves of a high street brand store up and down the country and, following his telephoned instructions, this had been confirmed in their Liverpool branch. His loot, a modest few hundred grand, was to be collected from the Glasgow store that morning, or the contaminated containers would be unleashed throughout the UK.

In the best traditions of the polis, we had a plan. To ambush the baby-killing bastard when he picked the money up (as if there would be any money in the bag) and send him off to prison for a stretch, ideally in time for us to get a late breakfast and celebrate in the normal fashion (in the pub).

The pressing tasks at that minute were to identify the team you were in and secure a decent motor, clock who was 'carrying' so that you could always be behind him, in order to minimise the chance of him shooting you in any excitement, and make sure you had a radio to give you some chance of figuring out what was going on.

Problem was that the surveillance unit were a tight bunch who knew their roles and were well used to working together, but we were mixed with the Stewart Street enquiry team, who spoke in open language on air, and by the nature of their day-to-day roles weren't accustomed to lengthy stake outs followed by intense activity, requiring precise and instant communication.

My team were in our unmarked, shabby works type van, parked in an alleyway giving us a direct eyeball of the store doors. Vehicles were plotted up around a tight perimeter, an OP (Observation Point) had been set up in a hotel nearby, the customer service staff had been replaced by a couple of our worthies, and our secret weapon was walking the street in disguise. George, or Baldrick as he was more commonly known, due to his ability to pass for a dosser (even at the Christmas night out), had secured the use of a street sweeping cart complete with brushes and shovels. His council overalls were a great improvement on his own choice of daily clothes.

As I watched him through the bitter cold rain, I was fascinated by the diligence he applied to the task and the obvious flaw in his disguise was clear to any Glasgow boy that winter morning. No self-respecting council worker of any description would be seen on the streets in that weather, but Baldrick was cleaning that pavement as if his life depended on it. At one point a passing pedestrian threw his cigarette butt away, and George pursued him and made him pick it up! Luckily, he resisted booking him, but only, I suspect, because he was too busy cleaning the street.

At the appointed time of nine-fifteen, we became anxious to pounce on our man and the standard comment was heard across the airwaves as we watched every vehicle in the vicinity with suspicion. Stand By.

The first understanding about proactive policing that separates the men from the boys is the realisation that police reports are always written after the event. This is the only reason that every police operation is presented as planned, coordinated, chronological, and with a rigid chain of command. Because it's written that way, presented to the Crown that way for consideration of prosecution, and backed up by all of the statements of those officers involved, statements that collate all of the individual actions of the police to make the report flow to its logical conclusion. Eventually, if a trial ensues, these witnesses then present these statements verbally to the hearing, panel, jury or court, and our justice system takes its due course. As it should.

During the occurrence of the actual event, there are only two priorities. Stay alive and catch the baddy, strictly in that order, which is exactly what stand by means. As we all stood by, other than George, who was now shifting a pile of muck into his wheelie bin, a motorcycle parked directly in front of the store, and the rider made his way indoors, still wearing his full-face helmet. He made his way directly to the desk and gave the pre-determined phrase required to acquire the fictional loot, and at this point the final instruction was given over the airwaves as the thief made his way back towards his bike.

Go!

This is the most dangerous part of any operation, not because the intended target is especially a threat, but because you risk being trampled, bundled, cuffed, punched or even shot if anyone remembers to produce their firearm. It's also the point where all sense of team work or coordination is lost completely and every man becomes manic.

How it must feel to have twenty or so frenzied maniacs run at you from every point of the compass, I can only guess, but from the look on the face of the biker, and many others over the years, I think it would be a life-changing experience sure to intrude in dreams for a long time to come.

In a split second, the people at the bus stop run at you with guns pointed at you, the street sweeper looks as though he's about to batter you with a giant shovel, men appear from a van together and run towards you and even the placid customer service staff who were so nice a few seconds ago suddenly want to kill you. All of them shouting 'freeze' or 'get on the ground, ya prick', or whatever appropriate phrase is chosen, designed to immobilise and stun a target into confusion, fear and surrender. No one ever remembers what they shouted at these times but in the subsequent report it will read: 'Armed police. Stop.'

Many times I've heard cops say that suspects can often seem relieved to be caught immediately following their arrest, as if subconsciously this is what they really wanted all along. Bollocks. They're just so glad that they only got arrested!

Our biker was floored, cuffed and searched within seconds, with four handguns trained on him throughout, and we congregated at a nearby city centre police office to tie up the loose ends and be told what to put in our statements. This is when the case unravelled and thoughts of a late breakfast drifted. The guy said he was a courier simply making a pick up. He had no idea what was in the package he'd just picked up. A likely story, but absolutely true. His instructions were to pick it up as he had done and take it directly to Edinburgh Airport where he would be met at the check-in. He had a description and name of the would-be recipient. A dastardly plan that no one had foreseen, and so, with real urgency, we all scurried into cars and made for the airport forty-two miles away, at breakneck speed and with all the finesse of the Keystone Cops.

A cop was now riding the courier bike – in this instance, 'Baldrick' was the nominated bike driver – and time was of the essence if we were to prevent the suspect being spooked by a late delivery. He obviously had an escape flight booked.

I would love to say that our arrival at Edinburgh Airport was a precision landing, capturing our man in a perfect pincer, but, in practice, we were a mob of frenzied madmen on a mission, still in go mode, but now hungry and thirsty. We clawed our way through the lounge ready to make a further scene, led by a half council cleaner, half bike courier, raging that he had left his street cleaning duties unfinished.

We were deprived of our mob takedown by Baldrick, who spotted the expectant suspect, approached him with the package outstretched, and recited the surname provided by the real courier. As the smiling and relieved extortionist put his hand out to take possession of the loot, and confirmed his identity, George slipped his cuffs onto his wrist and said, 'you're nicked, mate.'

How George still had cuffs, I'll never know, because I was sure the original courier still had about a dozen pairs on him, mine included. So a happy ending which would read rather differently in the subsequent report, containing all of the evidence gathered over the following week or so.

Some of us were sent to Liverpool to trace the movements of the accused in the weeks leading to his sting, and we found the hotel he'd stayed at. From there, we put together a string of damning evidence including the shop where he had hired the typewriter to write his extortion note and even the ribbon that had been in the machine. Our lab was able to prove that this typewriter had been used to write the actual notes.

Unfortunately, this was no ned. We searched his detached home in the west end of Glasgow and discovered the motive for his desperate effort at major crime. A wife, unsustainable lifestyle, and floundering business, which he had hoped to salvage with the two-hundred thousand pounds.

But Baldrick wasn't finished yet. Making his way through Glasgow city centre after a hard days street cleaning and arresting extortionists, he was contented, pushing his dust cart − full, of course − to return it to the cleansing department, when he passed his next door neighbour's, bore them a hasty 'hello', and continued on his way. They were last seen gaping after him, open mouthed, wondering what had happened to his police career.

CHAPTER 40:
THE CAMPSIE MURDER SUICIDES

This was a multiple murder, but when the first body was found naked in a stream up a mountain range, it was initially tagged as a suicide. Overtime was curtailed at that point, but only until the post-mortem uncovered the obvious ligature and binding marks on the body and the inevitable conclusion of strangulation. We then had a murder on our hands, and when a second body turned up a few miles away in a similar state, it became an all-singing, all-dancing major murder enquiry.

It wasn't a protracted murder enquiry from memory, and within a few days, we had locked up a boyfriend of one of the deceased, who unfortunately had admitted one of the murders almost immediately when detained, and the cops, in a panic, had charged him, locked him up and then called the CID. That's the thing about the Ten Percent. They can always be relied on when things need fixing. When the system has malfunctioned, or gone awry somehow, and the bad guy is going to walk free, some good cop has made a genuine mistake and it needs fixing, or some rascals are getting away with just too much. The truth is that, at times, we bend the rules just enough to get things back into sync. I know that some people, a lot of them police officers, find this whole idea abhorrent. They would say we are no better than the criminals if we operate outside of the rules.

When people need protection, when lives are at stake, when the system has malfunctioned, or someone's made an innocent error, or when some scumbag is distributing drugs through a community, we had no problem making sure that we could circumvent the rules and justify our actions in the witness box. The court or jury could then decide if we had crossed a line. That was when we believed justice was served and, in these times, it was always us they turned to, regardless of their opinions and moral high horses when everything was cool in the cold light of day. When someone or something had to be dealt with, by hook or by crook, it was invariably the ten percenters who were called on. I have strong opinions on this. In order to keep our society running, our children safe and the many 'freedoms' we like to believe are God-given, there has to be someone in the front line, keeping the absolute scum at bay.

In this case, all we did was use our charm. We were designated the task of conveying this guy from A to B, knowing that he had fessed up to one murder, but that the other was still under investigation. We were not allowed to discuss the first with him as he'd been charged with it, but we still had enquiries to make into the second. And he hadn't been charged with that yet.

After his lawyer had visited him later, and had left the building, he was to buzz for the turnkey until he or she appeared, demand to see the duty officer, the custody sergeant or inspector, and, in turn, tell him or her that he had something to say about another murder, but would only speak to the Crime Squad officers who had brought him here.

When the call came, we had left about forty minutes before, but were sitting round the corner at the shopping centre, drinking coffee. We acknowledged the instruction to head back and finished our coffees before returning. Our boy had played it perfectly and the duty officer was a great witness to speak to the fact that he had specifically asked for us, and that his lawyer was not to be told. What unfolded then was quite surreal. He told us that he would take us and show us where the murder weapon was, where he had disposed of the victims clothing, and where he had stashed the items he had stolen from them. He also maintained there was a third body and he would show us where.

By the time we had him out of his cell and ready to go, we had been joined by another two SCS officers, but there was no lot drawing this time. I was told to cuff myself to this character and get in the back seat. Off we went on a tour of the north of Glasgow and he took us to a lake where the underwater unit later retrieved the hammer. He showed us a pile of mostly ash where he had burned the clothes, and we later recovered and identified a belt buckle from one of the victims. He refused to take us to the third body, citing a headache.

We returned him to his cell and began the process of tidying up the paperwork associated with this confession. As he'd already been charged with one murder this was to take the form of a voluntary statement, and so had to be handwritten on lined paper, and be the exact words stated by the accused. To be honest the notes we had, scribbled by Michael Langford Johnston in the car, were a bit of a mess and we wanted to tidy them up for presentation in the High Court at any future date. This was when we rediscovered the dangers of indentation, a tool at the disposal of every detective, where writing is replicated through the sheet you're writing on, onto paper underneath.

We had spent at least a few hours preparing the sheets that would eventually accompany Michael's scribbles, when someone held a sheet up to read it aloud and we noticed the indented writing and changes we'd made all over the background. Fuck. We had to get fresh paper and take it one sheet at a time, then carefully put it aside and start the next totally fresh sheet. It was daylight by the time we headed back to the city, but had certainly been a good night's work.

The trial in this case was a media circus, as the accused offered to show the police where the third body was buried or hidden. The press were all over it but, again, I'm sure he was just seeking attention and limelight. What I do know is that when it went to trial, I was caught out badly. I was on standby with the Fiscal to be called and give my evidence but something went wrong at the court and I was needed in a hurry. We were tearing along the M8 at the time on a follow of some kind when I got the coded message to attend the High Court immediately. There was no time to change into my suit at the office. I was to go as soon as possible.

I peeled off out of our surveillance convoy and did as I was told, but it was a strange experience, giving my evidence in front of a jury in the High Court, the most formal of surroundings, dressed in a T-shirt and jeans. At one point, lawyers were debating some point of law regarding my evidence, probably the voluntary statement and, subsequently, I was asked to leave and sit in the corridor until called back. The jury were also sent out at this juncture. When I sat down, Mr Donald Findlay was also out there chatting to his assistants and hangers on.

'You'll never guess what that idiot asked me this morning, chaps. He asked me if I would take him up the Campsies and he would show me where he buried the other victim, for fuck's sake.'

'What did you say, Donald?' piped up one of his minions.

'Are you fucking joking? Nothing would get me up the fucking Campsie Hills with you, you fucking imbecile.' Guffaw, guffaw, guffaw.

The others burst out in adoring laughter at the tremendous wit of their hero and boss. I'm sure it was pitched to include me, and hopefully I didn't even smile at this lawyer's banter. True to form, a while later, Findlay was calling me all the liars under the sun. For some reason, it was much easier to refute this stuff and maintain a dignified posture with your suit on.

It took me many years to come to terms with criminal lawyers and their ways. They are most certainly a particular breed of person. Not so long ago I was sitting next to the Defence Advocate, a friend of mine, who shall have to remain nameless. As I was finishing a law degree, I was assisting him in the High Court on a serious rape charge against two men, and I had done all of the investigating work in the lead up to the trial. Now I was on the opposite side of the fence. For so many years, it was me in the witness box sweating over every answer, trying to gauge how the judge and jury were responding to my responses, and shitting myself if I saw the lawyers at the big take scribbling notes to each other during the course of my evidence. This was exactly what I did now. My note to my esteemed colleague said, 'Do you think they did this? I do.'

The response, passed back to me, read simply, 'Who gives a fuck?'

A reminder yet again that innocence and guilt have little, if anything, to do with court proceedings. Only the evidence allowed, its legality in law and its veracity is important. Everything else is irrelevant.

His next note said everything about the criminal process.

'What are you up to this weekend?'

With the same advocate, I had once visited his client in prison. Stepps or Falkirk, I think. The lad, only seventeen or eighteen, had been convicted of attempted murder in Clydebank, had appealed, and the appeal had not been upheld by the High court. We were going to break the news and I thought I was there to explain any questions about the extensive enquiry work I had done to build his appeal case.

He was brought into the wee room and my learned friend proceeded to explain to him this unfortunate development in the proceedings, but the lad just sat there with his mouth open and a puzzled look on his face. Realising what the problem was I stepped in.

'It's bad news, mate, your appeal's fucked.'

Understanding flooded his face and he thanked us for trying and for coming to see him. It transpired I was only the translator, you see, or 'Code Switcher' in modern parlance.

CHAPTER 41: THE BARLINNIE RIOT

A few months after locking up the Rothesay Flasher I had the pleasure of speaking to Charles Contini again, this time under much more pleasant circumstances – for me, at any rate. The Royal Bank of Scotland on Victoria Street had triggered their panic alarm the previous afternoon and when the uniforms arrived a few minutes later, the two would-be bank robbers were still on the premises. Well, sort of.

The bank had a revolving door and Contini, along with some hanger-on, had got themselves armed, donned ski masks and rushed in to make their fortune, only to get totally jammed inside the now non-revolving doors. Brilliant. Unfortunately, I had been off-duty, but was told about it shortly after his incarceration. You can be sure I was at my desk early the next day.

A CID function in those days was to take fingerprints and photographs of all criminals locked up, prior to their court appearance. Yes, we did use actual ink and rollers. I visited Contini's cell and just sighed as we entered and handcuffed him. Just for fun, really. We took him towards my offices at the rear of the building and, as we approached, he made as if to go into my actual office, where all CID interviews take place. He had been in there so often it was routine to him.

I took him in and placed him in his usual seat across from me, and by this time the uniform sergeant with me was puzzled. An accused person cannot be interviewed after he's cautioned and charged. Any reply he makes to the charge is noted verbatim and he is in the hands of the justice system. But Charles thought he was to be interviewed and I didn't want to disappoint the guy.

There was no caution. I said, 'Just one question today, Mr Contini. I am craving a warrant to search your house this morning.

Is there any message you would like conveyed to your wife and family?' Considerate, I thought.

If looks could kill, I would have been dead on the spot. I did note the lack of his customary smirk, though.

He was sentenced to five years, and Rothesay was a much safer place without him, although there are always wannabes ready to step up.

About two years later, I was a detective with Strathclyde Crime Squad when the Barlinnie Prison rooftop riot kicked off. Supposedly, it was started over a disputed fried sausage at breakfast. As good a reason as any, I suppose, but a whole crowd ended up out on the prison roof. It was January and the West of Scotland was not only freezing, but under a thick blanket of snow for a good few days. The only downside was that some prison officers had been taken hostage and some were injured so that these clowns could enjoy their few days in the spotlight.

They had perpetrated a lot of damage within the prison walls and terrified the vast majority of inmates, who wanted nothing to do with the madness unfolding around them. A horrible situation all round, but inevitably it came to an end after a few days, and the cleaning up process began, as well as the police investigation, which would determine criminal cases against the perpetrators of the violence and damage. This is where we came in.

A team of squad detectives were sent to Barlinnie (not before time, some would say) and were allocated sections of the prison population to interview. My neighbour at the time was the DS Michael Langford Johnson. If he could have squeezed another name in it would have been Overtime, and we were allocated the task of interviewing the prisoners who had ended up in the hospital wing of the jail.

We were given an interview room and taken just down a corridor to a large waiting room where thirteen prisoners were seated in a semi-circle. I have been in prisons many times – on a professional basis, of course – and it is a special atmosphere of hate and contempt. I always found it strangely gratifying. Almost complimentary, I suppose. In a large group of prisoners like this, it's almost a competition between them to see who can hate us the most with their looks and body language.

We were met with a wall of growls and obscenities which were quickly subdued by the prison officers escorting us and, would you believe it, Charles Contini was among the group. Patience is a great virtue, for sure.

The prison officer read from a sheet and called out the first name to be interviewed, telling him to go with the CID officers. This was met by a loud protest.

'Fuck off, am no speaking to the scum.'

The officers present simply picked him up by his oxters and transported him across the floor, delivering him to us. He shook himself free and faced up to my neighbour, telling him, 'Am tellin yous fuck all by the way.'

Michael simply blew some cigar smoke in his face and we took an arm each, ready to drag him back down the corridor to our interview room. This was shaping up to be a long day, but when we were safely in the corridor with the waiting room door closed behind us, the wee shit changed entirely.

'Any chance of a fag, big man, am gasping.'

We couldn't shut him up for the next twenty minutes or so. He told us everything he knew. He was our best pal in the world and it was an act of persuasion to get him back to the waiting room. As we approached the door, he stopped and put his arms out for us to play our part. With a shrug, we took an arm each as before and frog marched him into the room, where his demeanour entirely reverted to that of before.

'Fuck off, ya scum bags. You'll get fuck all in here.'

He went back to his seat and joined in with the emanating hatred. What a place.

I had a quiet word with Michael Langford and my plan for Contini was hatched. I asked the prison officer to keep him until last. Interestingly, Contini had shown no sign of recognition towards me, and I had in turn ignored him completely.

The pattern continued; reluctant submission in the room full of their peers, and blatant sucking up as soon as we were alone with them. As long as we played this game, the operation went smoothly. At last, it was the turn of Mr Contini. Now, Contini had a nickname, as most of his ilk have, but I had always felt that nicknames were for their scummy mates and the press, not police officers. Throughout my career, I endeavoured never to call any ned by his nickname. On the contrary, I would deliberately use their full given name, and there were some real crackers. I actually hated it when colleagues referred to neds by their nicknames. Call me old fashioned, but to my mind it gave them unwarranted recognition and credence.

When Contini's name was finally called for interview, I played it exactly as I had with all of the others, and once safely in the corridor out of hearing from his mates, he asked me, 'How's it going, big man, how's Rothesay?'

We spent a pleasant forty-five minutes or so, much longer than all of the others had taken. Michael Langford was well aware of my intentions and he was the perfect guy to play the part. When we returned him to the room, we weren't holding on to him at all. We were smiling with him, still all good pals. Michael followed him over to his seat and touched his shoulder.

'Cheers, Chic, we'll sort something out for you, mate,' he said, deadpan.

I'm sure I waved to Contini as we exited and burst out laughing as soon as we were down the corridor. My only regret is not knowing how much grief I caused him. Our prison escort nearly died laughing when I told him the back story, and he had no doubt about the consequences.

'We might need to put him in protection.'

Not good protection, I hoped.

On that same enquiry, Michael and I were sent through to Edinburgh to get statements from senior prison staff. HMP were based there. Of course, we had to fit our work around office hours and this entailed having a lunch break (not often a consideration for working detectives). Michael Langford knew somewhere where we could enjoy a 'great pie and beans with a pint of real beer.' It wasn't a hard sell.

I have no idea where we ended up. It's possible my brain has sealed the part where these memories lie in order to protect my sanity. It was a long bar down the middle of the premises with punters sitting and standing either side and a small stage at the far end with a curtain. There were actually a few seats in front of the stage but I didn't notice that until the action started.

The place was busy, and getting busier as it neared the peak of lunchtime. I remember feeling lucky that we secured a couple of stools at the bar just in time. We ordered two pies and two pints as people crowded in behind us, and no sooner had I supped the head off my beer, when music began blaring from the speakers, lights went on over the wee stage and the curtains opened. To a huge roar of approval, a partially-clad young woman strode onto the stage and began gyrating to the music. This was met with howls and roars of approval from the clientele, including those sitting in the area directly in front of the stage. I looked at Michael and he was grinning from ear to ear. He had obviously been here before.

In these days of #MeToo and male enlightenment, when everyone's looks and body is exactly the same in all men's eyes, and it's only talent, personality and character that the opposite sex are evaluated by (or the same sex, all in between sexes, those who choose to be no sex whatsoever and anyone or person I've unintentionally forgotten to mention), I would obviously walk straight out and report this to some authority or other, but in those dark ages, we knew no better.

My day was only spoiled when we went to leave the establishment and I discovered that I had spilled beans and sauce all down my shirt front and tie. Served me right.

CHAPTER 42: THE PERFUME TEST

All good things must come to an end, as they say, and so it was with my partnership of two years with Donnie McQuade. We had been 'neighbours' on many major enquiries, strike partners on many football trips and matches, and confidants in many sticky situations. But our time was up. The shift patterns of the SCS were being jiggled about. There must have been a new boss and one of the consequences was tried-and-tested partnerships being broken up, as the new broom cleared the decks.

Our last shift together was a back shift at Pitt Street, which was thankfully uneventful and we went for a few pints together. Not an altogether unusual occurrence anyway, but on this occasion well justified. We alerted the night shift as to our movements and the hope that we could maybe get a wee lift home later if things remained calm on the city streets.

I'm not sure where we started off but we ended up in the old Warehouse (known with little affection as the Whorehouse) down by the side of the Clyde. It was a Thursday night and only moderately busy. We knew the proprietor and so it was a relatively safe environment for our parting speeches. We weren't looking for any excitement or drama, just a quiet drink together and to wish each other all the best for the future.

I should say at this stage that Donnie was six-foot-three, medium build and with a head of golden blonde hair. I was six-foot-one (I've now shrunk at least an inch) and obviously we were both 'suited and booted', having just finished a shift at Pitt Street. We were stood at the bar, had shared a laugh and a joke with the owner, and were not really interested in our surroundings when the barman came over and handed us a drink each.

'Those two ladies sent these over for you, gentlemen.'

Now, much as we thought of ourselves as elite detectives, we knew that was really just a cover story. Both Donnie and I always referred to the Serious Drinking Squad. No one was more aware than we were of the truth behind the façade that was the image portrayed to the public. We knew the actual horror stories behind suits and badges. Some of our colleagues were real fuck ups of just about every persuasion possible.

So, it must have been with absolute mouth-hanging-open puzzlement that McQuade and I looked up to find out who our benefactors were, suspecting some candid camera moment of piss take. There, smiling at us from the end of the bar, were two gorgeous creatures. I mean really nice, proper like. Not what you would expect. They certainly weren't charging by the hour. What's more, they walked over and introduced themselves to us.

What a nice evening we had. It transpired that one of them was a solicitor and the other a model. I had no problem believing that. She was about my height and absolutely stunning. More importantly, they were really nice and good company. To this day, I'm not entirely sure what was going on. I suspect they were just having fun, and being with us meant they wouldn't get pestered by every Tom, Dick and Harry. Just the two Dicks.

We had a few dances, a few more drinks, and we all laughed plenty. I remember one incident when the lawyer, who was kind of pairing off with Donnie, asked him if he were married. Now, to his credit, I have been in these situations a million times with McQuade, and he famously always produced a photograph of his wife, Irene, and his young family. Always. I've seen him do it on dance floors from Fife to Islay. But he hesitated on this occasion. They really were stunning women and although I knew I was totally out of my league, Donnie maybe had a wee doubt.

Whatever was going through his head, she didn't wait long for a response. She was rummaging in her handbag when she asked the question, and produced a perfume spray, pointed it right at him and proceeded to let him have both barrels. Of course, he leapt back and away from it, trying to brush it off his suit as he did so. The girls thought this was hilarious and was a great way of establishing a man's attachments or otherwise, and the veracity of his story.

There was no pretending, anyway. We had a nice time and when it came time to leave, I established that there were two-night shift squad cars outside, making sure that we didn't drive and got home safely. I told my new girlfriend, the super model by now, the situation and explained the cost of a lift home. A bargain was struck and we strolled out at closing time arm-in-arm.

I swear I will never forget the look on DS Bob Barrowman's face, together with my big mucka, Mike McKenna. Totally priceless. They were both stunned beyond belief, their wee faces jammed against the windscreen. Totally flabbergasted to see me strolling towards them with Miss World in tow. I was cool and blasé, pretending hardly to notice them. I swear their eyes were bulging and mouths hanging open. I got in the back with my new 'bird' and Donnie got into another car with the lawyer. No doubt, his chauffeurs were equally impressed.

My new friend made a nice show of cuddling up to me in the back of the car and we whispered and giggled all the way through Maryhill, where we dropped her off on the way to Dalmuir, where I stayed. Although it was only referred to once or twice over the following weeks or months, I know that without doubt the whole of the Crime Squad and hopefully much of the force CID heard the story about the two beautiful women McQuade and McLean pulled on their travels.

Donnie's story that night became a bit more tricky and much funnier. Having dropped of his lawyer friend he was dispatched at his lovely home in Uplawmoor, where his equally lovely wife, Irene, was asleep. As he crept upstairs and tried to get ready for bed quietly, he woke Irene, and I suspect the kids and neighbours as well. Irene immediately put the light on and asked him where on earth he had been till that time of night. It would be two o'clock or later by then.

Emboldened by the booze and his newly discovered status as a stud to beautiful women, Donnie proceeded to tell the truth.

'I was out with Simon. It was our last night working together, and we ended up at a nightclub. We were dancing with beautiful women and we had a great time. Now, go to sleep.'

Anyone who knew McQuade would understand this outburst of total honesty. He always found it almost impossible not to burst out with the truth, even in the most inappropriate of circumstances. Like then, half-drunk at two-thirty, to his half-asleep wife. Irene had been a police officer – a detective, in fact – so it took quite a lot to phase her, and she knew Donnie better than anyone. She chose to bide her time.

Donnie relates that he woke in the morning and was immediately confronted by Irene, her face hovering above him.

'What happened last night, then? You were quite drunk?'

Totally forgetting that he had blurted out the truth some three hours before, he now told the more traditional lie.

'It was our last night at work and some of the boys put up a few bottles after the shift.'

'And what about the nightclub, the beautiful girls and the dancing?'

He then proceeded to cut his losses and tell her the truth, the whole truth and something like the truth.

To his absolute shock and relief, Irene simply smiled and nodded knowingly. She, of course, knew the truth when she heard it. She then produced the suit he had been wearing and threw it on the bed.

'I believe you, although you are an arse. This perfume on your suit is far too expensive for any woman you could pull.'

I liked that story because it proved to me that it did happen. Sublime.

CHAPTER 43: MAGNUS

Some days simply go from bad to worse. Things just won't sit right. Nothing falls into place. Everything goes wrong pretty much from the minute you step out of bed, like maybe you got out on the wrong side. The worst of it is that these days never get any better.

I reckon you know in your heart within the first half hour or so, but you either persevere in the vain hope that it will turn around, or because you don't have any choice. This was one of the latter.

A routine surveillance job in the East End. A bar manager taking the weekend's takings to the nearby bank on a Monday morning, he was going to be accosted en-route in a lane behind the pub when he came out. We even had the number and make of the getaway car.

The lad, John, who had received the information from his 'tout' was to be closest to the pub in the back of a nondescript works van, with the rest of us in three or four unmarked vehicles on a tight perimeter. We were there a good hour before anything was due to go down. So far so good, and plenty of time for breakfast.

The first hint that this job was to be different was when John told us in coded message over the radio that the registration number of the getaway car had changed. This was baffling as John was securely ensconced in the rear of a supposed works van and, being the days before the proliferation of mobile phones, had no way of communicating with his informant. It later transpired that the informant had discreetly shuffled up beside the van and banged on the side, whispering (no doubt out the side of his mouth):

'The motors changed, by the way, he's usin anuther wan, so he is.'

He then proceeded to give the new registration number. You really couldn't make it up.

At or near to the appointed time, the bar manager left the pub and headed for the bank, his planned route taking him a shortcut through a residential back lane, and it was here that the robbery was to take place. We obviously had men in the lane, lying in wait, as well as manned vehicles at its end, and nearby, ready to close the perimeter quickly. I was in one of the perimeter cars with my colleague, Donnie McQuade. What could possibly go wrong?

To be absolutely honest, I have no idea what went wrong. The robbery (a snatch, in effect), took place and the rascal quickly realised that cops were everywhere. He ran away, a real dastardly move that seemed to have caught us unawares, still clutching the bag of money. It was real money. The actual takings, as no one had alerted the pub manager of what was going on.

In fairness, he ran in an unexpected direction, and not to his getaway car as expected. He ran down the lane for a bit then cut across some spare ground, over a fence, and along a railway track. I know this because I saw him running along the track pursued by a colleague, John Jackson, who I played football with. I knew John would catch him.

As we watched from the car, trying to find a spot to alight and join the action, I saw John gradually gain on the ned, who was visibly wilting. As John came up behind him it seemed he was ready to grab him, but instead I saw John raise a baseball bat over his shoulder, ready to bring the scoundrel down, both of them still running at a fair speed. John took an almighty backswing over his shoulder, too far over his shoulder, and proceeded to trip himself up with the bat catching his moving legs. And over he went in an absolute heap. The thief seemed to get new wind at this point and disappeared over the other side of the embankment, and off with the loot.

I doubt if any of us could have reacted, anyway, either because of our absolute disbelief at what we had just seen (he really could have just put out a hand and nabbed the guy) or because those of us who had witnessed this Keystone Cop moment were paralysed with laughter. Not our best operation, but this was only the start of the day.

The clever thief who was also an extremely fast runner and managed to evade about twelve plain clothes officers in a lane, was arrested from his bed at six-twenty the following day. Some two hundred pounds of the stolen two-thousand plus was recovered.

It wasn't even mid-morning and things were to get a lot worse. We were summoned back to Pitt Street immediately as one of the city centre casinos had just been the target of an armed robbery.

From memory, about forty-thousand pounds had been stolen, and it seemed to be generally acknowledged that a well-known family from Possilpark in Glasgow were the culprits. We also had a list of safe houses where they were thought to be headed with the loot, and off we all went, armed to the teeth now. I was still with Donnie, and also Donnie Hardie, another DS. Our car, plus one other, was to head to a house in the Southside, just off Cathcart Road in Govanhill.

Both cars arrived at the same time but there had been no reconnaissance, no planning, nothing. I think two were at the front and two were trying to make their way to the back of the property, but Donnie McQuade and I were at the ground floor tenement door. We chapped a few times and could hear some movement inside. Enough for us to suspect someone might need help (we had no warrant) and crash the door in. As we did so we heard a gigantic crash of broken glass and entered just in time to see a figure jump out the broken kitchen window at the rear.

We couldn't get through the locked rear close door and so ran out onto the street, but Donnie Hardy had the car keys, and he was in hot pursuit of the robber. My neighbour McQuade made an instant decision and proceeded to commandeer a civilian vehicle. He just stopped a car in the street and jumped in beside the driver, shouting in his face, 'Reverse, reverse, this is police business.' The driver, no doubt in shock, immediately did as he was told and reversed the vehicle at speed right back out of the street and onto the main road, right into the side of another vehicle heading south. Donnie just jumped out and joined me in the chase on foot, alas to no avail. Yet again, the bad guy was off into the wind.

We did save face somewhat by recovering thirty or forty-thousand pounds lying on the floor of the not so safe house, and caught up with the clever robber a few days later. He was subsequently convicted of armed robbery. It usually transpired that things worked out all right. We were the good guys, after all. Even the biggest fuck ups can be re-spun in the cold light of day, especially where the bad guys are eventually caught or, at the very least, some property is recovered.

In this instance, our biggest problem was the civilian vehicles that had been quite significantly damaged. Luckily, no one had been hurt (this was before the days of immediate litigation) and Donnie had promised the respective owners that their vehicles would be repaired. The gaffers had told him to get it done on the fly and it would be paid from petty cash funds. When he looked at me, we both knew there was only one solution. We went to see Magnus.

The late Magnus Mowetta had a repair and second hand sales garage in Havelock Street in Partick, Glasgow, when I was first introduced to him. I was taken there by a Crime Squad colleague who shall remain nameless. Not to protect his identity, but because he might come looking for commission. I did a lot of business with Magnus over the next thirty-six years right up until his untimely death from cancer in 2016.

Magnus was flying high when I met him around 1984. He had a serious garage unit under the tenements in Havelock Street, just off Byres Road in the busy West End of Glasgow. He had eight to ten mechanics working there, a slick sales operation moving second hand cars of every description, and if I say that he wasn't encumbered too much by administrative burdens, you will get my drift. Everything was cash, done with a nod and a wink, and always with the intention of maximising the immediate profit. He was raking it in.

He had all the trappings of his new-found wealth. A yacht berthed down at Inverkip, a Rolls Royce with his own plate, a new detached house outside Glasgow, and so on. He naturally had the women, who will always find something cute about you when you have a few million in the bank, the cigars and booze, and the inevitable accessory for every wealthy 'businessman' or individual. The hangers-on. The shady guys who always seemed to be lurking in the background, quietly manipulating everything to their own agendas. In this case, it was easy.

This success had come quickly to Magnus. He was enthralled by his new found popularity. His ego grew much faster than the business ever could, and this made him such easy pickings for the sober guys awaiting their chance. Unfortunately for Magnus, these were serious people, a bank manager and an accountant who had quickly secured the ear and confidence of their mark, and eventually left him high and dry with nothing. In fact, much, much less than nothing. Nothing would have been acceptable, manageable, re-doable. But he was left with more debt than could ever be managed and from that day on lived hand to mouth.

Throughout all of that, and spanning many years, he was our go-to guy when someone had a bump and a motor needed fixing. When I eventually left the police and ran my own security company, Magnus supplied me with a never-ending change of car for any given scenario on a day-to-day basis. He had arrangements with all sorts of people and companies till the day he passed, and his connections in Glasgow and beyond really were amazing. More than anyone I've ever known, Magnus knew the benefit of favours owed. He had helped so many people out of tricky situations over the years, and he could remember every one of them when need be. This included a large percentage of Strathclyde police, especially detectives, and in particular the ones who flew by the seat of their pants – the Ten Percent.

When I left Her Majesty's employ, I became involved in private security and personal protection, as well as conducting surveillance regularly, which meant vehicles were in constant use.

Magnus made sure that I always had ready access to everything he could source, which was just about anything at all.

CHAPTER 44: SURVEILLANCE

Of all the skills, methods or techniques I acquired during my police service, this was the one that was to become my calling. Some people are lucky enough to find their thing in life and this was mine. It seemed that everything I had learned surviving those early years in Possil, the elements involved in team sport, the confidence and posture required to perform and speak in public, all of it came together and enabled me to blend in to almost any background, or adopt a posture as required.

Over the years I've been a drunk, a minister, a doctor, a woman, a tramp, an arms dealer, a soldier, a drugs dealer, a beggar, a taxi driver, the owner of a nightclub, a pimp, a gay person, and on and on. I would be quicker listing the impersonations or guises I haven't adopted, including the most important and tricky one: the invisible man who no one notices at all. This was my calling and was to lead me ultimately into a world of which only the tiniest percentage of even the Ten Percent know. But it all started with that first one-week training course to help form and shape what was to become the Strathclyde Police Surveillance Unit, and if the Crime Squad was the sharp end, this was the wee pointy bit right at the end.

On the Friday, the last day of the course and day of assessment, we were given a scenario at Glasgow Airport and it was generally accepted that whoever had excelled during the weeks field training would be allocated the Commander for the test operation. They picked two of us as joint commanders, me and a lad from the drugs squad. Politics. This backfired dramatically when, in the fog of the early morning, we totally missed the targets and had to start all over. This was a direct result of there not being one commander, an outcome I had warned about and been ignored.

From that day on, I spent the vast majority of my time undercover, in one guise or another.

I was to thrive in this environment from the day we went to London and saw how the Major Crime and SAS guys did things, adopting many of their principles and systems to our daily routines. The surveillance operatives nationwide form an elite and exclusive community and we would regularly come into brief contact if operations overlapped. All of this was to inform my future, another story entirely.

Everything we did daily was, of course, confidential. We worked with the Special Branch, a number of Drugs Squads, The Scottish Crime Squad, the RUC, HMCE and the MET, and we could end up anywhere in the UK with no absolutely no notice. Often, we had no idea why we were actually on a job, and sometimes, if the SB or SS were involved, we never did find out.

One Friday afternoon, we were told that our weekend was cancelled. We were working on a job for the branch and would be briefed by them at one o'clock. We all trundled up to their floor of Pitt Street at the designated time, and were admitted to their corridor via a scanner where we had to wait like schoolboys. We were then admitted to a room in threes, the teams that would be in each car going in together. We were then taken over to a big whiteboard that ran the full length of a side wall, maybe twenty feet, but we could only see about two feet of it. The rest was curtained off.

The bit we could see had the known details of the person we would be watching all weekend: his picture, address, known relatives and associates, vehicles, etc. We were then issued side arms and sent on our way, and the next three-man team went in to see their wee bit of the board. They never told us why this guy was of interest or what he was suspected of. Nothing. Thankfully, it didn't matter too much because we heard later on Radio Clyde that the police all over the UK were on major alert because of a suspected terrorist plot coming to a head. We gleaned ten times more from Radio Clyde than from the Special Branch.

That weekend culminated in us raiding a lot of houses across the city and bringing suspects in for questioning, implementing the anti-terrorism legislation in place at that time. We kicked in doors, dealt with the mayhem, pointed guns at people, arrested them and dragged them off in front of their hysterical families, searched their homes upside down, and then processed them at whichever station we had been told to take them to, usually Stewart Street at that time. That was our job over. We had been accompanied by a Special Branch Officer throughout, who only observed and said nothing, and when all of the hard lifting was over, these guys moved in to speak to the detainees. Or do whatever they did. We had been told not to talk to them any more than was necessary.

On one job, on a Thursday, I remember we were doing a job for the MET, I think, and ended up in Liverpool quite late at night. The target went onto the ferry to Ireland but we were stood down in no uncertain terms, and when we had seen him safely of to the Emerald Isle, we were told to stay over in Liverpool and come back the next morning. We had been on-duty and driving for about sixteen hours by that time.

We had no change of clothes or suchlike and one of us went into a late-night shop or chemist and bought some razors and basic clean up stuff. We then all congregated at what was a nice hotel and checked in. It was nice enough to have a bell boy, who appeared totally confused at the complete lack of luggage between these ten or twelve guys (and one girl). Seeing his confusion, Donnie Hardy took him aside and explained that there was no luggage, but we did have a change of clothes. Simon was changing with him, Bill was changing with Eddie, and so on. He then handed him our wee bag of toiletries to give him something to do.

Naturally, a night in Liverpool wasn't to be wasted and so we hit a nightclub late on and had a few beers. We were all standing together near the bar when one of our number, I'll call him Ian, became a bit agitated. It transpired that he thought a gorgeous woman at the other end of the bar was looking at him too much and that she was obviously interested. After another drink and suitable persuasion, he meandered over to ask her what was on her mind. When he came scurrying back five minutes later, his face was a picture. It transpired that she had wanted him. Her proposition was that they would go back to her place and she would ensure he had something to remember. She was stunning and Ian couldn't believe his luck. The catch was that after he had his way with her, the guy behind her would have Ian, pointing to a massive black guy smiling at him. He never left our side for the rest of the night.

At that time, I was working with a good like-minded friend we'll call Tam here, when, one day, we were both summoned upstairs at Pitt Street. We were on the fourth floor, so upstairs was never a good thing. Thankfully, I had to go to court right away so, in the best traditions of the job, I buggered off. Tam was not best pleased, but what a tale he had to tell, so much so that he came to the Sheriff Court to share it with me, unsure what to do.

He had a typed letter from the Chief, signed and witnessed; a disclaimer, in effect. They had asked him to go undercover in a city centre 'Sauna Parlour' and find out what was going on with a view to raiding it later. Obviously, some graduate type upstairs had heard about these seedy goings-on from a neighbour over a barbeque or from a golf buddy and wanted the police involved. Anyone who actually knew anything knew that the law was a joke in this regard, the Fiscal was subsequently reluctant to proceed with anything, and the penalties, if any, were so paltry it was a total waste of time. None of that helped Tam.

His disclaimer stated that he must tell his wife or partner what he was doing and that if he caught anything it was nothing to do with the police. I'm sure Tam will still have it somewhere. This put him in a tight spot whether to say no and risk affecting his prospects moving forward, or say yes and subscribe to this crap. Together, we decided he would sign the disclaimer and keep a safe copy, do the job with me outside, keep it strictly to ourselves, and submit a negative report that killed the upstairs interest stone dead. That was exactly what occurred but Tam's real story of his undercover visit might be of interest.

He had been warmly welcomed by a beautiful woman and taken into a sauna where he had a good steam, on his own, for about ten or fifteen minutes. As he describes, in came the most stunning Asian girl, wearing a white short button up dress that he judged to be at least two sizes too small for her. Maybe they were short of personal protective equipment? His description was much more detailed. She smilingly invited him to accompany her and they went in next door where he was directed to lie down on a big massage table.

At this point, he's on his front, wearing nothing more than a towel wrapped around his waist and she proceeds to give him a thorough toe to shoulder massage. He's loving it, even more so because this delight is being paid for by Strathclyde Police, although he's worried about what he can put on the expenses claim form. This angel then asks him to turn over onto his back and as he does so his smile and the bulge in the towel indicate just how much he's enjoying this, and the girl giggles. As expected all along, she asks him:

'Oh dear, you like wank?'

I think Tam had a giggle himself. 'Please, that would be great.'

At which point, she goes to the door and leaves, telling him, 'OK. I be back in ten minute.'

Whether true or not, it was great fun.

Tam also told me the story of another enquiry, when a well-known male celebrity was alleged to be picking up rent boys in Glasgow City Centre. This nefarious activity – pre-internet, of course – was known to be prevalent around public toilet facilities and the locus in this instance was supposed to have been the underground unit on St Vincent Street, central indeed. As Tam tells it, he and his neighbour were making enquiries here and went down to speak with the janitor/caretaker guy.

'Do you get any gay men meeting down here at night?'

'Are you fucking kidding me? They're in here night and day,

snogging, giggling, touching each other up. I'm fed up chasing them away. It's got to the stage that if someone comes in here for a shite it's like a breath of fresh air.'

You must admit, even if he makes them up, they are still good.

CHAPTER 45: THE HIGH JUMP

Sometimes there was no time for a formal briefing before an operation. Crooks rarely gave us any warning of their intentions, which was totally inconvenient, although we happily had a never-ending list of touts or snitches who kept us relatively well informed. On this occasion, we had sketchy information via the drugs squad, who shared a corridor with us at Police HQ. They shared little else.

They had learned that a wanted male who had escaped from custody was about to leave the city driving a red Ford XR3. Naturally, we were anxious to recapture him and have him complete the remaining part of his twenty-four-year stretch. The problem was that they had three possible locations in and around Glasgow and insufficient manpower to cover them all. And so, we were drafted in as a last resort. I'm sure they considered every other avenue.

This was a 'good ned', a term we used throughout the force as a code for a bad ned. Clever, eh? He had already been stopped in a routine roadside check outside Lochgilphead in Argyll when he had produced a sawn-off shotgun and discharged a few rounds towards the unsuspecting traffic cops. Myself, and most of my colleagues, felt that this activity was due for consideration of legalisation, or even nomination as an Olympic sport, but strictly by the book it was frowned on. Somehow, these cops had also gleaned that he had no intention of being 'taken alive' and was intent on a shootout if it came to that. Or so their report said.

Being a blatantly serious threat to our lives, you would suspect a proportional response, but we were sent there straight from some other mission, and had only enough firearms for half of our number. So, we 'plotted up' around a Southside tenement, four cars in the perimeter, with a static van providing a direct visual on the ground floor flat. We were so short on the ground that we were told the detective inspector was coming to join us and that he, too, was armed. This was to be the first and last time in two years with the surveillance unit that I saw him outdoors. Until that point, I'm sure that his career résumé listed a fire drill evacuation from HQ as his total street experience so this was serious stuff. He had a DS leave us to pick him up (perhaps he'd forgotten how to drive) and so, in effect, we were a car and one man down at that point, when, at three o'clock precisely, we heard the words that triggered an instant adrenalin rush, as surely as Pavlov's dog would slaver when his Winalot was produced.

'Stand by.'

A red XR3 had pulled up outside the target flat and a male fitting our man's description had gone into the close, leaving the car running and the hatch back open. He was ready to join Ronnie Biggs and resurface as a celebrity years down the line!

At this point I have to convey our state of readiness that day, as on many other days, when our natural scepticism and cynicism helped us convince each other that we would soon be in the pub after another non-event. We had been working all day, usually from seven, and knew that the pubs were open. We had been allocated this job by the drug squad, who would surely have ensured that we had little or no chance of success as we would have had, had we been in their shoes. We were light handed and resented being a back up to those would-be detectives down the corridor, and since it was no doubt information gleaned from some low life junkie, and not by us, the chances of us engaging in any meaningful activity were as low as a traffic cop's IQ. Wrong yet again.

As usual, when the code for standby was announced by our watcher, concealed in our works van in the same street as the XR3, my colleague and I were reclining with cups of hot tea in our car, happily bemoaning the using we were getting by the hierarchy at HQ. We were instantly alert and ready to go, but could hear a familiar sound tinkling in the background of the day's normal sounds. The rising crescendo of young happy voices celebrating their freedom – the primary school directly across from the target address was spilling just at that minute.

The original intention had been to ambush our man as he came out of his flat, hopefully laden with his worldly belongings, leaving him no hands to work his arsenal of cop-killing guns, but the thought of youngsters running around pointing at us and asking those daft questions put paid to that. No matter how hard-nosed a cop becomes, he will always respond to an innocent tot asking, 'Are you a real policeman?'

We would all have been kneeling, smiling and chatting as our baddie drove off.

And so, we had to follow him, as he appeared a few minutes later, packed his few boxes in the car and drove off without a care. He drove sedately, well within the speed limit, as a desperado anxious to avoid the attention of the police or any authority would, unwittingly closely pursued by a convoy of incredulous detectives. I was in the passenger seat of our car, with my mate, Willie Wilson, driving and it was only now that the flaw in our designations became apparent. Willie had the firearm. We had no time to dwell on that problem as we interfaced with our colleagues over the radio, switching pole position behind the target at every natural opportunity, such as lights or crossings. The most difficult follows are those at slow speeds.

That five- or ten-minute pursuit seemed to take forever, steadily heading south, knowing that at any time the target could get suspicious and speed off, or worse still get out and start blasting away at us and passers-by. I had little awareness of the convoy behind us as we took up pole position immediately behind the XR3 for the first time, but as we headed into the quieter suburbs I became acutely aware of the only tool at my disposal, an old and worn 'snoopy', as it was termed in those days (a baseball bat to everyone else). It would have given me more comfort if I could have figured out how to load it.

As the traffic thinned, we saw the XR3 indicate right into Waterside Street and it became obvious that this was as quiet a location as we were likely to find to effect an arrest. No sooner had we turned the corner behind him when the shout came over loud and clear.

'Take him, take him! Hit, hit, hit!'

Willie immediately gunned our old cavalier and overtook the target, who had thankfully maintained his speed in his confusion. And as we pulled ahead of the Ford, Willie yanked to the left, forcing the target into the verge and onto the pavement, jammed against our offside wing and a wall.

Remember, Willie had the gun and I was vaguely aware of him scrambling for his seat belt release as I jumped out, and if I said my actions were in any way considered or planned, I would be lying. Acting purely on impulse, I jumped onto the bonnet of the XR3 and proceeded to smash the XR3's windscreen with my trusty 'snoopy', my sole intention being to disorientate the scumbag inside until someone else could do something smart. I remember looking to my left expecting to see Willie pointing his shooter at the head of the driver. He was nowhere to be seen. I had heard a loud bang as I came out of the cavalier, and assumed that this had been caused by the unmarked car behind the XR3, as I saw that he had rammed into him from behind, seemingly with the same purpose of distraction as I had.

Within seconds there were colleagues in both sides of the Ford and the suspect was eventually prised from within. I say eventually because, as usual, he had been handcuffed by about at least two officers on each side and still had his seatbelt on. I don't remember who solved the Rubik's cube puzzle to disentangle him, but he was certainly going nowhere.

The relief at these times is immense. Feeling suitably elated, I casually placed the 'snoopy' back in the boot of our car and wandered up to the junction behind us to stop any civilian vehicles or pedestrians coming into the street, knowing that the forensic analysis of our actions would now begin. Followed inevitably by all of the criticisms and smart assed assessments of how things could have been handled so much better.

At times like these, and I was involved in many in my years in plain clothes, the follow-up investigation into the actions of the arresting officers is every bit as thorough as any murder enquiry and always with the benefit of hindsight. It is also conducted by senior officers who invariably have never ever put their own life on the line and been forced to make decisions away from their desk and without their telephone handy to consult, hold a few meetings, delegate as required or pass the buck upwards, and, in effect, make sure their ass is covered to the nth degree. The other Ten Percent ...

I was happily directing traffic away from the scene, where our whole convoy was concertinaed up behind the takedown site, when Willie, my chauffeur for the day, appeared in an agitated state. I hadn't seen him since I jumped out of the car wielding my 'basie', which, in my head, had already become my police issue truncheon.

'Where the fuck have you been?'

He began rambling on about guns and shots being fired but, to be honest, was making no sense. Reluctantly, I left my mundane and comforting task of traffic control to the many uniform units now in attendance and returned to the locus with Willie. He showed me a bullet hole in the passenger side of the windscreen of the second police car that had rammed the XR3 from behind. Only then did I notice our DI, who had been the passenger in this car, looking decidedly pale and shaken. To be honest, I first put this down to never having seen him in natural light before.

Then Willie told me about the takedown from his perspective. As he had got out of his side of the car, a few seconds after my exit due to having to bring the vehicle to a halt, he heard and saw a round being fired from the second police vehicle as it rammed the target car. He had assumed that whoever was in it had decided to shoot and ask questions later, which was certainly never in the plan, and wisely decided to get himself out of the firing line. He had run across the road for cover.

It transpired that our DI, being driven to the original stake out by the DS (no doubt in the safe knowledge that we had no chance of being involved in any action, given that the drugs squad had given us the turn), found himself tagging straight into the follow. He had his gun in his hands with his finger on the trigger when the takedown occurred. He had no experience of such intense action and was completely caught off guard when his driver, John Severiano Michael (he gave himself that nickname, but played off a poor sixteen), rammed the target vehicle without hesitation.

The DI's gun had gone off, shooting the hole in his windscreen, which was quite funny at first, until we figured out that I was, in all likelihood, jumping onto the bonnet of the Ford at that precise time. The bullet was later found in a garden a few hundred yards away and the ballistics boys took great delight in telling me that it had actually missed me by just over a foot.

Our trigger-happy DI was the only person missing when we congregated to debrief back at HQ, and discovered that our Superintendent Joe Jackson had left a massive carry out for us to do things properly. He made sure we were fully aware of the internal investigation already under way, and that the following day the report would have to be meticulous and rigid and that was the first purpose of these debrief sessions, to ensure that everyone knew their part and statement. This was second nature to us and much more galling looking back than at the time.

There's a general acceptance in the force, and in every law enforcement agency world-wide in my experience, that the only praise or congratulation comes from your immediate peers who were there when the action went down. Only they share the knowledge of the fear and rush involved in these activities and that can never be understood and, thus, acknowledged by someone with no such experience. We were fortunate that Joe Jackson understood these things fully and, like any exceptional leader, had our backs as far as was possible.

As I was to rediscover many times, the massive carry out had a real purpose to serve, allowing us to relax, unwind and go over the details from everyone's individual perspective. Effectively sharing the emotions we had all felt, but could never convey to outsiders who hadn't been involved. This includes spouses, family and the closest of friends, who could only relate the story to an episode of the Sweeney. By the time we had polished off the booze between us, we had found many funny stories and exhausted the jokes about the DI's premature discharge, but we had shared and come to terms with ourselves, and reinforced much about each other and the trust we had to have in each other for the next time, which was never far away.

The most incredible and hilarious story to emerge that day was from the vehicles making up the convoy behind us and the DI's ramming vehicle. As they turned that last corner, they saw that we had jammed the vehicle into a lamp post on the pavement (news to me) and they saw the second car ram into the target. At that point, all were aware of Willie getting out of our driver's door, taking one look at the XR3, and running across the road. He proceeded to leap over the hedge into a garden, his firearm flailing all the way. What made this extraordinary was that the hedge was at least eight-foot three-inches high, and they all swear that he cleared it comfortably!

The world record high jump at that time was two-metres forty-two, or almost eight feet, held by the Swede, Patrick Sjoberg, but we all know that Willie Wilson of Scotland was the unofficial high jump champion of the world. By a stretch.

CHAPTER 46: POLICE SHOOTINGS

A Spanish Policeman shot dead four terrorists following the horrific Barcelona attacks. This was announced on every news channel under the sun, but always as a throwaway line in the tale of the bigger picture. The many bereaved, the dozens injured, even the deaths of the terrorists themselves, being commented on, dissected, probed and scrutinized by the media – and rightly so. 'Four terrorists were shot dead by Spanish police', 'Police shot dead a suspected terrorist today on London Bridge' and, recently, here in Glasgow, 'Six people were injured today in a Glasgow City Centre Hotel where asylum seekers were resident. The culprit was shot dead by the police.'

I invariably find myself thinking about the police officers who had been forced to discharge their firearms and take human lives, in order to protect us all. I suspect their lives are also changed forever by those events and the decisions they had to make that day, but they only get a passing mention, as if that's just their job. It's routine. If putting someone in a cell can cause pause for thought and delivering a death message can be emotionally challenging, imagine having to pull the trigger and kill another human being. I can assure you that it is a life changing event. That was certainly the case in Glasgow when a friend of mine was forced to open fire.

There had been a series of armed robberies, all perpetrated on licensed premises around six on Sunday evenings, before opening time at six-thirty. In those days, pubs closed on Sunday afternoons. How old world.

The M.O was identical in each instance. They would enter while staff were getting organized for the Sunday evening shift, hold them at gun point before tying them up, gagging them and emptying the contents of the safe and tills, etc. This had happened two or three times on consecutive Sundays and the pubs targeted were spread all over Glasgow.

In those days, Crime Intelligence was localised. There were seven city police divisions: 'A' Division (The City Centre), 'B' (Partick/Clydebank), 'C' (Maryhill/Milngavie), 'D' (Baird Street and the north), 'E' (London Road and the east), 'F' (Craigie Street/Castlemilk and the south), and 'G' (Govan, Pollok and Giffnock). Each had its own collator, a senior cop who had usually worked the division for most of his or her service, and who kept a card index full of information he would glean from police reports and suchlike. I knew every collator and CID clerk in the city because I knew that the neds weren't aware of the divisional boundaries we had drawn, or if they were, they were deliberately flouting them over and over. This Sunday team certainly were.

The pubs they were targeting were all over the city, even into Lanarkshire, and so it was impossible for anyone from the CID office to investigate all of the robberies effectively and, rather than set up a designated team, they appointed one already in place: the Serious Crime Squad Surveillance Unit.

We treated it like a major enquiry, collating all of the information, working the streets, interviewing witnesses in minute detail and, after a few weeks and two more robberies, we had a solid lead. The barmaid, who worked in a city centre bar, had left one fingerprint on a plastic bag that we had found discarded in the bin outside the pub as they made their getaway. A witness at a bus stop on the last job had seen them leave the side door with their masks on and, before getting into a black Hack taxi waiting outside, the barmaid had thrown the bag into the bin. Despite having gloves on, she'd obviously handled the bag earlier.

We had no registration for the hack, and knew that it surely had false plates on at the time. Another baffling part was that the description of the taxi driver was of an elderly woman with a hat on. There weren't many of them about. With a lack of enough evidence as yet, we decided to 'take on' this woman (a surveillance operation) from her home address and see where she led us day-to-day. We had her home address in the West End and, about two o'clock on that first day, we followed her to that city centre bar. All good so far, but as we began to discuss who would be entering the bar undercover, there was one detail preventing a rush of volunteers. Even Baldrick and I weren't keen, and we were usually the first to step forward. It was a renowned gay bar, and there were actually only a handful of them in Glasgow in those days.

Our gaffers showed leadership and decisiveness, exerting their authority on the matter, and we drew lots. Out popped Arthur Chatfield and Eddie McCusker. They were immediately designated Art and Ted, which is, perhaps, what inspired Ant and Dec later. We concocted a simple cover story, and had great laughs doing so, but basically they were boyfriends with some time off, Chatfield with his long ZZ Top beard and Eddie with his boyish good looks. They made a lovely couple actually.

I'm not sure how long they drew this out. Drinking and playing pool all day seemed to suit the pair of them, but the target barmaid didn't make a move, a visit or talk to anyone that we weren't aware of that week. Although it's quite tedious hanging around in cars surrounding the pub, we were kept quite busy following punters, identifying them, as well as other staff members, and keeping meticulous photographic records of everyone, their habits and movements.

The only tricky incident they encountered inside the pub was again caused by drink and pool, similar to my experience in the Oban operation. Ted and Art fell out playing pool. They had a loud argument and were just getting to the point of exchanging blows when they were separated by concerned staff and clientele. Ted stormed off to the toilet, but as he was at the urinal, a regular punter came up behind him, put his hand on his shoulder, and told him not to be upset. Art was a bitch and he was too good for him. I'm not sure how much of the lengthy story I believe, as we were all good at stories, but I do believe the part where he rushed to make up with Chatfield as quickly as possible, and they never fell out in that pub afterwards.

On the Saturday we got the break we had earned. Among the plethora of statements and details gathered and collated was the fact that, on every job, witnesses described the guns having been taken out of a large black Adidas holdall, distinctive with the three-stripe logo. It was a feature of every robbery, but its significance only slammed home when a male was seen walking into the pub we had under surveillance, carrying what no one of us doubted was the actual holdall. It didn't leave with him later, but we certainly did.

We housed him in Maryhill in a busy street of big tenement buildings. There also happened to be a Hackney Taxi on the street, and so, after consultations with all sorts of bosses and the Fiscal, it was agreed that we would draw side arms, maintain a watching brief overnight, and have a full armed surveillance team in place the following day in order to catch them en-route to their next robbery. We wanted the whole team together, tooled up, and with all of their gear.

An armed hit is an unpredictable thing. I know it looks routine on the Sweeney, and it more or less is in the States, where everyone's carrying all the time, but in Scotland, it's something that only a few of us ever get involved in, and rarely at that. We just do our best and, on this occasion, we saw the bag leave the pub, we saw the robbery team get into the Hackney, and we followed it for a mile or so heading into town. It was there that the decision to intervene was made, as it was possible that their target pub was nearby, and we certainly didn't want civilians being involved, or a gunfight breaking out.

I was driving on this occasion and so was stuck behind the wheel (hoping someone would run and I could run him over), watching the whole thing unfold in front of me. When the Hack stopped at the lights, a car pulled in front of it, blocking its progress and I pulled up directly behind another of our cars which, in turn, was inches from the taxi's rear bumper. Our passengers then jumped out pointing their firearms and shouting at the occupants. The main bad guy, he who we'd seen with the bag of guns, then stood up and pointed a sawn-off shotgun at my colleagues on the offside. This happened to be a DS Les Darling.

Before he could discharge the shotgun, he was shot by another colleague on the nearside of the taxi by DC George Adair. One shot, in the backside, non-fatal unfortunately. George possibly saved Les' life, although Les always maintained he was just about to pull the trigger. The occupants were all quickly apprehended and whisked off to the nick, mostly by our uniform colleagues, who had been in and around the vicinity of Charing X. You see, we all had to remain in situ, pending bosses descending on the locus to second guess every decision made. This especially included George Adair, who had the audacity to actually discharge a firearm.

This case went to trial, and the High Court proceedings were flawless. We all gave evidence but last in the witness box was DS Donnie Hardie, who had been in charge of the takedown. He was superb. Our training was always to shout a warning 'armed police, stop' and to then double tap the target. Always double tap. Bang, bang. Always aim to kill, always double tap. If it's got to the stage where you have to shoot, you shoot to kill. Just like our baton training as rookies – if you take your baton out, you use it. You don't wave it about as a threat or it will be taken off you and used on you, so if it comes out, you are using it, end of. Same as the gun. If I really have to shoot you, I'm killing you. But George only shot him once. Not much of an anomaly, but anything can be used to cast reasonable doubt, and lawyers will do just about anything to do so. That's their job.

Donnie negated all of that by doing a clever thing. He told the truth. Yes, George and others had shouted 'armed police, stop' repeatedly, but when the ned bent down, George had shouted something like, 'Fucking freeze, ya motherfucker.'

This was real. This was believable. The jury loved it.

As for the one round discharged, Donnie explained that, because everyone had got out of their police cars, we had set up an Irish firing squad, with every officer having other officers in their line of fire. This is why George had only fired one round, against all protocol and procedures. George followed his lead in the witness box and told it as it was and, by the time the prosecution case was over, we had all resigned ourselves to whatever verdict the jury deemed fit. We didn't care. We were all alive and the job had been done the best we knew how. No one else in that esteemed room would ever put their lives on the line and make the hard decisions we had to make.

We needn't have worried. They were all found guilty, even the mother driving the taxi for them. The scumbag had refused to do a deal to help his mum, who had only gone along because she was so scared of him. The trial was, I suppose, a success, but as usual the whole thing was badly tainted by how it was handled by our hierarchy. They really were total wankers when it came to compassion, understanding or welfare. We were all taken to different offices to be interviewed, in order that there would be no collusion. George was treated as an accused for at least a month, only he was never afforded the rights that a ned would be. He was suspended and left at home. He was never counselled or shown any compassion. He was never even allowed to just talk it over with us and wind down.

George Adair was never the same man in my eyes. His health deteriorated; he became distracted all the time. I'm sure he began drinking more and basically the person we had known was replaced by a shell of the man. That's how I and many of his colleagues saw it and the blame was laid squarely at the feet of Strathclyde Police and, in particular, senior officers who had never done anything more risky than dodge a day at university, and had no idea how we looked after our own at the front line.

We knew this in the various plain clothes squads I worked with. We were the Ten Percent who were at the coal face, dealing with the realities of serious, organized and dangerous crime. But that was our choice and, in the surveillance unit, actively pursuing and hunting down the most dangerous of criminals, we knew that no one had our backs. No one even understood what we did on a day-to-day basis. How could they? They'd never been there. We didn't care. We were making a difference and, in our minds, living life to the full. At the sharp end.

CHAPTER 47: HOSTAGES

This day started like any other in the surveillance unit. You woke up and, from then on, it was mayhem, usually started by a phone ringing in your ear at stupid o'clock: 'Office, quick as you can.'

Here we go again. But this was different. Hostages had been taken, that much was clear, but the whole thing was just beginning to blow up as we hit the streets and, to be honest, it was an on-the-go briefing; things were developing so fast. We were all tooled up and plotted up in Ibrox, awaiting instruction. We were told that the family of a security van driver had been taken hostage at gun point and taken to an unknown location. The driver was then told to go to his work and drive his security van as normal, picking up all of the money he would normally collect on his round and, at the end of his shift, a car would be waiting for him to follow and hand over the cash. If he did so, his family would be released without harm, and he would be released. If not …

Bravely or stupidly, there's always a fine dividing line between the two, usually drawn after the outcome is known, the guard had called the police, and when he left the yard on schedule, he had an armed police officer driving, kitted out as a security man. By this time, I was sitting behind the wheel of a nice Ford Sapphire with DC John Gillan beside me. We had written down the brief details, including the reg number and identifier of the security van, and were waiting for it to come out of the nearby depot. The problem was that, as the day's business got under way, there were loads of these similar trucks on the move.

John and I had just settled with our McDonald's coffees, sports pages on standby, when another bloody security truck went by. John was spotting them with binoculars from quite a distance, but it wasn't ours. We let it go. For whatever reason, I took the binoculars to have a swatch and give John a break. I centred on that same van as it disappeared southwards over the horizon.

'John, I think that was it.'

'Fuck off, big man. Do you think?'

With nothing to lose, I was off in pursuit but it took us a good five minutes to catch the van up and, sure enough, it was the target. This turned out to be an insightful tactic of ours, as it transpired much later that the armed robbers were watching the van and its progress from nearby high flats, and they were reassured that there was no one following it. Little did they know that the followers were just idiots.

We were relaying our position, all in code, and our transmissions were being monitored by the bosses back in Pitt Street as our convoy of surveillance vehicles followed the truck all over Lanarkshire, making its routine stops and loading up with cash. It was a long, tense day, because as each drop passed, we were getting ready for the bad guys to make their move. It would have made sense for them to intercept the van in the countryside and take what had been collected, already many thousands of pounds. But, as always, they were greedy and waited until the last pick up had been made, in Motherwell, and the van was almost back at its depot.

They had just come off the M8 at Govan when a car pulled in front of the truck and hand signalled for him to follow, turning left towards Cardonald rather than right to the security yard. Again, this could be seen from the high flats. The truck then followed the car, with us ever closer together behind the truck, along Paisley Road and up Berryknowes Road, taking the entrance into the cemetery. The lead car stopped about fifty yards into the grounds and out the driver got from the truck, with his balaclava on, to collect his money. His face was a picture when he saw our cars come skidding to a stop beside and behind the security truck, and about a dozen armed madmen come running towards him. Rather than start shooting, because he had a hand gun in his hand, he did what I would have done and ran off into the graveyard.

All of our team gave chase, but I veered off quickly, realising that if he was going to shoot, it would be at the pack. My excuse later was that I was heading him off, which I did. It took the wee shit a while to progress through the grave yard, hiding behind grave stones, being shouted at to throw down his gun, and generally playing hide and seek, while he decided whether to shoot it out. At this point, he had no money, and obviously still had to answer to his pals who were holding hostages and expecting him to secure their pay day.

This gave me plenty of time to get ahead of him, and by the time he got near the exit gate, he could see me, gun pointed at him (or in his general direction) and he put his hands up. He was swiftly grounded, disarmed, cuffed and conveyed back to Orkney Street. John Gillan and I took a leisurely stroll through the gravestones, checking whether he had left any evidence behind, and, consequently, we must have been about ten minutes later arriving at Orkney Street than everyone else.

As we walked in to what was to become my work station soon, we could hear screaming coming from inside. Orkney Street had a huge marble staircase leading up to the CID level on the first floor, and the shouting and pleas for mercy got even worse as we entered the hall way. As we started to climb the stairs, I saw the source of the noise. The wee ned driver was hanging upside down over the banister with a senior detective holding onto his ankles.

'Let him go boss,' I shouted. 'He was gonnae shoot me.'

With some help from ashen faced detectives, he was brought back over the banister and, within a few minutes, we were told the address where the hostages were being held, seven flights up in the high flats. Off we all went again, this time surrounding the flats to keep them secure, while the police helicopter, the armed response unit, and every spare Tom, Dick and Harry created a perimeter around the flat in question. So started some serious negotiations.

I'm not sure what communications were set up or exactly how things went. We were really just providing the first ring of firearm cover until the proper guys for that role could be dispersed. That usually took about six hours to accomplish. No exaggeration. George (Baldrick) and I were sent to a stairwell. We jammed the door open and it was pitch dark inside. It was sunny outside so we were sitting targets right away. We took up positions either side of the door, guns drawn, ready to confront anyone trying to escape, and also prevent anyone from going up the stairwell.

We were there for ages, hours maybe, I don't know. It was warm and sunny. We were tired, hungry and really thirsty and the time just dragged by with nothing happening. I had a theory about police negotiators. I know that in movies they're usually charismatic, funny, brave and sharp witted. Ours were the most boring guys, who spoke only in monotones. They were the last guys you wanted to get lumbered beside in the pub or, God forbid, in a police car on a night shift. This was a deliberate ruse to bore the crooks into submission. Only a theory, but I think it stood up.

At one point, George and I were roused from our coma by footsteps coming down the stairwell. They were quite distinct but still some levels away. Perhaps seven? We could hear them get louder and we both stood back pointing our weapons at the dark void of the close. George started shouting.

'Armed police. Stop on the stairwell now. We are armed police.'

No effect. If anything, the footsteps were getting even quicker and certainly louder as they descended. My turn.

'Armed police. Will the person on the stairs stop? You are in danger. Armed police officers are here.'

All of a sudden, the moment was upon us and out of the pitch dark came a figure running straight past us, crying and in obvious distress. It took me until he was passing me to register it was a wee boy about ten years old. Why didn't we shoot him? If he had been carrying a shotgun, we would both have been in the city mortuary that night instead of the pub. We should have shot him, at least one of us. Did some subconscious process calculate that it was too light a footstep to be a grown robber? Did we get just enough of a glimpse as he came out to make a decision? Who knows? But we lived to tell the tale and that was always the yardstick with which I measured my success or failure in those days.

Around six-twenty, the hostages were released and we got to arrest the baddies; one was well-known to me. I had put him away for a long time for robberies, but he had escaped. I know the time of the release as we then learned that he had wanted to wait until the evening news before surrendering. He wanted to be on the telly. Not the brightest.

We were stood down, and George and I made our way to a well-known Govan shop where we could get some filled rolls and a coffee. We'd had nothing all day, and you don't want to be drinking copious amounts of celebratory alcohol on an empty tummy.

As we waited for the food, the woman in the shop went into the back and left us unattended for several minutes. This being Govan, and this being Baldrick, he said to the woman, 'I think it's a bit risky leaving the shop front and till unattended at this time of day with two strangers in the store.'

She just smiled and, pointing at his arm, said, 'If we cannae trust you guys, it's a really bad day, son.'

We still had our police arm bands on, worn by plain clothes officers when firearms are carried or drawn. Govan shopkeepers are astute.

I had now spent four years in the Squad, in a role that was normally a maximum three-year stint. I had spent time working with the drugs squad, with crime intelligence when football casuals were travelling the continent causing mayhem, and the last eighteen months or so as part of the target team or surveillance unit. I'd had enough. Even the high-octane operations we were mounting were becoming mundane to a degree and that is a serious and dangerous state of affairs. In these life and death situations, every member of the team has to be fully switched on and alert. I was losing that edge through a combination of factors.

A lot of my colleagues had moved on. We had instigated the surveillance unit and its day-to-day running, and it was time to pass that baton on. I was sick of carrying a gun. The incident with the wee boy had upset me because I knew that if one of us had shot him, we would have been castigated and thrown to the wolves, but also that we were wrong not to open fire. I was getting involved with the Cystic Fibrosis Research Trust and enjoying the fundraising and public speaking aspects of that cause, which was obviously dear to my heart. I also had three young children at home.

I was given a choice of office to move to as I had never worked a city office and, although I was tempted by Partick, closest to where I had grown up, I opted for the busiest division in the city, just across the water in Govan. This was to prove an inspired choice and I was given a licence to put all of my experience and skills to good use.

PART FOUR: GOVAN

CHAPTER 48: THE BEAUTIFUL GAME – GOVAN TEAM

By this stage, I was always injured. In actual fact, my left knee would swell like a balloon after games and I was walking with a pronounced limp. I had been climbing the old metal, spiral staircase at Orkney Street one night when the police casualty surgeon (the doctor on call) shouted me back down the staircase. The conversation went something like this:

'Why are you limping, Detective?'

'Am I, Doc?'

'Yes, you are. Now, what have you done?'

'Nothing, Doctor, just the usual sore knee after football.'

He sighed and proceeded to examine my knee and prescribed a drug that was to become my best friend and remains so till this day. I keep it in the cupboard for emergencies. God bless Ibuprofen. This allowed me to continue playing football then, although I did have a sobering chat with the police doctor not long after that. I had gone to him to perpetrate what to me was an elaborate scam.

We were swamped at Govan. It really was relentless and at Glasgow Sheriff Court one day I got chatting to an old football pal who had just come back from a place called Harrogate, in Yorkshire. There were two places where you could guarantee meeting cops from all over the force. The first was the Sheriff Court in Glasgow, where hundreds of cops would attend every morning at nine-thirty, ready and prepared, for the most part, to give evidence. The truth is that about five percent actually did so, and that may well be a gross exaggeration. The problem was that you couldn't ever assume that you wouldn't be called, and so the preparation had to be done in every case. There was no rhyme or reason and no cognisance given to shifts or other duties, and so you could be there every day straight off the night shift each morning. Just your luck, but when you were awake and functioning, it was a real catch up and networking opportunity.

The other place wasn't too far away, just down the road in Govanhill. Nan's Dairy on Inglefield Street was a famous rendezvous for cops of all ranks and from far and wide. East Kilbride, the West End, Shettleston even, and my one-time neighbour at Govan, Ross McLellan, needed a Nan's roll before he could function properly in the morning. Nan Caldwell had opened the dairy in 1973 and it was always queued out the door. She just had that cheeky no-nonsense way with her that appealed to the working men of the city and she once told me that they were shifting over a thousand rolls per day. She was a rascal and, although sadly missed by everyone since her passing in 2011, her son, Billy, and his wife, Marie, have maintained all of her standards, and Nan Caldwell's Dairy still thrives today.

Criminal Intelligence in those days was basic at best and still relied on index card technology. Each division had its own collator, making eight collators in Glasgow alone, each individual entity happily recording all sorts of information, but stopping at the imaginary boundaries invented by planners somewhere, as if the neds couldn't cross over between Maryhill and Partick, or Govan and Paisley. A joke, really, with hindsight. Places like Nan's, with its long queues of cops, were ideal places to exchange information, and I solved or helped solve many mysteries standing there. I also recruited a cop from Castlemilk who could pass for a junkie. He was totally emaciated and born for the role and, when I got him dressed for the part, he could score smack at any dealer's door. What an asset he was for a while. I wonder what happened to him. Back on the drugs, perhaps.

So, this lad in court told me about Harrogate and, more specifically, the police convalescence home situated there. He mentioned that the police doctor sent him because he was stressed and he'd enjoyed a fantastic week of rest, socialising, good food and even physio. He also told me how to play it with Doctor McLay, the police doctor, and so I made an appointment.

I thought I was at it. I thought I was acting. I told him about my swelling knee and my miracle drug, Ibuprofen, and also about the relentless pressure we were under at Govan CID. My cover story was to get help for my sore knee, but have him convinced that I also needed a break at Harrogate. I really just wanted a week 'off the book' and, in retrospect, I'm sure the old Doc knew just fine what I was up to. But I didn't have to fake my reaction when he told me that he had a cure for my knee that would mean no more pain, and no more Ibuprofen with all of its possible side effects, of which I was totally oblivious. This was really good news, even better than a week of leisure down south.

'So, what's this cure, Doctor?'

'Just stop playing football, Simon.'

That's what he told me. That was his cure. He was deadly serious. Just stop playing football. What a joke. He went on to explain to me that it was entirely my choice, but I should know the consequences of continuing to play. He obviously didn't grasp how integral I was to the team. How had that escaped his attention?

He explained that, in his judgement, if I kept playing at the level I was, I would need a new knee by the time I was fifty years old, which admittedly seemed quite far off at that time. It still does, looking back the way now. More sobering was the information that knee operations were not among the most successful procedures and that, in any event, I could only reasonably expect to get seven years or so from the replacement, when it could be done again, with all of the risks. Then seven years after that, I would be fortunate if there was enough material left around the joint to replace it for a third time. There would be no fourth replacement.

Dr McClay then asked me about work and, here, I could tell him the truth because Govan really was madness. I was so busy thinking about having to give up football that I almost missed

him telling me that I was to go the Harrogate for intensive physiotherapy and a change of scenery for a fortnight. I protested, and
must have done a good job.

'I couldn't possibly take two weeks away from work, Doctor,
we're far too busy.'

Just as I had been briefed, he was adamant and firm with me.
He ordered me to go. No one could argue with the police doctor.
If he said I was going on holiday for two weeks, then that was it,
job done. Ya beauty.

Harrogate: what a jaunt it was. Two weeks of convalescence,
full board, single rooms, fantastic sports facilities, a beautiful
pool, sauna, steam room, you name it. Even a crew of top-notch
physiotherapists on hand with all the mod cons of ultra sound
and electronic massage. Oh, and the laid-back attitude of the staff
and superintendent in charge, which we couldn't have made up if
we tried. Here's an example …

A lad who was to become a close friend over that period, and
way beyond, Gary Murphy, went for a pint on that first Monday
at lunchtime. A few of us congregated at the local and one thing
led to another. I do remember a few taxis appearing for Murphy,
and him going out, paying them the fare and coming back in
again. He was a real Irishman.

I also remember him telling us a story about his mate being
killed on the streets of Belfast. This was the mid-eighties. The
crowd of us lunch-time revellers, about six to eight of us, were
enthralled and hushed into respectful silence as he told us of how
his lifelong friend was shot in the head and died there in his arms.
Someone bought a round and the following comment was made:

'Who gives a shit about money when your colleagues are
being shot to death?'

That sentence cost me a lot of money over the next two weeks.
I also remember misquoting it when I eventually got back to
Glasgow:

'Who gives a shit about colleagues being shot to death when
you've no fucking money?'

That gives the reader a clue as to the misadventures of that fortnight, which was in no way a recuperation. Thanks to Gary and our partner in crime, 'Big Phil', I needed a rest when I got home. But, back to the first day and the superintendent's rules…

The main taboo was disturbing other inmates or guests. There were about sixty of us there, a number of them actually suffering real injuries or trauma from the streets of Belfast or elsewhere, and so this really was the first and most serious commandment, which Gary broke on the very first night. Actually, we were all late back, and had committed a few minor breaches along the way. We had missed dinner without informing anyone, stayed out after eleven without informing staff, that kind of stuff. But the major incident was Gary falling in the front door, going to the wrong room and waking half the place up with his Irish megaphone-whispered apologies to all and sundry. Bad form, indeed.

So it was that at breakfast we were all a bit sheepish, especially when Gary was summoned to attend the super's office immediately afterwards. We all, including Gary, assumed he was for the chop and would be packing his bags that morning. I also remember finding my allocated meal table in the dining room and introducing myself to the other three guys.

'Are you one of the few here who are actually injured, or are you just like the rest of us?' the oldest immediately asked me.

I must confess to a slight hesitation, suspecting a trap of some kind, but they all looked like typical hairy arsed coppers to me, so I smiled and said, 'Just one of the boys, my friend.'

'Great, badminton at eleven in the gym.'

And so the tone was set.

I was waiting outside Gary's room when he appeared back with a stupid big grin on his face.

'What happened? Are you no going home?'

'Home my arse, big man. You'll no believe it, so you won't. Come and see this.'

He then had me follow him to the basement area, and to another room, away at the back of the old property. It had sliding doors leading out on a paved area and the grounds of the building. The room was massive and the shower had a wee seat in it that I immediately thought would be great when hung-over. This was now Gary's room for the duration of his stay. There had been no chastisement for the previous night, just a change of room to a location where he could come and go without disturbing other residents. His room became our front door.

From then on, we totally obeyed what little rules were in place, realising that we really were in some other place from reality, where we were treated as proper adults who needed space and liberty to deal with stuff, and as long as we didn't upset or intrude on other people's same process, we could do as we pleased. Wow. That's why I had no money at the end of it.

As a footnote to Gary's story about his friend being shot beside him, I heard him tell it in company a week or so later, in Liverpool I think, and the punch line on that occasion was, 'It was me that fucking shot him.'

You had to take everything with a pinch of salt.

The days at Harrogate were full. Breakfast was at eight and was a full buffet spread. This was usually followed by a walk to the shops to get a paper, or whatever supplies were required and then a change for the pool. After a wee swim, and maybe a sauna, there was a regular badminton match at eleven, and lunch was at one o'clock prompt. Again, it was substantial.

After lunch, I would go to the gym and work my way round the machines, have a chat with the physio, and usually try out some fancy contraption on my gammy knee. After a few hours, and coffee at three, I would always go back to the pool area and read while mucking about in the Jacuzzi, etc. I remember once sitting in the steam room with a sergeant from Manchester.

'Where are you going next, big man?' he asked.

'A wee swim, few lengths, then the sauna. Why?'

'I'll just follow you. I can't be arsed with all this decision making.'

If anything can, that kind of summed up Harrogate.

Our three-course evening meal was served at six o'clock and afterwards we would always try to be busy. I got involved in a regular volleyball game that killed an hour or so, but the intention was always to put off as long as possible the inevitable: going out to the pub. Harrogate was marvellous. The main reason for this was that typical English reserved thing. You know, the half pint, not speaking to strangers, sitting in wee cliques. That was just never going to fly with an Irishman, Scotsman and a mad Yorkshire man on the premises.

We were like a light to the moths and anyone who was up for a laugh, a stranger in town, or just pissed, was drawn to our company and welcomed with open arms. This was mainly down to Murphy's ability (if that's the right word) to say almost anything to anyone and get a laugh rather than the slap or punch you and I would provoke.

There's undoubtedly something about the Irish accent, perhaps the tone or delivery, or maybe the look of devilment and mischief in the eyes, but he got away with murder. The fact that everything comes out at double volume must help. My Glasgow accent was a nice foil for this, or maybe no one understood a word I said, but Big Phil didn't have to open his mouth at all. He was an Adonis.

Everywhere we went, he was swooned over. I had never seen this at such close proximity. He didn't have to say or do anything. Women just came over and openly flirted with him. He was about six-foot-five and played rugby at a serious level (albeit Rugby League) around about Wigan, where he was a uniformed police officer. It was a total mystery to Murphy and me, but we quickly realised the doors we could open just by having Phil with us, and we became inseparable.

The stories of that two weeks could fill another X-rated book, but the truth is that they are mostly clouded in a haze of drink, and may not be taken in the right spirit by the 'victims' of our jovial exploits. Suffice to say, there was rarely a dull moment, so much so that, when everyone else went home for the weekend, we three decided to visit Liverpool, as it was Grand National weekend and promised plenty of fun. It really was tremendous and remains one of my favourite cities. Where to start?

Gary had 'organized' the accommodation and I remember accepting this without question, which seems totally banal now. Obviously, he had put us in a hotel that accommodated the Irish contingent travelling over for Aintree. And I mean all of them.

We had just arrived and were sitting in the lounge with our first of many pints when a troop of about a dozen of them came into the bar. They were as boisterous as, well, a dozen Gary Murphys, I suppose. Gary immediately got up and said, give me a minute, I'll find out what side of the fence they are, and went to greet them. They obviously passed or failed whatever test there was and, with big smiles, Gary brought them over to join us. Within seconds, we were all singing protestant songs, running through the familiar repertoire of historic and passionate unionist venom.

'Hello, Hello, we are the Billy Boys', 'The Cry was no Surrender', etc., always at absolutely full volume. This seemed to be some kind of greeting or welcome, but was certainly as much part of the process as buying a drink for each other. There was a real bonding going on here that could apparently only be understood when involved. We were all in full voice, smiling and back clapping, like you do, when Phil nudged me. I tried to ignore him as I proved my reluctance to surrender, but he was obviously agitated, and so at an appropriate lull, I asked him what was wrong.

'What's a Taig, Simon?'

Through the side of my mouth, and as discreetly as I could manage, and with some puzzlement at his question, I told him, 'It's a Catholic, Phil. It's just another word for a Catholic.'

'But I'm a Catholic, big man.'

'Do us all a big favour, Phil. Shut up and keep singing. OK?'

Needless to say we never got anywhere near Aintree. The TV in a pub was as close to a horse as we got, other than the police horses at Anfield, where we joined in with the Kop and sang ourselves hoarse.

When our stint at Harrogate's police convalescence home was

finally over and they threatened to have us physically removed, we all made our way back to our real lives. Over the course of the two weeks, we had made a lot of friends, just about anyone who was there basically, and one of the real good guys was a woman, Judith, who was a police officer in Newcastle. I never did find out why she was there because she looked absolutely fine to me. She and Big Phil had become good friends over our stay and when it came time to leave, she offered me a lift as far as Geordieland, and I could catch a train from there.

We shared the driving to Newcastle in Judith's white MR2, which was a flying machine, and the only stop we made was about half-way for lunch in some fine country hotel. When I got home, I realised that Judith had been at the toilet when I paid the substantial lunch bill. Although I thought it only fitting that I pay as I was getting a lift half-way home, she hadn't even commented on it. The truth is that women who looked like Judith seldom buy things like meals or drinks themselves, although I would never say that out loud these days.

From my office, I called Newcastle where I knew she was on a night shift and spoke to her shift sergeant, asking if he was up for a wind up. You bet he was. I told him the story and that he could summon her and make up a tale about the hotel manager tracing the car and reporting the theft of a twenty-five pound lunch. I gave him all the details and apparently she was mortified, gobsmacked and ready to resign before they told her the truth. My only regret was not being there to participate but it was almost as much fun listening to her shouting abuse at me over the phone. What a mouth.

Around this time, I was refereeing a lot more than I was playing football. It was good exercise without straining my knee too much and I enjoyed the banter. Don't get me wrong, it can get a bit heated at times even in amateur football, but I found that the abuse was water off a duck's back, and even quite funny sometimes. At one big game, through in Livingston, I was coming off the park when I almost got a compliment from one of the coaches. This is unheard of after a game, but they are always lovely people who want to be your new best mate before kick-off.

This coach or manager came straight over to me as I came off the park at time up and extended his hand for the shake. 'You played a blinder ref,' he said.

High praise, indeed, usually reserved for the man of the match or suchlike. Seeing my surprise, but pleased expression, he quickly followed up with, 'Aye, you saw fuck all.'

Now, that's more like it.

The pinnacle of my refereeing career was when I officiated in front of over forty-thousand fans at Ibrox stadium. At that time I was friends with the head concierge at police HQ, the late Bobby Dinnie. Bobby had spent his life in youth football running some famous boys' clubs and had been poached by Graeme Souness for Rangers as part of his revitalisation of the club. There were many age groups of youth development and, consequently, a lot of games being organised all the time, so it was quite normal for me to do two or three games a week for Rangers.

It was the last day of the Scottish league season, the 9th of May 1987, and Rangers had already secured their first league title under Souness with a 1-1 draw at Pittodrie the previous week. This was to be the day the flag was unfurled and the celebrations began in earnest and, with a final home game against St Mirren, and a packed stadium, the stage was set nicely. I got a call about ten or eleven o'clock.

'Simon, could you help me out and do a game this afternoon?'

A Rangers game for Bobby would normally be played on what was, at that time, the Albion training ground, diagonally across from Ibrox stadium but with a big game on at the stadium it seemed strange that we would be playing a game there on a Saturday afternoon. I was perplexed, and more so when he told me it was a two o'clock kick off and I was to come to the main entrance of Ibrox and ask for him.

When I got there, soon after one, there were already hundreds of Rangers' fans crowding around the barricaded entrance, hoping for a sighting of their heroes. I had to squeeze my way through the crowd. Bobby was there to take me down the home team corridor. He explained to me that he had been asked to put on an U17 match, leading up to the big games kick-off and that was my game. It was to finish at five to three, when the senior teams would take to the field.

I have to admit I was in my element. I'm not sure now if I needed tie-ups or if it was just an excuse to have a wander about, but I went to the first team changing area and poked my head in. I was in my kit by now, just looking for something to hold my socks up, but the whole first team gave me pelters. I asked for tie-ups and the guy that came towards me was Graham Roberts, the English centre back.

'Fuckin referees. Fuck sake, mate, you not got no gear. Fuck sake.'

I immediately drew out my yellow card and brandished it right in his face, and told him, 'I'm probably the only Scottish referee that hasn't booked you yet, Roberts, so that's sorted.'

The whole dressing room gave a roar of approval.

I then got my two teams of young lads lined up as if it was the world cup final and led them onto the park. I'd love to say a huge roar of excitement went up, but there were actually only about two thousand punters dotted about the stadium at that time. However, we kicked off, and the stadium began to fill as we neared three o'clock. I was wrapped up in the game to some degree. I had no linesmen or any assistance and was up and down the park like a yoyo.

I do remember standing under the Govan stand at a corner and thinking to myself, I must remember this properly, because it'll certainly never happen again.

I do and it didn't.

At one point, I gave an offside decision and knew immediately I had called it wrong. Not because of my own perception, but because about two thousand punters on either side of the park screamed in derision at me. You need to be thick-skinned to be a match official, but nothing prepared me for the next abusive interlude.

I was running west, past the enclosure, in front of the main stand, when a lone voice screamed at me, 'Ya fuckin fenian bastard referee.'

Whoever the idiot was, I was sorely tempted to drop my shorts and show him my rear end, but thankfully resisted. I should have realised that this wasn't really a comment on my religious background, schooling or general character, but simply a useful expression to shout at any referee.

When the game finished, the big players were waiting to come on and I recall Terry Butcher, England's captain at the time, saying well done to me. Next thing I knew, I was in the big team bath with a bottle of lager being delivered to me on a tray. I could get used to that.

On Monday morning, I was back at my desk at Govan CID when I took a call.

'DC McLean, how can I help you?'

'Ya fucken fenian bastard referee.'

My own Detective Inspector had been in the enclosure for the match. He could have got me killed, FFS.

CHAPTER 49: THE GOVAN BEAST

I have always got along with most people, but still find that the ratios previously stated apply, as a general rule. Three out of ten, you'll get along with fine, three out of ten you'll not like, and four you'll be ambivalent towards. In my experience, these same principles apply in the police, as they will do in most jobs, I suspect. But, occasionally, you come across someone who you just can't stand. In Govan CID, with about thirty detectives, there was one guy I clashed with every time we came within close proximity. Jim Moffat.

He was certainly outspoken. A real loudmouth, and he would honestly argue black was white. He was clever, sharp tongued, arrogant, bolshie and every barbed comment was made with a horrible sneering expression. He obviously didn't like me much either, so we avoided each other like the plague. He wasn't just like that with me, but with everyone he encountered. The trouble was that he was a damn good detective and, as they say, it takes all types. He was also a grafter. He had been told by supervisors, as I had, that he didn't suffer fools gladly, the only thing we seemed to have in common.

I came on-duty one morning and was called into the DI's office, where Jimmy Phelps (now deceased) told me that I was to work with a new partner, Jim Moffat. Our strained relationship was no secret. We were bitter rivals. As I protested and huffed and puffed, I was not reassured to learn that the DI had already had all of these tantrums and protestations with Moffat, but as of the following morning, we would be working together. End of.

We were so different. There was nothing subtle or measured with Jim. He only had one mode. Flat out. He treated everyone exactly the same: like idiots, whereas I was everyone's friend, or liked to think so. I was a negotiator, a compromiser, a wheeler and dealer. I enjoyed running informants, involving uniform cops and other detectives in my schemes, but Jim Moffat had no time for any of that nonsense. He was totally public and spoke his mind loudly and at full volume, all the bloody time.

A strange thing happened, though, because being a partner or neighbour is a special relationship in the police. Working together as a partnership is treated as a real privilege and responsibility, and even our animosity for each other was trumped by our unspoken understanding of that bond. On a day-to-day, hour-to-hour basis, your partner is the most important person in your life, and vice versa.

What I discovered was that Jim's mouth was like a machine gun. He just wound up everyone he came face-to-face with, all of the time. He just fired comments, jibes and put downs constantly and always had a smart retort to any sign of resistance. I had been a major recipient of this barrage many times, but now I was beside or behind the Gatling gun as it swept back and forward across his bows. I was his neighbour and so out of range. It was fascinating to watch.

Jimmy Phelps later told me over a beer that the hierarchy were tired of the constant niggling and competition between Moffat and I and judged that we might make a good team with our totally different approaches to the job. On one hand, they were proved absolutely right by the results we produced, but ultimately it was to blow up in their faces during a major enquiry out of Orkney Street, on the hunt for the Govan Beast.

Within the space of five days, three young lads between ten and twelve years old had been attacked and raped. Consequently, an incident room was set up and a large team of detectives drafted onto the case, including Moffat and me. The problem from the outset was that the OIC (Officer in Charge) of the enquiry was a DCI Dan Scott, who I doubt had ever run a major enquiry of any kind. (The detective super, Joe Jackson, was on holiday).

When you're inexperienced or new to a task, and unsure of your ground to some degree, you go by the book, and this was

Scott's solution. The incident room was processing paper, as it does, the leads and enquiries were being pursued and, although his daily briefings and debriefings were at best uninspiring, they were functional and by the book. Jim and I thought that due to the close proximity of these attacks over a short space of time there was more urgency needed.

Between us we had concluded that anyone who could perpetrate these types of crimes was a creep, a pervert, a total weirdo. A beast, as the press had tagged him. There was no way he wasn't in our files and records somewhere, and the obvious place to start looking was in the index card files held by the Female and Child Unit, or the Fanny Unit as it was more commonly known force-wide.

We trooped in to see Mr Scott, who really wasn't the brightest, and disclosed our thoughts, asking if we could take some time to look into these files while still carrying our daily workload of enquiries. His response was to nod, smile, and say, 'We'll see how it goes. Leave it just now.'

Wrong answer. He actually sent us to the shops to get an anniversary card for his wife, which demonstrates the character of the man!

Neither I nor Moffat were ever going to adhere to this. Even if he had given us some credence, and put one of the policewomen in the FACU on it, we would have been mollified to some extent. So, we made our own plan.

We agreed between us to come in at six instead of eight and finish an hour or so after the paid day. We would interrogate the Fanny Files, make a list of favourite suspects and pay them a visit early in the morning or in the evening, and do this until the beast was caught. We started the next morning and, within an hour, we had a list of about ten perverts. We had a reasonable description of the beast and so could narrow down our list as we researched, pulled records and confirmed the status of our suspects.

The list evolved and, on day three, we called on a Mr Jim Smith in the Pollok area. He was strange from the off, but had an alibi. He had been working on the day of the most recent attack, on a building renovation in the city centre, Buchanan Street to be exact. We visited the site and eventually tracked down a foreman. After some encouragement (no workplace really likes the CID hanging around for long), the foreman came up with time sheets for the day in question and, sure enough, there was Mr Smith working when we needed him to be in Govan doing beastly stuff. Shit.

These setbacks are not really seen as such by experienced detectives. We spend ninety-nine percent of our time eliminating suspects and lines of enquiry. It's what we do, in the certain knowledge that, if we do it properly and thoroughly, we will eventually home in on the culprit. We had his site manager telling us that he was getting paid for working that day, and his foreman or gaffer who had filled out the time sheet backing this up, and we returned to Orkney Street to revisit and select the next target on our list. We had no reason to stall at that point. The idea was to tear through the perv list and then take stock, but I must confess, grudgingly of course, it was Moffat. He wasn't happy. I knew this *because* he was quiet. He was never quiet. He wasn't complaining about anyone being an idiot. He was almost normal. After much teasing, he eventually came out with it.

'Something's not right about Smith.'

One thing I know for a fact: you should always, always follow that gut feeling, your subconscious mind flashing a warning or signal. No one knows where it comes from, but we ignore it at our peril, and I always had an understanding with my partner, and any boss worth his salt always allowed me to pursue that feeling, that gut feelings were times to stop and think.

Jim and I did that and brainstormed the whole Smith scenario from start to finish, and agreed to revisit the building site as they were about to finish the next day. I had been an apprentice in Yarrows Shipyard straight from school and, while working on a massive conduit job in the hangar of a Type 21 Frigate, I had been assigned two tradesmen. I can't remember their names or their faces. I never ever saw them both at the same time.

It transpired that only one of them ever came into the yard at a time, but both of their time cards were stamped for the day. At the same time, the other one was in the Albion works across South Street, having stamped them both in there. This had gone on for at least six months before they both disappeared, never to be seen or heard of again. Jim took that story as affirmation that Smith was our man and I was content that Moffat's instincts were worth pursuing. We decided on the direct arse-collapsing approach.

We were on site at five o'clock and told the manager that we were taking his foreman in for further questioning. We duly made a show of cautioning the guy and escorted him by an arm each to the nearby CID car. The trick is to keep it formal. No messing about, no answering questions. We're going to the cop shop. The message is that this is serious and needs to be dealt with immediately at the police station. I've seen it so many times, where you have interviewed someone initially, taken their statement and moved on, leaving them content to see the back of you. When you reappear the next day or so later, their demeanour is different – depending on how many lies they told the first time around, of course. Colombo used this trick in every episode I ever saw, and I modelled myself on him, especially my dress sense some would say. This guy's bottle completely crashed.

He had told us and his manager a pack of lies. Smith hadn't been at work that afternoon. He had left at lunchtime, 'feeling ill', and his gaffer had marked him as working. We had a suspect, but this is where we got too smart for our boots. This story might well have had a happy ending if we had gone to Dan Scott at that stage and given him the task of putting the next moves in place, but the thought never crossed our minds for one second. We were hot on the trail and Moffat and I just loved the hunt.

We went back to a deserted Orkney Street and while I dug out the information we needed from the last attack and telephoned the victims' parents to arrange a visit, Jim put together a collage of photographs. In those days before video fit, we simply attached eight or ten photographs on a brown A4 card, making sure they were of similar age and general description of the suspect, whose photograph was obviously one of them. We made these cards all the time. An identification of the suspect would give us enough evidence (alongside the broken alibi, etc.) to bring the suspect in, interview him formally and run a proper identification parade.

Off we went to the young lad's tenement house, where we were met by his mum. Victims are pitiful, sometimes. Especially young kids who've had their whole lives changed in a short space of time, when simply walking home from school in broad daylight. There's nothing you can say to make things better, especially as a policeman. Nothing will ever be the right thing and, in these cases, the parents are every bit as shattered, full of guilt and helplessness.

I explained that we were following a definite line of enquiry and were simply going to show the lad some photographs. The chances were that the boy wouldn't recognise anyone, and that was okay, it was all part of the process and would be just as helpful to us. By the time I had finished, I and everyone else was convinced that this was just boring routine and not dramatic or even important.

Jim came over, knelt in front of mother and son, and opened his folder with the photographs revealed. I can still feel the hairs stand up on my neck, the tears well in my eyes, and the glow of inner satisfaction when the prey comes into sight, as the youngster immediately pointed at Jim Smith.

'Mum, that's him, that's him,' he screamed. 'That's the man.'

He buried his face in his mother's embrace, sobbing uncontrollably. I think I nearly did, too. After a few minutes, I asked him to have one more look just to be absolutely clear and sure. (I wanted him to get a right good look at the bastard for future purposes.)

Eventually, he did look but took us all by surprise, especially Jim Moffat. He said, 'That's definitely him, but so is that there.'

The boy pointed at a second photograph further down the page. My heart sank until I looked at the second photograph. Jim

Smith with a beard. Moffat had put two mug shots of Smith on the card. Twat. We returned to the office, elated.

That wasn't to last long.

We then called a gaffer, a detective sergeant who came in and called Mr Scott. The Procurator Fiscal was consulted and plans for Jim Smith's arrest were made. Jim and I wrote statements and lodged our photograph folder and other evidence.

Not for one second did we even discuss or contemplate changing the second picture of Smith. This was unspoken between Moffat and me. It's just the way it was. We would never jeopardise any case, never mind one of this import, by tampering with evidence. We had made a genuine mistake and would stand by that error through thick and thin – the High Court, in this case, but it would be the truth. Any lie uncovered at a later stage could be catastrophic, would taint all of the other evidence and could see the whole case collapse. Not an option. We were sent home and told to be in the office early the next day.

I don't think Dan Scott spoke to Jim and me at all the next morning. We were there at seven o'clock, as instructed, but totally ignored. We then received the biggest punishment possible. We could have been suspended, I suppose, we could have even been charged with something criminal at a push, and I've no doubt we could have been disciplined formally. All of those possibilities would have been better than being told that two detective sergeants were going to detain Smith and bring him in for interview. We were totally excluded from the arrest of Jim Smith, who made a full confession before they even got him back to the office. We were then told to take two days off.

When a major enquiry comes to a successful conclusion, with the bad guy locked up and charged, there is always a 'payoff.' This is where the OIC books a suitable venue, like a bowling club, and every one of the enquiry team congregates to celebrate. The typists attend, the uniforms who assisted in a variety of ways, bosses from other departments, the support unit, maybe, anyone really who played any part in the major enquiry. Even bloody traffic cops if they had been involved at any stage. You get the picture.

The payoff in the Jim Smith case took place at The Neptune Masonic Lodge two days after he was incarcerated, but Jim Moffat and I were excluded totally. Instead, we went for a game of pool that night and had a few beers to ourselves, laughing and giggling the whole time. We were actually delighted. We caught the Govan Beast.

A week or so later, we were called into the DSI's office at the end of a shift. Joe Jackson was back from holiday behind his desk, suitably tanned. He got us to tell him the whole story. He then produced a bottle and the three of us had a dram together. I later learned that Dan Dumb Scott really had wanted Jim and I disciplined, but he had been slapped down.

Our disgrace had nothing to do with the two photographs of Smith shown to the young boy, but purely because we had pursued a totally rogue line of enquiry out-with the floundering major enquiry, gone off on a total tangent, and made Dan Scott look like the total incompetent that he undoubtedly was. We only ever wanted to catch the beast. And we did.

Together, Jim and I really were a force to be reckoned with, and we cleared up many crimes together. Jim also threw himself into the fundraising activities I was organising at that time in support of The Cystic Fibrosis Trust, but there would always be a price to pay. We were both driven and were always pushing our luck and operating on the fringes of the mainstream. We encouraged each other all the time and so could never be tamed. We were a bad match, being far too alike, as it transpired, rather than the opposites we thought we were, and so our partnership was broken up after six months or so when I was put back undercover. It was fun while it lasted, though.

CHAPTER 50: THE HERO

On taking up my CID duties at Orkney Street one midweek morning, I leafed through my allocation of Greens. This is the green copy of Form 3;24;1, otherwise known as a Crime Report. Every crime or offence recorded by the police went onto a triplicate crime report. The top part, which was white, was filed somewhere by somebody, the pink middle section was used for inputting data onto computers, and the green copy was a working copy for completing a report where someone was charged, or for follow-up enquiries or investigations where the perpetrator was unknown.

This is in the past tense because things are much more digital and paperless nowadays, but the principle is the same. The crimes being committed and the neds doing the committing are largely unchanged.

Anyway, a day-shift detective in those days, the mid-eighties, could expect an average of two to three greens each every day. We all had partners, or neighbours as we referred to each other, who would work as a pair virtually at all times. So, between us, we would have four to six greens per day. These greens had already been sifted and sorted by the DI who would allocate them and attempt to spread the workload as evenly as possible, giving cognisance to looming citations for court, days off, holidays or just workload being carried over on a daily basis. This would naturally take in to account his favourites –detectives, that is, not greens. He couldn't care less about them.

Greens dictated everything and contained all of the information required to proceed with an enquiry, provided the uniform cop had filled them out correctly (a rare occurrence). They told you the complainer (generally, the victim), the locus, the crime or offence committed, the times between when the crime had been committed and any enquiries made so far, including names and/ or descriptions of suspects. The detective's job was to continue those enquiries to conclusion, either when the perpetrator was charged or when all lines of enquiry had been exhausted, at which point he or she would return the green with a 3;24;2, or Crime Report Supplementary Report Form, explaining everything that had been done and the result thereof.

The length of enquiry and the resources expended on each green would be dictated by the seriousness of the crime, and some other factors, of course, such as political considerations or, indeed, the chance of an easy capture. Or simply who it was given to. Let's face it, in every walk of life, people have a useful shelf life. Some are charitable and call it 'burn out' when you no longer function properly or even give a toss. A friend of mine has a nice way of describing it. He'd say I think he's landed. As opposed to being on the runway ready for take-off, or even cruising at altitude. If you've landed, forget it. I've sure landed now, headed for the hangar.

A murder enquiry would be headed up by at least a DCI, usually a DSI, and he would command as much resource as deemed necessary, including a dedicated major incident room and team. With such major enquiries, the local CID was supplemented by detectives from the SCS, and possibly other departments, as required.

When a major enquiry had kicked off in your division, the short straw was to be left covering the book. The book is where the DI recorded all of the greens he allocated every day, but when a major enquiry burst, there were generally two DCs left to work a twelve-hour day-shift, and the same number to cover a seven till seven night-shift. This could mean juggling twenty or thirty greens per shift between two, as day-to-day crime continued uninterrupted during major investigations. The crooks were inconsiderate that way and continued to steal stuff, batter each other and sell their drugs. To be consigned to cover in such circumstances would attract looks of sympathy and pats on the shoulder from colleagues, as they had all been there, and knew what madness lay in wait for those left 'On the Book.'

A green could be allocated to a DI or DS if it was deemed sensitive in some way. Perhaps a dignitary or celebrity was involved or, God forbid, some spurious allegation had been made against a policeman. It could be allocated based on the geography, if there had been a spate of similar crimes in a particular area, or simply on the MO, which might suggest a link with other crimes under investigation. Such were the basic workings of the CID.

One of my greens that day was for an incident that had occurred at five o'clock the previous day. This was unusual because there had been a back shift and a night shift since then, and neither had made any reference to it in their summary notes of their respective shifts. The report had been put through as an assault, which again was highly unusual, because as a rule you don't get unsolved simple assaults, and only a serious assault would end up in the CID docket. The DI explained that a girl had reported being assaulted and the uniforms had submitted the report, but their sergeant, being ex-CID, had smelled a rat. He wanted the CID to check it out. He must have been too busy. What I discovered was a horrific unbelievable story of public disinterest.

It had happened on Paisley Road, almost under the Kingston Bridge, in broad daylight, at the busiest time of day. The woman, aged twenty-five, was walking west towards Harry Ramsden's to meet her mum and dad, when a guy a bit younger than her coming the other way asked her for a light. As she told him she didn't smoke, he grabbed her by the arm and frog marched her through some light bushes onto spare ground, now partially concealed from the busy roadway. He pushed her onto the ground and made a grab at her clothes but she kicked out, managed to get to her feet and ran onto the main road, where hundreds of cars were heading eastwards towards the city centre.

Her jacket was half off her shoulder, she was crying now, and she was screaming for someone to stop and help her. No one did. The scumbag simply walked into the middle of the road, grabbed her again and dragged her back into the spare ground. He had one arm around her neck and the other holding her arm behind her back. She struggled the whole way but he was much stronger. Although many of the cars had to slow down or stop to allow her to be dragged into the bushes, no one rolled their window down or got out to establish what was actually going on.

This time, he was angry, and much more violent. He got down on the ground on top of her, and told her that if she continued to scream and fight him, he would kill her. He said he had a knife, although it was never seen. She explained to him that she was pregnant, that she was meeting her mum and dad round the corner, but he was relentless and had her pinned to the ground with the full weight of his body, when he simply got up and ran off westward at full speed.

When I interviewed the girl the day after, she related the above story in some detail to the policewoman I had with me, but said that she got up and saw a young lad standing straddling his bicycle staring at her.

'Ur you awright missus?' he asked.

When she nodded that she was, he simply cycled away, also westward towards Govan.

I was there at five that night. It was mobbed. It's always mobbed, even to this day. I estimated that, over the timescale of the attack, there must have been between eighty and a hundred and twenty vehicles slowly passing the incident, or were actually at a standstill, waiting for lights to change. I was so baffled and enraged that I took the story to the *Evening Times*, who ran it on page two the next day.

That was a great success. Not. Naturally, no one was going to come forward and admit to being an absolute twat and a coward. The only person who did come forward was a young lad. He had come upon the scene just at the right time and had no hesitation in confronting the would-be rapist with the typically Glasgow reprieve: 'Lee hur alane, ya prick.'

This was a ten-year-old boy passing on his bike. He had seen the latter part of the assault from the west bound carriageway, and had realised something was wrong. He had made his way through the rush hour traffic to confront the would-be rapist, who confirmed what everyone in law enforcement knows as fact. That woman beaters, molesters, rapists, etc., are the biggest cowards ever created. From the threat of a ten-year-old, he got up and sprinted off at top speed.

I caught the culprit several months later for a similar type of approach to another unaccompanied victim under the Kingston Bridge at the riverside, but he never admitted anything, the pregnant complainer didn't want anything to do with identifying him, and our young hero couldn't be tracked down.

Do you know I still can't believe that no one helped that girl or at least made some effort to ascertain what was going on?

That was one of many, many greens, covering all facets of police work and all types of crime. Together with my then-neighbour, Craig Coid, we attended a routine housebreaking in the old Wine Alley high flats. The victim was an old man living alone who frankly had nothing to his name worth stealing. His door had been kicked in all the same and they had made a right mess of his wee flat. It transpired that his main sustenance was to make a right big pot of broth soup every week, and this pretty much kept him going. It was easily the most valuable thing in the flat, certainly to the old man.

Not content with messing up his house and smashing his door down, the idiots who had broken in had seen fit to put a big jobby into his big freshly made soup. He was distraught. It was the only thing he could talk about. I had no answer to his repeated question.

'What kind of arsehole would do something like that?'

None of this shocked us at all, as we were used to every kind of degradation and inexplicable behaviour. It's impossible to think of anything that could really have shocked us, to be honest, other than the parting shot from that wee old man.

'It took me ages to ladle that shit off the top of the soup, as well.'

Craig was my neighbour for about six months. What a pair we

must have made. Completely contrasting backgrounds, Craig had been brought up in Giffnock, a well-to-do area in the Southside suburbs. He had married his childhood sweetheart and still lived close to both of their parents (who were friends). His schooling had been top notch and I doubt if there was a more conservative detective in Strathclyde. I, on the other hand, although I could always pass myself off in decent company, was and am strictly working class. This is so engrained in me that there's a pride about it deep down. How working class is that? We were chalk and cheese and whoever decided to pair us up in Govan CID had a real sense of humour.

Mostly, we got on. We dovetailed quite well and, between us, we were effective. Craig was always on top of his paperwork. Everything had a place and his desk was always immaculate, with every note, form and piece of paper in its wee folder or drawer. Although I was on top of the paperwork, it was always highly visible. An inspector once told me that, if you want something done, ask the guy with the busy desk, because he will just do it; never ask the guy with the clear desk, because everything's out of sight. He'll forget or take ages to get round to it. I found that to be true with Craig and me. If it was filed, he was happy; if it was done, I was.

He had a great sense of humour and, of course, we knew we were opposites in many ways, but being neighbours superseded any societal differences we had, mostly. We only really fell out twice and the first was public, in the middle of the CID room at Govan, in the throes of a murder enquiry, with a room full of detectives. It would have started with a jocular comment from either of us, but just true enough to tickle a nerve and the reply would have been sharp and immediate. Off we went. We didn't speak for a few days afterwards and that is really difficult – nay, impossible – for police officers. He had accused me of caring about my informants more than I did him, of keeping him in the dark, not sharing information, cutting corners, holding him back and relying on him to keep things proper. (Filed, I suppose.) It most likely wasn't what he said that annoyed me, but the typical sneering supercilious way that he delivered it, in front of a room full of our peers. So, I responded immediately and totally sarcastically, telling him it was all right for guys like him, he wasn't from a council estate. (When I had previously called him a snob in similar circumstances, he'd retorted, 'I'm no snob. I once went out with a girl from a council estate.')

I went on to extol his good fortune and background, his higher education and privilege, but pointed out that here he was, in Govan CID, with me, his senior (by about six months). Me, from a scheme, brought up in poverty. I was overachieving. I could be proud of having got this far. He was underachieving by a distance. He must be a total disgrace and embarrassment to his family, the black sheep, whereas mine were proud of me. I immediately knew I must have reinforced everything his parents, wife and family said to him all the time. Oops.

We had both overstepped the mark, especially in public view. These things are normally kept for the pub, but we got eventually over it, so much so that a few weeks later Craig invited me to his wife's birthday party. Great, but it was about five months away, and I forgot all about it. No reminder, nothing. I don't think he ever forgave me for that, but we had gone our separate ways by then. We had some great laughs, captures and times, but, man, what a snob!

CHAPTER 51: BIG JOHN

Big John (or Cowboy to his pals like me) typified for me the transition from policing pre-regionalisation, before what we thought was the monster of Strathclyde was created. Of course, in the context of today's Police Scotland, Strathclyde was quite local. In the 'county' days, recruitment was a local concern, the exception being the Highlanders, who came to the Glasgow Polis, or indeed the many Scots who headed south to the real monster that was and is the Met. In those days, cops were mostly working class, earning what today would be classed as minimum wage or less, with unforgiving shift work and unpaid overtime. They all lived in tied police houses, which were rent free, but this negated any chance of ever owning property, leaving them able to be relocated at the will of their managers. It really was a poverty trap, the only consolation being that wearing the uniform in those far-off days brought with it a modicum of respect in the community served. Unbelievable now, I know.

With the advent of beefed up salaries, index linked wages, the ability to buy police houses or own private property, and a general boost to the police officers' terms and conditions of service, a new breed of young professional was attracted to the force. This coincided with a revolution in management techniques and strategies, all academic and based on modern theories which had nothing to do with policing at the sharp end, on the streets, or catching bad guys for that matter. This was all about efficiency, quality control and so for a lengthy period, from the mid-seventies until the mid-noughties, a real transition took place, and the old-school beat coppers disappeared through natural wastage, their like never to be seen again.

The beat man replaced by CCTV, the desk sergeant by civilians, the black note book by the PDR, and the jail cell by a social worker, a counsellor or a 'project' (or all three for that matter). Having said that, some things you could never ever replace, and Big John was certainly one of them. He was a Govan man, still lived in the division, had run the Govan Boxing Club for as long as anyone could remember, and had been a successful boxer back in the day. Or so the stories went. Regardless of his prowess in years gone by, there was no doubt that he still commanded a splendid right knockout punch. Whether he could follow that up or punch at all with his left was immaterial and never seen by anyone I knew. The one right to the chin did it every time, out for the count, a real sight to behold.

I befriended John. Or at least got as close as I can imagine anyone getting. We could communicate. Only a few could make that claim. A minority made the effort because he was equally dangerous to his colleagues as he was to crooks. Or so it seemed because he just went about his business, never bothered anyone, grunted replies to his gaffers, and didn't even bother grunting or acknowledging anyone he didn't have to speak to. I made the breakthrough due to a fatal stabbing outside the old Stadium Bar in the notorious 'Wine Alley' area of Govan one Friday night.

It was bedlam at the locus. Flooded by uniforms, drunks everywhere, the victim off in the ambulance with only a large pool of blood to mark where he had been. In those circumstances, the uniforms really kick into gear. The sergeant or inspector at the scene takes charge and everyone who needs to be informed is called pronto, the scene is marked and taped off, and we all start taking names of everyone in the vicinity. I liked getting to these places quickly, while all of the mayhem was ensuing. The scenes of arson, serious assaults, shootings, anything attracting crowds and mass disorder, even funerals. I had a way of keeping myself out of it and being able to observe the whole scene, often spotting the guy acting unnaturally, or in a case of mass disorder and fighting, the guy who was dangerous, who was inflicting real damage or carrying a weapon discreetly.

At this particular locus, I guessed that the culprit had made off after delivering what was to prove the fatal wound and the mob left behind were innocent bystanders caught up in the circus, patrons of the pub who had spilled out to see the commotion, or friends and associates of the soon to be deceased. After a few minutes' consideration, I quickly grabbed the lad I judged to be closest to the victim, frog marched him to our unmarked car and pinned him face down across the bonnet. I then whispered in his ear, 'I need a name and I need it right now, before I search you.'

I got the name. As I stood him up and pushed him away towards his mates and screaming women, one of his mates rushed towards me, obviously raging, and, I suppose, about to lamp me one. I never did find out because all I saw was a flash of a fist and the guy lying at my feet, out for the count. I turned in time to see our John slinking away, putting his glasses back on. This was the first time, but not the last, that I was to witness the phenomenon that was John's right fist.

I told the uniform in charge at the locus of the name I had gleaned as our suspect, and left him and the other detectives who had arrived, together with the Scenes of Crime, forensics, etc., and made my way back to the office. I had to get some background on our suspect and get a posse together as soon as possible in order to find him in time to salvage some of the trace evidence he no doubt had all over him. I made a point of finding John, just as he was leaving the office for the night, and thanked him for what he had done at the locus, possibly saving me a sore face. He went past me as if I wasn't even there. Maybe a grunt was uttered, but I might be imagining that now. I followed him towards his car and said I had to speak with him, maybe even tugging his sleeve, and he turned to speak to me. (I later learned that he had floored colleagues for less.) In a barely audible voice he said, 'I'm no doing any statement, big man. Sorry.'

And walked off again.

I'm not sure where the insight came from, but instantly I knew Big John. I understood. The lack of communication, the reluctance to engage, the refusal to provide a statement, the anger and frustration that emanated from the man. I went to the control room and had someone interrogate the system for a few seconds and confirmed all of my suspicions. John hadn't submitted a written crime report of any kind in over two years, and I would wager good money that even then he had gotten a young colleague to put his name on the paper. John was dyslexic or illiterate or on a spectrum of some kind. I didn't know of such terms back then, and I'm not actually fully conversant with them now, but I knew right away that he must be tormented having to hide such a handicap every day, fearful of discovery.

We didn't get our man that night. He was off and running, and when I came back on-duty on the Saturday back shift, he was still in the wind. It was now a full-scale murder enquiry and, after consultation with my gaffer Joe Jackson, it was decided that I would take a team and hunt him down that night. At the briefing, I asked if I could second a uniform cop from the shift who had helped me at the locus the night before, this causing some raised eyebrows, as uniform cops were generally kept well away from plain clothes work. They were a red flag to the neds and, more specifically, were an unknown quantity in the field. Those raised eyebrows became gaping mouths when I told them who the uniform cop was to be. I got my way. I'm sure Joe knew me well enough to trust my reasoning and instincts and he let me run with it.

Convincing John to join my squad was another matter. His sergeant looked at me as if I was stark raving mad when I made the request.

'Good luck with that, Simon, let me know how you get on.'

I personally went to get John. He was on a beat in Cardonald and he was told by radio only that a car was coming to meet him at his location. If spooked, he would have no doubt vanished. I drew up beside him and he jumped in.

'I'd like you with me tonight, big man. We're gonnae track down the scumbag from last night and I need your help. You'll just stick with me all the time, and any paperwork will be done by me, all of it. You don't get to put pen to paper. Will you help me out?'

Again, I might be imagining this. It might be what I would like to have happened, but my recollection is that it was as if an enormous weight had been lifted from John's shoulders. He almost smiled at me, but his eyes said it all. I didn't really need him to say, 'Alright, bud. Nae bother.'

I knew he was on board. I also knew that I didn't need to worry about anyone battering me that night.

We got our man in the wee hours, hiding in some 'burds' house in Linthouse. It was just the usual harassment tactics and someone gave him up pretty quickly. I don't think we needed to employ John's special skillset that night, but it was always good to have him beside you.

A few weeks after that, I was trying to track someone down, and had little or no idea what he looked like. Often, the photographs were years old, and of limited use on the street. Much better, a cop who knew the character, and so I went to see Big John, who was working in the uniform bar at this time. He was taken off the street periodically for the safety of the public. On this occasion a main index criminal (Bad Guy) had been found semi-conscious in a telephone box with a broken jaw and his Chinese carry out meal poured over his head. John was the main suspect and it certainly had his trademark one punch signature.

John knew the lad I was after and I managed to convince his inspector that I would bring him straight back and would keep him out of trouble. Fat chance.

My information was that this guy drank in the Stadium Bar in Wine Alley, John's old beat, and so we visited the pub, which was heaving. I was in a suit and John in uniform. Neither of us had even discussed or considered taking back up, although the inspector knew where we were. I swear that the second we set foot inside the door the place became hushed. We started to walk round looking for our guy, but the quiet was in no way intimidating. Just the opposite, in fact. Almost at every table, someone would acknowledge John, stating his surname with total respect, or simply saying, 'Officer.'

I had never seen anything like it. I'm sure I never did again. Here was a man who could hardly write his own name, who couldn't be trusted to go out of the station on his own, and he commanded total respect in his community. We approached the bar and the manager came straight over, also acknowledging John's presence as some kind of holy visit on a Saturday night. This must be serious. I noticed that John was slid a wee goldie without any comment or preamble and he told the guy what we were after. The whisky was dispatched and off we went. As previously stated, his like was not to be seen again. We checked a few other establishments with similar results and I dropped John off at the office in time for him to get changed and go home.

About an hour later, around midnight, an anonymous call was received at the office giving an address in Brighton Street where our fugitive could be found, and I had him banged up before signing off at two o'clock. I made damn sure to tell John's supervisors the next day. He really was an undervalued resource and I'm sure the anonymous tip was made to help ensure that Big John wasn't going to be roaming the streets anymore.

The stories about John were never-ending, mostly about his stupidity and propensity for sudden explosive violence. I can only relate the ones I know to be true because I was either with him or in close proximity when they took place.

He was certainly confined to the uniform bar for the latter part of his service, but I still managed to spring him now and again for special missions. On one famous occasion, he managed to convince the gaffer to let him out on his own, to the high flats in the alley (long demolished). This was to deal with a specific problem. An elderly lady had, over a period of weeks, been calling the office, hearing all sorts of noises and strange bangs. She was convinced that the place was haunted. She was often in a real state of anxiety when she called and would keep calling 999 until someone attended. This normally entailed five or ten minutes of soothing and reassuring, but was no guarantee that she wouldn't call again later that night.

This was occurring generally around ten or eleven o'clock, just as the shifts were changing, and was becoming a real pain. The pensioner was perfectly sound in every other aspect of her life and all of the cops who had attended had their own theories about the noises she was hearing. I was at or near the control room one busy night when she called and the groans were audible all around the switchboard and uniform bar. It really was a drain on resources and on everyone's goodwill and patience. John piped up, volunteering to go see the old lady, sure that he could 'sort something out.' I'm not sure what the inspector thought. Maybe he, like me, envisaged John scaring the old biddy into never calling the police again, but he was certainly not inclined to let John loose in Wine Alley. There were just so many tempting targets for him, especially on a Saturday night.

So, I volunteered to give John a lift up to the flats (a two-minute walk away) and bring him back. This seemed to convince the gaffer to take a risk. And so, John was set loose on the old dear. I simply waited in the car, and, after thirty or so minutes, John returned. He told me what he had done and I have never told a soul. John trusted me and that was important. Suffice to say that the woman never called again. No more ghosts or haunting. John had solved the problem.

What he had done was listened. The noises and apparitions were all coming from the heating vents in these old high flats. John got the hoover out, explaining that he knew exactly how to deal with these incidents and hauntings. He guaranteed that he could solve the problem once and for all and life could return to normal, guaranteed. His methods had never failed and he became an instant ally of the woman, instead of arguing with her. What did these young cops know, after all?

He got the hoover out, plugged it in and sat next to the vent in the sitting room, the root of most events. He put the lights out and told the woman to alert him when she saw or heard the ghosts. Anyone who's seen *Ghostbusters* will know how this went after that and, before long, John and the previously terrified and frustrated pensioner were happy that they had hoovered up all of the poltergeists. For completion, John had taken the hoover bag away with him, and was still carrying it when he got back in the car. I made him dump that hoover bag in a skip on the way back – just in case.

On an early shift one summer, we had gathered early to execute a search warrant for heroin and arrest the main dealer. We had spent weeks watching this place and not only knew everything about the dealer and the address, together with all of his associates and hangers on, but we knew that a delivery had been made the previous evening, and was still there. I had asked Big John to drive the marked Sherpa van, follow us into Wine Alley, and simply sit outside the address until we appeared with our haul of drugs and drug dealers. The perfect job for John, he simply sat in the van, read his *Daily Record* newspaper, and waited.

We got our man, together with a serious haul of smack (he later got fourteen years prison time) and we were all happy. We made our way back to Govan and got on with the task of writing the report and processing the drugs and prisoners for court the next day. I wasn't totally surprised when I got a call to go see the shift inspector a while later, thinking there was maybe some query with a prisoner's address or details. But that wasn't it at all.

He had a male in hospital with multiple facial wounds and a possible fractured skull. This guy had been picked up by ambulance, having been found lying on the landing of a common close in Wine Alley. The close next to where we had been a few hours previous. The elderly woman who had called the ambulance had actually seen the assault take place, and was stating that it was a police officer in uniform who had inflicted this damage. From the description she provided, we were quite sure who she had seen. Big John.

The inspector assured me that John had been at his desk in the uniform bar, surrounded by civilians and other officers, since his return with us. That was good enough for me to accept John's obviously rock-solid alibi, although I did find out what had happened.

John had remained in the marked van throughout our enquiries, just reading his paper. On his return to the office with us he had picked up a ringing phone in the uniform bar and heard, 'Is that you, ya bastard. I'm gonnae shoot you the next time ah see you in the Alley.'

John had simply hung up the phone, put on his jacket, and told whoever was in earshot that he was nipping over to the shop. He then walked into Wine Alley and went straight to the door of the caller, as he had recognised his voice. This imbecile was stupid enough to answer the door, at which point he was dragged onto the landing and battered even more senseless. The old lady had opened her door and was told to close it by John, who said please, apparently. He then left the scene, got back to the office, returned his jacket to the stand, and got on with his work, as if nothing at all had occurred.

He told me this later and unofficially. I don't believe he would have told another soul. He told me because I told him that the only way I could ensure his safety from any follow-up enquiry was if I knew the truth. This allowed me to visit the 'complainer' in hospital and come to an agreement, where he withdrew any complaint of assault, and I didn't need to follow up on the taped message of someone calling Orkney Street threatening to shoot a police officer. My life was full of these types of 'accommodations.'

The simple fact is that I was never going to allow some scumbag to jeopardise the career of an honest, hard-working police officer because he'd sustained a sore face for threatening to kill said officer. I have always been clear on these issues. There was never a moral or any other kind of dilemma for me. Probably because of my upbringing in Possilpark, I have always understood that the fittest ultimately will survive. It's actually only because of the Johns in this world that the rest of us can walk the streets safely. If we didn't have good guys willing to batter lumps out of the scum, the scum would quickly take over, something that seems to have been totally forgotten in today's environment of tolerance, diversity and equality. We can only be tolerant, diverse and equal when someone is willing to batter the bad guys, of which there are many. Many men and women fought and died for those human rights we now enjoy and many consider an actual right. They're only rights when we have the strength, might and desire to defend them. First and foremost, thank you, John.

I can also allude to a story that left us all speechless at the time. I happened to be in the control room at Orkney Street when John came off the telephone, obviously really angry. He slammed the phone down. Never a good sign, and I could see the inspector and other bar staff wondering what was amiss.

It soon became apparent that the telex machine, which was a real mod con of our communication system pre-internet, had run out of paper. John had taken it upon himself to resolve this situation, and promptly phoned Pitt Street, our HQ some five miles away in the city centre. I can only imagine the confusion of that call's recipient, when John informed him that he needed to put more paper in the telex machine. John seemed to think that the paper wound its way all the way from HQ to Govan to be spat out from our machine.

You can rest totally assured that there wasn't even one hint of a smirk or smile in that control room. Not just right then, anyway.

CHAPTER 52:
DAVIE'S TRIBUTE GAME

Davie McTaggart was a friend of mine in the Squad and at Govan CID. We played football together many times and I think it's fair to say that he was 'Rangers Daft.' We would go to Ibrox together sometimes when working Saturday day shifts, because Govan CID were given two free tickets for the enclosure at home games, in order that we could prevent and detect pickpockets who were rife in those days in the standing area. Unfortunately, Davie had his warrant card and wallet stolen on one of those days in the enclosure. Those Govan pickpockets were something else.

Davie was killed in a tragic accident on holiday with his wife and young family. It really was a sad time for everyone who knew him. He was definitely one of the good guys. At times like these, people feel a need to do something or to express their remorse and, at Govan, we decided to put on a charity football match, have a raffle and a wee disco afterwards, and make some kind of token presentation to Davie's family, just to show how much he had been respected by his peers.

One thing about being a copper is that it is effortless to organize such things. There were many DJs in our ranks, and raffle prizes and suchlike can be gathered up with a few telephone calls, especially for an event such as this. From memory it was the SCS v Govan CID, but I'm not even sure who I played for (although I do know I scored the winner).

On the afternoon of the game, which was to take place at the police sports facility at Lochinch, in Pollok Park, I received a telephone call from Ibrox. Whatever player, official or ex, I had arranged to attend our event had called off, leaving me a bit in the lurch. I had really wanted a Rangers presence on the night, given

Davie's allegiance. I went to see the boss, Joe Jackson, who also had some contacts in Ibrox. He told me to leave it with him and within an hour he had made a plan for John 'Bomber' Brown to be there, a perfect choice.

Joe asked me about the event, which had somehow escaped his notice, and he said he would like to make an appearance, himself, to pay his respects; a bonus, for sure.

The game took place with the usual high-spirited enthusiasm and we all retired to the lounge of the Lochinch Police Social Club for refreshments. The evening went smoothly, with only one real incident of note to my knowledge. Joe Jackson hauled me aside at some point and told me that his wife had turned up. When he had told her about the event, obviously at the last minute, because he hadn't known about it until that afternoon, she had accused him of not telling her. She was convinced he was taking some other woman and so he had told her to come along. She did.

He asked me to dance with her, chat to her and make sure she knew I had organised the event, but had only told Joe about it late on that day, in order to get some help. This was the truth on this particular occasion. I had only met Joe's wife a few times, but I could tell that she had had a few drinks prior to arriving at Lochinch, and that she wasn't in the best of moods.

Anyway, I did my duty. We had a few dances; I bought her a drink at the bar and we had a carry on and a laugh. She was easy to amuse, my distinct impression being that she hoped to upset Joe by flirting openly with me. After the best part of an hour, I made my escape and didn't give it another thought. Job done.

The following day, I was in Govan CID office with my neighbour, Ross McLelland. We had just fallen out over my smoking cigars. That would have been fine, but our fall out had been tape recorded as we'd been interviewing some ned at the time.

'We all have to put up with stuff we don't like,' he'd said to the interviewee. 'Simon here smokes cigars all the time, but I just have to live with that.'

He had never told me there was a problem, and we proceeded to have a heated discussion while the tape ran on and on. The debate we were now having was whether we should start the interview all over again, legally problematic, scrap the tape, or submit it to the Fiscal as it was. I don't remember the outcome of that debate, but I do remember Joe Jackson popping his head in the door and asking me to come to his office. This usually spelled trouble.

As it happened, he explained that he had been speaking to his solicitor regarding his marriage, which was on the rocks. He was gathering evidence to use in future proceedings, and asked me if I would write a statement regarding the hour or so I had spent with his wife the previous night at Lochinch. He would be interested in any remarks she made about him, suspicions she harboured, her general behaviour, state of intoxication and demeanour, etc.

I wrote the statement immediately, but then I did another statement, this one much more colourful and entirely fabricated. In the second statement, I took Mrs Jackson out 'for some air' and, when in the car park of the social club, she had asked if she could sit in my car. From there, things went quickly downhill and she ended up committing a terrible sex act on me, right there in the car park. I must confess that this much-embroidered story had a few contributors including my neighbour, Ross, and, by the time I handed this second statement into Joe, most of the office knew what was afoot.

I nonchalantly dropped the envelope containing the lies on his desk and left. He mumbled some thanks. We waited.

From memory, it took about twenty minutes and, by that time, the whole of Orkney Street were primed for the eruption. I was told later that when he came out of his office, statement in hand, his face was beetroot red and his cheeks puffed out like a puffin. He stormed into the general CID office and I must confess I almost regretted the prank. He looked genuinely upset. He simply said, 'McLean. We need to talk, now.'

I think everyone realised that he was ready to blow, and I think if I had gone into his office, he might well have hooked me. We never got that far. As I walked towards him, I couldn't keep the smirk from my face and could hear the suppressed laughter in the room from my colleagues. Before I had reached the door being held open by Joe, the room had folded over in laughter, and Joe immediately joined in. I handed him the proper statement.

I just hope he submitted the right one to his brief.

CHAPTER 53: KALASHNIKOV

In 1993, Strathclyde Police ran a six-month operation designed to get as many firearms off our streets as possible. In conjunction with a gun amnesty, when members of the public could hand weapons in at their local cop shop, no questions asked, we had two detectives in each division designated to focus exclusively on retrieving illegal guns. I headed up this mission in what was G Division, based at the old Orkney Street Station in Govan.

I worked with Jimmy Miller from the Pollok office and we ran riot. We recovered sixty-seven firearms of all varieties, the highest in the force, and cleared up numerous crimes in the progress. Guns ranging from high powered air rifles, low and high calibre rifles, hand guns, shotguns of every length and variety, imitation firearms that are just as effective as the real thing when pointed in your face. But the prize capture was a working Kalashnikov.

Our tactics were simple, as always. When you make a ned's life miserable by breathing down his neck, he'll do anything to shake you off. This was a tactic we had recently seen the legendary detective, Joe Jackson, use when murder enquiries were grinding to a halt due to the wall of silence often met in schemes. When no one wants to speak to the police, mainly because the last thing they want to be is a Crown witness in a murder trial. They don't have a reason to get involved. Much easier to lie low and say nothing.

Joe would muster the enquiry team, supplement it with plain clothes and uniform cops from any source possible and saturate the targeted scheme, with instructions to use all of our powers to check identities, stop and search and book anyone for the slightest offence. This always resulted in a quick stream of information, simply because, with movement restricted, no one with an outstanding warrant of any description could venture outdoors. Vehicles with as much as a light out were grounded. You couldn't even kick a ball in the street. The steady flow of minor contraband, and certainly drugs, was severely restricted. In short, life was coming to a standstill, or certainly lowlife. There was now a good reason to speak to the police.

Jimmy and I did exactly the same, only on a much smaller scale. Although the police nationally were only just beginning to acknowledge the severity of the drugs problem (ten years too late), and how it pervaded every aspect of criminal activity, we knew that the world of drug dealing was the sure route to everything we wanted to achieve, not only because of its propensity in Govan at that time, but because everyone knows that junkies will 'shop their granny' in order to stay on the street, using.

Through this process of harassment and blackmail, the lines of enquiry were completely endless, as one small result almost always leads to another, as you work your way up the supply chain and onto other small-time street dealers. This was how we came to be offered a Kalashnikov rifle, but at the cost of a thousand pounds.

We waited three days to get any money, and in the end had to settle for two-hundred pounds from the police, after an embarrassing and tedious series of negotiations including threats, promises, and everything in between. The deal was off several times, but by the time I had made up some of the gap with fags, booze and impossible promised favours in the future, we were told where to pick up the weapon: in a bin behind a pub at lunchtime.

I travelled with my then-DI, Pat Durkin, and we returned with an authentic Kalashnikov machine gun in the boot, cheesy grins across our coupons. This was an excellent result.

We took it straight to the super's office upstairs at the old Orkney Street Office, where the whole CID department quickly congregated to marvel at this tool of destruction. There were numerous AFOs (Authorised Firearm Officers) there, but none of us had seen such a firearm in real life.

Everyone had a wee shot of it. We had fun scaring the uniforms downstairs and the duty officer almost had kittens when we blew the whole control room away in one fake sweep of the barrel. This was a real boy toy, and if it hadn't been so early we might have had some prisoners to sober up with it as well. We were actually venturing into the back yard to scare the typists through their ground floor window when we received word that the ballistics team were two minutes away, coming to make a formal inspection and identification.

We quickly ran upstairs and put the Kalashnikov on the floor of the super's room, on top of brown bags to save his old carpet, and when the imposing firearms boys came in, we were circled around it, looking suitably serious and grave. What followed ensured some sleepless nights.

'Big Billy' stalked the gun where it lay and, after a few minutes' visual examination, took a pencil from his pocket and, with gloved hands, began to inspect it closely. After some ten minutes, he pronounced it safe, explaining that these guns were generally smuggled from the Falklands by serving officers, primarily as trophies, but of obvious value on the black market.

The problem was that the Argentinians knew this, and when leaving or surrendering them, were known to pack the stock with explosives. This meant that if someone pulled the trigger, even with no ammunition, the resultant explosion could blow the holder's head clean off.

He obviously didn't know that we had already checked all that while running about the corridors blasting all and sundry. Idiot.

CHAPTER 54: THE TEN PERCENT

We started out as rascals and, over the course of a year or so, got much worse. We had a free hand, you see. Our remit was simply to deal with the pesky drugs stuff, in order that the Division could cover its ass. They could claim to have dedicated valuable resources exclusively to the problem and thus fend off any future questions or criticism. It still wasn't real police work to them. It was for us.

We already knew most of the existing dealers and, due to the bank of 'touts' (informants) that we had nurtured by that time, our only concern was that there weren't enough hours in the day. At one stage, McLucas and I managed to close Govan down again for the supply of any drugs, albeit briefly.

We were aware of a steady supply of smack (heroin) coming out of the old Teucherhill scheme. We were reliably informed that the guy responsible was cautious, and had a sophisticated supply chain in place that was impossible to fathom out. We knew that he had already served a few years for supply, and was looking at a hefty sentence when we got him. He became our number one target that week.

The Teucherhill scheme was tricky. It was full of neds and lowlifes and was nicely contained with only limited access points. They could spot the polis a mile away. As always, we had to get creative.

I managed to get us the keys to an empty council house in the heart of the scheme, giving us a good view of the main street of interest, where we knew our man stayed in a bottom flat. Somehow, McLucas came up with a BT van that we could park not far away.

We watched for days, gradually building a picture of the supply and selling system. The problem with drug users and suppliers is that they are so random. They are stoned most of their lives, sleep at the craziest times, do some normal things in between, and they, too, are at the vagaries of their suppliers. Nothing is routine or predictable, other than the constant visits of dependent junkies trying to score.

We had devised a routine of being dropped off early by the bin lorries or other council workers visiting the scheme on a daily basis. Dressed in overalls, we were simply two of their crew on the way in, and we didn't come out. We created all sorts of diversions to get back out of the scheme later in the day. We were also gathering valuable intelligence throughout our stake outs.

On one such job, I was watching an address in Elderpark from a top floor corner flat, and became aware of a well-known scumbag cycling around the junction. Every few minutes he would stop, get off the bike, and pick up empty Embassy Regal cigarette packets. After inspection, he would either discard them, or keep them and move off on his bike. Weird. As he disappeared up the street, I gave it no more thought, as we were waiting for a large delivery of smack across the road.

Weeks or months later, I was made aware that a respectable male had made a complaint of fraud. He had been sold a carton of two-hundred Embassy Regal for a tenner in a local pub. When he opened them, he discovered only packets stuffed with paper and cigarette butts. I laughed for some time.

To my mind this was a victimless crime, and the cyclist had gone up in my estimation just a notch. He was being creative. Almost productive. Simply utilising the greed of his customers who were happy to buy what they perceived to be cheap stolen cigarettes, but thought it a police matter when it transpired they had been duped. I wondered how many others had been exploited by this scam, but had wisely decided to take the hit and learn from it without telling anyone.

Anyway, back to Teucherhill, where, by comparing notes and photographs taken, we now had a rough picture of the setup. It really was amazing. Our target rarely handled the drugs himself. He had a system of selling where his hangers-on would do the actual transaction, and there were regular delays in the process. He could move about the scheme on foot and monitor business, occasionally popping into his close, no doubt to collect the takings. The delays worried us, as people were sent away and told to return an hour or so later.

We saw one lad, who seemed to be the main gofer and kept disappearing into a common close across the road from our target's abode. These common closes were three stories high with eight individual flats in each block. The next day, we positioned the BT van in order that we could see the rear of this second close, hoping to watch which house this young man went to frequently. A few hours later, when business was about to start, I alerted McLucas that the same young guy had left the target house and was crossing the street to enter the second close. McLucas then said, 'He's climbing the fucking building, shimmying up the drain pipe.'

The young lad, who turned out to be the target's son, had climbed up to a top flat of the building and squirmed through an open window. He was a monkey. I must admit I was beginning to think McLucas was winding me up when, about forty minutes later, he reported that the lad had now come out the same way and slid right down the drainpipe into the back yard. Sure enough, I then saw him cross the street and go back to his fathers' house. Not surprisingly, business soon commenced.

McLucas and I had few miss hits because our information channels were just so good. We were acutely aware that our work was regarded by most coppers, especially 'gaffers', as futile and troublesome, and that any use of resources on this drugs stuff was only granted grudgingly. So we were always careful before committing any additional manpower to a job.

As usual, we had a friendly junkie on hand to visit the address and 'make a buy', that way confirming that the heroin had arrived and was on the premises. It cost us a tenner each time, as the 'friendly junkie' got to keep the bag of smack. As soon as this buy was confirmed, we called up the troops into Teucherhill.

Now, to dispel any illusion that we were working as two lone rangers, I should acknowledge that we had always made provision, mainly in case things went pear shaped and we needed help pronto. We had a tight group of colleagues, mainly community police officers and usually one or two cops on each shift, as well as a detective or two on-duty who were aware of our stake out, and the probable need for trusted help at some stage. They were usually on hand and, when they heard our call for a van and four uniforms in Teucherhill, they knew to be in the vicinity; passing by, if you like.

When your door crashes in off its hinges and six or more burly coppers rush into your house, most people tend to react hysterically. Not in this house. Our target and his wife were so gripped by the vice of drug addiction that they hardly raised an eyebrow. The children were a bit upset, but our target was resigned to his fate, content that we were only going to find a minimal amount of smack that any good lawyer could contest was for his personal use.

Having quickly found the heroin, wrapped in about twenty-five 'tenner bags' ready for sale, the troops were carrying out a methodical search of the house, recovering the usual booty of stolen property traded for drugs, and other substances, such as 'reefers' and 'jellies,' used to supplement a smack habit. While this was going on, I had a word with our target, alone.

He was quite arrogant and resigned to begin with, but I had his undivided attention when I told him we were about to hit his safe house across the road. And so, as usual, we made a deal. He knew that he was looking at more than ten years jail time. I also reminded him that his son was on camera helping his supply of drugs, and he was tasked there and then with telling me where he was buying his supply, with details. Names, descriptions, location and time of the next buy. All were forthcoming and, in my estimation, detailed enough to be true.

For my part, I promised not to mention the safe house in the police report. There was no warrant for it, only McLucas and I knew of its existence and this would keep his son out of the picture. He even told me where to find his stash in the safe house, under some floorboards. When he was transported away to Orkney Street, McLucas and I paid a visit to the now unsafe house, using the conventional method of going up the stairs as opposed to the drain pipe, of course.

We tanned the door and immediately recovered a 'poly bag' containing a substantial haul of heroin, much more than I had envisaged when I made the deal. It was never weighed or analysed by any laboratory. This was ours and no one knew we had it. A good result all round.

As I put pen to paper that night (I was, invariably, the author of such cases) there was the usual flurry of activity in our wee office, processing property and evidence, arranging transport to the lab, etc., when it suddenly dawned on me that we hadn't retrieved the BT van. This caused much hilarity and someone was dispatched to recover it from the streets of Teucherhill.

About ten minutes later, that someone called to report that the van was gone from where we had left it. Oops.

Police offices have a way of emptying quickly when such events occur, so it was left to me to call the BT depot and break the news of their lost van. We were lucky. A concerned elderly resident had become worried by its presence and had called BT. They had dispatched a crew and, finding it open and abandoned (by McLucas in his rush to arms), they had taken it back to base, safe and sound. Happy days. I'm sure I didn't impart this news to McLucas and co. immediately, as there was much more worrying to be caused.

As the dust settled and the wheels of justice were set in motion, McLucas and I decided how to best use our recently acquired bag of heroin. On our day off (Sunday), we had arranged to meet an informant, who was an eighty-pound per day smack abuser, and would do anything to maintain his crippling habit. He had no idea why we had arranged to meet. At the arranged bus stop, we pulled up, grabbed him, cuffed him and I joined him as he was buckled into the back seat and whisked away, all for the benefit of any onlookers. We took him to Mugdock Bank in Milngavie, far away from prying eyes, and well off our Govan beat. By the time we got there he was totally bewildered. I think we might have blindfolded him too, just for effect.

Whatever we did, it had the desired effect. He would have agreed to anything by the time we stopped in our wild country location. His job was simple. We provided magazines, scissors and gloves, and told him to make 'tenner bags' of the smack I produced. He was too nervous at first, but quickly warmed to his task, which he was obviously well practiced in.

McLucas and I watched on from outside the windows, so as not to be contaminated by the shit, and were delighted when he announced that he had finished, an hour or more later. We had him place them in batches of twenty in sealable plastic bags and gave him a few for his efforts. I'm sure he had already blagged a good few, but we were delighted. We now had nearly five hundred tenner bags of smack ready for sale on the streets. Result. (At that time, anything over ten bags could attract serious jail time.)

We dropped our wee helper off in Govan with strict instructions to tell no one of our mission, in the certain knowledge that he would be desperate to impart this story, or his version of it, to his junkie mates.

Our final task that day was to visit the spare ground next to Orkney Street Police Office, dig a two-foot hole, and bury our bags. We never ever revisited this site. There are now modern flats built on top of our hard-earned smack, and I think of that every time I drive along Govan Road.

The result was miraculous. Every dealer or lowlife prospective dealer in Govan and far beyond became aware that McLean and McLucas had almost five hundred (grossly exaggerated in every telling of the tale) tenner bags. This was enough to attract many life sentences. It was real and never denied; merely laughed off by McLucas and me.

All of a sudden we commanded instant respect from every

ned we spoke to. We became Mr or sir. We were welcomed with open arms into dealer's homes, who were at great pains to protest that they were going straight, getting clear of drugs, and would be happy to assist us in any way they could. Govan was closed for business again.

You see, they were scared shitless that we would take it into our heads to plant a sizeable amount of heroin on them or in their home and arrest them accordingly. I can honestly say that the thought never once crossed my mind, and was never discussed by Davie McLucas and me. Never. The knowledge that we had the bags and the possibility that we could use them anytime was much more useful than actually doing so, and carried no risk.

We may have sailed close to the wind on occasion, or even crossed a few dubious lines at times, but we were even more scared of prison than *any* ned alive. We had far too many clients incarcerated there to ever join them.

Although we didn't consider it at the time, McLucas and I were at one end of a scale in the police force, together with about ten percent of our colleagues, where the overriding criteria – apart from staying alive and keeping out of prison – was to get the job done. Catch bad guys. I could never adequately describe the buzz I got from catching neds and locking them up. In our minds, that's what we were paid for and that was what the police did. How naïve we were.

At the other end of the scale were officers who had a completely different outlook. The police service was a job with a clearly defined career path of promotion and advancement and the way to achieve progress was not by getting involved with criminals. That only led to complaints, court appearances and trouble of all descriptions. Some of this minority were fresh from university or on accelerated promotion routes, earmarked for leadership and management roles that required only cursory knowledge of grassroots policing. I believe that the modern thinking is that management of any corporation or endeavour is a specialist function, and the incumbent need not have any specific knowledge or experience of the day-to-day jobs involved on the factory floor or workplace.

I should also point out that I had the pleasure to work with Ten Percenters at my end of the spectrum, who were also high ranking. They had managed to balance their inherent desire to lock up bad guys with a flair for leadership and man management. The fact that they continued taking risks, put their neck on the line, and supported the cops on the street doing the same, speaks volumes for their outlook and resolve. After all, they had much more to lose at that point in their careers. Gaffers like Joe Jackson and Ian Hosie had come through the ranks being operational and so had a real empathy and bond with those of us who were operating at street level, and especially those of us who were proactive.

I think that is the one word to sum up the Ten Percent. Proactive. The careerists, academics and managers to be would actively avoid any possible contamination of themselves or their prospects by dealing with criminals and suchlike. God forbid. In fairness, that was never asked or expected of them.

The bulk of the police force, eighty percent in my model, but probably more, responded to the needs of the public and the routines of policing a modern society, whereas my Ten Percent were much proactive when possible and would go looking for crime and those behind the criminality with gusto. Of course, there were no actual dividing lines, and we were all experts at recognising like-minded souls, who, over time, would be recruited and utilised as situations dictated. The vast majority simply did their jobs, walked their beats, trained their dogs or rode their horses, administered the whole force, or manned their desks and kept everything afloat, responding to the calls for assistance from the public. Only when this function was in place could we employ the luxury of my Ten Percent, who enjoyed the back up and support of all of that, but were given a more specific remit to tackle the sources of crime at root level and were allowed to shed the shackles of the uniform, the suit and short haircut.

We attracted the Ten Percent to our work, guys who wanted to be at the sharp end, risk takers, and rascals. We enjoyed 'Creative Policing', as I called it at the time to wind up my detective peers. As time went on, we sunk to the lower extremities of even the lowly ten percent but this is where danger lies and the lines of crime, morals and even sanity become blurred in the constant pursuit of adrenaline. It is only with hindsight that I can see how close we were to those trap doors. But, boy, were we having a ball.

Post script: The information provided by our target was acted on. We involved the Drugs Squad from Pitt Street and staked out the gates of Craigton Cemetery on the appointed day. Sure enough, a major dealer arrived with his entourage, waited for five minutes or so, and then headed off, closely (but not too closely) followed by a whole surveillance team. In typical drug squad style, we were never involved in the follow-up or formally told of the outcome.

I did learn a few weeks later from an old colleague that a major shipment of cannabis and other drugs was intercepted at Greenock Docks as a direct result. A resounding result at the time, credited to Customs and Strathclyde Drug Squad officers. Fair enough. Like our Teucherhill junkie dealer, we were just cogs in a wheel.

Unfortunately, I do need to clarify something here, because, although I enjoy disparaging my uniform colleagues and I regard my position with the Ten Percenters as being esteemed and 'where the rubber meets the road' and all of that nonsense, the truth is that there would be no such thing as a ten percent at either end of the scale, without the eighty percent who carried out the day-to-day policing duties that keep us all safe. They were and are the lads and lasses who walk the beats, help our kids across the road, deal with the accidents and deaths that are going on all around us all the time. All year round they are chasing thieves, carolling rioters and solving disputes, and the truth is that we could only be risk takers and chancers in the certain knowledge that, if and when the shit hit the fan, we could call upon the eighty percent to bail us out. They were always there, thank goodness. Of course,

I have never admitted any of this before and will certainly deny it in future …

CHAPTER 55: FINE MARGINS

My manufactured Ten Percent is just that, of course, but I feel it's useful in understanding the different kinds of police officers that make up a force. It's a huge generalization and, although I pretend that the category I fell into was superior in some way, I realise that, in order to be effective, a police force needs all types of individuals. Without the vast majority who deal with the routine, attend calls for assistance and reports of crimes committed, and deal with accidents and incidents, there would be no place for anything else. They are the backbone of the service that allows every other function to take place, and enables us all to go about our daily lives.

The place where the differences of my make-believe Percenters are glaringly obvious to all is in the courts, both Sheriff and District. The Ten Percent with leadership credentials and aspirations would rarely be seen at a court. Perhaps a licensing or administrative matter, or a civil procedure against the police, for example, but, in general, if they ended up in the criminal courts as a witness, they had slipped up somewhere along the line.

The district, or JP court, is where the lower level matters such as drunkenness, Breaches of the Peace or minor traffic offences are heard, and we were rarely if ever cited there. The Sheriff Court, we were never out of, along with the cops working shifts day after day and dealing with all sorts of crime and traffic offences along the way. The High Court was invariably where you would find my Ten Percent, giving evidence against the murderers, drug dealers, armed robbers and rapists. The more serious the crime and possible sentence involved, the more all of the stakes go up for everyone. The more scrutiny, the better the defence attorneys, and so on. The front line to me.

A courtroom is a unique environment. I always felt that it

was the perfect setting to conduct an interview or interrogation because you have to be an accomplished type of liar to do so in there. Especially in the High Court, with a jury watching your every inflection. To me, it feels forensic, and when you're telling the truth, it's intimidating enough. Lies, prevarications and denials have to be good indeed to convince anyone in there and that's why few accused go in the witness box, and why my policy was always to tell the truth, the whole truth, and something like the truth.

A colleague and friend, albeit a traffic cop, produced his notebook when giving evidence and then recited some reply to the charge. He read from it and, as sometimes occurred, the defence lawyer asked to see the notebook during cross examination. No big deal. Watty handed over the book, the lawyer looked at the appropriate page, and handed it back, at which point the officer simply fainted. Collapsed right there in the box. He was seen to and the trial ran its course with no more drama made of the incident, but it transpired that Watty had nothing noted in his book about that particular case. Not a thing. The lawyer, for whatever reason, never brought it up. The witness box is a lonely and scary place.

Lawyers assumed that police officers always made up these replies to charges, comments made under caution and confessions to crimes. After all, it was a simple matter of writing it up, putting inverted commas around it, and *voila*. Often, the comments (or no comments) of the accused felt like the tipping point in the case. The icing on the evidence cake that took away any niggling doubt as to guilt, and the key to this was that the court had to accept the word of the police officer. I took that trust seriously. So, when tape recorded interviews were introduced around 1990, criminal defence lawyers thought that the pendulum was swinging firmly in their direction. Not so. What a surprise they got when it became clear that their clients actually did admit things, make damning replies and spill their little hearts out, even on tape under proper conditions. Tape recording became a huge tool of the police and mostly took away the tedious allegations that we were making up all of these verbal responses.

I'm not suggesting here that every officer played with a straight bat. Just as there were lazy cops who never lifted a finger and avoided work at all costs, there were the overzealous that went over the mark in order to clear a crime or secure a conviction. I know for a fact that evidence was tampered with or omitted, that confessions were extracted by less than scrupulous means, and that 'reasonable force' was, on occasion, exceeded in the arrest or detention of a suspect. Of course, these things occur regularly where a force of six-thousand officers is working round the clock on city streets full of violence, drug dealing, theft and abuse. What was always paramount was that these incidents were acceptable encroachments over the line in the heat of the moment or in unusual circumstances; that it never became the norm and the officer involved was always made aware of where the lines had to be drawn.

There was and has to be a realisation that tracking down and bringing to justice violent and desperate criminals, often carrying weapons or guns, is a physical, as well as mental, task. If everyone could be on a hit team about to smash down the door of a drug dealer with dogs, weapons and who knows what waiting on the other side, they would surely attain a fresh perspective about how an arrest is affected. The truth is that every decision, every action and every order given is scrutinized with hindsight in the cold light of day and every officer is answerable under the law of the land for his actions and deeds. As long as they were acting in good faith, they will be given some leeway, but we should all know that these men and women are operating at the front line, making instant decisions under the most severe pressure, where the margins are fine indeed.

With regard to deliberate tampering with evidence, or planting evidence in order to incriminate a person, again the common perception in my day was that the police, especially the Ten Percent, had no compunction in doing this. They would verbal you up, stick some drugs or a weapon in your pocket and trot you off to jail without a second thought. The real problem here was that anyone I worked closely with, and where I was calling the shots, knew for a fact that I didn't want to go to jail and wouldn't engage in these perversions of justice. Not only was it self-interest, but I hated the idea of abusing the powers we had and of locking up an innocent person. The trouble was I didn't want the neds to know that.

For us to be effective, and we really were, we needed to appear ruthless, capable of anything at all, and totally without scruples. We made such a fine job of this that most of our colleagues believed this as well. I remember a senior officer telling me that a change of image and a move away from the front line was required if I wanted to progress in rank. The crooks and, in particular, the drug dealers who underpin most crime on our streets had to be under no illusions that we would do anything to close them down. It was this perception and fear of us that secured our constant flow of intelligence and information. Nothing else. The price we paid was that our distant bosses in their ivory towers perceived all plain clothes operatives as rogues and a liability to the force. I must confess that the Strathclyde Police Drugs Squad in the late eighties and early nineties did nothing to dispel this impression, as a few of their number crossed over those invisible lines into the dark side. They were casualties of the job, collateral damage in the fight we wage against crime, and to be mourned with sympathy.

Not so the parasites that chose to visit the dark side and collude with the worst among us while acting a role day-to-day, pretending to be upstanding officers of the law, family men, churchgoers and people to be trusted and relied upon. They abused the trust invested in them. A trust hard-won by generations of honest hard-working police officers. They take it, use it to build a façade of integrity, and betray everything and everyone who came before them; everyone who relies on their decision making and honesty and everyone who will come after and try to uphold the institution of the Constabulary.

They are worse than the most professional lifetime criminals operating in our society, because they are traitors, users and snakes. They've no place in my tale here, because bringing them down is a complex, confidential and sometimes dirty process. Those matters are best left for another day.

As I explored earlier in 'Fishy Business', the moral margins of a police officer's day-to-day decision making are muddy waters. So much has to do with intent, motive, reward, self-interest and the 'Big Picture.' The latter is the most common excuse or justification I've heard given by officers who are caught manipulating outcomes to suit their own personal agenda. Where some crook is given a free pass because they grassed someone up or gave information about some pending criminal activity. This starts at grass roots, where petty crime is not acted upon in exchange for information deemed more important to the common good, and this goes on at all levels into the court itself, where the prosecutor will 'do a deal' in order to secure a conviction. I think everyone understands this trade and accepts that, in a less than ideal world, sometimes priorities have to be decided.

Away from traffic wardens jeopardising their lift to work, or property and business owners looking after their beat man, or even keen young detectives trying to clear up local crime, we have to acknowledge that there are much more serious levels of corruption within the ranks. At the extremes where officers are 'on the take', lining their pockets or offshore bank accounts, as a reward for turning a blind eye or providing information. It shouldn't really be news to anyone that this goes on and I have to admit straight off the bat that those of us who make up what I perceive as the Ten Percent are much more likely to be seduced by these obvious temptations. This is simply because we are a constant source of disruption to the crooks and dealers. We are their biggest problem and so we have the closest dealings with them and their type, making us a problem to be ridded of at any cost or payment.

These officers who did were a blight on all of us, a disgrace to the job and a source of embarrassment and shame to every single right-minded copper, undermining the foundation of the job entrusted to officers worldwide.

I think that was the main cause of sadness and anger to the vast majority who wore the uniform, carried the warrant card or presented the badge: the undermining of the trust those credentials invested in you. It was made clear to me from an early stage in my career that the office engendered real responsibilities, because most would open their doors, entrust their most valued possessions, or impart the most personal information to someone filling the role of a police officer. That office holds a unique standing in society and, to most of us, a breach of that trust was the most heinous of crimes against us all.

In my time in Strathclyde Police, I only got involved in the periphery of such corruption, usually because an operation we were conducting had been undermined or compromised by some officer with an entirely conflicting agenda. This often entailed informants who were high rankers in the criminal world and had forged long term relationships with now senior officers. Sometimes those informants were the main reason those officers had become high ranking and they would be protected at virtually any cost. They rose through their respective ranks together. I worked with a detective inspector who, when it came time to leave the Crime Squad, wasn't wanted in any division, because he would bring a crime wave with him. Such was his bond with his informants that they and their criminal activity moved with him.

There's no doubt that many officers, me included, had close relationships with informants and snitches, but the danger lies in the longevity and familiarity that invariably builds. In many cases, those once small-time crooks or dealers become 'legitimate' businesspeople. Wealthy business and property owners who are well able to oil the wheels of justice when required and 'look after' those who look after them. Often they will provide detailed information into serious criminal activity in order to clear out opposition or rivals, or indeed settle old scores. The bent copper is rarely concerned as he or she will glean the credit for such a capture, as well as the holiday, new car or monetary reward being proffered. It should be noted also that these activities rarely start at that level, unless blackmail is involved, but grow from the petty favours and deals struck over many years. Just like many crimes, such as theft from the workplace or embezzlement, they usually started off as a minor pilfering and grew as they remained unde-tected and became habitual.

I had a case where a business owner friend asked me to make enquiries into anti-Semitic graffiti being painted on his gable end walls. It was costing a fortune to remove it, but he was worried that there were underlying problems that might escalate into further more serious incidents. I watched the place for a while and established the cause. I stopped it and established that it was only really vandalism and there was nothing more sinister, but in the process, I clocked activity taking place in the back yard late on a Sunday evening. It transpired that the manager of the premises, who had been employed for twenty-seven years and was a personal family friend of the owner, had been stealing systematically from the business for many years, effectively running his own separate business. Over the years, and starting with a few items here and there, he had stolen over two hundred thousand pounds in stock.

In my experience, officers 'on the make' are few and far between. Nevertheless, they do and, I suspect, will always exist. There are also sexists, racists, homophobes, liars, thieves and those who will regularly use too much force, but they are always in the margins and required to conform by the regulations and laws that apply to the police at all times.

All of this nefarious activity takes me back to my pet subject, that of illegal drugs. I maintain that virtually everything in our materialistic world is controlled or at least hugely influenced by the laws of commerce and trade. As long as these substances, such as heroin and cocaine, are illegal, we have no control over the supply chains at all. It is part of the unregulated black market and so forms part of the underground where corrupt activities will thrive. If I steal your bag of heroin, you can't go to the police. It is a non-crime just between you and I and so the laws of the jungle apply.

We all know that the rewards of dealing at a certain level are enormous, only because of the market our drug laws have created. But with the resources available to these guys they can and do offer rewards that could never be earned in a lifetime of dedicated and successful police work. They are masters of spotting weakness, need or greed and manipulating it to suit their own ends. An officer with debt, perhaps from a marital breakdown or gambling/drink addiction? Maybe a sick loved one requiring special and expensive care? Whatever the angle I know for a certain fact that there are opportunists trying to find these conditions and use them to suit their own nefarious ends.

I have seen countless honey traps set and sprung in almost every setting imaginable simply to compromise an officer and use the underlying threat of exposure to curry the simplest of favours. The thin edge of the wedge. I should also state that the same tactics are used to enrol doctors, lawyers, accountants, politicians, bankers and, indeed, any professional who can help keep business thriving. The criminals have no rules to play by, no boundaries to constrain them and, left unchecked, would undermine everything we hold dear. Be in no doubt that there is real evil around us and such is the reach of their tentacles that, in the corridors of our services battling to contain them, everything is compartmentalized. Information is guarded at every possible opportunity but still they – organised crime, terrorists and foreign interests – manage to infiltrate at every level. This is a constant running battle of wits and brawn.

There is no conclusive summing up on this topic. In the real world, the levers of power and wealth are complicated and control over them is constantly being fought over by any means possible. Police officers are an integral part of that struggle and often are the only dividing line between such factions. The fact that they suffer casualties of every kind is no surprise to those involved. Suicide rates in the service are high, marital harmony almost unheard of, and problems such as alcoholism are rife. This is the price paid by many of the men and women who choose to man these particular barricades, behind which most of us go about our daily lives, oblivious to the battles being waged. These are undoubtedly the Ten Percent risking everything.

The truth that transgressions by our police officers still make unwelcome and uncommon news is to be celebrated because they are rooted out by their vigilant colleagues who do nothing more than protect all of our interests, often with their own lives. The only surprise is that so many, the vast majority, never succumb to the array of temptations, the easy road to material wealth and riches by the simple betrayal of their colleagues and service. Thankfully, they continue to address their duty, their sworn oath and simply get on with what we call The Job.

CHAPTER 56: DRUGSFEST

Orkney Street was really busy in the eighties. Crime was fuelled by the growing need for illegal drugs, mainly heroin, and as always, the police were way behind the curveball. The consensus among the hierarchy and, indeed, older cops and those officers with rank was that it didn't count as crime and hardly as legitimate police work at all. This was frustrating, as all young officers and detectives knew for a fact that most of the thousand-plus crimes per month reported in G Division alone were motivated by the drug habits of the perpetrators.

The then Commander of the Met (McNee) had even announced publicly that there was no relation between illicit drug use and crime, and he had been the Chief Constable of Strathclyde Police; unbelievable now, but true! This ignorance was being duplicated all over Scotland; in fact, throughout the UK.

On my detective training course, I had made friends with a lad, Tam Sneddon, who worked in Central Scotland. At Tulliallan, we had shared many a pint and jaunt across Fife and, together with a few others, had resolved to do something about the drugs issues we encountered and that we knew were underpinning most of the crime we investigated. This was so obvious to us as front-line detectives who were also living within the communities as young single men, socialising and mixing with our peers.

Tam returned to Stirling and secured a meeting with his force commander, where he asked for a week to investigate the growing drugs problem. Tam was so sharp. He had secured top student on the detective course and, like all of us in our early years on the job, was enthusiastic. His commander saw fit to indulge him, in order to shut him up and keep him onside, I suspect.

Tam reported to me daily. He had instant success. It wasn't hard, to be fair, as everyone knows that druggies will 'shop their granny' if need be, and what we discovered was that the hierarchy had been right to a degree. These weren't 'good neds' or hardened criminals we were initially arresting. Not at the user level at any rate. They were often young people who had never been in any trouble with the police before, and so they were putty in our hands when detained and confronted with time in police cells or even prison.

I don't recall Tam's exact results that week but he re-entered his commander's office, as appointed, glowing at the figures he had produced. Dozens of people charged with possession, numerous with intent to supply, an Aladdin's Cave of stolen property recovered, offensive weapons seized, and a wealth of information promising even more progress to come. Tam was convinced, as was I, that he was about to be put in charge of a drugs unit or team, which, until that point, did not exist in Central Scotland. He was not only to be disappointed, but crushed, humiliated and threatened with his job.

His commander was livid. Tam had created a crime wave. There had been no drugs problem in Central Scotland until then. Drugs use or supply can never be a 'reportable crime' and so, until that moment, it did not feature anywhere on any police radar. So, it was not a problem at all. Then along comes Tam Sneddon and, within a week, the courts have a wave of drugs cases, the administration staff are snowed under with laboratory reports (which are expensive) and evidence, complaints have soared and, before long, the press will be asking about this sudden wave of drugs into Stirling.

Tam was left in no doubt that he was not to follow up on any of the work he had done, he was not to pursue any of the leads or information he had gathered and if he submitted one more drugs-related case he would find himself in a uniform. Now, I knew Tam really well. He was no shrinking violet and would have stood his ground if possible, but such was the dressing down he received he had absolutely no option but to bury his head in the sand and return to his detective duties, and ignore the root source of much of the crime he was investigating.

Thanks to Tam Sneddon, I had the heads up in Govan, a totally different environment than Stirling, where we were regularly investigating major crimes, and were always looking for ways to circumvent the criminal fraternity in order to clear up murders, robberies and the like. And so, I received a much more considered response when I approached my DCI, Joe Jackson. I was also armed with an impressive back story due to my success in Rothesay and my stint with the SCS, where Joe had been my superintendent. He trusted me and I had been recommended to him at the squad by his peer and good friend, Willie Anderson.

I related Tam's experience in Stirling, explained that the legislation (The Misuse of Drugs Act 1971) was there to be used, and maintained that this was a chance to police proactively, to our agenda, and that the rewards would give us great leverage into the crime world. Joe studied me intently, no doubt gauging my sincerity. He told me to go and see the Divisional Commander, Mr McLaren, with my case for action, but with one word of caution.

'Make sure you're prepared, son. If he likes it, he'll fire it straight back at you and ask you for your plan. Have one ready.'

So I made a plan.

Stage one was to gather some stats to back up my initial premise: that there was a problem and the public were surrounded by junkies, dealers and drug related crime. I wanted a public helpline. My idea was simple. A free phone number directed to a dedicated line in the CID office, and posters displayed over a manageable area asking for any information about drugs and their misuse.

The Commander was agreeable to this approach but said there was no money available for such a scheme, never before attempted in Scotland or, as far as I could establish, in the UK. I recruited my mate, Charlie Carlton, who was a uniform cop in the community police, with a wealth of local knowledge. He was also like-minded.

He introduced me to Jim Sillars, who was the prospective SNP MP for Govan at the time and, within days, we had funding for our 'community project.' The phone line was quickly established and the community police department put our new posters up, primarily in Govan itself. This was viewed with ridicule by all of my detective peers, and certainly all of the senior officers in Govan and beyond. The undoubted consensus was that we all had enough work (we really were stretched all of the time in Govan) without actively generating more.

I remember retrieving the answering machine from the divisional collator's cupboard in the main CID room early that first day, and seeing the red-light flashing, indicating that we had at least one message. In fact, we had thirteen messages. A handful were spurious, a few of no use, and a few backed up already known intelligence, but the rest were from obviously distraught, and sometimes elderly, members of the public, who were besieged by obvious drug dealing and user activity on their doorsteps, leaving them feeling totally helpless.

Realising what a powerful tool I now had, I followed up on some of these reports, and took some action where appropriate, but mainly took statements and details, collating them into some order. Every day, we had more and more messages and, after a week, I had an impressive pile of information, portraying an undeniable tale of misery and intolerable frustration throughout the Govan area to which the police were totally oblivious. It soon became a daily ritual for the day shift detectives to crowd round the collator's desk and listen to the night's messages. Some of them were hilarious, some abusive. But, mainly, they were a cry for help.

The fact that a local politician was also party to our project obviously did my call for action no harm and so I entered the Commander's office one Monday morning in April, well-armed to make my case. Mr McIntyre was a formidable character. I perhaps met the man five or six times throughout my career. I had retired from the police some six years when I had occasion to telephone Ibrox Stadium (the home of Glasgow Rangers in Govan) about some security issue, and was put through to their Head of Security, Mr McIntyre, who had obviously also retired. He answered the telephone.

'Can I speak to the Head of Security please?' I asked.

His reply?

'Simon McLean, how the hell are you, son?'

Formidable.

But, well warned, I had a plan that day as I sat down in front of him. I had a vision: Drugsfest. (The timing coincided with what was then Mayfest, a cultural event in Glasgow, hence the name.)

I laid my impressive pile of paper on his desk and proceeded to divide it into types of information, geographic area, etc., but he quickly stopped me. He had read over my summary report, read a few telephone messages, and needed no more prattle from me. He had obviously been speaking with my boss, Joe Jackson, as well.

'What do you intend to do about this problem, son?'

The way he said it made it sound as if I had created drugs, or at least been totally negligent in not having solved this issue by now, without troubling him with such things. I then produced my detailed plan and, to my total amazement, got everything I asked for.

In four weeks', time, I would take charge of a team of eight. This would be made up of one other detective (John Ramsay), a young uniform cop from each of the four shifts (which would include at least one female officer), and two experienced and hand-picked community officers. We were in business.

The next month was spent preparing files on specific targets; transport to be used, including public service vehicles; observation points, which were empty council houses or vacant business premises; and, of course, Sheriff warrants to be executed during Drugsfest.

We ran riot that week. We actually closed Govan down for the sale of heroin. By Saturday lunchtime, we had submitted over fifty cases, eleven of them being serious petition cases where the accused were remanded in custody. The intelligence we had gathered would have kept us going for the rest of our careers, as the enforcement of drugs crime is self-perpetuating in nature.

We knew every dealer, and had made good inroads into their

supply chains as well. Much of this was passed to the Force Drugs Squad in Pitt Street for enquiry on a force or nationwide level, but locally in Govan, the police were back in charge, briefly.

The stories generated during that week of Drugsfest would fill a book on their own, but, despite the unprecedented success, and the incredible fun we had, it was all tainted by a horrible incident at the very end. Our colleague, John Ramsay, slipped in his shower on the final Saturday and sustained a horrible injury, resulting in the loss of an arm. It could have been much worse but for him running naked into his street and receiving expert first aid from a neighbour who had forces – and hence first aid – experience.

The outcome of Drugsfest was disappointing. A drugs unit of two plain clothes officers was established at Govan, and I was put in charge to work with a cop, Davie McLucas. We shared the community police office, which was a godsend, as the community cops saw little operational work and were always up to lend us handers. They also bore the brunt of complaints about drug crime from their neighbourhood beats and meetings, and so had a vested interest in our work. They could justify time spent with us. They were all experienced coppers with superb local knowledge and were highly trusted.

Drugsfest would never be repeated in my time. Policing was changing. We had created a mountain of paperwork. We had also made every other department busy with the arrests we made, with the court appearances we all stacked up, precognitions, dealing with productions (evidence for production in court), and on and on. All of this on top of the normal daily workload being dealt with by the busiest division in Strathclyde.

The truth was that the police just didn't have the resources to tackle this tsunami of illicit drugs washing over the country. It was a social problem driven by the simple and irresistible forces of supply and demand. The solution was, and remains, a political one, but there are no politicians, especially these days, with the balls to actually address the issue. Although we had shut down Govan for a few weeks at most, we knew fine well that we had simply moved the problem into neighbouring areas, such as the Gorbals.

That's all with hindsight, as McLucas and I pursued our plain clothes mission with real gusto from day one.

CHAPTER 57: FRENCH STREET

This information came from a hopeless addict, found in possession of a stolen television, who couldn't bear the thought of a night in the cells – or, more likely, a twelve to fourteen-hour stretch without a hit. I was lucky that I met him on my own. The chances of nurturing an informant increase a thousand-fold when there's no witness to the deed. It's that type of intimate process, and a unique and special relationship. Most cops and detectives avoid them for that reason. They always end in heartache.

Being comfortable with fucked up relationships, I had many touts, and enjoyed everything about it. No, that's not right. I loved it, thrived on it.

The information given by an informant can be quantified as it relates to the collateral being dealt by the cop. Often, it's a straightforward cash transaction. Sometimes, early release when an overnight lie in the cells is on the cards. Or simply the offer to submit a report case to the PF. Whatever makes a win-win trade off will do the trick. In general, the scale of the 'turn' (information) imparted will be tailored to the favour being considered by the good guys and, of course, both parties are exaggerating throughout.

Let's be honest, the reset of an old telly isn't much of a hand. There were no warrants for this guy, and having confirmed his identity and address, I would have pushed the boat out just by taking him to Orkney Street. But, as any poker player will confirm, it's not the hand that matters, but how you play it.

He immediately told me the name of the thief that I had seen delivering the TV and the location of the housebreaking. A useful start, but I was totally unimpressed. Desperate now he proceeded to tell me a story that beggared belief. This concerned named major criminals who were running an operation within an industrial estate in Renfrew. Apparently, firearms and drugs were stashed here, and almost every unit within the large estate was involved in major crime the length and breadth of the country.

In my experience, people are vague when they lie. 'Tuesday or Wednesday', 'In the morning, I think', 'a big guy with a dog', that kind of shit. On the other hand, when being truthful, details are inserted, such as, 'It was Monday just after ten because I was watching Jeremy Kyle.'

This guy was full of details. The guns were kept in a cellar under the gatehouse. The drugs were stashed in a loft space over Unit 1. That sort of stuff, with numerous names included – strange. His only stipulation was that I had to protect his identity as he was adamant that he would be killed if these people learned of my source.

That night, and the following morning, I checked out this information, and at every turn verified his information. Some of the crooks involved were of interest to CID officers throughout the UK, the Drugs Squad, Stolen Car Squad and so on, but before going with this, I wanted some verification of my own, and also some protection for my informant, who, after all, could be of great use in future if this was genuine.

That day, I visited the French Street industrial estate, accompanied by my trusted colleague, Davie McLucas. We had selected a name from the information who was supposed to be 'ringing' a stolen Cosworth at the time, according to my new best friend. We knew the unit number, and simply drove straight to it, detained him, and took him and the vehicle back to Orkney Street. This was done with little fuss and in full view of anyone wandering about the estate or in neighbouring units.

It emerged quickly that the Cosworth had been stolen five days previous in Perth and, at a meeting later that day, it was decided that an operation would be mounted the next morning involving several divisions, the Support Unit, Dog Branch, etc. After much persuasion I managed to convince the Super and the Stolen Car Squad to let me release our detainee and the Cossie, and tell him it had a clean bill of health. I let him go with no fuss after nine that night, when his six-hour detention had expired. To be absolutely candid, I never really gave it another thought. I was only trying to protect the actual informant.

After a busy night, warrants were in place and a team of over sixty officers were arranged to meet at Paisley Police Office the next morning. This included two Support Unit vans, Drug Squad officers, CID officers from five divisions, the Dog Branch, traffic officers, firearms officers and umpteen uniform divisional personnel with police vans and vehicles to transport prisoners and property.

Everything went as smoothly as could be expected. The proprietors of this estate were serious criminals who also owned several hotels and numerous 'legit' businesses across the country. We seized a significant haul of drugs, a case full of handguns and a sawn-off shotgun. The problem was that the estate was so big that it actually took days to search. We recovered articulated trailers that had been hijacked in England at gun point, a stash of forged tax discs, countless stolen cars, even a stolen fork lift truck. The seized documentation alone took up an office at Partick CID office.

The subsequent enquiries went on for many months, being delegated to offices where the original crimes had been perpetrated, and I attended court cases across the land for years, all from spotting a stolen television being delivered in Govan.

But this wasn't a happy ending for everyone involved. A few months after this operation, I came on-duty one morning only to be hauled into the DI's room, not an unusual occurrence, and I was asked if a name rang a bell, and it really didn't. I was shown a report submitted overnight by the police in Inveraray. It related a horrifying incident when the local police had rescued a male dangling by his neck from Inveraray Pier. He had been heard by a passer-by at six-twenty, screaming for help. He had been twenty minutes away from drowning in the rising tide. I relaxed somewhat at this point, as I hadn't been in Inveraray for a few weeks.

He had eventually related a story borne out by all of the facts. He had been abducted into the rear of a van the night before. He had several fingers removed (not surgically), had been raped repeatedly, battered senseless and driven to Inveraray. His captors had then tied him to a stationary vehicle by his ankles and to their van by his wrists, and proceeded to attempt to tear him apart.

Only succeeding in dislocating a few joints, and worried about the noise they were making they had then dragged him down the pier and tried to hang him. This was the young guy we had released with his stolen Cosworth as a distraction from the real informant. As my kids say: oops.

CHAPTER 58: FISHER'S BOLT

Geoff Fisher was certainly a Ten Percenter. In fact, he was in the marginal two-percent, or nut job category. He played football for both Govan and Strathclyde Police and was as fast as lightning. He was also a natural plain-clothes operative, who loved the subterfuge, the running of informants, and the physical side of the job when we executed warrants and harassed all sorts of scumbags. He became a regular on our missions and was later to join McLucas in my place when I moved back upstairs.

One mid-week, we received reliable information that a delivery of acid, amphetamine and ecstasy was to be made that night to a house in Arden, on the south of our division. A right good ned was to be present to take his share and it was a great opportunity to nail him and get him off the streets. He was a real up-and-coming sort, who, while staking out his territory, had been directly and indirectly responsible for some really serious assaults in recent times.

So sure were we of the information, that I let the back shift duty officer (an inspector) know of our planned job in Arden. He said he had no men to spare. There was a football match on somewhere and he couldn't guarantee any resources. We were strangely undeterred. We surrounded the flats that night. Our target was ground left. The plan was that I would be at the front in our unmarked car (my own car, I think) and McLucas would lurk in the back-court darkness, while Geoff went into the property to buy drugs. Simple. When he scored the drugs at the door, we would rush in and arrest the bad guys. We must have felt invincible back then. (I can't rush a pint these days.)

The plan went awry from the off. The door was answered and Fisher disappeared inside the house. Shit. The problem with any of our well thought out plans was that Fisher always had his own plan. Life was never dull, that's for sure.

Time goes by slowly sometimes – waiting for a woman to get ready, or the last few minutes of a football match when your team is one up. But, I swear, we were sat outside for hours that night wondering what had happened or was happening inside that flat. We were both gradually moving towards total meltdown. Eventually another wee guy went to the door. He got an answer, made a buy, and left via the back court, where he was jumped by McLucas, quickly interrogated, and sent packing at speed minus his drugs. The waiting had to be over.

We chapped the door meekly, like a junkie, and when it was answered, we steamrolled our way in. The scene that we confronted in the sitting room was of total calm and tranquillity. Geoff sitting with three other spaced out druggies, all of them comfy round a coffee table littered with a variety of illegal drugs and drug para- phernalia. No one moved when we made our dramatic entrance. They were too stoned, all except Fisher.

No one else uttered a word other than 'Awright, big man' or 'Nae bother, mate' as we quickly cuffed the two biggest guys and called for transport urgently. Other than Geoff, that is; he decided to stay 'in character' and gleefully began slagging McLucas.

'Have you nothing better to do, ya fat fuck?'

'You think you're a big man. You're worse than us, ya prick.'

And so on.

At one point, one of the genuine detainees tried to calm Geoff down, telling him, 'Chill man, it's only procedure, like.'

Alas, it was to no avail. Geoff was enjoying himself immensely, but McLucas was getting riled, and things could have gone downhill fast. In the event, I grabbed mouthy Fisher and dragged him into a bedroom to be 'searched.'

Thankfully, a marked police van with four uniform cops from Pollok arrived a few minutes later. We told them to take the four neds, plus Fisher, to the station and more cuffs were applied. We took them out in convoy with Fisher at the rear. The problem was that the cop escorting him hadn't cuffed him. He was holding him lightly by his sleeve and, just as Geoff was about to make the step up into the van, he broke free and bolted down the street.

Some cop made as if to chase him but I quickly told him to leave him and get us out of there pronto. Geoff was last seen belting down the street, being cheered on by our captures and people hanging out the windows. Prick.

I'll never forget the faces of those four druggies eight months later at their trial, when Geoff appeared as a police witness in their trial, suited, booted and clean shaven and identified himself as a police officer. He was definitely a Ten Percenter.

The next day, Geoff and I were in an empty council house across the landing from a known smack dealer, Sparra. Geoff had given a 'friendly' junkie, James, ten pounds to go to Sparra's door and buy a bag of smack, our intention being to ascertain he had 'stuff' and, on our friends departure, smash his door down and take it all from him.

We were frozen in there and took turns to monitor Sparra's door through the peep hole. Sure enough, at the appointed hour, James appeared at Sparra's door. But he couldn't raise the dealer despite repeated knocking. I can still hear him shouting over and over through the letterbox.

'Spaaaara, Spaaaaaaarra, Spaaaaaaaaaaaarra.'

Eventually, he turned to our door, with me looking out the peephole and Fisher through the letterbox. Geoff said, 'Gies ma tenner. He's no in.'

James had the tenner in his hand, but was reluctant to hand it over. There then ensued a hysterical whispered argument with Geoff's hand out the letterbox trying to get his tenner back. I swear he could have been a gynaecologist. He could have strangled James through that letterbox.

James disappeared and Geoff gratefully pocketed his money, and him and I got packed up and left the empty frozen flat, but just as we approached the front close door, we saw the bold Sparra trying to get the controlled entrance lock open. The instant he opened it; he was dragged into the landing by us. He must have been at the shop or making a delivery but we found a dozen tenner bags of smack in his pocket and a further two dozen in his house. Geoff saved a tenner and we got our result. Sometimes you're better being lucky than good.

The bugger did come to my rescue one Sunday afternoon, though. I had gotten myself into a right jam. In plain clothes, heading back to the office, I heard a call for an alarm activation on Craigton road. I was on my own but thought it must be a false alarm, something fallen off the wall, or someone had leaned on the button and I would help out by stopping by. What a tube. When I got there, it was all quiet and I got out, opened the pub door expecting to see a staff member attending to the alarm, but the place was mobbed. There had been a fight, the alarm had been pressed and everything was just calming down when I popped my stupid smiling face in the front door. All heads turned and someone immediately recognised me as the filth.

'That's a copper at the door.'

Not for long. I was half-way back to the car, where I had left my radio, when the baying mob came out, the leader coming straight up to me and getting into my face. I couldn't turn my back on him because they are total cowards, and I had to face up to him, give him a stern no messing about warning, stating what I would do to him, and hope to delay him for a minute or so. This put him on the back foot for the few seconds it took for me to reach in my window and transmit a Code 21 message. The cry for urgent help.

By this time, he had re-evaluated and was coming towards me, so I went straight up to him, hands raised, and got him to stop. I read the riot act. There were about a dozen or more by this time and I swear this felt like my last stand. One of them would make a move soon and I would be overwhelmed quickly. I was just thinking of my options when I heard it. The happy distant sound of police sirens getting louder. I now pushed him, confident that, if it kicked off, I could hold onto him and use him as a shield for the next thirty seconds or so.

What a lovely feeling. The last thing I remember vividly is the smiling faces of my mate, Big Willie Stirling, driving the fast-approaching Sherpa van, with Geoff Fisher sitting in the middle grinning from ear to ear. I now knew the outcome of this unfortunate incident, caused by my stupidity, and I grabbed the idiot threatening to kill me by the two collars of his shirt, and hit him with the best ever headbutt you can imagine. My old grand-dad would have been proud. As his nose and the crowd erupted, the lads jumped out and turned it into the usual slaughter. The good guys have to win. Thanks, Geoff.

CHAPTER 59: INTERROGATIONS

Now, just hold on a minute. When the police or any government body indulge in 'interrogations', it conjures up all sorts of images. Of police states, torture, lost toe nails, or worse, and all with big shiny lamps in your face. I am here to state that these methods have no place in a civilised society. Not on a day-to-day basis, anyway. Oh, come on, there has to be some instances when just about anything goes to get the required information? Can the means never justify the end?

Regardless of our views on this, and they will cover the whole spectrum of moral opinion and division, yet again there are times when some of us have to act rather than comment or debate. For the protection of the masses. This is unfortunate. It's also unpleasant and, I would suggest, damaging for everyone involved and I for one definitely sign up to the oft-cited belief that when we resort to physical threats or actual violence we've lost already. Mostly.

Let's first put this in perspective. When does an interview become an interrogation? I still carry out interviews from time to time for High Court cases, major incidents or high claims. I have never met the witnesses or accused before, never will again, and they are always volunteers who know why I'm there and what I'm doing. I simply record their statement, regardless of my view, with as much detail as possible. This can take several days, especially with an expert witness. My job is simply to get down as much detail as possible, but it's the statement of the witness, not mine. My most common phrase throughout the process is: 'And then what happened?'

I just write or dictate it. No controversy there and the court or lawyer or investigating body gets an untainted account of that person's testimony. If they're telling lies? I don't know or even care.

If their dates or times are wrong, if their descriptions of people or events are in contrast to other evidence? Not a problem. I want to know what they say or think they remember. That's all.

Let's move to the suspect for an assault or a theft. The crime is almost irrelevant, although the seriousness will determine how much time, preparation and thought I will put into the interview. Is it still an interview? Just as above, I want to get down the statement, untainted by my bias or preconceived ideas about what occurred, only now the lies, lapses of memory or inaccuracies are much more important. I actively want these to come out. I want the downright obvious lies, and the last thing I will do is contradict them or show, in any way, my scepticism. Again, my dead pan response should be of total impartiality and neutrality, but this time I have a purpose. Now I'm investigating.

'And then what happened?'

When I have that detailed statement down, read over and signed or, better still, on tape, I now have something to work with, but are we moving into an interrogation yet? You be the judge.

After a break and the gathering together of CCTV, documents, photographs, forensic evidence, or whatever constitutes the hard evidence so far, I want to go over this statement, but this time point out the anomalies, and give this person a chance to reconsider.

'Oops, I must have been mistaken about that.'

Or:

'Oh, yes, that's right. Now I remember...'

Or, better yet, keep denying. I've gone into countless interviews, knowing fine well that the individual concerned would rather die than ever tell the police anything, far less the truth. It was never going to happen. So, what was the point of the interview? Countless colleagues have asked me the same question. Because a denial is almost as good as a confession if the evidence all points the other way. A fingerprint or a credible eye witness. That gives the judge and jury a decision to make between the two.

What was even harder to convey was that an interview in front of a lawyer where I ask questions and only ever get 'no comment' answers can be the clincher in a case. Some cops considered this a waste of time or a negative outcome, but it often proved to be exactly the opposite. How more damning in front of a jury to be exposed as a person who, asked if he raped a woman, molested a child, or stabbed someone, responded 'no comment.' Wouldn't an innocent person deny such allegations? Surely, an innocent person would give an account of himself and at least protest his innocence, given the opportunity?

So, with the witness, no problem, open questions, almost verbatim answers noted. With an accused, where you have other evidence, no problem. Get the denial recorded. I think we're still in the interview part of the spectrum. The tricky stuff comes when we have little or no direct evidence, but a suspicion, and, without a confession, we'll struggle to make a case at all.

A notorious Glasgow gangster once told me that, if the police interviewed him, he sussed right away that they had nothing on him and wanted some purchase. He would just sit it out. He was right to a degree, but wrong to tell me. I once locked him up at London Road and put him straight in a cell. No questions. I made sure that he learned we had a sidekick of his, an Irish terrorist, locked up down the corridor. He sure wanted to talk to me then, not knowing what the other guy was saying to us.

This kind of sums up the whole complicated world of interviews, questioning, interrogations, and so on. It is psychological warfare from the minute you first make contact with the person of interest. Body language, posture, throwaway remarks, chit chat and courtesies. They all play a part. One slip up or throwaway casual comment, or even a look, can shatter the rapport required. A top QC once told me that most accused were convicted in the first thirty seconds following their arrest by opening their mouths. Of course, he was over-simplifying the matter, because he only ever questioned people when he knew all the answers and they were under a big spotlight in a witness box. The truth never mattered to him, only the outcome – and his pay day.

The truth was that the damning comments were usually the result of some clever foreplay by the arresting officer, and some subtle manipulation of the circumstances. A real skill. So much so that, when you became proficient, you had to be extra careful, because you could extract confessions from innocent parties, so desperate were they to please or obtain the promised incentive, such as an early release, a visit from a loved one, or even a paltry Embassy Regal. Most police officers never study these things at all. They are just natural communication skills that you have, or not, and they are actually difficult to train, because, to be effective, they have to appear natural. Most officers have little patience, would not speak to these 'scumbags' at all, and will leave such matters to others.

I, on the other hand, loved the joust. The foreplay, the dance, the tease, the play-acting on both sides, the half-truths and lies, all of it. In any walk of life, if you find something that you love to do and have some proficiency at, you're on a winner, and I would always put myself forward for interview jobs. I loved it, was invested in the whole process, and really enjoyed the feeling of success. It's like winning a chess match. Magic. I had much more than my fair share of success in interviewing for all of these reasons and I had no problem changing my language to suit the interviewee. You had to speak the same language.

I once did an attempted murder interview in Govan with a Chinese man, and he had an interpreter. My Cantonese was and is pretty poor. The interview was a disaster because all of the nuance and implications of questions were lost in translation, and the time between asking, it being translated, the reply, and it being translated back to me, gave him too much thinking time. This shows that interviewing is not just a case of asking the right questions. I would go as far as to say that, to me, and any other professional interviewers, it is an art form at its highest level, when the stakes on both sides are extremely high and you only have one shot at it. What a buzz.

My conclusion, then, is that any questioning, of a wife to her husband when he comes home late, to a mother of a child re his or her internet use, to an employer trying to make a judgement about who to hire, is interrogation. The thing that makes it so is not the shouting or the big light shining in the subject's face, but the assessment of the answers given. This judgement, not only of the words, but the tone, eye contact, body language and context will determine the future, and whether a further sculpted supplementary question is required. These questions often lead down a path where a trap door awaits, and this, to me, is an interrogation. We are all experts without even realising it.

Here are some examples of interrogation situations, and you can decide what is justified or not. These are all absolutely real scenarios that I was involved in, back in the day. For once, I will keep my view to myself.

Terrorists have hostages on a plane, on the tarmac at Glasgow airport. You capture one of them. You have no idea if there are explosives planted somewhere or what they plan to do. How far does interrogation go?

Your ten-year-old son has money he shouldn't have. A twenty-pound note. He says he found it but can't explain further, and you know he's lying. Do you let it lie or do you need to get to the bottom of it? How do you get there?

A family are held hostage at gun point. A mother, grandmother and three children, aged two, five and seven. You have one of the baddies in custody, but no idea where the family are being held or what will happen to them now that you have interrupted their plans. How far would you go in questioning the guy you have?

A suspect is being held for interview re the rape and murder of a girl, her body dumped in Pollok park. You have little other evidence, but are pretty sure he's the guy. Will you try some additional methods of interrogation to find out the truth?

A young woman, about eighteen years old, says her boyfriend raped her. He maintains it was totally consensual, but her mother found out. How far do you question either of them to find out the truth?

These are just five of thousands of scenarios faced by law enforcement, parents, teachers, partners and all of us every single day, but the hard ones are where there are lives at stake and you have a choice to make. It's easy for the watchers, behind their big desks or laptop screens, especially with hindsight. Thankfully, only a few of us have to make these calls when the chips are down and I would stand by every decision taken for the right reasons. The decision is made on behalf of us all, but only one person has to bear the consequences of judgement after the event, often having to live with that call forever.

In number one above, it was a training exercise. We were based at Gartcosh old steelworks for a few days, playing out a major incident terrorist scenario. I remember during the course of the last day, it was all coming to a head. We had been running about the city, carrying out interviews, kicking in doors, tracing cars and making worldwide enquiries and now it had come to a climax. The terrorists on the plane (who were in an outbuilding in the middle of the huge car park) had set an eight o'clock deadline. (Come on, we all had to get to the pub at a decent hour.) If whatever they were demanding hadn't been sorted, they would start shooting hostages. Everything ramped up a notch.

I was walking through the massive hangar on some paper chase when the huge doors opened a notch and a bus came in slowly. It was blacked out with wee curtains drawn across each window. I think I subconsciously knew what was going on, but was left in absolutely no doubt when, about twenty minutes later, a Range Rover appeared from somewhere. It had wooden scaffolding mounted around it, like a glazier's van, but, rather than glass window panes, there were men holding on. Fully armed, balaclavas, the lot. The hairs still stand up on the back of my neck at the recollection. What a sight. Awesome. Our special forces going into action. Thank goodness they were on our side.

After they had done what they do out on the 'tarmac', we then had the task of interviewing the terrorists who hadn't been killed. It really was make-believe now. I was told to accompany a DI who was a trained negotiator in conducting one of these interviews. What a laugh. The interviewee was, we later learned, an SAS soldier selected for the job. I have no idea what nationality he was, or where he was from, because he never uttered one word throughout. He was a lawyer's dream. I swear I detected a slight trace of a smile across in his eyes at one point, but I may have made that up.

There's a reason why the 'good cop, bad cop' interview format is a thing. It's so well-known as to be a joke. Well, the reason is that it works, always has, and always will. Not on this occasion. Both of the good guys in the room were on our side of the table, and the bad guy was saying absolutely nothing. So bad were we that we failed to even ascertain his name, rank and number, which is supposed to be a given.

In scenario number two, my son had been given money by his mother, but she had forgotten to mention it. He didn't want to cause any hassle and planked it somewhere. Split loyalties and confusion caused by adults, but a lecture about trust and the threat of being grounded did the trick. No need for a beating on this occasion.

Number three is related earlier in my story and resulted in the baddy hanging upside down over a high banister at Orkney Street. This had the desired effect and the family of hostages were then recovered safe and well. Justified?

In number four, I wasn't party to the interrogation of a suspected murderer taking place at Pollok. I was in Govan minding my own business when the phone rang on my desk.

'McLean, bring me some jellies to Pollok. Quick as you can, son.'

I couldn't believe it. My boss, and I mean high ranking detective boss man, had just ordered me to deliver controlled drugs to him at another police office. What the…? How did he know I could get them at such short notice? Why did he want them? I knew he could drink with the best of them, but jellies? FFS. (Jellies is a slang name for diamorphine capsules, popular with the junkies of the day.) What to do. I couldn't ignore him. It could be a trap, but of all the men I worked with over the years, he was the last I believed would betray a fellow Ten Percenter. He would batter lumps out of me, but he would cover my ass, and never sell one of his own down the river.

Still, I had to be cautious. You just never know who knew what was going on and what price your head or even the head of a senior detective might have. I simply got some plastic bags, put a variety of seized drugs that I had been saving as payment or bait, and labelled them accordingly. If anyone asked, they would be for training purposes. When I arrived at Pollok, I insisted on speaking to the boss myself. I wasn't passing anything through a third mouthpiece. I mean party. This was tricky because he was in the interview and disturbing any interview is fraught with danger. You never want to disturb the flow at any stage but my assurances that the boss wanted to see me eventually got through the barriers and he came out.

He took me aside and told me to make three coffees and he proceeded to put at least four of the jellies into one of them. I dealt with the sugar and milk, and we went back into the interview room together. I made damn sure I drank the right coffee, but I only stayed for five or ten minutes and it was made clear I should bugger off and the DI I had replaced went back in, throwing me daggers. He had no idea what had just occurred.

Whether this dubious tactic worked or not is neither here nor there. He'll have been released long ago, anyway. Your job, should you choose to accept it, is to decide if the means justified the end. It could have been your daughter or wife found naked, abused and strangled in that park, and we may have prevented many more needless deaths and devastated families.

Number five is, perhaps, the hardest of all. Rarely do you get confessions in these cases. Men hate to admit sexual failings, or assaults on women, far less crimes against children. HMP Barlinnie is full of robbers, murderers, conmen and fraudsters but not one of them says, 'I'm in for battering my girlfriend senseless.'

Unusually, in these cases, you have two parties whose stories have to be verified, as there are rarely any witnesses. The complainer, normally a girl or woman, also has to be interrogated in order to ascertain the veracity of her allegation, and, in my day, we would make a judgement as to whether we thought her story and, indeed, her personality would stand the rigours of a High Court interrogation by a defence lawyer. Should the woman's story be verified by officers interrogating her appropriately? Or should her story be believed without question?

Even more complicated is when children are the complainers. To what degree should we test their allegations? After all, in both of these instances, the crimes alleged can prove to be life changing for the person accused.

Such are the issues and daily dilemmas considered and argued over by those tasked with keeping us all safe, of wheedling out the bad apples and putting them out of our way. On one occasion at the High Court, the Fiscal came into our waiting room and told us that the accused in our case had pled guilty and we could all go home. The DI who'd worked the case with me when we had recorded a full confession turned, his mouth open in surprise, and said to me:

'Wow, it must have been him after all.'

You just never know for sure about anything, and all you can really do is your best and hope not to be judged too harshly in the final analysis, which usually takes place in the pub.

The definition of an interrogation is a verbal questioning of someone. 'When the police ask someone a series of tough questions to determine if he robbed a store, this is an example of an interrogation', according to Wikipedia.

Of course, interrogations can go too far or, rather, further than the situation warrants, and, in some instances, so far as to make any information gleaned not only unusable, but entirely unreliable. There was an infamous case in Glasgow in the early nineties when a divisional detective constable in the city centre began to accrue a fantastic clearance rate. Everything he touched was detected, mostly through confessions from the neds he was detaining and questioning. They were confessing to everything. Rather suspicious.

It came to a head when the officer involved was charged using a procedure called the Moorov doctrine. This is a special rule in evidence that can allow a single witness' evidence to be corroborated by the evidence of another witness in certain situations, in order to prove that the alleged offending was part of a course of conduct, systematically pursued. A key part of this rule is that the individual witnesses must be entirely independent of each other.

I should explain that, uniquely in Scots Law, corroboration is a foundation stone of all evidence allowed in court. Crucially, a confession alone cannot convict, and neither can the word of only one witness. There must be corroborating evidence of some kind, and the Moorov rule helps provide that in particular circumstances. (Samuel Moorov was convicted of interfering with a number of young girls, who didn't know each other, but gave similar accounts of Moorov's behaviour in the circumstance.)

In our case, the detective was accused of putting a hand gun to the heads of the suspects when questioning them. No wonder his clearance rate was exceptional. The story was leaked to the newspapers before any trial could take place, the story ran, and the Moorov doctrine was of no use, because the details were now public knowledge. That was my understanding and I was glad to have my faith in police integrity restored.

Without jumping to producing firearms, there are higher levels of interrogation and interview than the police employ investigating domestic crime and criminals. All sorts of tactics and devices can be employed, such as sleep deprivation, disorientation, repetitive questioning, and so on, eventually moving into areas of real torture such as the Americans' apparent favourite, water boarding.

For me, the upper echelons of interviewing takes us into the realm called the debrief, where the game is played in a civilised manner, sometimes over protracted lengths of time, with subtlety and decorum, but with the highest stakes. That's proper interrogation, where national security is at stake and there is no real end, just more of the never-ending game.

CHAPTER 60: MARTI PELLOW

I was ultimately scunnered in Govan CID. It all became a boring blur, a groundhog-day dealing with much the same crimes committed by the same type of scumbag. I was just fed up. I had also now passed my inspector's exam and so pushed myself into contention for promotion. I realised that to secure that I would need to get out of the firing line, become one of the ninety percent for a while, at least, and effect a change of image. My daughter, Louise, was starting to need hospitalisation more often, and my kids all lived with their mother in Campbeltown, so there were many factors aligned that suggested I needed a change.

It came to a head one night when Scotland was beating Sweden in the World Cup. Now, you realise that really was a long time ago. At some point, all hell broke loose in Ibrox, on Paisley Road West. It transpired there was a racial riot. At one stage, we had two white guys trapped in a chip shop, every window being smashed and the crowd attempting to put these characters in the fryers. It was mayhem. Cops appeared from everywhere. We had an estimated five-hundred Asians on the street at one point. Someone had assaulted and attempted to rob an Asian senior and all hell broke loose. There were running battles in the street, cars speeding in and out of the area, and guns were mentioned at one point. It went on for a few hours and I ended up in Kilmarnock, having pursued a car load of white Scottish neds who had joined in and caused a lot of injuries, damage and grief.

I was lucky to catch a glimpse of them, and saw them leave two young Asian lads for dead on the street and head off onto the motorway. I was on my own and couldn't get any back up as all hands were needed to quell the ongoing riot. They were picked up by me and Kilmarnock CID in a local Ayrshire pub and both later convicted of attempted murder.

The next day, I spoke to my DSI, at that time Jack Baird. I had worked with his brother, Allan, in the Crime Squad. Good people. I explained to Jack how I felt. I wanted out. I wanted a uniform. I was bored and nothing I was doing was stimulating. With hindsight, I had overdosed on adrenalin in plain clothes, but knew I needed a change. Jack quite rightly made me think about it for a week or so. This was a big deal. I was unaware of any detective asking to get back into uniform, ever. But, eventually, I convinced the gaffers that I was serious. This included a summons to Pitt Street and an in-depth interview by an Assistant Chief Constable. What I didn't know was that there was a plan in place for me, even then, and somebody somewhere was checking up on me. I was appointed the community police officer for Cessnock and totally delighted.

My first day in uniform for almost fifteen years, proudly patrolling my beat along Paisley Road West, I must have lit up my patch with the smile on my coupon. It felt like total freedom. No greens or pending enquiries. What a hoot. I was only just out the office, walking along PRW, near the Swallow Hotel (going for a coffee), when I bumped into a well-known face. She was a hopeless junkie with a hundred pounds a day habit, and we knew each other well. I was aware that an old woman in the sheltered housing next to the Swallow had lost her pension book to some couple who'd faked their way into her house on some pretext, and this was a prime suspect right here.

I shouted her over and immediately saw the choice being made whether as to run, or stay and tough it out. She chose the latter, knowing I would have caught her, anyway, and came across to chat to me.

'Angela, I need the Monday book back. Where is it now?'

She was funny. All of the junkies were – with hindsight, of course. They never spoke at normal volume for some reason. You hear them shouting at each other a mile away, and it sounds really aggressive, as if a domestic is about to break out. But that's just them talking normal. They also seem to have smack blinkers on.

Like a mouse that hides its head and thinks you don't see it. They think they can swan about shoplifting and stealing, shooting up and sleeping wherever they want, and no one can see them.

She started spouting the usual drivel as soon as she got within bawling distance, about where she'd been, her terrible health, who she was helping, who was dying, why her brew money hadn't come through, and on and on.

'Am no kiddin, big man. Av no goat time fur this, by the way.'

I listened for a few minutes and then got fed up and, without thinking, took my police hat off in the process. Her face lit up immediately.

'Mr McLean, what the fuck happened to you?'

Suffice to say, I was just about to call up a van to lock her up, or so she thought, when she told me where she had sold the Monday book. It was such an interesting piece of information that the resulting operation deserves its own chapter (see Knotty Green).

I once interviewed a junkie on my Govan beat, who told me that she was doing well on her methadone project. She was down from 140mls per day to only 100mls. I was quite impressed till I asked her how long she'd been on the programme.

'Thirteen years,' was the shocking reply.

Not quite so impressive. Especially when you knew, as we all did, that the methadone was only a ground base that took the edge of their addiction, to be topped up at every possible opportunity with smack or whatever they could get their hands on at any particular time. Securing drugs wasn't at the top of a junkie's list of things to do – it was the *only* thing on the list, and everything they did was designed to acquire them.

For some clarity here, I had absolutely no prejudice or especial dislike for drug users or addicts. I hated that they were so selfish, untrustworthy and sometimes violent, all driven by their crippling habit, but they were still victims to us. The people we really despised were the dealers and, even more than them, the government system and policy on drugs, which was to deny it existed, underplay its existence, or ignore it completely and hope it went away. The only government intervention I remember was when they ran a TV campaign warning about the dangers of controlled drugs. I heard somewhere that, when Saatchi & Saatchi assessed this campaign, they concluded that they couldn't have designed anything better to encourage the abuse of drugs than this campaign. I would contend that nothing has changed.

Apparently, all over five hundred US congressmen, and about a hundred Senators all believe in God and practice their faith. Does that not tell us that politicians just follow the routes that they believe will get them elected? Or, more pertinently, won't expose the truth about their thoughts, beliefs and feelings if it might risk their political futures. I would suggest that the same is true of many subjects that they think are too risky and, moreover, I would put drug policy right at the top of that list of shame. I use the word 'shame' deliberately because these politicians mostly have no idea the misery, heartache, poverty and devastation caused by drug misuse and addiction. Not a clue. Even if they did, it wouldn't influence them enough to risk their cushy ego-driven careers to actually try and make an impact. I might be cynical, but I really believe that we are governed by the least among us, for the most part.

Jack Baird, the detective super, told me the day I started on my uniform community beat, when he came across me speaking to the divisional collator in the CID room, that rather than losing an experienced detective, he now felt that he had gained a detective in deep disguise, which is really exactly what I had become.

During that first few back shifts, I was walking towards Paisley Road Toll, and at that time there was a Bank of Scotland on the corner at the lights. As I approached, I could see from quite a distance that there was a 4x4 vehicle double parked right outside the bank, causing mayhem as the filter traffic behind it tried to get past. What a selfish idiot. It took me a couple of minutes to get there and, when I did, I got my notebook out to note the vehicle details, and show the passing public how diligent the local Bobby was. Just as I was doing this, out came the guy from the bank, red faced and rushing suitably. It was Marti Pellow of the Clydebank super group of the day, Wet Wet Wet.

He was all apologies, of course, grovelling as he jumped up into the vehicle ready to drive off. I still had my notebook in my hand and I started the procedure.

'Is this your vehicle, Sir?'

A big sigh was followed by more timid apologies. I carried on regardless.

'What is your full name?'

'Occupation, please?'

'Home address?' (I thought that might be useful.)

'Now, if you could just sign under those details for me, sir, my daughter will be most impressed, as she's a huge fan.'

That famous Pello smile was a thing of real beauty up close. He had some kind of CB-radio thing on his dashboard and immediately grabbed it and spoke to a girl in what I guessed was their office and, taking my address, he promised to have a bag of goodies sent to my daughter. And he did. He was a nice guy, then at the peak of his powers, and who apparently went on to fight his own addiction demons.

I became quite the autograph hunter on my beat. One time I was refereeing a charity game between Strathclyde Police and Dukla Pumpherston (a celebrity and ex-professional players team) at Benburb Juniors ground. It was for cystic fibrosis, on a lovely day, and I would guess a few thousand punters were out to watch, mostly crowded under the old covered terrace. As the game progressed, I became aware of collective giggling behind my back, but every time I turned round to face the terrace, where the bulk of the crowd were congregated, it stopped. I also saw that a Dukla substitute, Tony Roper (actor and comedian), was running up and down that touchline and had a decidedly guilty look on his face. I was still a detective, after all.

I let this play out for a while, realising that when my back was turned Tony would jump onto the playing surface and wave his arms about frantically, as if looking for a pass out wide. Then, when I turned round, he would jump back trackside and make as if stretching and warming up. Eventually, at a suitable moment, I blew the whistle and summoned him over.

'Me?' he exclaimed, feigning innocence as only footballers can, and turning to the crowd for sympathy.

They were all booing me, which is not an unusual occurrence. I met Roper half-way and got my notebook out and made as if to note his name, then gave the pen and book to him for his signature and shook his hand. The crowd loved it.

Around this time there was a lot of racial tension in the air, apparently more so over on the south side of the city. There had been a few incidents and the media are never slow to pick up on easy headline grabbers. For my part, my beat was, at that time, a real centre of the Asian community and I made many lifelong friends there in Cessnock and Ibrox. On one occasion, I was asked to take a young reporter out with me on my beat, as he was doing some kind of Radio 4 programme about race relations. When he appeared with all of his kit, we walked up to Paisley Road West, where most of the businesses were owned by Asians, and I knew most, if not all, of them. He got a few interviews, visited Bellahouston Academy, and we had a few laughs. All positive, I thought. Then we came towards Percy Street, where a group of Asian lads were playing football. We were across the road and they hadn't seen us approaching and, truth be told, they were being a bit rowdy. As I made to cross the road, I felt my journalist friend tense up.

'Is it okay, do you think?' he asked, holding back a bit.

I told him not to worry, I knew all of these Asian gangs. He then dropped a full ten feet behind me, fumbling with his recording gear as an excuse. Still unnoticed I shouted in my best PC Murdoch voice:

'Right you lot, what's going on here?'

They all stopped, stunned, and simultaneously broke into big smiles, shouting hellos and mild piss take obscenities at me. All good banter that I was never slow to return. One of them kicked the ball to me and I kept it up, crossing the road, and put it in their makeshift goal on the gable end. I was still the keepy-uppy king, even with my Dr Martens on. Mostly, they called me Mr Simon, or Uncle, but my nickname in the area was Kakaspyee. I've never seen it written but, supposedly, it meant some kind of esteemed, handsome and brave law enforcement person, and had been used affectionately, I think, since I took over the community beat.

We had a bit of banter and mutual piss take and then I made my usual threat to go speak with their fathers about this hanging about on street corners terrifying the locals. Although said as a joke at the time, it was the ultimate sanction and threat. If I had a word with their fathers, they would have been grounded, or much worse, for disgracing the family and community. This was a real tool in my armoury, which ensured total, if grudging, respect from these teenagers, and on the occasions I had to use it, the retribution was always swift and effective. That said, the only person terrified on this evening was my journalist friend, who was visibly stunned by this encounter. I should say that he was an Asian lad, but he had obviously gone to a private school or had somehow avoided the daily street life of a city boy. I don't think it ever made the radio, which I suppose shows that our adventure was a success.

I was friendly with and knew most of the Asian shopkeepers on PRW and around the Cessnock area, making some lifelong friends such as Harry Burmy (now passed away, sadly) and Harry Singh of Harry's Hardware on the PRW. Harry being our version of Harbinder. These people became friends. I refereed their football, went to engagement and wedding parties that lasted for days, and was a confidant when things went badly and advice was sought.

I took my kids to meet a butcher friend and introduced them. His name was Shaheed, but when I said that, my youngest promptly corrected me.

'Dad! It's Shahead.'

I was determined that my kids would never be lumbered with a broad Glaswegian accent, but my corrections came back to haunt me occasionally. Bellahooston got the same treatment. She was mortified at me when she told me it was obviously Bellahooston.

Shaheed's Butchers was in the heart of my beat, and a meeting point for many of the shopkeepers and businesspeople in the area. I regularly had many a lunch there, cooked in the homes with chapattis, brought over piping hot in dish towels. I also had too many meals sitting on the floors of my parishioners' homes with the whole family around me. I think I was a natural at the community policing lark, as well.

One night, I was at the office when Shaheed called me. There had been some kind of robbery and he needed me there at his shop. He was rambling on, but sounded cheery. I thought he's won the lottery or come into some other good fortune.

When I got there, I was confronted by about twenty or more local Asians, all trying to speak to me at the one time. When I could eventually get a word in, I pieced together what had got them all in a tizz. Earlier, two Jamaican gentlemen had gone into one of their shops, asking where he could find the local jeweller. After a bit of persuasion, the shopkeeper had established that these two had some good jewellery that they wanted to sell quickly, and thought that a jeweller would be most interested. More arm twisting went on and, after much begging, the lads made an exception and showed the shopkeeper some of the beautiful stuff they had and shared the minimum prices they were prepared to accept.

This was such a chance, to get in before the jeweller and get this gold at bargain prices, that not only did they buy some, they immediately shared their good fortune with other family members and friends in the neighbourhood. Such is the networking in the Asian community that the Jamaicans were sold out of their bargain gold within a few hours and were gone. Only now had the buyers discovered their folly, when an actual jeweller came over from Shawlands and broke the sad news to them. It was not much better than costume jewellery. Oh my goodness gracious me, phone Simon.

Shaheed was hosting this non-party in his shop and was the only one on my side. Everyone was irate, some of them having parted with a few thousand pounds, every transaction in cash. Shaheed understood what I was struggling to impart to these would-be complainers. No crime had been committed. Even if I caught the culprits, who were half-way back to Jamaica (or London) by now, there was nothing with which I could charge them. They had only taken advantage of human greed. They hadn't misrepresented themselves or the jewellery, and no one could ever prove that they knew its actual worth. I was not a popular community policeman that night.

A few hours later, I was driving along PRW when I spotted Shaheed, slowly heading towards home with his head bowed. I stopped, and saw he was almost crying.

'What's wrong, Shaheed, is everything okay?'

'No, my wife spent eight-hundred pounds on jewellery that is worth about twenty pounds'

Not much I could say to that.

These are the perfect crimes, when you could never be arrested or charged with anything. One time, in Rothesay, I was called to a big house outside the town where an elderly man lived on his own. I'd say he was in his eighties and suffered from dementia. When I arrived, his daughter was there and she reported that her dad had been visited by a thief, who had taken a valuable painting from him, and I should get on the case immediately and have it returned. She pointed to a light patch on the wall where said painting had hung until recently.

It transpired that this was a Koekkoek painting (a Dutch landscape artist and lithographer born in 1803, Barend Cornelis Koekkoek) and was, indeed, of significant value. While attempting to interview the gentleman, however, I discovered that he was totally relaxed. It also became apparent that I would not be able to get a worthwhile statement from him. He was wearing a sports jacket and collar with tie, as that generation tend to do, and on a whim, I asked the daughter to go through his pockets for me.

She did so reluctantly, displeased that I hadn't caught anyone yet, and, sure enough, from his right-hand pocket she removed eighty pounds in cash and a business card.

I would have no trouble catching up with the guy who had taken the painting, but alas, he would not be going to a cell. No crime had been committed. He maintained that he had simply bought the painting in good faith, paid for it in cash and left his card for future business purposes. Perhaps you can see why some people would take the law into their own hands. I can assure you that this particular art dealer did pay a hefty price some years later at the hands of Her Majesty's Revenue but it wasn't through karma. It was through me.

We had an amazing case in Govan. An old man, or at least someone acting like an old man, went into the bank across from the Swallow Hotel on PRW. He then told the few customers to lie down on the floor, which they all did. This was all on camera. He proceeded to go to the young teller, hand over a plastic bag, and tell her to fill it with five thousand pounds, which she duly did. He left.

This landed on my desk as a robbery, but I didn't spend a minute's effort trying to catch this guy. I spoke to the Fiscal instead and confirmed that, as there had been no threat of violence or actual violence, no weapon or threat, only a request, there had been no theft, and certainly no robbery. If you ask someone to give you money and they do, where's the crime? Thankfully, no one can yet be charged with stupidity, or many of us would be doing life.

CHAPTER 61: KNOTTY

Remember my first day on my beat back in uniform as a community police officer? When I was told where the stolen Monday benefits book had been reset or traded. Well, it was supposed to have gone to a guy, Knotty Green. That on its own was no big revelation. Only the fact that he was out of prison was news, having served a good few years for the manslaughter of his father. He was a well-known scumbag, drug user and dealer and all-round piece of vermin. What was newsworthy was that he was just about to score a large quantity of smack and cocaine, any day now apparently.

This was my first day in uniform, but I had to go see my new gaffer about this. It sounded true and checked out as far as I could tell.

'It didn't take you long then,' he said. 'Do what's required, but keep me in the loop.'

So we did. We set up an observation point on Clifford Street, where with binoculars we could watch Knotty's fourteenth floor balcony. He was supposed to be going across the balcony to cut the gear next door. We took it in turns and I secured sheriff's warrants for both flats – his own flat and that of his next-door neighbour. I think we were a few days into our watching brief when my own informant, who I had sent up there to make a buy, came back and said the stuff had just arrived. We were on.

A few hours later, we could plainly see the bold Knotty walking back and forward across the balcony between the two flats. I got a team of about five trusted guys together, some of who knew Knotty of old, and were ready for him, because he was a violent individual. I had decided to wait until he was safely inside what he thought was a safe house along the landing, and affect the warrant there in order to catch him red handed. A cunning plan, but not so clever in the execution. We could tell from the change in activity that something was going down. Knotty and his wee girlfriend, Janet, were trekking along the landing, her going to and fro, no doubt supplying tea and fags for our man while he got down to the serious business of cutting and wrapping.

Leaving a spotter in place watching the balcony, off we went, straight to the door of the safe house. We would generally knock the door, just for good form, and it's always nice to see their faces when they opened it to us rushing in on top of them, but no answer on this occasion. So, boots to the fore, we almost took the door off its hinges in one swoop and made our move for Knotty. Imagine our surprise when all we saw just inside was an old woman sitting in front of her telly, oblivious to anything going on behind her. If we were surprised, it was nothing to the fright she got when she spotted us, half a dozen coppers with batons drawn and cuffs at the ready, expecting a crazed madman, confronted by a much more scary proposition: an old deaf lady minding her own business. Fortunately, she didn't have a heart attack, but I thought her son might when he appeared, ranting and raging. Someone tried to fix the hanging door, but I was determined to make this right, by catching Knotty.

What had happened was that each apartment within the high flats was on two levels, with stairs up to the sitting room and kitchen area, with the bedrooms all downstairs at door level. All except the homes at the gable end of the building. These were reserved for elderly or infirm tenants, so there were no internal stairs. We had raided the door adjacent to Knotty's, but he was in the one directly above. We quickly retreated, and I'm not sure what Knotty saw as we rushed through the door and onto him in his safe house, but the adrenalin was pumping by then. It must have done the trick, because he surrendered like a big pussy and there it was. Enough smack and other drugs to keep the whole of Govan going for a week. All in the process of being cut or mixed and packaged, his scales, magazines for preparing the wraps, gloves, the whole shooting match on the coffee table. We called that bang to rights.

We then searched his house along the landing and what an Aladdin's Cave we found. Monday books and other giro slips, cheque books, domestic items, about twenty-five car radios with cassettes, a lawn mower, three bicycles, a shelf full of jewellery, it just went on and on. He had been trading drugs for just about anything that could be stolen and it was a two-week job identifying where a lot of it had come from and reconciling it with the rightful owner. A lot of the property the police recover is never returned because people tend not to keep serial numbers or other identifiers, even a photograph, and so the police auctions were always busy.

This was all well, and just to have someone like Broon locked up was considered a good day's work, but he was looking at a right good stretch if we could get over the one obvious flaw in our, otherwise, water-tight case. We had no warrant for the house where we had entered by force and where we had recovered the drugs, and before Knotty appeared at court, I was summoned to Ballater Street to speak with the Fiscal – never a good sign.

I was initially told by the PF that she could not take proceedings in this case and would have to throw it out. Funny. I had come prepared. I showed her the warrants that I did have and explained the layout and the fact that an old woman and her son would be witnesses in the case. Everyone knows that nice old ladies are great in the witness box and generally just tell it as it is. I also produced the drugs we had seized, all packaged and ready to go to the laboratory. And when I told her we would have to give them back, she visibly wilted. I emphasised that I had the full backing of DSI Jackson and that we should let the court decide if I had acted improperly.

In due course, we went to trial, and I spent a long time in the witness box, but I stood my ground, and I felt that every angle the defence tried to use to attack our actions gave me an excuse to reiterate that I acted in good faith. There was no time to retreat, as the drugs were above us and could be gone or even destroyed imminently. It felt as though it was on a knife edge for a while, but eventually the judge saw fit to allow it, and the jury only took a few hours to agree with him. Twelve years was the outcome and, after an appeal, there was some case law evolved from it.

His girlfriend, Janet, was kept out of the trial, ostensibly being a Crown witness who was never used in court. I judged that she was as much of a victim as anyone in this case and, during the lead up to the trial, I had visited her where she stayed with her mum and sister in Whitelock Street. Her sister was Jade, and I say sister, because I never knew Jade as anything other than a beautiful young woman. She had a sixteen-inch waist (apparently) and was always meticulously turned out, as transgender people generally are, in my experience. She also had the most bubbly, likeable girly personality and was a magnet for attention.

Jade accompanied Janet to the High Court for the trial and, when she walked through the front door, every single male head was turned. She had made a special effort and was loving it. I made sure she and Janet were safely seated in the civilian Crown witness room and returned to the police waiting room. Jade was the talk of the steamie. Who was she; did you see her, big man; what a body; and on and on. One lad in particular, Stevie, had obviously been stricken big time.

'She's a witness in our case Stevie,' I said. 'Do you want to meet her?'

'Honestly, big man. You know her? Fuck sake, aye, let's go.'

Off we went to the civilian witness room. I made up some pretext to speak with Jade and Janet and introduced Stevie. He could hardly talk, but he was a good-looking guy and Jade grasped what was going on immediately. Before long, they had exchanged numbers and might have eloped right then if I hadn't brought this fledgling romance to an end. Back in our own room, as Stevie was boasting to all and sundry, I broke the news to him that Jade was actually a man going through the changes required to change sex. I think that's how I put it. The place was in an uproar, but I must give Stevie his due. He stuck to his guns and made a great and eloquent on-the-spot defence for himself that shut everyone up instantly.

'I don't fucking care. I'd shag her, anyway.'
I never found out if he used that number.

CHAPTER 62: LOUISE

When my beautiful daughter, Louise Jane McLean, was born on 28th April 1988, my life turned upside down. Her mother had known something wasn't right midway through her pregnancy. Don't ask me how. When she appeared, she was perfect in appearance, and went on to become a beautiful young woman, both inside and out. But over that first six months of her life, her mum fought tooth and nail with the doctors and specialists because she knew Louise had problems. Eventually, when she was six months old, the medics were persuaded to carry out a test for cystic fibrosis, which unfortunately proved positive. One of the things we know for a fact is that early treatment in any serious illness or disease is of great benefit. Don't start me.

When we got home, with heavy hearts, I realised that we knew hardly anything about cystic fibrosis, and would have to wait until an appointment was made for us to attend a clinic to find anything out. It's hard to believe that, in those days, we had no Google. We relied on family and friends to find things out from the collective knowledge, if you will, and so I phoned my mate, Stan, as his stepfather was a GP. Old Arthur came on and, after much humming and hawing, he told me that Louise would do well to reach the age of five, such was the seriousness of the diagnoses.

This was in September, 1988. Arthur was nearing retirement and CF was quite a new disease, in that it had only been discovered relatively recently. For clarity, here it is the most common genetically inherited disease affecting children and young adults. What a bombshell at the time, but I think old Arthur unwittingly gave us a gift that day. The whole day was just so profound and emotional that I think that five-year prognosis hit home and that, for the remainder of Louise's life, had been our deep-seated expectation. In actual fact, she lived to be twenty-three, and so those additional eighteen years could be seen as a fantastic bonus. You grab any comfort you can.

Having been diagnosed, Louise now stabilised and, although you could never claim that she thrived (she was always underweight), she just got on with growing, with a relatively strict regime of drugs, physiotherapy and hospital visits for those first five or so years. A feature of cystic fibrosis is that the patient often looks perfectly healthy and, although this can allow normality to a great degree, it can also lull everyone into a false sense of security.

Living with CF and a terminally ill daughter obviously takes a toll, but the price paid isn't always apparent and creeps up over a long period of time. My doctor once described it as a dripping tap, which I found quite apt. When Louise was five years old, her mum decided she wanted to return to Campbeltown. Her grandfather had just died and she went to live with her mother. Truth be told, I wasn't surprised and the reasons are of no interest here. The problem was she took our kids with her, and so I was forced to drive over a hundred miles just to see them. I did this every weekend or on days off, if possible, and was still much part of their lives. We went on holiday together regularly and they came to stay at mine a lot.

I was heading down the A83 on one occasion when I heard a feature on the radio. It was about estranged fathers and how almost fifty percent of them lose contact with their children and often never see them again, or only much later in life. I couldn't fathom this at all. I treasured that time and still do. It was only on the way home on the Sunday, as I drove along the Tayinloan straight, with tears rolling down my face, that I realised: maybe they don't see them because the pain of leaving them again every time is just so hard to bear.

It's difficult to write this section at this particular time, in the middle of a global pandemic, when NHS staff are risking their lives daily in order to help us fight off COVID-19, but it's the truth and is perhaps pertinent. In the eighties and throughout my dealing with hospitals, firstly Yorkhill Children's Hospital, and, secondly, Gartnavel General Hospital, both in Glasgow, the standard of simple hygiene to prevent cross-infection was staggeringly poor. It was an absolute joke. I must be clear that this was not a wilful act of neglect or stupidity. Far from it. It was actually a simple case of poor training.

Let's be clear, although the specialists, consultants, experts and doctors like to proffer an air of knowledgeable professionalism, the truth is that many times they learn by their mistakes, and in many cases they don't, but in order to maintain that reassuring posture of expertise, they have to appear all-knowing. They never, in my experience, admit being wrong. Equally, for all of the above reasons, they will rarely give a straight answer to a question, always covering themselves from criticism, because often they just don't know.

A case in point: in the early nineties, the children in Yorkhill with CF were all on the one ward. From babies to young adults up to fifteen years, together on open wards, they shared the same toilet facilities, had the same nurses and doctors doing their rounds, went to play classes together, and so on. Their respective parents shared all of their facilities such as the kitchen, showers and bathrooms, as most of us stayed with our children. These are irrefutable facts.

Another fact is that we have always known that the biggest danger to a CF patient is infection and, in particular, lung infections. We could even, in those days, name the germs that were known to be killers, and still are to this day. Well-known everyday organisms, relatively harmless to you and me, but deadly to a person or child with a compromised respiratory system, the most common that I had become scared of being *Pseudomona* and *Cepacia*.

I had read an article about cross-infection and, while on the ward that evening, I spoke to the specialist and asked if it wasn't desirable to prevent such contamination between patients. Surely, there were some basic precautions we could take. At this point, my five year old daughter had four other children on her bed playing with her.

'Nothing but scare-mongering, Mr McLean,' the CF consultant told me.

If I had a pound for every time I had to ask a nurse to wash her hands before dealing with Louise, I would still be a wealthy man. I only recently visited a friend in hospital, the New Royal Infirmary on High Street. On the way into the ward, the dispenser of alcoholic sanitizer was empty, so when we eventually got access, I told the staff nurse at her station.

'Okay, thanks,' was the polite reply.

She didn't make a move or offer me facilities to wash my hands, and when I came off the ward ninety minutes later, it was still empty.

'We've been very busy, sir,' was the curt response when I reminded her.

Yes, busy spreading fucking germs all over the ward. I didn't say that; I'm too old for confrontation now.

I became a hand wash and hand hygiene expert. I can't help that. We wanted Louise out of hospital as much as possible for all the obvious reasons and too minimise the risk of cross-infection, but when she was on Intravenous Antibiotics (IV treatment), this posed a problem. In order to get her home, her mum and I had to be trained to administer the drugs, which were injected into her IV line three times a day. It was a long drawn out procedure and had to be conducted under the strictest regime of cleanliness in order to prevent infection of the line. We were, essentially, pushing drugs directly into her heart.

We needed special taps fitted at our homes, sin bins, drapes, all sorts of cleaning mixtures and wipes, and an area that could be made completely sterile for the preparation of the drugs. It required extensive training that had to be refreshed and signed off on every time Louise required a two- or three-week doze of IVs. We had to change gloves twice during the set-up. Believe me, I knew how to wash my hands and keep germs at bay.

I more or less lived with Louise during the last two years of her life, a large proportion of that being on the floor of her hospital room. By this time, patients with different bugs were totally segregated. Adult CF patients were advised never to meet. Certain bugs were even kept at separate hospitals and no patients on a ward were allowed to go into the room of another patient. So much for scare-mongering twenty years before.

To my mind, and that of my daughter, who was the one at risk, the wards were a disgrace. We always had to have them cleaned before we would stay in one. And we often had to ask for cobwebs or just dirt to be removed from fans and corners and plugs. I can safely say that the state of cleanliness in both Yorkhill and Gartnavel were a joke. If I said it was worse than the food, then you'll begin to realise the severity of the issue.

My final word on this is that even then, in 2011, when Louise passed away, the ward at Gartnavel had a chart on public display showing how staff were doing with hygiene issues, what percentage each shift was achieving, etc. For God's sake, why was it so hard to wash your bloody hands?

I've had a rant. I could rant all night and day. I was so numb when Louise passed away that I was like a zombie for a long time, and only now, nine full years later, can I even be arsed thinking about some of this stuff. I'm not going to, firstly, because Louise wouldn't want that at all, and, secondly, because down the road of bitterness and reprisal lies heartache and misery. Louise lived life to the full and crammed much into her twenty-three and a half years, and it's much better to reflect on the hugely positive influence she was to so many. On her headstone she is referred to as inspirational and she remains so to this day. Her acceptance of her condition and fate, her refusal to seek or receive sympathy or special treatment, and her desire to minimise her problems and their effect on others, all indicate the exceptional child, girl and young woman she was. No one was more inspired over the years by Louise than me.

When she was diagnosed in 1988, I immediately joined the

West of Scotland Branch of the Cystic Fibrosis Trust, soon after took on the head of fundraising duties and, after a few years, became the Chairman. Ultimately, I went on to the Scottish Council for CF and spoke at events all over the UK. I organised and helped with fundraising wherever it was going on, but like everyone else I had to start at the beginning, and it's not as easy as it sounds for some people. I hated asking for money or donations – until I met Ralph Slater.

Ralph had not long founded his men's tailoring empire here in Glasgow, and on my first exploration into organising charity events, I naturally went to see Ralph at his office in Howard Street. He took me into his big office, we had the usual chit chat, and then I told him about Louise and why I was there. He chatted a while and then handed me an envelope and sent me on my way. Half-way down the stairs, I checked the envelope, expecting vouchers or suchlike, and there was a hundred pounds in cash inside. I immediately ran back up and told Ralph I thought he'd made a mistake. There was a hundred pounds here.

'You've not been doing this very long, Simon, have you?'

He ordered tea and biscuits and proceeded to educate me about fundraising.

'You don't want this money for yourself, Simon. Do you? It's going to be used properly. It will change some people's lives for the better, help find a cure for your daughter and children like her or maybe make someone's life easier just for a while. Why would you hesitate to try to do that? Why would you be shy about trying to do that?

'I'm lucky that I happen to be in a position to help just now. If you had come at another time, I may have had to say, I'm sorry, I can't help just now. But that would have been my problem, not yours. I would still have been grateful to you for having given me the opportunity to help. It needs you asking to find the people who can help. Because they all surely would if they could.'

He changed my whole outlook. It was a total paradigm shift for me and, from that day onwards, I never hesitated to ask for donations or cash or favours. What a gift Ralph gave me, and I have since passed it on to many, many people, always in his name. On the foot journey back from Ralph's, through the city centre to Pitt Street, I had to call up a police van to collect all of the donations I had gathered from sports shops, book shops, restaurants, you name it. I never looked back after those words of wisdom from my old friend, Ralph.

One of my more innovative and successful events was The Cow Dung Drop. Fundraising was simple for me. It was about using the things that you had to hand, in this case a police force, a rugby squad comprising officers from every division in that force, an enormous sports facility in Pollok Park, including rugby pitches and, as everyone knows, loveable Highland Coos that graze in said park. So, there you have it. I only had one prize on offer, five hundred pounds that first time. So I didn't have to gather presents and gifts. I simply sold as many tickets as possible for a pound each and distributed them as far and wide as possible. If the internet had been a proper thing then, I would have cleaned up.

On the designated day, the prize was decided at the police sports ground and recreation club, Lochinch in Pollok Park. I had a seven-a-side rugby tourney, Scottish International and British Lion, Doddie Weir, presenting prizes, and all sorts of challenging physical strongman stuff for the adults, together with face painting, a bouncy castle, and an air rifle shooting gallery set up by the TA. A great day was had and a lot of money raised and it culminated in establishing the winner of the five hundred pounds. This wasn't achieved by drawing a ticket, though.

I had made a plan of a rugby park on a big sheet of paper, and divided the park into square yards, a lot of them, and each square created had a number, corresponding to a raffle ticket. So far, so good. What we then did was have the parkies bring a Highland Cow onto the rugby park. It was on a long length of rope and was allowed to wander about until it did its business and, after a few simple measurements, I could plot the winning spot and number on the plan. It was a hoot. It took the cow about thirty minutes to decide on a winner, but this was inevitable, I was told, as it had a deferred feed, ensuring a bowel movement was imminent. A rugby player and retired cop, Mike Harkins, won the money and we were friends for many years. Most importantly, this event provided the sure-fire ingredient to any event raising money: an awareness of our cause. It was *fun*draising.

Among the many new skills and attitudes I had to learn as I became more involved in the charity was that of public speaking. I had to attend all sorts of events and ceremonies, accepting checks, thanking people and organisations, speaking to charitable groups, such as the Round Table, and I can safely say that, although I started off as badly as anyone ever could, I acquired some competence and became comfortable, sometimes speaking to many hundreds of people.

During the course of my fundraising and charity activities, I met and befriended many people, and was constantly surprised by the offers of kindness and support I received, and, during the course of this, I was lucky enough to meet a certain Ross McInnes, who was the UK Professional Pool Champion at the time, and also held the World Speed Pool Record. Ross approached me and explained his personal interest in CF and offered to help in any way possible. Now, that was interesting, and here's what I came up with.

I had every publican in Campbeltown that owned a pool table hold a competition with an entry fee. They were to run it to the final and whether they played a final or not, send their best two players, their finalists, to my Campbeltown Pool Championship Day, a Sunday afternoon upstairs in the Argyll Hotel. I had four tables set up there and we played off the tournament all afternoon and into the evening. In attendance would be the UK pro pool champion, and he would play challenge matches against all four semi-finalists and give an exhibition after the final, attempt to break his world speed pool record, and play charity challenge matches. What a long but brilliant day we had.

This was only the second time I had met Ross. He flew down with his wife and I picked them up at Machrihanish Airport, with the Campbeltown tournament already underway. We had a detour to make. The night before the event, I had received a call from the social organiser at the American Social club on the Machrihanish RAF base. He had seen the publicity and wanted me to bring Ross to the airfield to do a session with the American servicemen based there. I explained that our plans were all in place and it was a tight schedule, but when he said they would donate two hundred pounds for the visit, I found some time from somewhere. When I told Ross, he was delighted. Let's make as much as we can was his attitude.

So, off we went to the club, which was on the base, but was like a part of America, using dollars as currency and speaking a funny language. When we went in the door, it was a wall of sound. There were about two hundred American soldiers screaming their approval at Ross, who looked just as he had on the poster with his tuxedo and bowtie. Ross immediately went over to the table centred in the bar, and turned to me, frowning. What was wrong?

He proceeded to show me his cue, which had the tiniest of tips on it. He explained this was an American pool table with much bigger balls and pockets. The table was about twice as big and he didn't know the rules and his cue was useless. Everyone was concerned, until he asked if he could borrow a cue and play a practice game to get to know the rules. I was so relieved. I sure didn't want to give back the two hundred pounds. I then watched in horror as Ross proceeded to get thumped by the guy the Yanks put up, much to the noisy approval of the watching crowd. What a nightmare.

I then told Ross that I had to rush back into the town to make sure the tournie was on course. He was happy; in his element, of course. I asked him how he made any money for the charity doing this and he told me, 'I get them to put money up on the table, and if they beat me, I double it, and if I win, the charity gets the wager. Simple.'

'How much have you got on you, Ross?' I asked.

He showed me a wad of maybe one hundred pounds in his pocket.

'Do you want me to leave some money, in case you need it?'

He didn't answer me. He just had the strangest look on his face, screwed up, like when you've heard something really, really stupid. He shooed me off and I left him to it.

I must admit I was busy and I forgot all about him until he strolled into the Argyll a few hours later. The atmosphere lifted immediately when he arrived, as the tournament was getting near to its climax and a few drinks had been consumed by now. When I eventually got him clear of the crowd, I asked him how he'd gotten on at the base and he casually emptied his pocket of at least another two hundred pounds. I remember thinking he must have got the hang of that American table pretty quickly.

Some people just don't cotton on well.

I repeated this format many times. Back in Rothesay, where Neil Robertson pulled it all together, we held the event in the Esplanade Hotel, owned by my friend, Billy, and his lovely wife, Angie. I had every police office in Strathclyde hold a tournament and send their finalist to Lochinch, where we had a great night, and I won the doubles with my now pal, Jim Moffat. We made a lot of money for the charity and we sure made sure that the FUN part was included.

Talking of the Esplanade Hotel, just across from the pier in Rothesay, Billy had called his son Jethro and we shared a love for the rock band, Jethro Tull. They were good people and, after I left the island, I always kept in touch and stayed there often when visiting for court or with my kids. So, when I visited with three friends to play a charity golf match over a weekend, it was an obvious destination.

Unfortunately, on that first night after doing our rounds of the local pubs, we stayed up a bit too late with Billy and were much the worse for wear at the breakfast table, prior to heading off for our tee time at the golf course. Billy was obviously suffering the same headache and proceeded to produce pie and beans for us all for breakfast. What a man, but there was much apologising and he assured us that he would make up for it with our Sunday breakfast. He was true to his word. After another late night locked in the lounge, we sat down for our lavish Sunday treat to be served pie, beans and chips.

We played golf from dawn to dusk, snooker for twenty-four hours, jumped out of aeroplanes, played countless charity football and rugby matches, anything where people could have fun and raise money and awareness for the cause. It got to the stage, however, where some of these events were ongoing annual or regular happenings that required managing. I put together a concert in the Glasgow City Halls that became a major undertaking. I was starting to bite off more than I could chew, and the whole charity endeavour is like a snowball, as the more you do, the more you generate to be done, and each event feeds contacts and offers into the next.

A great example was a summer football tournament in Campbeltown, where I managed to get Glasgow Rangers to send an U17 team. Steven (Elvis) Presley was the captain. There was a local team and a team from Islay, as well as a Hearts Boys Club team. Brian McGinlay, was arguably our top Scottish referee at the time and travelled down, paid his own hotel and food, and refereed as many games as he could. He was brilliant and I learned much about refereeing from him in that short weekend.

It was a huge success; Rangers won the final 14 – 0 and we made a lot of money and friends. I was watching the Rangers team together with their coach and I asked him how many of these lads would go on to be professionals. His reply shocked me. If only one went on to get near the first team squad, it would be classed as a successful year. To my eye, they were all outstanding, but such are the fine margins involved.

With the charity work and everything else, something had to give and I eventually made a fateful trip to speak with my Divisional Commander, Lawrence McIntyre, who I respected and trusted implicitly. I explained how I was feeling and he put a number of ideas in my head, but basically said that whatever I wanted to do, the police would try to accommodate me. My idea at that time was to take a year off and make a fortune for the charity. You see the charity at that time was called The Cystic Fibrosis Research Trust, their focus being entirely on finding a cure. The rogue gene that causes the condition had just been identified and the cure felt within touching distance. I was sure they would let me take a wage from the money raised as a commission to help me keep my family.

Underlying all of this was a desire to spend as much time with Louise as possible, and not even my career, that I loved throughout, could ever replace that time. I would only get one shot at it, and had no idea how long we had left with her. I left his office with all of this jumbled in my head, but his wisest council was to think things over, because, in the event, the decision was made much simpler. I was offered a job I could never refuse.

A few weeks after my conversation with Mr McIntyre, I was heading back to the office about ten o'clock. I had been hosting a neighbourhood watch meeting in Ibrox and was sauntering, away in my own wee world, like you do. Next thing I knew, there were two guys standing in my path, and before I had a chance to check my stride, a car drew up beside me with the rear door already open.

'Simon, in you get, son. I need to speak to you.'

There was no debate offered. The voice was vaguely familiar. The timing was spot on, the entire episode of pure military precision. Before I knew anything about it, I was on a twenty-minute drive that changed my life. This imposing man knew everything about me. Could name my family, knew where I lived, and that my kids were in Campbeltown with their mother. He seemed to have been well briefed and knew all of my circumstances and current conflict. What he basically gave me was a solution that would allow me to keep working, doing what I loved to do, albeit at a different level entirely. Still working for the establishment, but free of the shifts and ties currently limiting my options.

I would be able to spend much more time with Louise and my other two children, would maintain my income level and more, and would be free to retire much earlier than previously scheduled through the normal course of things. The only real catch here was that I couldn't tell anyone about it. A full cover story was in place, but it included me retiring on ill health grounds. I was to make myself available for intensive training and be prepared to live a double life from then on. He gave me a number to call and leave a yes or no answer the next day before midnight. He made it clear that this was a one-off opportunity. He wouldn't be coming back. It was a no-brainer for me. I waited until nearly two, but couldn't put it off any longer. I couldn't wait to see what lay in store for me.

This is almost where this story ends. I say almost because I was given a fantastic gift that night that I couldn't possibly appreciate at the time. Yes, I got to do what I was built to do and go undercover. I got to risk everything, travel extensively, meet amazing people and even help thwart a few bad guys. But the real gift wasn't quantifiable. I got to spend loads of time with Louise as she got her own wee house, her wee dog, Charlie, and passed her driving test just after her seventeenth birthday. I got to drink and party with her friends, meet and spend time with her handful of boyfriends, go on holiday with her to the sun and create memories that sustain me to this day.

I was with her in the best of times and through all of the worst, sleeping on the hospital floor, bringing her carry out food at midnight, helping her thwart the nagging ward sister's rules and regulations right till the end. I was right there for the week we spent at Freeman's Hospital in Newcastle getting assessed for the lung transplant programme, and celebrated with her when she was accepted on the list. We thought it only a matter of time till she got 'shiny new puffers' but, alas, it wasn't to be. I spent two years waiting for the call that never came.

We shared so much and crammed as much in as was humanly possible. Latterly, she was staying with me so as to be handy for the hospital and, in early October 2011, was rushed back onto the ward in the middle of the night. I was with her throughout the next two weeks and must tell one last story of the ward. Louise had asked if her bed could be moved into the middle of the room, in order that visitors could sit around the bed properly. A simple request but, as a matter of course, denied by the sister. No surprise. She then asked if she could have a wee glass of Bailey's to help her sleep. The answer was the same, but I was set to smuggle it in that night, anyway. The ward sister was just a jobsworth, to be honest, with not an ounce of apparent compassion – the only kind that counts, in my book.

Anyway, this is what happened. I was at Morrison's getting some snacks for Louise, when the doctor gave her a surprise visit at the end of his shift. Sister was with him. After a chat and brief examination, he asked Louise if there was anything she needed. Big mistake. I'd fallen into this trap many times.

'Yes, please, Doctor. Do you think it might be possible to move my bed into the middle of the room? That way I can see what's going on, rather than being stuck in this corner.'

'I don't see any problem with that, Louise. Sister, will you have someone sort that out, please?'

Ya beauty. Just the look on the sister's face was reward enough, but Louise pushed the boat out, as always.

'One more thing, Doctor, would a wee Bailey's be okay last thing at night, just to help me sleep?'

'I've got no problem with that. Where is your dad?'

'He's at Morrison's round the corner, Doctor,' says Louise.

I can still see that mischievous glint in her eye, as can anyone reading this who knew her.

'Can you phone him and let me speak to him?'

I was happily gathering the cheesy strings, Monster Munch and all of her favourite snacks and drinks when I answered the phone, expecting Louise to give me further instructions. It was the doctor.

'Mr McLean, I've decided to write a special prescription for

Louise, and it requires you buying it at the supermarket. Could you get a nice bottle of Bailey's for her?'

I swear I laughed out loud all the way back, not at the audacity of Louise. I was used to that. Not at the compassion of the doctor playing along. No, what was and is so funny is the thought of total resignation on the face of the sister.

It was only two nights later that we lost her. She was taken from us at a quarter-to-five on the 15th of October 2011 and I'm crying as I write this almost nine years later.

The next day, in the bedside cabinet of her room in my flat, I found a now much treasured handwritten note from Louise to me. It simply said:

'Hey Dad, you've been the best Dad ever. Don't ever doubt that ok. Now I'm gone, but I'm not really gone. I won't be there for you to see or cuddle but I will be with you in spirit. I don't want you to be sad. Be happy that I am free.'

What a girl. Without doubt, her spirit sustained me during those first dangerous months, when I had every excuse to prop up a bar and slip down the road so many before me have travelled. They're all at the bottom of that road waiting, beckoning you on to join them down in the depths of despair, where few ever escape back into the light. I couldn't possibly succumb to those temptations, given that Louise had been so strong. And so everything I did and every decision I made was informed by how she would have wanted me to behave. They still are.

She would be bemused to know that I'm back playing football – walking football, of course – but some people insist that was all I ever played. I actually have a wee coaching job with Glasgow Life that keeps me busy and involved in the sport I love. I still help a friend who is 'in the game' now and again, and my old paymasters still keep in touch obscurely, but those stories are for another place and time. When I learned to become the One Percent of the Ten Percent. This is in loving memory of my baby girl.

LOUISE JANE McLEAN 28/04/88 TO 15/10/2011

The End

GLOSSARY

A fry – a free parcel of fish
A hauf – a measure of Scotch
AID – assistant to the CID
alain – alone
awright – all right
bam – (pot) an irrational person
barny – a rumpus or fight
basie – baseball bat
big man – endearment to someone of any size
blagged – misappropriated or misrepresented
blether – chat
blue trains – West of Scotlands over ground rail network
cannae – cannot
carrying – in possession of a weapon
coonty – The County
coos – cows
coupon – mouth or face
copper – police officer
daft – stupid
dram – glass of Scotch
dodgie – suspicious
doon the watter – the river Clyde estuary
doss – a place to hide or skive
drapped aff – dropped off
driech – damp, dull, miserable weather
drookit – very wet
drooth – thirst
druggie – illicit drug user
dubbed up – in prison
dug – dog

fag – cigarette
fearty – easily scared
Fenian – Irish Republican
fessed up – told the truth
Firhill – esteemed home of Partick Thistle
Fir Park – Dump
fitba – soccer
flapper – someone who tends to panic
flog – sell
flutter – small wager or bet
freebies – attained at no cost
front room – kept for visitors
fur a shag – for copulation
gaspin – desperate for a smoke
gear – drugs
gie driech – very damp, dull miserable weather
gies peace – stop annoying me
a git – not an endearment
gonnae –will you please
goony – woman's night dress
gormless – not the brightest person
gubbed – broken, finished, done for
Hogmanay – New Year's Eve
hoot – a laugh, amusement
hoovered up – cleaned up off the streets
humphed – lift or carry
Hun – Protestant
hur – her
huv – have
jist – just
jobby – number two
junky – heroin addict
keepy uppy – keeping a ball above ground with feet
kerry oot – take away alcohol
ken – know

knackered (knocked) – physically exhausted
lee – leave
lum – chimney
menchie – scots term for graffiti
miffed – displeased
moturs – cars
mucka – close friend
nae bother – not a problem
ned – with criminal or loutish behaviours
nedess – female version of above
neighbour – police partner
neeba – Fife version of above
Ne'rdy – New Years Day
nicked – arrested
numpty – idiot
Old Firm – Rangers and Celtic
oot – out
ovies – overtime
parkie – park attendant
pay off – police social gathering
pelters – abuse
pig – farm animal
planked – hidden
plot – area around a target
plotted up – police surveillance cordon
polis – The Police
pre fab – prefabricated aluminium house
Proddy – Protestant
punter – customer
punting – selling
rozzer – police officer
scheme – council estate
screw – prison officer
scum bag – not a nice person
scunnered – fed up

shell – temporary coffin used for transport
shifty – suspicious
skint – no money
slapper – a woman of loose morals
smack – heroin
Snoopy – baseball bat
sookin up – currying favour
stick – slag or abuse
tenner bag – a wrap of heroin costing £10
teuchter – Highlander
toonie – from the city
touts – informants
tun – a lot of
the Wee Toon – Campbeltown
Tim – Catholic
up the swanny – gone, lost
usin – using drugs
verbal – a response under caution
wantin – wanting
weans – children
wee – small
weegie – from Glasgow
well-kent – well-known
white hat – worn by traffic cops
wisnae – wasn't
wooden tops – uniform police officers
Woolies – Woolworths
woose – a softy (see fearty)
workies – manual workers
ya – you
yur – you are

ACKNOWLEDGEMENTS

To all of my police colleagues and my friends over the years who made these stories possible with their unquenchable thirst and never-ending quest to see humour in almost every situation, no matter how sad, cruel or unpalatable.

To those I've verbally regaled these stories to over the years and whose regular comment "You should write a book, big man" rang in my ears throughout the process. Most especially my friend Bobby Preston who has been a reliable and trusted sounding board as well as a great encourager.

The Cystic Fibrosis Trust staff and Daisy in particular who helped make this project so personally important and poignant, and to my grand-children Fallyn Louise and James Simon for unwittingly giving me the motivation to leave some kind of legacy for them to ponder and question in years to come.

Sandy Jamieson of Ringwood Publishing, for his initial willingness to explore the possibilities, his patience over the years since, and his help and advice as I stumbled over the finish line. Mostly for his strange confidence and faith in me and in the Ten Percent project.

Also at Ringwood, thanks to Ruth McQueeny who has been and is amazing, Kevin McGowan for his editing skills and understanding, and Nicola Campbell for her imagination and artistic talent on the cover.

My children Simon, Tracy, who have been listening to these stories all of their lives and still try to laugh at the right bits, and my brother and sister Dermot and Jane, who somehow resist laughing at any bits at all.

My long-suffering partner Fiona who has cajoled, listened, laughed and cried with me all the way. She has spent months watching me hunched over the PC cursing and slurping coffee, but without her constant, unflinching faith and encouragement I would never have completed this work. Ever.

Thanks to you all. I hope it was worth it.

ABOUT THE AUTHOR

Simon was born in Possilpark, one of the notorious housing estates of north Glasgow where he soon learned of the divisions inherent in our society, but an unconditional love of football helped steer him through the hazards lying in wait on both sides of those divides.

Placed in an apprenticeship when told to leave school and 'get a trade', a freak football injury led to a chance visit to police HQ and he found himself in the Highlands of Argyll as a rookie police officer, in Campbeltown on The Mull of Kintyre.

His journey across Scotland as a plain clothes officer and undercover operative involved many exploits and tales, some sad, some uplifting but all of them thought provoking in their way.

He now coaches and plays walking football, helps run an amateur side Lomond Vale AFC, and until recently enjoyed world travels with his partner Fiona, who has taken early retirement. With all of their globe-trotting plans on hold during the world pandemic, writing has been a saviour and resulted in his debut memoir, The Ten Percent, reaching completion. He hopes there will be more opportunities to tell the truth, the whole truth, and something like the truth.

OTHER BOOKS BY GADFLY PRESS

By John G Sutton:
HMP Manchester Prison Officer: I Survived Terrorists, Murderers, Rapists and Freemason Officer Attacks in Strangeways and Wormwood Scrubs

By Lee Marvin Hitchman:
How I Survived Shootings, Stabbings, Prison, Crack Addiction, Manchester Gangs and Dog Attacks

By William Rodríguez Abadía:
Son of the Cali Cartel: The Narcos Who Wiped Out Pablo Escobar and the Medellín Cartel

By Chet Sandhu:
Self-Made, Dues Paid: An Asian Kid Who Became an International Drug-Smuggling Gangster

By Kaz B:
Confessions of a Dominatrix: My Secret BDSM Life

By Peter McAleese:
Killing Escobar and Soldier Stories

By Joe Egan:
Big Joe Egan: The Toughest White Man on the Planet

By Anthony Valentine:

Britain's No. 1 Art Forger Max Brandrett: The Life of a Cheeky Faker

By Johnnyboy Steele:

Scotland's Johnnyboy: The Bird That Never Flew

By Ian 'Blink' MacDonald:

Scotland's Wildest Bank Robber: Guns, Bombs and Mayhem in Glasgow's Gangland

By Michael Sheridan:

The Murder of Sophie: How I Hunted and Haunted the West Cork Killer

By Steve Wraith:

The Krays' Final Years: My Time with London's Most Iconic Gangsters

By Natalie Welsh:

Escape from Venezuela's Deadliest Prison

By Shaun Attwood:
English Shaun Trilogy

Party Time
Hard Time
Prison Time

War on Drugs Series

Pablo Escobar: Beyond Narcos
American Made: Who Killed Barry Seal? Pablo Escobar or George

HW Bush
The Cali Cartel: Beyond Narcos
Clinton Bush and CIA Conspiracies: From the Boys on the Tracks to Jeffrey Epstein
Who Killed Epstein? Prince Andrew or Bill Clinton

Un-Making a Murderer: The Framing of Steven Avery and Brendan Dassey
The Mafia Philosopher: Two Tonys
Life Lessons

Pablo Escobar's Story (4-book series)

By Johnnyboy Steele:

Scotland's Johnnyboy: The Bird That Never Flew

"A cross between *Shawshank Redemption* and *Escape from Alcatraz*!" – Shaun Attwood, YouTuber and Author

All his life, 'Johnnyboy' Steele has been running. Firstly, from an abusive father, then from the rigours of an approved school and a young offenders jail, and, finally, from the harshness of adult prison. This book details how the Steele brothers staged the most daring breakout that Glasgow's Barlinnie prison had ever seen and recounts what happened when their younger brother, Joseph, was falsely accused of the greatest mass murder in Scottish legal history.

If Johnnyboy had wings, he would have flown to help his family, but he would have to wait for freedom to use his expertise to publicise young Joe's miscarriage of justice.

This is a compelling, often shocking and uncompromisingly honest account of how the human spirit can survive against almost crushing odds. It is a story of family love, friendship and, ultimately, a desire for justice.

By Ian 'Blink' MacDonald:

Scotland's Wildest Bank Robber:
Guns, Bombs and Mayhem in Glasgow's Gangland

As a young man in Glasgow's underworld, Ian 'Blink' MacDonald earned a reputation for fighting and stabbing his enemies. After refusing to work for Arthur "The Godfather" Thompson, he attempted to steal £6 million in a high-risk armed bank robbery. While serving 16 years, Blink met the torture-gang boss Eddie Richardson, the serial killer Archie Hall, notorious lifer Charles Bronson and members of the Krays.

After his release, his drug-fuelled violent lifestyle created conflict with the police and rival gangsters. Rearrested several times, he was the target of a gruesome assassination attempt. During filming for Danny Dyer's Deadliest Men, a bomb was discovered under Blink's car and the terrified camera crew members fled from Scotland.

In *Scotland's Wildest Bank Robber*, Blink provides an eye-opening account of how he survived gangland warfare, prisons, stabbings and bombs.

By Michael Sheridan:

The Murder of Sophie:
How I Hunted and Haunted the West Cork Killer

Just before Christmas, 1996, a beautiful French woman – the wife of a movie mogul – was brutally murdered outside of her holiday home in a remote region of West Cork, Ireland. The crime was reported by a local journalist, Ian Bailey, who was at the forefront of the case until he became the prime murder suspect. Arrested twice, he was released without charge.

This was the start of a saga lasting decades with twists and turns and a battle for justice in two countries, which culminated in the 2019 conviction of Bailey – in his absence – by the French

Criminal court in Paris. But it was up to the Irish courts to decide whether he would be extradited to serve a 25-year prison sentence.

With the unrivalled co-operation of major investigation sources and the backing of the victim's family, the author unravels the shocking facts of a unique murder case.

By Steve Wraith:

The Krays' Final Years:
My Time with London's Most Iconic Gangsters

Britain's most notorious twins – Ron and Reg Kray – ascended the underworld to become the most feared and legendary gangsters in London. Their escalating mayhem culminated in murder, for which they received life sentences in 1969.

While incarcerated, they received letters from a schoolboy from Tyneside, Steve Wraith, who was mesmerised by their story. Eventually, Steve visited them in prison and a friendship formed. The Twins hired Steve as an unofficial advisor, which brought him into contact with other members of their crime family. At Ron's funeral, Steve was Charlie Kray's right-hand man.

Steve documents Ron's time in Broadmoor – a high-security psychiatric hospital – where he was battling insanity and heavily medicated. Steve details visiting Reg, who served almost 30 years in a variety of prisons, where the gangster was treated with the utmost respect by the staff and the inmates.

By Natalie Welsh:

Escape from Venezuela's Deadliest Prison

After getting arrested at a Venezuelan airport with a suitcase of cocaine, Natalie was clueless about the danger she was facing. Sentenced to 10 years, she arrived at a prison with armed men on the roof, whom she mistakenly believed were the guards, only to find out they were homicidal gang members. Immediately, she was plunged into a world of unimaginable horror and escalating violence, where murder, rape and all-out gang warfare were carried out with the complicity of corrupt guards. Male prisoners often entered the women's housing area, bringing gunfire with them and leaving corpses behind. After 4.5 years, Natalie risked everything to escape and flee through Colombia, with the help of a guard who had fallen deeply in love with her.

By Shaun Attwood:

Pablo Escobar: Beyond Narcos

War on Drugs Series Book 1

The mind-blowing true story of Pablo Escobar and the Medellín Cartel, beyond their portrayal on Netflix.

Colombian drug lord Pablo Escobar was a devoted family man and a psychopathic killer; a terrible enemy, yet a wonderful friend. While donating millions to the poor, he bombed and tortured his enemies – some had their eyeballs removed with hot spoons. Through ruthless cunning and America's insatiable appetite for cocaine, he became a multi-billionaire, who lived in a $100-million house with its own zoo.

Pablo Escobar: Beyond Narcos demolishes the standard good versus evil telling of his story. The authorities were not hunting Pablo down to stop his cocaine business. They were taking it over.

American Made: Who Killed Barry Seal? Pablo Escobar or George HW Bush

War on Drugs Series Book 2

Set in a world where crime and government coexist, *American Made* is the jaw-dropping true story of CIA pilot Barry Seal that the Hollywood movie starring Tom Cruise is afraid to tell.

Barry Seal flew cocaine and weapons worth billions of dollars into and out of America in the 1980s. After he became a government informant, Pablo Escobar's Medellin Cartel offered a million for him alive and half a million dead. But his real trouble began after he threatened to expose the dirty dealings of George HW Bush.

American Made rips the roof off Bush and Clinton's complicity in cocaine trafficking in Mena, Arkansas.

"A conspiracy of the grandest magnitude." Congressman Bill Alexander on the Mena affair.

The Cali Cartel: Beyond Narcos

War on Drugs Series Book 3

An electrifying account of the Cali Cartel, beyond its portrayal on Netflix.

From the ashes of Pablo Escobar's empire rose an even bigger and more malevolent cartel. A new breed of sophisticated mobsters became the kings of cocaine. Their leader was Gilberto Rodríguez Orejuela – known as the Chess Player, due to his foresight and calculated cunning.

Gilberto and his terrifying brother, Miguel, ran a multi-billion-dollar drug empire like a corporation. They employed a politically astute brand of thuggery and spent $10 million to put a president in power. Although the godfathers from Cali preferred bribery over violence, their many loyal torturers and hitmen were never idle.

Clinton, Bush and CIA Conspiracies: From the Boys on the Tracks to Jeffrey Epstein

War on Drugs Series Book 4

In the 1980s, George HW Bush imported cocaine to finance an illegal war in Nicaragua. Governor Bill Clinton's Arkansas state police provided security for the drug drops. For assisting the CIA, the Clinton Crime Family was awarded the White House. The #clintonbodycount continues to this day, with the deceased including Jeffrey Epstein.

This book features harrowing true stories that reveal the insanity of the drug war. A mother receives the worst news about her son. A journalist gets a tip that endangers his life. An unemployed man becomes California's biggest crack dealer. A DEA agent in Mexico is sacrificed for going after the big players.

The lives of Linda Ives, Gary Webb, Freeway Rick Ross and Kiki Camarena are shattered by brutal experiences. Not all of them will survive.

Pablo Escobar's Story (4-book series)

"Finally, the definitive book about Escobar, original and up-to-date." – UNILAD

"The most comprehensive account ever written." – True Geordie

Pablo Escobar was a mama's boy, who cherished his family and sang in the shower, yet he bombed a passenger plane and formed a death squad that used genital electrocution.

Most Escobar biographies only provide a few pieces of the puzzle, but this action-packed 1000-page book reveals everything about the king of cocaine.

Mostly translated from Spanish, Part 1 contains stories untold in the English-speaking world, including:

The tragic death of his youngest brother, Fernando.

The fate of his pregnant mistress.

The shocking details of his affair with a TV celebrity.

The presidential candidate who encouraged him to eliminate their rivals.

The Mafia Philosopher

"A fast-paced true-crime memoir with all of the action of Goodfellas." – UNILAD

"Sopranos v Sons of Anarchy with an Alaskan-snow backdrop." – True Geordie Podcast

Breaking bones, burying bodies and planting bombs became second nature to Two Tonys, while working for the Bonanno Crime Family, whose exploits inspired The Godfather.

After a dispute with an outlaw motorcycle club, Two Tonys left a trail of corpses from Arizona to Alaska. On the run, he was pursued by bikers and a neo-Nazi gang, blood-thirsty for revenge, while a homicide detective launched a nationwide manhunt.

As the mist from his smoking gun fades, readers are left with an unexpected portrait of a stoic philosopher with a wealth of charm, a glorious turn of phrase and a fanatical devotion to his daughter.

Party Time

An action-packed roller-coaster account of a life spiralling out of control, featuring wild women, gangsters and a mountain of drugs.

Shaun Attwood arrived in Phoenix, Arizona, a penniless business graduate from a small industrial town in England. Within a decade, he became a stock-market millionaire. But he was leading a double life.

After taking his first ecstasy pill at a rave in Manchester as a shy student, Shaun became intoxicated by the party lifestyle that would change his fortune. Years later, in the Arizona desert, he became submerged in a criminal underworld, throwing parties for thousands of ravers and running an ecstasy ring in competition with the Mafia mass murderer, Sammy 'The Bull' Gravano.

As greed and excess tore through his life, Shaun had eye-watering encounters with Mafia hitmen and crystal-meth addicts, enjoyed extravagant debauchery with superstar DJs and glitter girls, and ingested enough drugs to kill a herd of elephants. This is his story.

Hard Time

"Makes the Shawshank Redemption look like a holiday camp."
– NOTW

After a SWAT team smashed down stock-market millionaire Shaun Attwood's door, he found himself inside Arizona's deadliest jail and locked into a brutal struggle for survival.

Shaun's hope of living the American Dream turned into a nightmare of violence and chaos, when he had a run-in with Sammy "the Bull" Gravano, an Italian Mafia mass murderer.

In jail, Shaun was forced to endure cockroaches crawling in his ears at night, dead rats in the food and the sound of skulls getting cracked against toilets. He meticulously documented the conditions and smuggled out his message.

Join Shaun on a harrowing voyage into the darkest recesses of human existence.

Hard Time provides a revealing glimpse into the tragedy, brutality, dark comedy and eccentricity of prison life.

Featured worldwide on Nat Geo Channel's Locked-Up/ Banged-Up Abroad Raving Arizona.

Prison Time

Sentenced to 9½ years in Arizona's state prison for distributing ecstasy, Shaun finds himself living among gang members, sexual predators and drug-crazed psychopaths. After being attacked by a Californian biker, in for stabbing a girlfriend, Shaun writes about the prisoners who befriend, protect and inspire him. They include T-Bone, a massive African American ex-Marine, who risks his life saving vulnerable inmates from rape, and Two Tonys, an old-school Mafia murderer, who left the corpses of his rivals from Arizona to Alaska. They teach Shaun how to turn incarceration to his advantage, and to learn from his mistakes.

Shaun is no stranger to love and lust in the heterosexual world, but the tables are turned on him inside. Sexual advances come at him from all directions, some cleverly disguised, others more sinister – making Shaun question his sexual identity.

Resigned to living alongside violent, mentally ill and drug-addicted inmates, Shaun immerses himself in psychology and philosophy, to try to make sense of his past behaviour, and begins applying what he learns, as he adapts to prison life. Encouraged by Two Tonys to explore fiction as well, Shaun reads over 1000 books which, with support from a brilliant psychotherapist, Dr Owen, speed along his personal development. As his ability to deflect daily threats improves, Shaun begins to look forward to his release with optimism and a new love waiting for him. Yet the words of Aristotle from one of Shaun's books will prove prophetic: "We cannot learn without pain."

Un-Making a Murderer: The Framing of Steven Avery and Brendan Dassey

Innocent people do go to jail. Sometimes mistakes are made. But even more terrifying is when the authorities conspire to frame them. That's what happened to Steven Avery and Brendan Dassey, who were convicted of murder and are serving life sentences.

Un-Making a Murderer is an explosive book, which uncovers the illegal, devious and covert tactics used by Wisconsin officials, including:

– Concealing Other Suspects

– Paying Expert Witnesses to Lie

– Planting Evidence

– Jury Tampering

The art of framing innocent people has been in practice for centuries and will continue until the perpetrators are held accountable. Turning conventional assumptions and beliefs in the justice system upside down, *Un-Making a Murderer* takes you on that journey.

HARD TIME BY SHAUN ATTWOOD

CHAPTER 1

Sleep deprived and scanning for danger, I enter a dark cell on the second floor of the maximum-security Madison Street jail in Phoenix, Arizona, where guards and gang members are murdering prisoners. Behind me, the metal door slams heavily. Light slants into the cell through oblong gaps in the door, illuminating a prisoner cocooned in a white sheet, snoring lightly on the top bunk about two thirds of the way up the back wall. Relieved there is no immediate threat, I place my mattress on the grimy floor. Desperate to rest, I notice movement on the cement-block walls. *Am I hallucinating?* I blink several times. The walls appear to ripple. Stepping closer, I see the walls are alive with insects. I flinch. So many are swarming, I wonder if they're a colony of ants on the move. To get a better look, I put my eyes right up to them. They are mostly the size of almonds and have antennae. American cockroaches. I've seen them in the holding cells downstairs in smaller numbers, but nothing like this. A chill spread over my body. I back away.

Something alive falls from the ceiling and bounces off the base of my neck. I jump. With my night vision improving, I spot cockroaches weaving in and out of the base of the fluorescent strip light. Every so often one drops onto the concrete and resumes crawling. Examining the bottom bunk, I realise why my cellmate is sleeping at a higher elevation: cockroaches are pouring from gaps in the decrepit wall at the level of my bunk. The area is thick with them. Placing my mattress on the bottom bunk scatters them. I walk towards the toilet, crunching a few under my shower sandals. I urinate and grab the toilet roll. A cockroach darts from the centre of the roll onto my hand, tickling my fingers. My arm jerks as if it has a mind of its own, losing the cockroach and the toilet roll. Using a towel, I wipe the bulk of them off the bottom bunk, stopping only to shake the odd one off my hand. I unroll my mattress. They begin to regroup and inhabit my mattress. My adrenaline is pumping so much, I lose my fatigue.

Nauseated, I sit on a tiny metal stool bolted to the wall. *How will I sleep? How's my cellmate sleeping through the infestation and my arrival?* Copying his technique, I cocoon myself in a sheet and lie down, crushing more cockroaches. The only way they can access me now is through the breathing hole I've left in the sheet by the lower half of my face. Inhaling their strange musty odour, I close my eyes. I can't sleep. I feel them crawling on the sheet around my feet. *Am I imagining things?* Frightened of them infiltrating my breathing hole, I keep opening my eyes. Cramps cause me to rotate onto my other side. Facing the wall, I'm repulsed by so many of them just inches away. I return to my original side.

The sheet traps the heat of the Sonoran Desert to my body, soaking me in sweat. Sweat tickles my body, tricking my mind into thinking the cockroaches are infiltrating and crawling on me. The trapped heat aggravates my bleeding skin infections and bedsores. I want to scratch myself, but I know better. The outer layers of my skin have turned soggy from sweating constantly in this concrete oven. Squirming on the bunk fails to stop the relentless itchiness of my skin. Eventually, I scratch myself. Clumps of moist skin detach under my nails. Every now and then I become so uncomfortable, I must open my cocoon to waft the heat out, which allows the cockroaches in. It takes hours to drift to sleep. I only manage a few hours. I awake stuck to the soaked sheet, disgusted by the cockroach carcasses compressed against the mattress.

The cockroaches plague my new home until dawn appears at the dots in the metal grid over a begrimed strip of four-inch-thick bullet-proof glass at the top of the back wall – the cell's only source of outdoor light. They disappear into the cracks in the walls, like vampire mist retreating from sunlight. But not all of them. There were so many on the night shift that even their vastly reduced number is too many to dispose of. And they act like they know it. They roam around my feet with attitude, as if to make it clear that I'm trespassing on their turf.

My next set of challenges will arise not from the insect world, but from my neighbours. I'm the new arrival, subject to scrutiny about my charges just like when I'd run into the Aryan Brotherhood prison gang on my first day at the medium-security Towers jail a year ago. I wish my cellmate would wake up, brief me on the mood of the locals and introduce me to the head of the white gang. No such luck. Chow is announced over a speaker system in a crackly robotic voice, but he doesn't stir.

I emerge into the day room for breakfast. Prisoners in black-and-white bee-striped uniforms gather under the metal-grid stairs and tip dead cockroaches into a trash bin from plastic peanut-butter containers they'd set as traps during the night. All eyes are on me in the chow line. Watching who sits where, I hold my head up, put on a solid stare and pretend to be as at home in this environment as the cockroaches. It's all an act. I'm lonely and afraid. I loathe having to explain myself to the head of the white race, who I assume is the toughest murderer. I've been in jail long enough to know that taking my breakfast to my cell will imply that I have something to hide.

The gang punishes criminals with certain charges. The most serious are sex offenders, who are KOS: Kill On Sight. Other charges are punishable by SOS – Smash On Sight – such as drive-by shootings because women and kids sometimes get killed. It's called convict justice. Gang members are constantly looking for people to beat up because that's how they earn their reputations and tattoos. The most serious acts of violence earn the highest-ranking tattoos. To be a full gang member requires murder. I've observed the body language and techniques inmates trying to integrate employ. An inmate with a spring in his step and an air of confidence is likely to be accepted. A person who avoids eye contact and fails to introduce himself to the gang is likely to be preyed on. Some of the failed attempts I saw ended up with heads getting cracked against toilets, a sound I've grown familiar with. I've seen prisoners being extracted on stretchers who looked dead – one had yellow fluid leaking from his head. The constant violence gives me nightmares, but the reality is that I put myself in here, so I force myself to accept it as a part of my punishment.

It's time to apply my knowledge. With a self-assured stride, I take my breakfast bag to the table of white inmates covered in neo-Nazi tattoos, allowing them to question me.

"Mind if I sit with you guys?" I ask, glad exhaustion has deepened my voice.

"These seats are taken. But you can stand at the corner of the table."

The man who answered is probably the head of the gang. I size him up. Cropped brown hair. A dangerous glint in Nordic-blue eyes. Tiny pupils that suggest he's on heroin. Weightlifter-type veins bulging from a sturdy neck. Political ink on arms crisscrossed with scars. About the same age as me, thirty-three.

"Thanks. I'm Shaun from England." I volunteer my origin to show I'm different from them but not in a way that might get me smashed.

"I'm Bullet, the head of the whites." He offers me his fist to bump. "Where you roll in from, wood?"

Addressing me as wood is a good sign. It's what white gang members on a friendly basis call each other.

"Towers jail. They increased my bond and re-classified me to maximum security."

"What's your bond at?"

"I've got two $750,000 bonds," I say in a monotone. This is no place to brag about bonds.

"How many people you kill, brother?" His eyes drill into mine, checking whether my body language supports my story. My body language so far is spot on.

"None. I threw rave parties. They got us talking about drugs on wiretaps." Discussing drugs on the phone does not warrant a $1.5 million bond. I know and beat him to his next question. "Here's my charges." I show him my charge sheet, which includes conspiracy and leading a crime syndicate – both from running an Ecstasy ring.

Bullet snatches the paper and scrutinises it. Attempting to pre-empt his verdict, the other whites study his face. On edge, I wait for him to respond. Whatever he says next will determine whether I'll be accepted or victimised.

"Are you some kind of jailhouse attorney?" Bullet asks. "I want someone to read through my case paperwork." During our few minutes of conversation, Bullet has seen through my act and concluded that I'm educated – a possible resource to him.

I appreciate that he'll accept me if I take the time to read his case. "I'm no jailhouse attorney, but I'll look through it and help you however I can."

"Good. I'll stop by your cell later on, wood."

After breakfast, I seal as many of the cracks in the walls as I can with toothpaste. The cell smells minty, but the cockroaches still find their way in. Their day shift appears to be collecting information on the brown paper bags under my bunk, containing a few items of food that I purchased from the commissary; bags that I tied off with rubber bands in the hope of keeping the cockroaches out. Relentlessly, the cockroaches explore the bags for entry points, pausing over and probing the most worn and vulnerable regions. *Will the nightly swarm eat right through the paper?* I read all morning, wondering whether my cellmate has died in his cocoon, his occasional breathing sounds reassuring me.

Bullet stops by late afternoon and drops his case paperwork off. He's been charged with Class 3 felonies and less, not serious crimes, but is facing a double-digit sentence because of his prior convictions and Security Threat Group status in the prison system. The proposed sentencing range seems disproportionate. I'll advise him to reject the plea bargain – on the assumption he already knows to do so, but is just seeking the comfort of a second opinion, like many un-sentenced inmates. When he returns for his paperwork, our conversation disturbs my cellmate – the cocoon shuffles – so we go upstairs to his cell. I tell Bullet what I think. He is excitable, a different man from earlier, his pupils almost non-existent.

"This case ain't shit. But my prosecutor knows I done other shit, all kinds of heavy shit, but can't prove it. I'd do anything to get that sorry bitch off my fucking ass. She's asking for something bad to happen to her. Man, if I ever get bonded out, I'm gonna chop that bitch into pieces. Kill her slowly though. Like to work her over with a blowtorch."

Such talk can get us both charged with conspiring to murder a prosecutor, so I try to steer him elsewhere. "It's crazy how they can catch you doing one thing, yet try to sentence you for all of the things they think you've ever done."

"Done plenty. Shot some dude in the stomach once. Rolled him up in a blanket and threw him in a dumpster."

Discussing past murders is as unsettling as future ones. "So, what's all your tattoos mean, Bullet? Like that eagle on your chest?"

"Why you wanna know?" Bullet's eyes probe mine.

My eyes hold their ground. "Just curious."

"It's a war bird. The AB patch."

"AB patch?"

"What the Aryan Brotherhood gives you when you've put enough work in."

"How long does it take to earn a patch?"

"Depends how quickly you put your work in. You have to earn your lightning bolts first."

"Why you got red and black lightning bolts?"

"You get SS bolts for beating someone down or for being an enforcer for the family. Red lightning bolts for killing someone. I was sent down as a youngster. They gave me steel and told me who to handle and I handled it. You don't ask questions. You just

445

get blood on your steel. Dudes who get these tats without putting work in are told to cover them up or leave the yard."

"What if they refuse?"

"They're held down and we carve the ink off them."

Imagining them carving a chunk of flesh to remove a tattoo, I cringe. He's really enjoying telling me this now. His volatile nature is clear and frightening. *He's accepted me too much. He's trying to impress me before making demands.*

At night, I'm unable to sleep. Cocooned in heat, surrounded by cockroaches, I hear the swamp-cooler vent – a metal grid at the top of a wall – hissing out tepid air. Giving up on sleep, I put my earphones on and tune into National Public Radio. Listening to a Vivaldi violin concerto, I close my eyes and press my tailbone down to straighten my back as if I'm doing a yogic relaxation. The playful allegro thrills me, lifting my spirits, but the wistful adagio provokes sad emotions and tears. I open my eyes and gaze into the gloom. Due to lack of sleep, I start hallucinating and hearing voices over the music whispering threats. I'm at breaking point. Although I have accepted that I committed crimes and deserve to be punished, no one should have to live like this. I'm furious at myself for making the series of reckless decisions that put me in here and for losing absolutely everything. As violins crescendo in my ears, I remember what my life used to be like.

Printed in Great Britain
by Amazon